Ernest William
GOODPASTURE

Ernest William GOODPASTURE

Scientist, Scholar, Gentleman

ROBERT D. COLLINS

HILLSBORO PRESS
Franklin, Tennessee

Printed in the United States of America

06   05   04   03   02   1   2   3   4   5

Library of Congress Catalog Card Number: 2001099118

ISBN: 1-57736-251-9

Cover design by Gary Bozeman

Cover photos by Dr. Samuel Paplanus and Mr. Brent Weedman

Hillsboro Press
PROVIDENCE PUBLISHING CORPORATION
238 Seaboard Lane • Franklin, Tennessee 37067
800-321-5692
www.providencepubcorp.com

To
Vanderbilt Medical Students

CONTENTS

LIST OF JOURNAL ABBREVIATIONS

The following abbreviations are used for medical journals in the text.

American Journal of Diseases in Children	*Am J Diseases Children*
American Journal of Hygiene	*Am J Hyg*
The American Journal of the Medical Sciences	*Am J of Med Sciences*
American Journal of Pathology	*Am J Pathol*
American Journal of Physiology	*Am J Physiol*
Archives of Pathology	*Arch Pathol*
Bulletin of the Johns Hopkins Hospital	*Bull Johns Hopkins Hospital*
Journal of the American Medical Association	*J Am Med Assoc*
The Journal of Experimental Medicine	*J Exp Med*
Journal of Laboratory and Clinical Medicine	*J Lab Clin Med*
Journal of Medical Research	*J Med Res*
The Philippine Journal of Science	*Philippine J Sci*
Proceedings of the Society of Experimental and Biological Medicine	*Proc Soc Exp Biol Med*
Southern Medical Journal	*Southern Med J*

PREFACE

W e should begin by reading carefully the definition of the word *biography*: it is an account of a person's life written, composed, or produced by another.[1] Biographers are more difficult to describe precisely as they assume the role of judge and jury, of filter and sieve, of reporter and analyst in their account of a life they can know only secondhand. No less an authority than Mark Twain has written: "Biographies are but the clothes and buttons of the man—the biography of the man himself cannot be written."[2] However, histories are often written by those who did not experience the events described, and biographies, imperfect as they may be, similarly offer perspective by opening a window into the past. This biography of Ernest William Goodpasture is justified by the character and accomplishments of the subject, as well as by an attempt to understand the profession and institutions that were integral to his life. It would be particularly inappropriate to have this biography misinterpreted as a worshipful or idealized account, that is, a hagiography, because there is abundant evidence that Dr. Goodpasture led an exemplary life and that he made significant contributions to the welfare of humankind. We are further justified in treasuring his memory because of his idealism, humanism, and intellectual curiosity.

My chief sources are as follows: Dr. Goodpasture, who was my mentor during the thirteen years I was privileged to know him; Sarah Goodpasture Little, who as our friend has provided reminiscences and other factual material about her father and mother; other members of the Goodpasture family, especially Dr. Joseph Little Jr., Sarah's husband; Katherine Anderson Goodpasture, his collaborator and second wife, who was our friend and frequent companion; the Vanderbilt faculty—many with a role in this biography were known by me; the papers of Dr. Goodpasture, given to the Vanderbilt University Medical Center Archives in 1988 and 2000; the papers of Chancellor Kirkland and of Deans Robinson, Leathers, Goodpasture, and Youmans in the Vanderbilt Archives.

Biographers at the outset should declare their intentions and interests. Mine are to document the life and accomplishments of one of the most distinguished graduates of Vanderbilt University and to describe his contributions to Vanderbilt Medical School and to medicine worldwide, with the intention that these accomplishments and contributions will be ingrained in institutional and personal memories for our guidance and inspiration. The timing of this biography is related to the availability of block time for the author; there have been no recent scientific developments enhancing or diminishing the justification for Dr. Goodpasture's biography. This work is perhaps more timely now than if it had been written closer to his death. Medicine has changed so much since Dr. Goodpasture's time that it is worthwhile to emphasize that the profession was once more idealistic and humanistic. To read about his life now may make that message clearer and more poignant. The only known loss in written source material over the past decades is the loss of most laboratory notebooks prior to 1959.[3]

ACKNOWLEDGMENTS

For authorizing this biography, providing historical materials, photographs, and other memorabilia as well as personal reminiscences: Sarah Goodpasture Little.

For providing information about the Goodpasture family: Joseph Little Jr.; Joseph Little III, who also made the logbooks about Basin Spring available and provided photographs of Basin Spring and their legends; Sarah Little Glover; Susan Little Berry; Ann Wilson Goodpasture, who provided photographs of the Goodpasture family, genealogical information, and the biography of J. D. Goodpasture.

For providing information about Dr. Goodpasture, the Goodpasture family, and early Vanderbilt faculty: Mrs. Albert J. Evans Jr.; Margaret Dawson, who also provided information about her husband, Dr. James Dawson; Alice Clark Coogan, who also provided memorabilia about her grandfather, Dr. James Dawson.

For editing the manuscript: Elizabeth Cate Collins, who also helped maintain the files of background information, interviewed several Goodpasture family friends, and made many helpful suggestions about textual tone and organization; Elizabeth Landress Collins, who generously provided professional editing of the text and made major improvements in its presentation; Dr. Robert Merrill, who critically (of course!) reviewed the manuscript, suggested key revisions in approach and organization as well as enforced precision in word usage. His attention to these matters in the year 2000 is particularly appreciated.

For reading portions of the manuscript and providing suggestions about style and content: Robert McGaw, who also provided historical information about Vanderbilt; Samuel Paplanus; Charles Randall; Judson Randolph; Roscoe Robinson; Preston Russell; Bertram Sprofkin.

For organization of the Goodpasture memorabilia donated to Vanderbilt after 1988: Harwell Wells.

For providing information about the Goodpasture family, particularly in reference to the homes on Fairfax Avenue and the Monteagle cottage: family friends Peggy Wemyss Connor, Miriam McGaw Cowden, Susie Sims Irvin, Grace Benedict Paine, Laura Whitson Sharp.

For maintenance of archives, finding and copying source materials, the archivists of the Heard and Eskind Libraries of Vanderbilt University: Randy Jones; Cathy Smith; Jeremy Spector; Mary Teloh, who also provided expert guidance in the history of Vanderbilt Medical Center and its faculty; Jim Thweatt, who was especially helpful in tracking references, finding photographs, and finding materials in the Special Collections files of the Eskind Library.

For help with archival material, Tennessee State Library and Archives: Genella Olker.

For help with archival material, Armed Forces Institute of Pathology: Michael Rhode.

For help with archival material, University of Alabama: Donnely F. Lancaster.

For providing archival material, Johns Hopkins Medical Archives: Nancy McCall.

For help with Buddingh material: Dr. Adele Spence, L.S.U. Medical Center.

For information about Dr. Glenn Millikan: Dr. George Millikan, Berkeley.

For providing material about tissue culture laboratory at Vanderbilt, Department of Pathology: Dr. Charles Randall.

For providing information about the history of the Cytology Laboratory at Vanderbilt, Department of Pathology: Dr. Lily Mauricio.

For providing information about the operation of Vanderbilt Hospital 1947–49, providing memoirs, and reading portions of the manuscript: Dr. Henry Clark.

For providing information about financial matters of Vanderbilt Hospital: Mr. Richard Wagers, chief financial officer, Vanderbilt University Medical Center.

For providing materials from Singer Research Laboratory and guiding us to the Goodpasture home in Sewickley: Dr. Robert Hartsock.

Illustrations: The illustrations in this book came from several sources, and many have appeared in previous publications. We are particularly indebted to Sarah Little for photographs of her father and other memorabilia used for illustrations. All of the illustrative material was prepared for scanning and then scanned into files by Mr. Brent Weedman. He deserves special thanks for removing scratches and other imperfections from old photographs so that they were more usable as well as for careful editing of all illustrative material. In addition, thanks are due the following for selected pictures:

Joseph Little III for pictures of Basin Spring.

Samuel Paplanus for photographs of Drs. Goodpasture, Clark, and Christie; Hopkins Archives for picture of Johns Hopkins Hospital.

For help with archival material and design: Robert Vantrease.

For transcription of the curriculum vitae and other portions of the manuscript: Amy Verheide.

For assistance, guidance, and support in developing computer literacy: Deborah Himes.

For assistance in preparing the CD of Dr. Goodpasture's lecture: Joe Goff and Jeff Gordon.

For support and facilitating the transmittal of this book to Vanderbilt alumni: Mr. Joel Lee, executive director of Medical Center Communications; Mr. Robert Feldman, associate vice-chancellor for Medical Development; Dr. Harry Jacobson, vice-chancellor for Health Affairs.

Chapter One

THE MEASURE OF
THE MAN

A man should be measured by a yardstick contemporaneous with his time as well as by the judgment of history. In the case of Ernest William Goodpasture, those who knew him might wonder if there were in addition a higher standard, a bar he set for himself, composed of values that cannot be quantified and are difficult to document. At a personal level, these values would certainly have included integrity, devotion to family, valued friendships, and loyalty (Fig. 1-1). There were also professional values, partially made apparent in his writings and fully evident in his actions—chief among which was his conviction that academic institutions and particularly universities were the highest manifestation of civilization,[1] and that as such their major responsibility was maintaining independence to seek the truth, followed closely by their proper training of young people.[2] In academic institutions Dr. Goodpasture singled out the medical profession as having "so great an opportunity and with it so profound a responsibility for leadership along paths of sane and healthful living in the broadest sense."[3]

Fig. 1-1: This photograph of Dr. Goodpasture was taken around 1945.

Ernest William Goodpasture was born on a working farm near Clarksville, Tennessee, on October 17, 1886. He had four siblings, first a brother and sister who never married, and then a brother and sister who did. Altogether there were six nieces and nephews. His father was a lawyer, farmer, politician, scholar, historian, and owner of a highly regarded secondhand bookstore in Nashville. His mother was credited with Ernest's "quiet and pleasant sociability and his characteristic enthusiasm, whether for work or play."[4]

Ernest's formal education began in 1893 in the public schools of Nashville, continuing at Bowen's Academic School from 1899 to 1903 and Vanderbilt University from 1903 to 1907. He enrolled in Johns Hopkins Medical School in 1908 and received his M.D. degree in 1912, staying there for graduate work in the Department of Pathology until 1915. Fellowship and junior faculty positions were taken at Harvard Medical School from 1915 until 1922. In 1915, he married Sarah Catlett of Clarksville, Tennessee, and their only child Sarah was born in 1919. During World War I he was called to active duty at the Chelsea Naval Hospital where he served from 1918 to 1919. From 1921 to 1922, on leave of absence from Harvard, he served as head of the Department of Pathology at the University of the Philippines in Manila.

The Goodpastures returned to the United States in 1922 when Dr. Goodpasture became the director of the Singer Research Laboratory in Pittsburgh. After two extremely productive years, he accepted the position of professor of pathology and head of the department at Vanderbilt University School of Medicine, for which new facilities were under construction. Along with several other recent recruits to Vanderbilt, he had the opportunity to work abroad until construction was completed in 1925. Dr. Goodpasture chose to work at the University of Vienna.

He remained at Vanderbilt until 1955. For the decade of 1930–40, Dr. Goodpasture's laboratory was in the forefront worldwide in the study of viral diseases. In the thirty-year period of his professorship, Vanderbilt flourished as a medical school, becoming for a time the premier medical school in the South and one of the best in the country. The declines in status of the medical school and in his productivity were probably related to financial pressures on the school as well as shortage of personnel due to World War II; additional factors contributing to his decreased productivity were the illness and death of his wife in 1940 and the assumption of a crushing administrative load (associate dean/dean) from 1943 to 1950. Katherine Anderson became his second wife in 1945. He was elected to emeritus status in 1955, at age sixty-eight.

The remaining five years of his life were spent as scientific director of the Armed Forces Institute of Pathology (1955–59), as visiting professor of pathology at the University of Mississippi (December 1959–March 1960), and as emeritus professor of pathology at Vanderbilt. Dr. Goodpasture was almost seventy-four years old when he died suddenly and unexpectedly on the afternoon of September 20, 1960, while working in his backyard in Nashville.

Dr. and Mrs. Goodpasture had recently returned to Nashville and Vanderbilt, where they had resumed their investigative studies in the Department of Pathology. Their research appropriately was on a pox-virus they isolated from warty nodules on the legs and feet of a junco trapped in Jackson, Mississippi. Their last paper was published in 1962 in the *American Journal of Pathology* and dealt with the distinctive features of this virus.

During his years at Vanderbilt, he had numerous intramural administrative responsibilities before assuming the deanship. He was recognized repeatedly with the most prestigious scientific awards and honors from the scientific community. Although he was quite appreciative of such recognition, he would probably have preferred to be remembered for his role in placing Vanderbilt in the first rank of medical schools.

There are no written or oral self-assessments by Dr. Goodpasture, nor were such likely even had he anticipated death. However, in terms of the personal and professional measures above—those values of most importance to him—he would have been contented with the depth of respect by family, friends, colleagues, and students, at a level that remains undiminished forty years after his death.[5]

The traditional measures of academic accomplishment may be summarized under the following headings: significance of research; quality of teaching; and respect by peers as manifested by appointments, professional responsibilities, recruitment by other institutions, honors, and awards. The success of trainees and administrative abilities are other indicators of academic accomplishment. These are listed in their likely order of importance to Dr. Goodpasture. Before considering these measures in more detail, we must define the yardstick appropriate for his time.

A Perspective of His Time

Imagine a time, if you can, when the function of DNA was not known, when the very nature of viruses was unclear, when the light microscope was arguably the most sophisticated diagnostic and research tool, when tissue cultures were difficult or impractical due to bacterial contamination, when the tubercle bacillus and spirochete of syphilis had recently been identified and bacteria were in their heyday as human pathogens, a time that included the last decades of the nineteenth century and the first half of the twentieth. It was during this period that Dr. Goodpasture was most productive. Only in the last ten years of his life, when his research had essentially ground to a halt, were methods for studying the molecular biology of viral diseases developed.

The major accomplishments in virology from 1890 to 1960 are outlined in Table 1-1. Many scientists believe that the discipline of

Table 1-1
Landmark Events in Virology, 1890–1960

1890

Filterability of tobacco mosaic virus demonstrated by Ivanovski, 1892, Beijerinck, 1898

Filterable animal virus (foot and mouth disease) found by Loeffler and Frosch, 1898

1900

First human virus (yellow fever) found by Reed et al., 1901–1902

Inclusion bodies demonstrated in rabies by Negri, 1903

Polio virus found by Landsteiner and Popper, 1909

1910

Virus-producing solid tumors (Rous sarcoma) shown by Rous, 1911

Tissue culture of chick embryo explant by Carrel, 1912

Discovery of bacteriophage by Twort and d'Herelle, 1915

1920

**Axonal transmission of herpetic infection by Goodpasture and Teague, 1923

1930

**Proof that elementary bodies of fowlpox are infectious unites by Woodruff and Goodpasture, 1929–30

**Use of chick embryo for studying viral diseases and vaccine production by Woodruff and Goodpasture, 1931

Swine influenza virus demonstrated by Shope, 1931

**Proof that mumps is a viral infection by Johnson and Goodpasture, 1934

Influenza virus grown in chick embryos by Smith, 1935, and Burnet, 1936

Crystallization of tobacco mosaic virus by Stanley, 1935

Attenuated yellow fever strain 17D developed by Theiler and Smith, 1937

1940

German measles proven to induce congenital malformations by Gregg, 1941

Influenza virus grown for vaccine in chick embryo by Burnet, 1941

Ultrastructure of influenza virus demonstrated by Mosely and Wykoff, 1946

Polio virus grown in explant of human embryonic tissue by Enders et al., 1949

1950

Plaque assay in tissue culture developed for viruses by Dulbecco, 1952

Bacteriophage reproduction shown to be dependent on DNA by Hershey and Chase, 1952

Varicella cultured in roller tubes by Weller, 1953

Measles propagated in tissue culture by Enders et al., 1954

Viruses defined as infectious agents composed of nucleic acids and proteins, but unable to grow autonomously or reproduce by binary fission by Lwoff, 1957

**Indicates contributions by Dr. Goodpasture and associates

virology was initiated by the discovery in 1892 by Ivanovski (with independent confirmation in 1898 by Beijerinck) that tobacco mosaic disease was due to an agent that passed through a filter capable of blocking bacteria. On the other hand, no less an authority than Sir Macfarlane Burnet claimed virology did not become an "independent science" until the 1950s, when viruses were defined as infectious agents that grew only in the presence of living tissue.[6] Independent science or not, the basic clinical and pathological manifestations of many viral diseases were defined before 1950, as were methods developed to study viral diseases in the laboratory (*in vitro*) and *in vivo*. More importantly, effective immunization programs were launched for prevention of such devastating diseases as smallpox, rabies, poliomyelitis, and yellow fever. Dr. Goodpasture's research played an important role in these advances prior to 1950.

The opinion of the eminent scientist Sir Macfarlane Burnet has been emphasized to make the point that virtually all of Dr. Goodpasture's work in virology occurred before the life cycle of viruses was known. The judgment of the authors of a current text[7] is that the *modern* period in the study of animal viruses began in 1960. This text diplomatically assigns the work summarized in Table 1-1 (as well as the Goodpasture studies described subsequently) to the "Early Period" of virological research.

In addition to the conceptual gaps in viral biology (not understanding the basics of viral life cycles), investigators such as Dr. Goodpasture were also limited by the paucity of methods. Diseases were grouped, and specific viral agents evaluated, by clinical features (for example, was a disease associated with pox production?), by filterability of the infectious agent and by microscopic changes indicating viral infection such as pattern of cell death and inflammation or production of inclusion bodies (structures in nucleus or cytoplasm with a specific microscopic appearance). Scientists are always limited by the methods available to them, and the accomplishments during this "Early Period" become more impressive when we take into account the methods available then.

This was also a time when the recognition of the central role of the scientific method in medicine had recently led to the formation of the Johns Hopkins Medical School, the fountain-head for development of modern medicine. Many faculty members at Vanderbilt and other medical schools seemed to have measures of idealism and sense of purpose that modernists can envy but seldom emulate. In those times, the pace and quality of life were even more enviable. In comparison to the present, there were infrequent department, medical school, and national meetings. It was particularly helpful for the *esprit de corps* at Vanderbilt that faculty and house staff routinely had lunch together in the doctors' dining room (Fig. 1-2).

This type of gathering was possible because the full-time faculty at Vanderbilt during the 1930s and 1940s numbered fewer than forty. Apparently united by the challenge of developing Vanderbilt as a leading academic medical school, their clear sense of purpose was strengthened by an ideal academic setting in which faculty could concentrate on research, teaching mechanisms of disease, and health care. Not only were they in a compact physical facility that fostered interactions among clinical and basic

Fig. 1-2: Doctors' dining room at Vanderbilt Hospital, circa 1930. Faculty, residents, and university officials routinely met for lunch. Tables were unassigned in theory, but senior faculty probably had preference.

sciences, but the endowment allowed free access by patients to the hospital.

Imagine practicing medicine before Blue Cross and managed care, without the welter of competing economic interests that now control and distort care of the sick. There was only a handful of journals, and the pace of publication was more leisurely, even dignified. Competition for priority of discovery may have been less keen, in part because information was transmitted less rapidly. Yearly national meetings apparently served as the major mechanism for information exchange. Before air-conditioning was available, work in the summer months slowed or ceased altogether, with retreat by senior faculty to mountain or beach homes as the order of the day.[8]

In short, academic life in those days had a more sustainable pace and was focused on gratifications in the home university and less on travel. As for deadlines, they were more self-imposed than externally enforced. Finally, many academic transactions now associated with elaborate and time-consuming procedures were effected by a handshake. The support of the chief, whether in a letter or at dinner in Atlantic City, opened doors, secured the plum appointments, and facilitated publication in prize journals. Virtually all of the publications from the Department of Pathology were accepted forthwith on the basis of Dr. Goodpasture's recommendation.[9] This was not academic cronyism in action. An informal system of this type worked because one's reputation was dependent on reliability and usefulness of recommendations as well as altruism. The system was more effective because many of the leading faculty had known each other at Hopkins or other major medical schools.

It was a time when financial resources were sharply limited. The budget of the Department of Pathology in 1925 was $20,000; this amount included salaries, supplies, and expenses for research. This budget in 1940 totaled $36,562.18,[10] and in Dr. Goodpasture's last year as chairman (1955) had reached $57,240.[11] Admittedly during these times of austerity, one could travel round-trip to New York from Nashville for $59.10; this figure included sleeper accommodations. Hotel and meal expenses for six days might boost the grand total by an additional $61.90. Nevertheless, there was a constant battle for funding during the years when Dr. Goodpasture was most productive. Fortunately, some research grants were available. In 1940, Dr. Goodpasture's research program was completely dependent on a $5,000 grant from the Markle Foundation.

Dr. Goodpasture's career may be considered as extending from 1912, the year of graduation from Johns Hopkins Medical School, until 1960, the year of his death. In those forty-eight years, the United States was indirectly and/or directly involved for a total of thirteen years in major wars, with World War I from 1914 to 1918, World War II from 1939 to 1945, and the Korean War from 1950 to 1953. At a personal level, no close members of his family were lost during these wars, and his only tour of duty was stateside at the Chelsea Naval Station near Boston from 1918 to 1919. Dr. Goodpasture made good use of this time to become thoroughly familiar with the pathologic anatomy of influenza. After World War I, Germany was no longer the dominant force scientifically, as the balance of power shifted to England and the United States.

World War II completely altered the framework of academia in the United States. During the war most medical schools were drained of their professional life-blood—young physicians—leaving the undrafted and essential faculty to carry on. For the first time in the United States, government began to fund science programs in universities in an organized way, a process that obviously continues to the present with its advantages and disadvantages over the previous more private system.

For most of Dr. Goodpasture's life, health could not be taken for granted, even by the young. Pharmaceutical wonders became generally available only after 1950, and there were no effective treatments for many diseases, such as the malignant hypertension responsible for the death of his wife in 1940 at age fifty. Immunizations were available against only a few infectious diseases, and it was by the luck of the draw that Dr. Goodpasture and his immediate family were spared in the great influenza pandemic of 1918–21. It is worth recalling that at least twenty-one million people died worldwide in that pandemic.

As devastating as these wars and illnesses were, there was yet another malignant force that drastically affected his life personally and professionally. This was the conjoined economic disaster known as the "Great Crash" of 1929 and the following Great Depression that lasted, with varying severity, for ten years.[12] The crash and depression were spawned in the speculative frenzy of the Roaring Twenties that followed the vast economic expansion associated with World War I. Although the number of active speculators in 1929 was probably less than a million (from a population of approximately 120 million), the crash and depression spared few in the United States or worldwide. In 1933, the total production of the U.S. economy (gross national product) was a third less than in 1929,[13] while the average number unemployed was greater than eight million between 1930 and 1940. Prices on the New York Stock Exchange did not bottom out until July 8, 1932, when the Dow-Jones industrial average was 58, down from a high of 452 in September 1929.[14] Banks failed at a horrifying rate across the United States, with 659 banks going under in 1929, 1,352 in 1930, and 2,294 in 1931.[15] The first run on a bank in Nashville occurred on November 14, 1930, immediately after Caldwell and Company declared insolvency. All in all, this was a miserable, dreary period for most, with hopes, resources, and/or reputations lost. Farmers were not exempt, with many farms lost owing to defaults on mortgages.

The searing experience of the Great Depression undoubtedly affected investment strategies of Vanderbilt University into the 1940s, accounting in part for the low rate of return on the university's endowment. One of the aftershocks of the depression was the financial shortfall of the medical school endowment in the 1940s as prices began to outpace return. (See chapter 5 for details.)

With these perspectives, Dr. Goodpasture's academic accomplishments should now be analyzed in light of the judgment of history.

SIGNIFICANCE OF RESEARCH

Although Dr. Goodpasture is best known for developing the chick embryo technique for culturing viruses, he and his staff made other significant contributions, particularly in elucidating basic pathogenetic mechanisms in certain viral and bacterial diseases. They also discovered the causes of several diseases, including mumps. The highlights of his work are given in this chapter under the headers of pathogenesis and prevention of viral disease, the cause of cancer, and the pathogenesis of bacterial infections, while the details are covered in chapter 3. Please be reminded that the goal of this chapter is to analyze the significance of his work, and how his conclusions have held up over time, as a measure of the man.

Pathogenesis and Prevention of Viral Diseases

Mode of transmission of herpes simplex virus from periphery to central nervous system

Doctors Goodpasture and Teague first addressed this question in 1923, when they were coworkers at the Singer Research Institute in Pittsburgh.[16] Dissemination is an infrequent complication of herpes simplex infection, but their studies were probably undertaken to address a broader issue: how do viruses travel from the portal of entry to reach target organs such as the brain? Goodpasture and Teague demonstrated that rabbits universally developed a fatal encephalitis within a few days following an infection of the cornea and conjunctiva with herpes virus isolated from a typical "fever blister."

It was fortuitous that this strain of herpes was particularly likely to affect nervous tissue. By carefully dissecting the brain and major nerves, they showed that the initial site of brain involvement was *anatomically* related by nerve branches to the initial focus of infection. In order to detect the pathways by which virus spread, they searched microscopically for inflammation in which there were cells containing typical inclusion bodies.

In their most significant experiments, corneal inoculations resulted in apparent transmittal of virus along the *sensory* fibers of the fifth cranial nerve to the brain stem, with a local unilateral acute inflammatory reaction produced in the nerve at the point of entry into the brain stem. On the other hand, if herpes virus were injected into the jaw muscles, the nerve affected was the *motor* branch of the fifth cranial nerve, and the first central lesion was in the motor nucleus of this nerve. After conducting extensive variations of these experiments, Goodpasture and Teague concluded that the virus grew in the connective tissue sheaths around the nerves, the axis-cylinders, propagating therein until it reached the highly susceptible cerebral tissue.

Because of this work, Dr. Goodpasture has been described as the founder of axonal spread of some viral infections.[17] Studies using currently available techniques have confirmed his conclusions that were dependent upon his interpretation of histologic sections.[18] Different conclusions have been reached when other animal models are studied. Using suckling mice as the experimental host, Johnson[19] showed that the herpes virus might gain access to the central nervous system by blood-borne as well as neural pathways, and that the major neural pathway was via supporting cells of nerves rather than in axons as proposed by Dr. Goodpasture (for rabbits).

These studies are of historical as well as scientific importance, in that Dr. Goodpasture stated that his interest in viral diseases was based on this very productive collaboration with Oscar Teague at the Singer Laboratory,[20] rather than being due to his experience with influenza in the 1918–19 pandemic.[21]

Chick embryo technique

Dr. Goodpasture is best known as a scientist for developing the chick embryo technique because its use greatly facilitated the study of viral diseases and for the first time enabled large-scale production of viruses. His first publication about chick embryos was in 1931 and the last was in 1959; from 1937 on, Dr. Goodpasture and collaborators used these embryos to focus on bacterial infections and to investigate immunity. The original publication in 1931 was an extension of eight years of research on viral disease, with papers on herpetic encephalitis (1923), rabies (1925), yellow fever (1927), molluscum contagiosum (1927 and 1931), and fowlpox (1928–31). During this time, in part because of Dr. Goodpasture's efforts, the concepts of viral biology had become more true-to-life, while the methods of study had not changed appreciably. Viruses were known to pass through earthenware or porcelain filters, they usually were preservable in glycerol, and they resisted drying. Individual viruses had clear preferences for specific tissues (cytotropism), and the lesions produced included necrosis of tissue, tumorous proliferations, and inclusion bodies. Viruses could not be cultivated in lifeless media. Some viruses causing diseases in humans affected other animals naturally or could be passed experimentally to them. Recovery from viral infections was usually associated with lasting immunity.

Visualization of viruses by electron microscopy did not occur until the 1940s; the biology as well as mechanics of viral reproduction were a mystery. Answers to questions about the nature of viruses awaited, in Dr. Goodpasture's terms, the "great desideratum,"[22] which was the successful cultivation of the active agent in artificial media. He recognized that cultivation would serve two purposes: to determine whether viruses were living agents capable of existence free of host cells, and to facilitate their study in the laboratory.

Fig. 1-3: Dr. Goodpasture is working on an embryonated egg, in which a window has been cut and covered. Laboratory equipment in the picture includes egg-holder and Bunsen burner. Shell-cutting equipment is not shown. This photograph was taken in 1955 and is available through the courtesy of Dr. Samuel Paplanus.

The embryonated egg proved to be an invaluable laboratory tool in virology, although it was not artificial (Fig. 1-3). Eggs were cheap, readily available, and tolerant of various manipulations. They were susceptible to infection with many viruses and promoted the reproduction of viruses free of bacterial contaminants (a very important consideration before antibiotics facilitated general use of tissue cultures). For all of these reasons, the chick embryo technique is generally regarded as a landmark development in animal virus research.[23] Perhaps the greatest value of this technique was in vaccine development, a potential clearly recognized by Buddingh and Goodpasture in their studies on smallpox vaccines.[24] Both viral and rickettsial agents could be grown in relatively pure cultures in large quantities, thereby facilitating their use as the antigenic material in vaccines. Vaccines made with Goodpasture's techniques were extensively used to immunize against yellow fever, influenza, rickettsial infections such as typhus, and to a lesser extent, smallpox.[25]

Of these vaccines, the immunizations against yellow fever and typhus were particularly effective, protecting millions of Allied troops during World War II. By 1965[26] more than forty million people had received the yellow fever vaccine,[27] judged to be one of the most successful attenuated viral-immunizing agents. After 1949, tissue culture techniques for viral propagation became available and largely supplanted chick embryos in vaccine work.

Chick embryos were also used by Dr. Goodpasture and associates to study bacterial infections. Among these infections, chick embryos were particularly useful in understanding the pathogenesis of whooping cough and meningococcal infection as well as finding the infectious agent in granuloma inguinale.

Infectious potential of viral inclusions

Nuclear or cytoplasmic inclusions are important morphologic features of viral infections, and their presence was one of the mainstays in recognizing viral infection during Dr. Goodpasture's lifetime. Because of their importance to morphologists, he focused his attention on the nature of viral inclusions. It is further to be expected that such an analysis could occur only after he had perfected certain staining techniques and his abilities to recognize inclusions in their various guises. To quote Dr. Goodpasture, "It was only natural that the morphologist should have sought in the study

of these intracellular bodies to find their relationship to the etiologic agents at work . . . "28

He (and others) considered two possibilities: that inclusions
represented wholly or in part a virus itself, or that inclusions
consisted of constituents or products of cells resulting from viral
infections. Both circumstances hold true if we consider all viral
inclusions. Dr. Goodpasture, however, focused on the inclusions
of fowlpox.

As described in chapter 3, fowlpox was one of his favorite experimental subjects. Working with C. Eugene and Alice Miles
Woodruff from 1929 to 1931, he progressively dissected the fowlpox
inclusion body, establishing its infectiousness at each stage. Finally
able to disrupt individual inclusions by simple air-drying, they were
able to prove that the inclusion bodies of fowlpox represented
colonies of minute microorganisms (Borrel bodies) "believed to
represent the actual virus of fowl-pox."29 In meticulous experiments
one of these inclusions or a few of the minute bodies placed into a
feather follicle were shown to reproduce the lesion of fowlpox.
These studies thereby established that inclusion bodies in viral
infections might contain an extremely small living agent that was
capable of causing the disease. Paschen, working twenty years
earlier with the vaccinia (cowpox) inclusion, had also seen in the
inclusion enormous numbers of minute granules that he postulated
were the etiological agent of vaccinia, but the work of Doctors
Goodpasture and Woodruff30 represented the first proof that a
living, infectious agent was present in an inclusion closely associated
with a specific viral disease. At least for the disease fowlpox, it was
no longer tenable to consider viruses as *inanimate* proteinaceous
materials, a view held widely at that time.

Significance of cytotropism and mutability of viruses

Two of the most fundamental as well as puzzling attributes of
viruses are their predilection to affect specific tissues (cytotropism) and their apparent ability to change over time (mutability).
The term "cytotropism" had been coined for viruses by Philibert
in 1924. Dr. Goodpasture shortly afterwards recognized that this

feature of viruses had fundamental significance. As he put it in his lecture at Duke Medical School in 1932,[31] "Viruses generally speaking manifest a very clear, specific and perhaps an essential relationship with certain cells of the infected host." Further, viruses induced recognizable cellular alterations in specific tissues with such predictability that the type of virus might be identified thereby.

Despite this very close relationship with living cells, the main feature allowing viruses to be distinguished from other infectious agents was their filterability through porcelain filters that held back bacteria as well as cells. It seemed paradoxical that viruses needed living tissue in which to grow, but they could be separated from cells and still induce infection. The phenomenon of cytotropism implied that there was a specific relationship between the cells of the host and the virus, leading to his suspicion that viruses may reproduce "exclusively in the interior of cells," and that they have a "highly selective adaptation to a restricted environment."[32] In this statement Dr. Goodpasture anticipated in broad outline the modern concept of viral biology established in 1957 by Lwoff,[33] that host cell metabolism may be manipulated by viral genetic material. The interaction between cell and virus culminates in the production and release of infectious material that may pass through filters easily. More significantly for natural infections of humans and other animals, infectious material must be released into the environment, often as droplets or fomites, for infections to spread.

This fundamental predilection of viruses for specific tissues was also used by Dr. Goodpasture to study their mutability, as none of the techniques of molecular biology now in use was available to him. He recognized that changes in preferences for tissues by viruses (their cytotropism) could be analyzed as a manifestation of a fundamental change in viral biology induced by mutations. It was known that bacteria and viruses evolved, as do all living things, and that this evolution was probably responsible for dramatic shifts in virulence of infections such as in the devastating influenza pandemic of 1918–21. Such changes in pathogenicity of bacteria and viruses might be studied to understand their biology as well as for the more immediate value of developing vaccines. As an example of the latter, Pasteur had induced changes in anthrax bacilli and rabies viruses in order to develop vaccines that were effective against these agents. Dr. Goodpasture's interest in mutation in viruses extended from 1923 until his death. His initial work with Teague was based on a strain of herpes virus that was distinguished by its ability to spread to the nervous system. In 1939 Katherine Anderson made an extensive analysis of this property in Dr. Goodpasture's laboratory, showing that herpes virus could be induced to become more virulent for the chick, while its harm to rabbit brain decreased.[34] Mutations in fowlpox were evaluated in one of his last papers.[35] Although cytotropism and mutability were studied thoroughly by Dr. Goodpasture for thirty-five years, his research offered no insight into the basic mechanisms of either phenomenon, as such insights awaited the methods of molecular biology.

Determining the cause of mumps

Determining whether a particular disease is infectious, and then establishing that the disease in question is caused by a specific bacterium or virus, seems simple to us today. We are accustomed to thinking specifically about such entities as tuberculosis, typhoid fever, syphilis, and viral hepatitis. However, it has taken more than one hundred years of study to arrive at our present enlightened state, and, surprisingly, attributions of bacterial causation are still being made for long-known diseases such as peptic ulcer (*Helicobacter pylori* is the usual cause) and multiple sclerosis (recent evidence links this disease to chlamydial infection). Rules were established to ensure that specific bacteria were correctly assigned responsibility for given diseases; these rules generally bear the name of Koch, although Henle[36] had priority for espousing such rules. Koch's postulates, as they are known, state in part that the infectious agent occurs in every case, that it accounts for the clinical and pathological features of a disease, and that it is not found in other circumstances as a nonpathogenic agent. These conditions have been difficult to meet in every bacterial disease, but Koch's final condition is even more demanding: the infectious agent must be isolated in pure culture and be able to induce the disease anew in man or other experimental animal. This last condition is extremely stringent, in part because humans for ethical and practical reasons are usually not used as test subjects.

It is pertinent that satisfying Koch's postulates in viral diseases has been far more difficult than for bacterial diseases, a circumstance justifying a brief consideration at this point. Huebner, in a paper titled "The Virologist's Dilemma,"[37] summarized the difficulties as follows: "virus infection" is a common diagnosis, particularly for minor illnesses; and new techniques readily isolate viruses from patients with fever of various types, but clinicians or laboratorians rarely prove that the virus isolated actually causes a particular illness. The extent of the problem is illustrated by Huebner's studies of a Washington, D.C., orphanage during the months of September and October 1955. The fifty or so children studied in September had few febrile illnesses, but an ECHO-like virus was isolated in 100 percent of the children at two times during the month. In October there were numerous febrile illnesses, and the same or a similar ECHO virus was equally prevalent. Had Huebner studied these children for only one month, he might have reached diametrically opposing conclusions. As it is, proving whether the ECHO virus was a normal inhabitant in these children or was responsible for some of the diseases is difficult if not impossible. Separately, Huebner and Rivers[38] modified Koch's postulates to meet these viral caveats. The conditions Huebner believed should be satisfied include:

- beginning with a homogeneous patient population (that is, all patients must have the same clinical illness)
- isolating a virus reproducibly from their tissues or blood (a common problem in this regard is that contaminating viruses may be found sporadically in the culture media)
- characterizing the virus in terms of its nature so that it can be studied in various laboratories

- showing that an appropriate antibody response is produced after infection. If possible, viral inoculations in human volunteers should reproduce the clinical disease, and specific vaccinations should prevent it.

Huebner recognized that many of these conditions bordered on the unrealistic and that they were more useful as guides than as strict criteria.

Dr. Goodpasture was able to meet these conditions fully in proving that mumps was a viral infection; this work was confirmed shortly afterward in several laboratories. In reviewing the literature on mumps in 1934, Johnson and Goodpasture noted that the causative agent of mumps at different times had been identified as a bacterium, filterable virus, and spirochete. However, no one had unquestionably produced the disease experimentally or clearly demonstrated its cause. Various experimental animals had been used and a standard model of study had not been developed. In contrast, Johnson and Goodpasture reliably reproduced the disease in monkeys, in which striking enlargement of the parotid glands was produced by injecting the ducts of these glands with saliva from patients with mumps. After seventeen passages,[39] filtrates from affected glands produced mumps in human volunteers who had previously not had mumps. All in all, this was an elegant set of experiments that clearly established the viral etiology of mumps. Dr. Goodpasture stated that this study was one of his "proudest achievements,"[40] as mumps had been known since antiquity and his experiments established the cause for the first time.

Pathogenesis of Bacterial Infections

Although best known for his work on viruses, Dr. Goodpasture was also an expert in bacterial infections. His studies on cholera described in chapter 2 showed the importance of autopsy technique in studying mechanisms of disease. The studies on pertussis (whooping cough) and granuloma inguinale described in chapter 3 were exploitations of the chick embryo as an experimental animal. For pertussis, the predilection of the causative agent for growth in ciliated epithelium was studied in developing chick embryos. These experiments showed that some bacteria had growth requirements *in vivo* as specific as those in viral infections. For granuloma inguinale, he and his associates found that the etiologic agent required living cells for growth, a phenomenon also similar to the culture requirements for viruses. These studies on bacterial infection, taken together with those on viral diseases, show a deep understanding of the range of possible interactions between living things. In this work, Dr. Goodpasture drew on the important studies of Theobald Smith as summarized in 1934 in Theobald Smith's book *Parasitism and Disease*.

Causes of Cancer

Cancer was less of a problem during Dr. Goodpasture's career than it is now, and his studies on tumors of aged dogs reveal an interest in biological phenomena per se. His demonstration in the late 1910s that tumors of various types were the rule in aged dogs anticipated the cancer problems of aged humans now. He also attempted to repeat in mammals experiments Peyton Rous had performed in fowls that showed filterable agents might induce cancers. Although bold in concept and reasonable in design, Dr. Goodpasture's experiments did not provide additional evidence that viruses might cause cancer.

QUALITY OF TEACHING

There were better, or at least more memorable, teachers at Vanderbilt than Dr. Goodpasture. Among the clinicians, Katie Dodd in Pediatrics, Tinsley Harrison in Medicine, and Barney Brooks in Surgery are usually cited for their ability to teach undergraduates. Many students found that instruction in the basic sciences was laissez-faire, as in anatomy, or excessively lecture-rich until they came to pathology. Much of the routine teaching from

1935 until 1955 in that department was the responsibility of Dr. James Dawson or Dr. John Shapiro.

Dr. Goodpasture is remembered by the students graduating during those years as reserved, dignified, and soft-spoken.[41] His lectures were given in a monotone, somewhat obscuring their richness in concept and understanding. Students probably had only the sketchiest understanding of his scientific accomplishments but knew he was highly respected within and outside the Department of Pathology. In any case, education of medical students in the basic principles of pathology has been exemplary since the reorganization of the medical school. Dr. Goodpasture recognized that the act of teaching and inspiring students was one of the chief functions of academic institutions. This goal was consistently met in his department, and it would be a mistake to assume his role in teaching was only that of a facilitator.

RESPECT BY PEERS AS MANIFESTED BY APPOINTMENTS, PROFESSIONAL RESPONSIBILITIES, HIS RECRUITMENT BY OTHER INSTITUTIONS, HONORS, AND AWARDS

Appointments

The premier medical school in Dr. Goodpasture's time was Johns Hopkins, and its school also contained the premier Department of Pathology, chaired by William Welch, avowedly the founder of academic medicine in the United States. It is possible, even likely, that Ernest Goodpasture's admittance to Johns Hopkins Medical School in 1908 (at age twenty-two) was the crucial appointment on which his career was based. After graduating from Hopkins in 1912, Dr. Goodpasture remained there on the house staff for three years before accepting an appointment at Harvard Medical School, then and now a most prestigious university. At Harvard the chief was William T. Councilman, perhaps the only pathologist in the same league with William Welch.

Dr. Goodpasture had three other major appointments, as professor of pathology and head of the department at Vanderbilt from 1924 to 1955, as dean of Vanderbilt Medical School from 1945 to 1950, and as scientific director of the Armed Forces Institute of Pathology from 1955 to 1959. His *modus operandi* as head was to participate as fully in departmental teaching and service activities as his travel schedule permitted, but day-to-day responsibilities in these areas were necessarily delegated to his chief assistant (Dr. Dawson or Dr. Shapiro, for example).

In addition to having the responsibility for directing the affairs of the pathology department, Dr. Goodpasture routinely sat on, or chaired, several medical school committees including the admissions, promotions, and library committees.

He served as associate dean from 1943 to 1945 and was dean from 1945 to 1950, with Sam Clark as associate dean. During these seven years, he continued as head of pathology.

Dr. Goodpasture had an active role in professional societies, with a forty-five-year membership in the American Association of Pathologists and Bacteriologists (president 1948–49) and a thirty-seven-year membership in the American Society for Experimental Pathology (president 1939–40). During the war and early post-war years, he held two posts of great significance in relation to medical concerns. The first was membership on the Board for the Investigation and Control of Influenza and Other Epidemic Diseases, established in January 1941, by the secretary of war, to investigate outbreaks of infectious disease. Secondly, he was on the board of directors of the Institute for Nuclear Studies from 1946 to 1952, serving in 1950 on the Atomic Bomb Casualty Commission. Other positions were held that were important to the war effort. He was a member of several National Research Council groups, particularly those that dealt with infectious diseases. He served from 1939 to 1944 on the Board of Scientific Directors of the International Health Division of the Rockefeller Foundation. He was a member of the Medical Advisory Committee of the Office of Scientific Research and Development under the direction of Vannevar Bush.

Professional Responsibilities

The appointments with the greatest responsibility were as chairman of the Department of Pathology at Vanderbilt from 1924 until 1955 (the position was titled head during his tenure), and as dean of the Vanderbilt School of Medicine from 1945 until 1950. For a discussion of his activities as head of pathology and dean, please see chapters 4 and 5, respectively. In the former position, Dr. Goodpasture was successful by all standards; his department was preeminent in research and managed a very successful educational program for medical students and residents. The major service responsibility was the performance of autopsies. Information derived from this service was effectively used for quality control of patient care, for teaching students, residents, and faculty, as well as for research.

In his role as head of pathology, Dr. Goodpasture had considerable autonomy by today's standards. As dean, he was responsible for the School of Medicine and Vanderbilt Hospital but was severely limited in options by a financial crisis described in detail in chapter 5. This crisis was so severe that the survival of the school was in doubt. That it survived is due in part to his arranging that the proceeds of the entire endowment come to the medical school, and in no small measure to trust and confidence in Dr. Goodpasture by the faculty, Chancellor Branscomb, and the Board of Trust.

The other major professional responsibilities of Dr. Goodpasture involved wartime assignments to important committees that dealt with control of infection in the armed services, the effects of atomic bombs on civilian populations, and the relationship between scientists and the government after the war. His positions on these committees were a reflection of his national stature; these activities are discussed in chapter 6.

Recruitment by Other Institutions

Johns Hopkins Medical School, October–December 1942[42]
His recruitment by Hopkins for the chairmanship in pathology was probably the most tempting offer he received while at

Vanderbilt. A veritable blizzard of telegrams and letters, originating from Baltimore on October 12 and October 13, bore the names of close friends and colleagues, including Longcope (physician-in-chief), Chesney (dean), Weed (professor of anatomy), Blalock (surgeon-in-chief), and Smith (director of hospital). Isaiah Bowman (president, Johns Hopkins University) followed on October 19 with affirmation of their unanimity in choosing Dr. Goodpasture for this important post and in cordially welcoming a visit for discussion of "any or all aspects of the question."

Dr. Goodpasture responded on October 21, as follows:

My dear President Bowman:

Your telephoned message informing me that I am the choice of your Committee of the Medical Faculty for the Professorship of Pathology at Johns Hopkins affected me deeply; and the telegrams and letters from Professors Longcope, Weed, Chesney, Blalock and Dr. Winford Smith assured me of the cordial spirit in which this great honor was tendered me. Some of these men were my medical classmates and others were recent and more remote associates on the medical school faculties and hospital staffs of Johns Hopkins and Vanderbilt. All of them I know are my friends.

It is not necessary for me to tell you how profoundly grateful I am to them and to you for this expression of esteem, confidence and friendship, which feelings I reciprocate in full measure.

You will know very well how concerned I have been to arrive at a right decision under these circumstances where distinguished traditions, old ties and happy memories pull so hard for renewal under such favorable auspices. Also you will understand the nature and strength of my ties here at Vanderbilt both professional and personal, and my realization on mature reflection that they are impellent.

I have decided that it is not best for me to accept the Professorship at Johns Hopkins, and I have so decided with a full realization of the greatness of Johns Hopkins University, and the eminent place its medical school holds in American Medicine. The rejection of the possibility of reuniting with my many friends on the Medical Faculty and of cooperating with you in your efforts to sustain the university's prestige and to lead it effectively on its great mission in these uncertain and often bewildering times was a difficult personal experience.

Please express to those most concerned in my decision my sense of appreciation for the honor of their consideration, and tell my friends of my feeling of personal loss in realizing my inability to work beside them again at Johns Hopkins.

Thank you very much for the favor of your communications and for your expressions of friendly and professional interest.

Sincerely yours,

Ernest W. Goodpasture

President Bowman urged reconsideration in a telegram dated October 26; a dinner was arranged at President Bowman's home on November 15, but Dr. Goodpasture warned that "I do not feel it would be well for me to change my decision." After this meeting, in expressing his thanks on December 2 to President Bowman, Dr. Goodpasture asked that he be allowed to confer with friends in New York on December 18. President Bowman may have misread the man with whom he was dealing, writing on December 10, "I do not see how you can resist the rising tide of sentiment in favor of your appointment here."

Dr. Goodpasture apparently finalized his decision over the Christmas holidays, with cordial letters of rejection to President Bowman on December 31 and to his colleagues at Hopkins on January 2. In contrast to the Harvard invitation described next, there is only one local response in the files, this from Dean Leathers on December 1, 1942. This letter carries rather oblique references to salary adjustments and arrangements to continue research interests. It is surprising that there are no other letters on file about Dr. Goodpasture's remaining at Vanderbilt, but the 1943 departmental budget showed significant changes in his salary ($10,000 to $11,000), Dr. Dawson's ($4,000 to $4,500), Dr. Buddingh's ($3,500 to $4,000), Dr. Anderson's ($1,800 to $2,250), and Miss McGovern's [the departmental secretary] ($1,600 to $1,800). The overall departmental budget[43] remained at $39,310, so the above raises were possible due to a reduction in technical staff and house staff.

The reasons why Hopkins would have recruited Dr. Goodpasture so heavily are easily understood. He had trained there in the glory days, he had created a very strong department at Vanderbilt, and his research credentials were impeccable. His overall reputation was perhaps more impelling; Alfred Blalock wrote Dr. Goodpasture that "every person questioned [by Bowman] has replied that you are the leading pathologist in the world."[44] His rejection of the Hopkins offer is a conundrum, to which there are no helpful leads in his papers. His wife and father had died within the previous two years, but there were no family responsibilities that impelled him to stay. Daughter Sarah had recently married and was self-sufficient. The decision was probably due to his assessment that Vanderbilt Medical School would be seriously weakened if he left, as the decimation of the faculty by wartime service was already a major problem. The invitation to Hopkins might therefore have been even more attractive had it come before the war, but concerns about his wife's health then would have likely led to the same decision.

Early in 1943, Dr. Goodpasture outlined for Dr. Longcope the type of academician Hopkins might attempt to recruit as the professor of pathology. A portion of his letter is quoted, as the opinions show the high qualifications he felt were called for:

> In the first place there are qualifications for a prospective occu-
> pant of the Chair of Pathology at Johns Hopkins transcending any
> that may appear readily available in any candidate, for those qualifi-
> cations would naturally be in the nature of ideals and one can only act
> on faith.
>
> I should hope the successful candidate would be a reasonably young
> man so that he might develop with and into the future, which just now
> would seem to be exceptionally obscure. A capacity for development
> however far outweighs the nature of changes in the days to come, and for
> development there must be a basis in the past and present. It seems to me
> this grounding should be primarily an appreciation of and a proven facility
> in the method and spirit of experiment. Secondly, though not essentially,
> the professor of pathology should have a feeling for and an experience of
> pathological anatomy, histology and cytology. It would be best I believe if

interest in the morphological aspects of disease could constantly be maintained and stimulated by applying experience of them in experimental work . . . With these qualifications should go those aspects of character and personality that are inspiring to colleagues and students.

Dr. Goodpasture then listed (alphabetically) the men who might be considered, including Doctors Buddingh, Dawson, and Arnold Rich. The latter was ultimately appointed chairman of pathology at Hopkins.

Harvard Medical School, February–March 1941[45]

The recruitment by Harvard may have been initiated by an invitation dated January 9, 1941, to give the Cutter Lecture in Preventive Medicine there. Dean Sidney Burwell issued the invitation at the request of Dr. John Gordon, professor of preventive medicine and epidemiology. This invitation was followed shortly by letters from Burwell and President Conant on February 6 offering the professorship of comparative pathology. President Conant recognized that there was overlap between his Departments of Pathology, Bacteriology, Comparative Pathology, and Epidemiology and indicated that the faculty of medicine was considering the "possibilities of closer arrangements" among the four. The relationship of the four departments was said to be in a "fluid state," so desirable modifications might be introduced when the various department chiefs were "ready for such cooperative efforts." Dr. Goodpasture flew to Boston in mid-February and returned to give the Cutter Lecture on March 7.[46] On March 10 he wrote Dr. Burwell to decline the offer, without giving specific reasons. In retrospect, the Harvard arrangements probably lacked the clear lines of responsibility he preferred; Dr. Goodpasture might have been more interested if the four departments had been fused *per dictum* and he had been offered the opportunity to head a more cohesive academic unit. The Vanderbilt community heaved a collective sigh of relief, with complimentary letters from Chancellor Carmichael ("the need here is greater and the opportunity for service more significant. The fact that you have decided to remain here will encourage others to do the same"), Sam Clark ("It is an encouraging thing to have you decide that this is a good place to be, and as long as you are here I'm sure it is a better one"), Paul Lamson ("It is a wonderful thing to be liked and appreciated as you are . . . I just received a note from Frank Rackemann in which he said about you 'We of Harvard are sorry that he will not come to us, but I have been to Nashville and tasted of the life and hospitality there, and I am not surprised that Ernest Goodpasture refuses to move away. He is a wise man, full of great common sense.'"), and Dean Leathers ("It gives me the greatest satisfaction that you have decided to remain at Vanderbilt . . ."). On March 27, Dr. Goodpasture thanked Dean Leathers (and certainly other colleagues) for a silver coffee set bearing this inscription:

Ernest William Goodpasture

Aestimatione amicitique summa

Socii ordinis medicorum

Universitatis Vanderbiltiae

Die Martii XXV

Anno MCMXII

Those needing help with this will learn that the translation reads: "With the highest esteem and friendship of the comradely society of medical doctors of Vanderbilt University, 25th day of March, in the year 1941." The Vanderbilt colleagues and Goodpastures had apparently celebrated at dinner as well, as there were thanks for "such an enjoyable evening and happy memory. Sarah and I will always take pride in the coffee set."

Offers or tenders of professorships were also made from George Washington University (1932), Stanford University (1934), McGill University (1938), and Cornell University Medical College (1940). The most specific reason for his rejection of these offers was expressed to Dr. Fleming at McGill in 1938: "My relations with Vanderbilt University however are such at the present time that I would not like for my name to be considered by your selection committee. Tennessee being my native state and Vanderbilt University my Alma Mater, I have of course many ties here . . ."

Honors and Awards

Dr. Goodpasture was elected to the most prestigious societies open to academicians (National Academy of Sciences, American Philosophical Society, Association of American Physicians), received honorary degrees from elite institutions (Yale University, University of Chicago, Washington University, Tulane University), was awarded the most important medals by such distinguished organizations as the American College of Physicians (John Phillips Memorial Award) and Association of American Physicians (Kober Medal), and received the ultimate recognition by his peers in the American Association of Pathologists and Bacteriologists (Gold Headed Cane) in addition to other citations from academia. (See chapter 9 for a full listing of his honors and awards and his curriculum vitae in the appendix.) Nevertheless, in Vanderbilt as well as in other academic communities, reminiscences and written accounts[47] about Dr. Goodpasture usually speculate as to why he did not receive a Nobel Prize as well. There are no written comments about the Nobel Prize in his correspondence, nor is he known to have expressed his views on this topic to colleagues or family. Indeed, when nominated by Shields Warren in 1953,[48] Dr. Goodpasture's response was very reserved:

> It was an especial pleasure during the holiday season to receive your greetings and good wishes. Needless to say it was also an uplifting experience to know that you were thinking of the work of this department in connection with the Nobel Committee for Physiology and Medicine. I greatly appreciate, I assure you, your high estimate of our efforts.
>
> I regret to say that many of the reprints I would like to send you are no longer available . . .

His lack of self-aggrandizement was genuine, and he doubtlessly believed it was unseemly for academicians to seek such awards in any way. Also he would have been concerned about appropriate recognition of his collaborators. In every speech accepting awards or honors, Dr. Goodpasture gave generous credit to his predecessors and colleagues. The intensity of feelings generated by the Nobel Prize, when awarded to an individual rather than a team, is exemplified by the award to Max Theiler in 1951 for his work on the yellow fever vaccine. Dr. Goodpasture was probably aware of the distress expressed by a Theiler colleague when the latter was not included as a Nobel laureate.[49] There is another ramification of Theiler's receiving the prize. The development of a successful yellow fever vaccine was based to a significant extent on the chick embryo work at Vanderbilt. Although Dr. Goodpasture might have felt slighted by the singling out of Theiler for the prize, there is no written or oral evidence to that effect.[50]

To put the Nobel Prize issue in some perspective, 169 prizes have been awarded in medicine from 1901 to 1999. Rather egregious mistakes have been made: the codiscoverer of streptomycin was not recognized in 1952; the English neurologist Charles Sherrington was nominated 134 times over a thirty-year period before finally receiving a prize in 1932 when he was seventy-five—apparently a single committee member blocked his recognition for seventeen years.[51] More recently, the discoverer of the underlying transmitter deficit in Parkinson's disease was not recognized while a colleague was given all of the credit, provoking an open letter to the award committee from 250 neuroscientists.[52] Closer to home, the head of zoology at Washington University for twenty-five years was passed over in 1986 when medals were awarded to two junior collaborators for their work on growth factors; one of the two recipients was Vanderbilt's Stanley Cohen.[53]

Now we should try to deal with the Nobel issue objectively. The Nobel Prizes are not awarded posthumously, so in fairness to others we need to consider the achievements of other awardees during the period when he was a potential candidate (Table 1-2). The deliberations of the Karolinska are held secret for fifty years, so we may not be able to come to closure on this matter until 2010 (fifty years after Dr. Goodpasture's death). What we do know is that he was nominated

Table 1-2
Nobel Prizes 1945–60 in Medicine and Physiology

1945—Florey, Fleming, and Chain for penicillin

1946—Muller for inducing mutations in drosophila with X rays

1947—Cori and Cori for synthesis of glycogen *in vitro*; to Houssay for discovering anterior pituitary hormone

1948—Muller for showing that DDT was an effective insecticide

1949—Hess for showing that specific loci in brain influenced behavior; to Moniz for discovering effects of prefrontal lobotomy

1950—Kendall, Reichstein, and Hinch for isolation and use of cortisone and ACTH

1951—Theiler for prophylaxis against yellow fever

1952—Waksman for isolation of streptomycin and use in tuberculosis

1953—Krebs for discovery of citric acid cycle; to Lipmann for coenzyme A

1954—Enders, Robbins, and Weller for growing polio virus

1955—Theorell for discovering oxidation enzymes

1956—Forsmann, Richards, and Cournand for cardiac catheterization

1957—Bovet for discovering antibacterial properties of sulphanilamide

1958—Beadle and Tatum for elucidating roles of chromosomes in heredity; to Lederberg for microbial genetics

1959—Ochoa and Kornberg for artificial synthesis of nucleic acids

1960—Burnet and Medawar for discovering acquired immunological tolerance

eight times between 1937 and 1949, with six of these nominations from overseas.[54] We also know that he was nominated at least once in 1953 by Shields Warren.[55]

The *Nobelkommiten* at the Karolinska does not provide details about awarding individual prizes, but one may comfortably assume Dr. Goodpasture was on a very short list, perhaps more than once. In the *Biographical Memoir*, Esmond Long states on page 122 that: "The eminent virologist F. Macfarlane Burnet (Fig. 1-4) went so far as to say that 'nearly all the later practical advances in the control of virus diseases in man and animals sprang from this single discovery [the embryonated egg technique].'"[56] The reference cited was *Encyclopedia Britannica*, 1954, 9:237, although the text in that volume does not give attribution for the statement. Sir Macfarlane Burnet did write later that "It has given me great satisfaction to pay my tribute to one of the masters of the great age of medical science. Goodpasture was one of the few dozen men from Pasteur and Koch to Florey and Enders who provided the basic discoveries that gave us, by 1955, control over disease that came from outside ourselves."[57] His work was Nobel-worthy indeed! It should also be recognized that Dr. Goodpasture did not receive a Lasker Award for Basic Research, while some of his colleagues in the infectious disease area were so recognized. The Lasker Awards often anticipate awarding of a Nobel Prize, and some of the recipients in the times under consideration were: Thomas Francis Jr. (1947), Oswald Avery (1947), Rene Dubos (1948), Sir MacFarlane Burnet (1952), John Enders (1954), Alfred Hershey (1958), and Peyton Rous (1958).

Perhaps we should all be content, as Dr. Goodpasture doubtlessly was, with the expressions of respect as recorded in the presentation of the Kober Medal in 1943.[58] The presentation speech by Dr. Sidney Burwell, and acceptance by Dr. Goodpasture, are cited in full. These speeches are a distillation of Dr. Goodpasture's accomplishments in the view of a colleague, and of his values as expressed by him. These few words should be read carefully for their mutual expressions of respect, dignity, motivation, and philosophy; it is a matter of record that Dr. Burwell,

Fig. 1-4: Dr. Goodpasture and Dr. Macfarlane Burnet. This photograph was made at the symposium on Immunity and Virus Infections held at Vanderbilt May 1–2, 1958.

although a close friend and former colleague from 1928 to 1935, did not give praise lightly.

Presentation of the Kober Medal to Dr. Ernest William Goodpasture
By C. Sidney Burwell, M.D.
Boston, Mass.
Mr. President, Dr. Goodpasture, Members of the Association:

The Kober Medal is awarded annually to a member of the Association of American Physicians "who has contributed to the progress and achievement of the medical sciences or preventive medicine."

Dr. Goodpasture, the custom of this Association and a decent respect to the opinions of mankind justify an inclusive recital of the achievements which led to the award of this medal to you. But time does not permit, and your fellows in this Association are already aware of these achievements.

As you have followed "the varying tide of battle between the active agent and the host," you have illuminated the natural history of host-parasite relationships. Thus you have added to that knowledge of pathogenesis which is basic to the understanding of immunity and to the institution of rational therapeutic and preventive activity.

It appears that you are of that succession of great naturalists whose virtue is that they know what questions to ask of Nature. From the answers to your questions have come: proof that the elementary bodies of fowlpox are really infectious units; knowledge of the spread of herpetic virus; demonstration of the etiologic agent of mumps; light on the pathogenesis of typhoid fever; and development of the fruitful concept of cytotropism of viruses. Your skillful development of the chick embryo as a living host has had great practical and theoretical usefulness. Viruses, rickettsiae, bacteria, even human skin grafts grow happily on the series of animals, with different susceptibilities at different stages, represented by the developing egg. Vaccines against yellow fever and typhus are possible, and the specific relationships of parasite and tissue are explored.

What are the characteristics of one who thus permanently enriches our understanding? Quality and continuity of thought, patient and resourceful skill, of course; also, and perhaps fundamentally, a deep delight in understanding the ways of living things for their own sakes. One is sure that you have as much interest in *H. sapiens* as in *P. pestis* and that you take as much pleasure in the successful transplanting of *Iris cristata* as in the transmission of the virus of epidemic parotitis.

Ernest, here is your medal, thriftily and legally made of silver and accompanied by a check to bring its value up to the gold standard provided for by the donor. Accept it as a symbol of the admiration and affection of your fellows; keep it as a perennial inoculum of their good will.

Reply to Kober Medal Award
By Ernest W. Goodpasture, M.D.
Nashville, Tenn.
Mr. President, Dr. Burwell, Members of the Association:

It is with a very natural feeling of pleasure and pride that I accept the George M. Kober Medal with which, for reasons better known to your committee than to me, you have seen fit to do me honor. I accept this medal, I hope in the same spirit of idealism that inspired Dr.

Kober to found it and you to award it, animated by a desire to encourage Medicine's high mission to serve the welfare of mankind through knowledge.

I realize that you have it in mind, by means of awarding this symbol of your concern for the promotion of medical research, to recognize and to honor all of those earnest investigators who have devoted themselves to the advancement of knowledge for human needs; nevertheless I feel it would be no infringement upon the special privilege you have allowed me today if I should mention a few of my own past and present associates who have made possible my preferred status on this occasion. Only a deep sense of indebtedness to their friendship and their comradeship in research could prompt me to call the names of Watson Sellards and Oscar Teague, and to add likewise with affection those of Alice and Eugene Woodruff, James R. Dawson, John Buddingh, Katherine Anderson and Claud Johnson, for I know all of them would have preferred at this time to maintain a generous anonymity.

By means of this beautiful medal you would honor also those institutions of learning that foster medical research, especially those institutions whose purpose it is to preserve, to acquire and to transmit knowledge and values—namely, the universities, and among them my own alma maters.

Our universities are in need of your special interest today for, in the arid deserts of our complex social and industrial life they must be the green oases of impartial intellectual growth and development; and lest they, too, parch in the withering heat of competition, they must be watered by every spring of our hope for improvement through research and proper assessment of values.

We are committed to research for we know well its power; but with this added strength come broader fields of influence and usefulness. Medicine in the days to come will make no greater extra-professional contribution to human well-being than by the application, as never before, of its great spirit and moral prestige to the cause of justice and righteousness among men and nations. One may even hope that, in the course of time, the traditionally high purpose of Medicine to serve mankind through knowledge and by means of a great body of trained and devoted men, will inspire similar groups endowed with wisdom and as assiduous in learning and practise, to apply themselves more and more to the ends of good government and social justice.

Even at the risk of chauvinism I would say that no other group of human beings in our midst by personal aptitude, by selection, by opportunities, training, traditional humanitarian objectives, ethical standards and preference in the hearts of mankind, has so great an opportunity and with it so profound a responsibility for leadership along paths of sane and healthful living in the broadest sense, in this sick world of ours, as does the medical profession, of which this Association is so distinguished a representative. All people will look to them for help and understanding, and they will not fail.

Sidney Burwell, let me thank you especially for your words of presentation and the friendship that lay behind them. Among the many bright facets of this medal, that which reflects your esteem will add much to its luster.

Mr. President and Members of the Association, I will always treasure and be uplifted by the honor of your respect and by this especial manifestation of your interest in my efforts at medical research. In behalf of my colleagues and for myself I thank you with all my heart.

The Success of Trainees

A total of twenty-one faculty were appointed from 1925 until 1955 in the Department of Pathology. Two of these (Doctors Dawson and Shapiro) became heads of Departments of Pathology, and two (Doctors Buddingh and Randall) heads of Departments of Microbiology. Several headed laboratories in community hospitals. Two medical students at Vanderbilt who trained elsewhere (Doctors Joe Grisham and David Walker) became heads of academic Departments of Pathology.

Administrative Abilities

It is difficult to pass judgment on this issue because conditions are so drastically different now as to the expectations for chairmen (heads) of departments. Salaries and space were fixed during Dr. Goodpasture's tenure, and space altercations in those days dealt with closets rather than floors or wings. As for management of personnel, there are no hints in the correspondence of personnel crises, while there is evidence the department was a happy place to work, and the staff was proud of their chief.

The success of Dr. Goodpasture's research program enabled the department to obtain its share of block grants available to the school for research. He was consistently able to recruit key personnel and to retain them in the department until it was in their interest to move elsewhere.

This chapter should close with the fitting tribute paid to Dr. Goodpasture by Dr. John Craighead on the frontispiece of his book *Pathology and Pathogenesis of Human Viral Disease*.[59] Please bear in mind that this book was published in 2000, forty years after the death of Dr. Goodpasture.

> Generally acknowledged to be the father of viral pathology in the United States, Dr. Ernest William Goodpasture was also recognized world-wide for his contributions to our understanding of the pathogenesis of viral diseases. An expert microscopist and microbiologist, Dr. Goodpasture made important discoveries by studying human tissue in influenza, respiratory syncytial pneumonia, measles, giant cell pneumonia, and cytomegalic inclusion disease. He was also a dedicated, insightful, and painstaking investigator in the research laboratory, where his work significantly contributed to elucidating the pathogenesis of herpetic encephalitis, mumps, and fowl pox. His most important research contribution was the development of the chicken embryo as a model for the study of virus diseases as well as a medium for vaccine development.
>
> His guiding hand can be detected in many chapters in this book.

One additional comment should be made. Many scientists, while achieving success professionally, are diminished personally. By every measure Ernest William Goodpasture grew in stature.

Chapter Two

STUDENT IN TRAINING

T his chapter covers the period from 1903 until 1922. Ernest Goodpasture entered college in 1903 and nineteen years later was superbly trained and ready for a professional appointment. He was at five educational institutions during this time: Vanderbilt, Allegheny Collegiate Institute, Hopkins, Harvard, and the University of the Philippines. The title for this chapter is justified by the evidence that he was preparing for a specific professional role throughout the undergraduate and graduate experiences described in those institutions. Based on family recollections, he had a long-term interest in medicine, and in medical school voiced his hopes to return to Vanderbilt as professor of pathology.[1]

His intentions to pursue an academic career are clearly apparent in the choice of Hopkins for his medical school, and of Harvard for fellowship and junior faculty appointments. These two institutions collectively offered the best educational opportunities available in medicine at that time. His reasons for going to the Philippines in 1921 are not recorded, but his interest was probably stimulated by the then-active collaboration in tropical medicine between Harvard and the University of the Philippines. This appointment also afforded an opportunity for the Goodpastures to see the world before settling into a stateside position; and several of their friends, including Watson Sellards,[2] had elected to work in the Philippines when the Goodpastures were there.

Ernest Goodpasture presumably chose Vanderbilt University for his undergraduate experience because of its location in his hometown and its reputation in the South. He entered at age seventeen, a mature young man particularly gifted in sense of purpose and a strong sense of values, a teenager with the additional advantages of an enriching and stable middle-class home life, a teenager grounded in the classics with a deep interest in information of all types. Nineteen years later, he was ideally prepared for a career in academic pathology, having seen the best of academe and a good part of the world.

VANDERBILT UNIVERSITY 1903–07

In 1903, Vanderbilt University was only slightly older than its students, having been founded in 1873.[3] Chancellor Kirkland, ambitious, competent, and respected, had been in office for eight years. Despite some major improvements under his leadership, the university was seriously underfunded, and he still had his major battles before him. Nevertheless, Vanderbilt was arguably the premier university in the South, with a faculty of twenty-six, a budget of $169,190,[4] and a student body of about 250.

The university's annual, *Comet,* in 1904 lists eighty-eight members in Ernest Goodpasture's class; forty-two of these were from Nashville and the remainder (save one Michiganite) from southern states. Attrition was formidable in those days, as three years later there were only thirty-eight graduating seniors. One of the missing was John Crowe Ransom, who graduated in 1909 summa cum laude, and was respected later as a founding Fugitive.[5] The 1907 *Comet* lists Ernest Goodpasture as a member of the Commodore Club (a quasi-honor club for seniors), Bowen School

Club, Kappa Sigma fraternity (Fig. 2-1), and class historian (with Katie Guill). He was not elected to Phi Beta Kappa as a student.

His scholastic record is difficult to translate into modern terms; the strength of later recommendations (cited below) when he applied to Hopkins in 1908 indicate a commendable performance with appropriate recognition of his personal qualities. When "Goodpasture, EW, of Nashville,"[6] registered on September 26, 1903, he had his choice of six courses: chemistry 1, chemistry 1 laboratory, history 1, English 1, Latin 1, and mathematics, of which he took the latter three.[7] His Latin first term grade has been saved on microfilm and looks suspiciously like a "55," this followed by an examination grade of 48! His Latin teacher may have been personally responsible for a significant portion of the exodus of freshmen to less stringent environments, as a second-term class grade of 68 and examination grade of 76 left "Goodpasture, EW," with a final grade (average of class and examination) of $61^{3}/4$—this the precise average of class and examination grades. At least his mathematics 1 teacher had the good grace to round $83^{3}/4$ to 84, and a 90 in English must have been consoling. English, Latin, and mathematics occupied the sophomore year, while he took geology, philosophy, and physics as a junior and biblical literature, biology (probably

Fig. 2-1: Ernest with Kappa Sigma fraternity members, circa 1903.

including botany and zoology), chemistry, and French as a senior. A total of twenty courses were available to seniors, including astronomy, economics, elocution, German, Greek, Italian, Latin, Spanish, philosophy, and physical culture.

College life in those days seems more than a century removed from the present experience. Ernest Goodpasture's senior year began on September 18, 1906, with a chapel ceremony. Dean Tillett of the theological department gave a discourse on the importance of character-building by "reading, thinking, loving and serving." Dr. Reynolds of West End Methodist Church offered a prayer, followed by Chancellor Kirkland's welcome for old and new students. The chancellor acknowledged that many problems in college life here were unsettled, but that some had been "fully and finally" (!) settled. Then he made these statements about the goals of the university, as reported in the September 27 *Hustler*: "This university is a place for earnest, hard work. We have no room for triflers. Vanderbilt is interested only in honorable, scholarly young men, scholarly in instinct, impulse, and desire. Character is even more important than scholarship, and we emphasize personal integrity."

It was necessary for Chancellor Kirkland to return to this theme a week later, as he lectured the assembled (by fiat) student body on October 4, 1906, in an attempt to deal with the problem of hazing, mostly by sophomores of freshmen. This problem apparently did not fall into the category of those settled fully and finally, because the whole student body was taken to the Kirkland woodshed two weeks later when retaliating freshmen tied a sophomore to a tree in Centennial Park.[8] One R. S. Henry, carelessly walking alone, was overpowered, blindfolded, led to a desolate spot in the rear of Centennial Park, subjected to "mild corporal punishment," and stripped of outer clothing; but he later allowed the worst feature, from his standpoint, was "being powerless in the hands of freshmen." Chancellor Kirkland did put this problem into the settled category in the fall of 1907, shortly after the sophomores issued an inflammatory proclamation that began with:

"WHEREAS: There has suddenly appeared in our midst an unseemly host of various kinds of diverse and sundry creatures of doubtful appearance," that continued with other such phrases and ended with eleven rules to guide freshmen in their behavior, dress, attendance in chapel, and how to comport themselves "with utmost humility" in the presence of sophomores. Warfare erupted shortly in Kissam Hall, leading to considerable destruction of university property, this in turn caused great distress to Dr. Tillett, dean of the School of Religion. Dr. Tillett was the administrative officer in charge of this unruly student body but immediately called for reinforcements in the form of Chancellor Kirkland, who was away on a treasured hunting trip. His mood was sour when all classes were called to chapel for an "important announcement," which was brief and substantially as follows:[9]

> Young gentlemen, your activities and demonstrations have clearly shown that many of you are incapable of self-control, as evidenced by recent episodes in connection with hazing. If let alone, you will likely advance from the cutting of hair to the cropping of ears. Tomorrow morning, from 8 to 9 o'clock, all freshmen are to meet in the lecture auditorium of Furman Hall for the purpose of signing some cards which will be provided by me. The sophomores will meet from 9 to 10, at the same place and for the same purpose. It is my understanding that some of the upper classmen were observers and perhaps aiders and abettors in the ceremonies that took place. The juniors, therefore, will meet from 10 to 11, and the seniors from 11 to 12 at Furman Hall tomorrow for the purpose which I have already indicated. Those of you who are not present or who fail to sign the cards, will cease to have any connection with Vanderbilt University. Chapel is dismissed.

At the safe distance of Alderson, West Virginia, the recently graduated Ernest Goodpasture was undoubtedly apprised of these campus developments.

Football was king, with Hustlers in November 1906, exulting in a hard-fought loss to Michigan and a 4–0 victory over the Carlisle Indians (the "greatest game played in the South"). The *Hustler* in November did note that the commission of the Methodist Church reported that Methodist bishops on the

Vanderbilt Board were not *ex officio* and had visitorial rights, a prelude to the highly charged and publicized rupture of the Vanderbilt-Methodist Church relationship.[10]

The Bachelor of Ugliness election in 1907 is of interest as it may be taken as a microcosm of Vanderbilt University campus life. The designation Bachelor of Ugliness then and later was awarded by students voting in assembly for the most popular and respected senior. As the highest nonacademic student award, it represented a test of values and of the quality of the graduates of the university, when the university was small enough that most seniors were known by their classmates. In view of its importance as an award, it is not surprising that Chancellor Kirkland was in the chair when the election was held. Three candidates had been properly nominated by their peers with virtues extolled humorously, if not eloquently. The two finalists were Max Souby and Dan Blake, the latter a natural for selection; he was voted twice all-Southern as a standout on a popular and successful football team, captain of the baseball team, and a member of the Glee Club. Max Souby, erstwhile cowboy, railway clerk, and general salesman, had come with his brother James from Karnes County, Texas, to seek their education. They were steered to Nashville by their minister, a Vanderbilt alumnus who was also a friend of Professor A. G. Bowen, for many years head of the Bowen School in Nashville.

Virtually penniless, the Souby brothers were admitted to Bowen School in September 1902. Subsisting we know not how or where, they were fiercely devoted to their studies, with Max graduating from Bowen in two years and from Vanderbilt in three. At Vanderbilt, Max was involved in numerous student activities and held several leadership positions, including election to Phi Beta Kappa. The election for Bachelor of Ugliness was held on May 30 and required three ballots, with Souby finally prevailing 152 to 119. This was a significant honor for this highly motivated and capable man. There is more to the story. In 1915, he married Susie Smith of Winchester, and in 1919 he returned to Vanderbilt to take the important post of alumni secretary. Max Souby apparently viewed his responsibilities in that role as encompassing campus life as well as interaction of the university with the community. Clearly successful in these roles, he became a highly respected campus figure, secretary of the Rotary Club, and a key member of the Coffee Club, a local men's discussion and dinner club. Then in March 1922, he developed pneumonia and died after a one-week illness in the prime of his life.

His death was a shock to the university and to the community; classes were suspended for the day of his funeral, and eulogies were given by Chancellor Kirkland and now Professor of English John Crowe Ransom. His benefactor and teacher A. G. Bowen was among the pallbearers. Max Souby's widow and their two small children remained in Nashville where Mrs. Souby had a distinguished educational career at Ward-Belmont, ultimately becoming headmistress of Harpeth Hall School. And then there is this interesting footnote to the Souby story. In 1920, as alumni secretary, Mr. Souby wrote Chancellor Kirkland to recommend his classmate Dr. Goodpasture for a position, presumably the professorship, in the pathology department in the medical school. This letter was sent on to Canby Robinson with these comments from Chancellor Kirkland:[11]

> I do not remember Dr. Goodpasture, but I have confidence in the judgment of Mr. Souby and think his opinion is worth something. Of course he can not testify to Dr. Goodpasture's ability as a pathologist. I presume that the proper line of procedure will be to wait until we get a pathologist-in-chief and then refer this letter to him for further investigation. Naturally I assume that Dr. Goodpasture would not be mature enough for the head of our department.

There are several places in this biography in which the various boys' schools in this region might be considered. Hopefully, this is the most appropriate because of the importance of Bowen School in the lives of Max Souby and of Ernest Goodpasture and in the early development of Vanderbilt. Basically, they were feeder schools for universities, and many had almost exclusive relationships with Vanderbilt. Classical education was the order of the day, with equal emphasis on character development and assumption of responsibility as citizens and as Christians. Here in Nashville, the schools were Bowen, Duncan,

Fig. 2-2: Kissam Hall, shortly after completion. This was the main residence hall for men.

Wallace, and Montgomery Bell Academy; nearby in middle Tennessee, there were Webb, Morgan, Branham and Hughes, and Vanderbilt Training School was just across the state line in Kentucky.

Most secondary schools in this region were named for their founders, and many closed when the founder died or retired from education. Chancellor Kirkland clearly recognized their vital importance in terms of higher education in this region and was instrumental in their legitimization by establishing the Southern Association of Colleges and Secondary Schools in 1895.[12] The Webb School, in Bell Buckle, may be the prototypic secondary school in view of its importance to Vanderbilt, in part because the two institutions opened for classes almost simultaneously. When founder William R. Webb died, Chancellor Kirkland stated: "The history of Vanderbilt University could not be written without alluding to Webb School. The roll call of Vanderbilt's distinguished alumni would also be in large measure the roll call of Webb School."

Our consideration of these schools should close by returning to A. G. Bowen, who received this tribute from Dr. John Crowe Ransom, Bowen School 1905,[13]

> Mr. Bowen's own pupils in Latin and Greek were recalled on Saturday to make up what they should have learned during the week [Ernest was probably also susceptible to recall, had Mr. Bowen heard of that 61³/4 in first-year Latin]. Otherwise Mr. Bowen was in the habit of spending Saturday in Goodpasture's second-hand bookstore, an ancient landmark in the city's culture, located on the north side of Church Street between Fourth and Fifth Avenues. He would hold forth with certain highly literate cronies on the classics and other topics. It was there that I gradually became familiar with the true geniality of his disposition.

In later years Dr. Goodpasture referred with affection to his undergraduate alma mater,[14] and he backed this affection with intensely loyal actions. His association with the Kappa Sigma fraternity was clearly meaningful as he participated actively for years as a distinguished "brother" in the affairs of this fraternity. However, there are no records of specific recollections about campus life.[15] He probably lived in the recently completed Kissam Hall, the showpiece of

Fig. 2-3: "Old Main" (now Kirkland Hall) after the fire that destroyed most of the interior.

Vanderbilt dormitories (Fig. 2-2) and must have helped save books and laboratory equipment from "Old Main" when it burned in 1905 (Fig. 2-3).

Commencement in June of 1907 as reported in the *Commencement Courier* on June 15 has the appealing aura of a better, albeit simpler, time. The highlights were an oratorical contest in the chapel on Friday, June 14, a reception at the chancellor's home [then located on the campus] from

8:00 to 11:00 P.M. on Saturday, chapel at 11:00 A.M. on Sunday given by Reverend H. S. Bradley, and conferring of degrees on Wednesday June 19 in Wesley Hall. The reception Saturday night was graced with a clear sky and young moon, while the beauty of the chancellor's walk was enhanced by "artistic drapery and Japanese lanterns" as well as by booths for the respective sororities.

As for the seniors, they gathered in cap and gown under a display of "incandescent" lights arranged in the figure "1907." The program began at 8:30, with

Fig. 2-4: Ernest Goodpasture upon graduation from Vanderbilt in 1907.

music, song ("Stars of the Summer Night"), and a class poem (by R. F. Vaughn); the program ended with a "wonderful history of the course of human events (in several volumes) and a much-needed complement to human knowledge divulged by "Doc" Goodpasture, a nickname by which he was known to friends and family because of his long-standing interest in becoming a physician) (Fig. 2-4). His words of wisdom would be of great interest and perhaps of value now, but the text is not available. Afterward there was a promenade, during which participants were served frappe by members of the Kappa Alpha Theta and Theta Delta Theta sororities.

ALLEGHENY COLLEGIATE INSTITUTE, ALDERSON, WEST VIRGINIA, 1907–08

The Allegheny Collegiate Institute was in fact a high school that in 1907 had approximately one hundred students and eight

Fig. 2-5: Students and faculty at Allegheny Collegiate Institute, 1908. Ernest is in the back row wearing a pork-pie hat.

teachers.[16] Most of the students were boarders. Tuition at the turn of the century was forty to fifty dollars per year, with one hundred dollars the yearly charge for boarding. There were three main buildings: a Boarding Hall (for young women), a Calisthenics Hall, and a Classroom Hall, all valued at $7,000 when purchased by the Methodist Church in 1900. This school existed for thirty-six years, closing its doors after the 1924–25 session.

There are only a few clues as to how Ernest learned about Alderson, why he spent a year there, and what he taught. Long's *Memoir*[17] states the reason for teaching was: "To add to his experience and to secure funds for expenses ahead." Alderson seems a little off the beaten path, but it apparently had a reputation as a "school town" and Allegheny Collegiate Institute had "huge fame."[18] We have a picture of Ernest with the men's basketball team, this presumably a secondary responsibility, and a picture with his students and fellow teachers (Fig. 2-5). The experience in

Alderson may have been enriching, but his salary for the year could hardly have exceeded five-hundred dollars, while the tuition at Hopkins was two hundred dollars per annum from 1893 to 1912.[19]

JOHNS HOPKINS UNIVERSITY SCHOOL OF MEDICINE 1908–12

Attendance at Hopkins was essentially inevitable for this particular student. In those times, students selected their school and were accepted "if they met the entrance requirements."[20] Its innovative curriculum was energized by a faculty with a national and international reputation for excellence. Despite the departure in 1905 for Oxford of the premier physician and teacher in the western world, William Osler, this school deservedly was acknowledged as the best in the United States, if not the world, for those interested in an investigative career in medicine. Goodpasture's application to Hopkins was buttressed by letters of recommendation[21] from George Martin, professor of biology, and L. C. Glenn, professor of geology, who had received a doctorate from Hopkins in 1899. Dr. Martin's letter was dated July 7, 1908:

> Director Johns Hopkins Laboratories:
> My Dear Sir:
>   I am pleased to state in Mr. E. W. Goodpasture's behalf what he has done in my department. He has had one years work in Botany with me and about one year and half in Zoology. He did much excellent work with me, one of my very best students. In fact he was so good I had him to assist me one year. Any favor you show him will be greatly appreciated by me, and I am satisfied you will have no regrets. By favoring him I am positive any institution will not regret it, because he is a man who will honor any institution. I think he has a bright future before him.

The letter from Dr. Glenn was dated June 2, 1908:

Fig. 2-6: The central buildings of Johns Hopkins Hospital, circa 1910. Courtesy of archivist, Johns Hopkins University Medical Center.

Medical Dept, Johns Hopkins Univ,
Baltimore, Md,

Sirs: This will introduce to you Mr. E. W. Goodpasture of this city and a B.A. graduate of 1907 of this university. Mr. Goodpasture is filing application for entrance to your department and I trust he may be successful as I know him to be a young man of much promise as a student and of fine character as a man.

There are no records of application to other medical schools, and very few letters, pictures, or other mementos from his time at Hopkins. We know that our little Tennessean found himself in a very large pond in the fall of 1908 (Fig. 2-6). Hopkins attracted students from across the country, as twenty-eight states and the District of Columbia were represented in the class of 1912.[22] More impressively, the class came from forty-seven universities, nine graduating from Johns Hopkins University, five from University of Chicago, four from Stanford, three from Harvard, five from Yale, and one from Colgate. Fourteen members were from Maryland;

nineteen were from the South and twenty-four from west of the Mississippi. Goodpasture was the only Tennessean. On the assumption that Helmina, Willa, and Rolla were females, there were eight women in the class (Fig. 2-7). Most of the students lived in nearby boarding houses; Ernest Goodpasture resided at 518 N. Broadway in 1912 with five other seniors. Almost fifty years later, these were Dr. Goodpasture's recollections about the decision to go to Hopkins:[23]

> I wish I could unravel from my own early experiences the thread of thoughts and events which led to my decision (and I'm sure I had had no other) to attend Johns Hopkins Medical School. I feel sure that eventually it was my impression of the scientific approach to the problems of medicine which influenced me most. But had I had any inkling of the wonderful class and body of students with whom it was my cherished privilege to be associated there, no other consideration would have had any comparable attraction.

As mentioned previously, William Osler had left for the Regius Professorship at Oxford in the spring of 1905. (See color

Fig. 2-7: Johns Hopkins Medical School class of 1912. Faculty and students are shown. Ernest Goodpasture is number fourteen. From Chesney, *Johns Hopkins Hospital and Medical School,* Volume III.

section for Osler's textbook *Principles and Practice of Medicine, Seventh Edition Thoroughly Revised, 1909* used by Dr. Goodpasture. This volume is housed in Eskind Library, Special Collections; it contains a few marginal notes in Dr. Goodpasture's hand and sections on typhoid fever and mumps that are underlined.) Indispensable is a notoriously inaccurate characterization of academicians, although for good cause William Osler has been virtually sanctified and was knighted. His absence must have been the subject of discussion in 1908, but the remaining faculty was truly impressive and clearly met highest expectations. Faculty from that period included these notables:[24] Welch in pathology; Kelly in obstetrics and gynecology; Abel in pharmacology; Howell in physiology; Meyer in psychiatry; Howland, Park, and Blackfan in pediatrics; Barker in medicine as well as Halsted, Bloodgood, Finney, and Cushing in surgery. These names resonate even now in academic medical circles. Lewellys Barker as Osler's successor developed three clinical research laboratories, all headed by full-time clinical scientists, and quickly established an extensive private practice. Harvey Cushing was yet another dynamo, who founded the Hunterian Laboratory as a center for experimental studies and surgical instruction using animals. The hospital superintendent was Dr. Henry Hurd, who was succeeded in 1911 by Dr. Winford Smith; both were heavily involved in the affairs of the hospital as well as in the educational program.

Johns Hopkins Medical School was still in its youth, or perhaps adolescence, when the class of 1912 arrived; they became the fifteenth graduating class. The physical plant was also in evolution: the Phipps Institute for Psychiatry was constructed in 1908, and the Harriet Lane Home for Pediatrics was under construction. Other memorable events in the 1908–12 period include the death of Johns Hopkins University's President Gilman on October 13, 1908; the installation of the first electrocardiograph in 1909; a visit by Sir William Osler in late April 1909;[25] celebration of Dr. Welch's sixtieth birthday on April 2, 1909;[26] and a site visit by Abraham Flexner as a part of his evaluation of American medical schools in December 1909.

The resultant *Carnegie Report on Medical Education in the United States and Canada* authored by Flexner was published in 1910. Hopkins was judged the model institution in this report, although it did not escape unscathed in Flexner's evaluation, as he urged that the clinical staff become full-time. In 1911, Flexner met with Welch, Mall, and Halsted about obtaining one million dollars in endowment from the Rockefeller Education Board to facilitate such a transition by the clinical faculty. This shift in funding strategy for the clinical faculty was strongly opposed by Osler and Kelly, who favored retention of private practice arrangements. They were so gifted as teachers and clinicians that they did not appreciate why academic medicine would require full-time people for success. Sir William Osler sent a fourteen-page letter to Remsen, the president of Johns Hopkins University, to trustees of the university and hospital, to various professors as well as to Flexner, in which he castigated the report, condemning in particular Flexner's "very feeble grasp of the clinical situation at Hopkins."[27]

Students were probably blissfully unaware of this high-level thundering, which did delay the acceptance of full-time status by the clinical staff until 1913. Students had more immediate concerns, such as a cluster of cases of tuberculosis in medical students in 1908. Frequently used boardinghouses around Hopkins were reviewed by authorities in that year to ensure their safety.[28] In fact, Ernest was admitted to the sanatorium at Lake Saranac in April 1909, for suspected tuberculosis and remained through June.[29]

An even greater threat to student health surfaced on January 25, 1911, when the medical school was closed for a month because of a diphtheria epidemic that ultimately caused sixty-six cases in students, staff, and patients.[30] Students were urged to stay in Baltimore, avoid public places, and keep in touch with the school.

The curriculum[31] available to the class of 1912 emphasized anatomy, physiology, and biochemistry the first year, with all of these courses continuing into the first trimester of the second

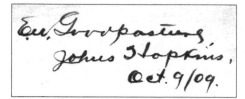

Fig. 2-8: Ernest's signature from 1909 is in *Epitome of the History of Medicine* by Roswell Park, published by F. A. Davis in 1908. This volume is in Eskind Library, Special Collections.

year (Fig. 2-8). Pathology, pharmacology, and physical diagnosis were the major courses in the second and third trimesters of that year, with pathology scheduled from 2:00–5:00 on Monday, Wednesday, and Friday both trimesters. The class was divided into sections in the third and fourth years for various required and elective clinical assignments.[32]

For the budding pathologists, there were abundant opportunities in clinical microscopy and surgical pathology in the third year and several pathology electives in the fourth year. Ernest's notes[33] from the pathology course show that the first lecture was given on January 3, 1909, by Dr. Welch (Fig. 2-9); the subject discussed was "cloudy swelling," which was also the first topic covered in the Vanderbilt course in pathology forty to forty-five years later. Lectures in the first trimester dealt with degenerative changes such as cloudy swelling, with acute and chronic inflammation, with blood clotting and embolism, and with several specific infections.

The second trimester was devoted to pathologic changes in major organs, with emphasis on the lung, liver, and gastrointestinal tract. Infections were discussed repeatedly, with Dr. Welch recorded in the lecture notes as stating: "The four important diseases are pneumonia, syphilis, tuberculosis, and typhoid." Welch apparently did not stop during lectures to help with spelling, as the word cirrhosis was written as "scirrosis" by Ernest. During these two trimesters, Whipple gave seventeen lectures, Welch gave seven, and Winternitz gave three; the lecturer was not identified in four cases. Surprisingly, there were no lectures on cancer and only a fleeting mention of atherosclerosis. Many organs now viewed as important, even vital, were not discussed, including the endocrine glands, brain, male or female genitalia,

Dr Welch.   Pathology.   Jany. 3/09

Cloudy swelling. (Parenchymatous degeneration). A disturbance in cell, swelling and increase in granular part of
cell. As distinguished from fat they
dissolve in acetic acid, not sol⁰ in alcohol
Found in practically all infectious
fevers, and in poisons phosphorus,
arsenic etc. About same changes
occur in fatty degeneration which is
an advanced stage. In fevers probably
the poison is due more to cause
swelling more than the temp. Very
high temp. may cause cloudy swelling
however. The parts affected are the
active tissues, i.e. Liver cells +
secreting tubules of Kidney, may occur
however in epithelium, muscle fibre (esp.
heart) salivary gland etc. Kidney for
instance cha. appearance is swollen
one, chiefly in cortex (losses slightly
cooked, boiled) paler + somewhat more
opaque. Change is entirely cellular. In
kidney the Epithelium of convoluted tubules
most affected. These however are normally
granular hence the change microscopically
slight, change more evident macroscopically
Granules more coarse than normal and
arranged irregularly, a disorganization
of cell substance, (paraplasmic granules)

and the bone marrow. Very few clinical manifestations of disease were mentioned, and no laboratory findings were presented. It was a course built on microscopy; presumably the gross changes in disease were shown by demonstration of affected organs in the laboratory sections. In these times before color microphotographs, students often prepared their own class sets illustrating the classical diseases and prepared portfolios of drawings. Ernest's portfolio[34] contains sketches nicely portraying pneumonia, atherosclerosis, and other diseases. (See color section for a sketch drawn by Ernest Goodpasture as a student at Hopkins.) Whipple's biography by Corner[35] describes the mechanics of instruction in the pathology course of that period. Whipple and Winternitz had full responsibility for the autopsy service, in which the students were presumably actively involved, and they lectured as demanded by Dr. Welch's travels and other commitments. Scheduling to accommodate the vagaries of his schedule was difficult at best, so Winternitz and Whipple each prepared half of the lectures and were thereby ready for last-minute changes.[36]

To have studied pathology under this trio was an extraordinary opportunity. The redoubtable Welch epitomized power, tradition, and scholarship in academic medicine, while functioning as a major driving force at Hopkins. Whipple, ultimately a Nobel laureate, was quiet, reserved, and factual. Winternitz was dynamic, quick-tempered, even volatile, but effective in teaching and research. Here was a superior breeding ground for academic pathologists.

Twelve members of the class of 1912 were ultimately cited in the *Who Was Who* series.[37] The best known, in addition to Dr. Goodpasture, were Mont Rogers Reid, longtime professor of surgery at University of Cincinnati; Oswald Swinney Lowsley, urological surgeon in New York; Louise Pearce, member of Rockefeller Institute where she investigated the pathogenesis of syphilis and trypanosomiasis (African sleeping sickness) as a longtime collaborator of Dr. Wade Brown, who was considered in 1920–23 for the professorship of pathology at Vanderbilt; Lewis Hill Weed, professor of anatomy at Hopkins 1919–47 and director of the School of Medicine, 1929–46; Alan Mason Chesney, dean of Hopkins Medical School 1929–53; and Harry Christian Schmeisser, long-term chair of pathology at the University of Tennessee in Memphis.

Residency, Fellowship, and Junior Faculty Appointments in Hopkins Department of Pathology 1912–15

Professional life

Departmental responsibilities presumably were limited to performance of autopsies, research, and education of students, residents, and faculty. The departmental faculty still consisted of Welch, Whipple, and Winternitz, the latter two having graduated from Hopkins in 1905 and 1907, respectively (Fig. 2-10). Departmental research was carried out in the Hunterian

Fig. 2-10: Pathology staff, circa 1913. From left, back row: Stevenson, Reid, Schmeisser, Davis, Lueback, and Goodpasture. From left, front row: Winternitz, Whipple, Welch, Ford, and Kline.

Laboratory, a two-story building designed for experimental work on animals by the Departments of Surgery and Pathology. Harvey Cushing was in charge of the surgical floor, and MacCallum's departure in 1909 for Columbia University left Whipple in charge of the pathology floor.[38]

In the three years of 1912–14, Whipple and coworkers published twenty-one research papers, all concerned with liver function, blood coagulation, pancreatitis, and intestinal obstruction. In 1914, Dr. Whipple accepted the directorship of a recently funded research institute in San Francisco, the Hooper Foundation, and the accompanying position of professor at the University of California. Further excitement was generated by his marriage on June 24, 1914, to Katherine Ball Waring of Charleston; among their wedding gifts was an etching from Dr. Welch and another from seven members of the Hopkins Department of Pathology. In early August, they returned to Baltimore for more parties and for packing before leaving for San Francisco on August 8.[39]

From the first, Dr. Goodpasture's publications dealt with investigations rather than with case reports. His first four papers came from the Hunterian Laboratory; three of the four investigated basic phenomena such as morbidity in experimental acute pancreatitis, the mechanism of production of a protein involved in blood clotting (fibrinogen), and the cause of defective blood clotting (fibrinolysis) in liver disease. George Whipple was clearly instrumental in guiding these initial investigations; Dr. Whipple was the first author on Dr. Goodpasture's first paper, and, as noted above, independently published other studies on fibrinogen.

These three papers are an indication of Dr. Goodpasture's investigative philosophy rather than significant contributions to medical knowledge. All three dealt with problems that were extremely complex and not subject to solution with methods available at the time. Nevertheless, he made a valiant effort to produce useful information by experiments rather than by the easier and more popular reporting of patients with naturally occurring diseases.

His fourth paper dealt with a problem that is now a major health issue in developed countries—cancer in aged populations. In 1910, life expectancy in the United States was about forty-seven years, and infectious diseases were overwhelmingly the principal cause of death. Although the number of aged patients was limited, it had nevertheless been recognized that cancer was much more likely to occur in the elderly than in youths.[40] Dr. Goodpasture became interested in this problem undoubtedly as a by-product of autopsying many dogs while conducting the experiments reported in his first three papers.

Postulating that the many tumors observed in old dogs had relevance to the increased incidence of cancer in aging humans, he recognized that the sequence of structural changes in developing tumors would be much easier to study in the dog than in the human. Tumors of several organs were found in all fifteen dogs, although "in hundreds of normal younger animals we have never observed a similar condition."[41] The authors concluded that the degenerative changes associated with aging created an abnormal environment in which local proliferation led to tumor formation. Most of the tumors in this study were benign, but the authors recognized that benign processes might degenerate and become cancerous.

Publications While at Hopkins

1913   With G. H. Whipple. "Acute haemorrhagic pancreatitis." *Surgery, Gynecology and Obstetrics*, 17:541–47.

1914   Fibrinogen. II. "The association of liver and intestine in rapid regeneration of fibrinogen." *Am J Physiol*, 33:70–85.

       "Fibrinolysis in chronic hepatic insufficiency." *Bull Johns Hopkins Hosp*, 25:1–17.

1916   With G. B. Wislocki. "Old age in relation to cell-overgrowth and cancer." *J Med Res*, 33 (3):455–73.

Personal life at Hopkins

Only scraps of information are available about Ernest's personal life at Hopkins. He was a member of the Nu Sigma Nu medical fraternity. Tuberculosis was a significant threat to students and faculty in those days, and you will recall Ernest was admitted to Lake Saranac Sanatorium for suspected tuberculosis in April 1909 and discharged in June. His memories of that event forty years later were cited in a letter to his friend and classmate Lewis Weed in 1949. (See footnote 29.)

On a lighter note, the archived Goodpasture papers contain an article from the *Baltimore News* of Thursday, May 11, 1911, with this headline: "Good Pasture and Weed On Grass Plot"; these two boardinghouse mates had been arrested for witnessing a carnival from the off-limits grass parkway rather than the pavement of Broadway. The news story set a record in word-play with rural connotations before closing with the good news that Judge Llewellyn "squashed" the case and freed the students after a lecture. Other residents of 518 Broadway were caught in the same net but escaped notoriety because of the plainness of their names. One residuum of this episode might be the acquisition by Ernest of a second nickname. Coming to Hopkins as "Doc," he left as "Parson," a play on the pasture-to-pastor theme.

Ernest's younger sister, Sarah, (nicknamed "Sook") came to Hopkins Nursing School in 1913, became a registered nurse in 1916, and ultimately the night nursing superintendent for the hospital. There are very few letters from Ernest to the family at home, but this one describes some of the events in the life of the Goodpasture siblings at Hopkins. It was addressed to Mrs. A. V. Goodpasture, RR number 3, Clarksville, Tennessee, and was dated 10/26/13:[42]

My dear Mom:

Sook and I have just returned from a little walk up to North Avenue. She has been telling me all about her nurses, their work and funny experiences. She has gained about twelve pounds since she came up, so I judge the life is agreeing with her pretty well.

We are all very proud of the donation of a million and a half to the medical school by the Rockefeller people. It establishes the greatest epoch in medical education in a good many years. The professors of Medicine, Surgery, and Pediatrics will now have to devote their entire time to teaching and research and renounce their private practice. It won't affect our department except that the Hunterian

Laboratory will be enlarged and better equipped as a result.

I have just finished one of my papers and sent it off yesterday to the *American Journal of Physiology*. When it is published I'll send you a reprint. Last night I went over to the fraternity house and saw all the boys. They had a little smoker and Dr. Clough gave a talk. It is very much like it used to be when I was a student.

How are you getting along with your farming? We haven't been visited yet by a snow. Give my love to the Dutch [probably sister Mattie, also known as Dutchess]. Affectionately, Doc.

Sook did not confine her interests to nursing school. In 1914, the two siblings returned to Tennessee to visit their parents after the move by the senior Goodpastures from Nashville to their farm in Montgomery County. On this visit, Sook introduced her good friend Sarah Marsh Catlett to Ernest at a house party at Dunbar Cave. No correspondence from or about their courtship

Fig. 2-11: Sarah Catlett and Ernest Goodpasture, wedding portraits. There are no extant photographs of their wedding ceremony.

has been saved, nor do we know how many times he was able to visit Sarah in Clarksville. He was evidently persuasive in person or by mail, for they married on August 11, 1915, just as he assumed a faculty position as instructor in the Department of Pathology at Harvard (Fig. 2-11). (Please see chapter 8 for additional details.)

Peter Bent Brigham Hospital and Harvard University Medical School 1915–22

- Instructor Department of Pathology, Harvard Medical School 1915–19; assistant professor of pathology, Harvard Medical School 1919–22
- On leave Chelsea Naval Hospital, March 8, 1918, to April 14, 1919
- On leave as assistant professor, then professor of pathology, School of Medicine and Surgery, University of the Philippines and Philippine General Hospital, 1921–22

Professional life

Departmental responsibilities in pathology at Harvard were presumably similar to those at Hopkins, concentrating on the performance of autopsies, research, and teaching. William T. Councilman, the head of the department, had worked with Welch from 1886 to 1892 at Hopkins, where he had developed innovative programs in investigative pathology. As the third Shattuck Professor of Pathologic Anatomy at Harvard, he was in the only position comparable to that of Welch; and, as such, Councilman was equally instrumental in training men who became leaders in American pathology.[43] Dr. Goodpasture's appointment as instructor in pathology in 1915, and as assistant professor of pathology in 1919, were steps up the academic ladder at another prestigious institution.

Dr. Goodpasture's most significant research at Harvard was the completion of the study of neoplasia in aged dogs and a focused autopsy study on the pathogenesis of influenza. In the former, a total of fifty old dogs was examined, fifteen from the previous study in

Baltimore coauthored with Wislocki, and thirty-five from Boston. The tumors were all incidental in the sense that none of the dogs had been suspected of harboring tumors before autopsy. In sharp contrast to the experience with young dogs, in which malignant tumors were exceedingly rare, 24 percent of these old dogs bore malignant tumors, with testes the most common site. Neoplasia in these circumstances was attributed to senescence and associated degenerative changes in multiple tissues ultimately leading to malignancies.

This study of neoplasia in aged dogs was extended to humans in a fashion that illustrated Dr. Goodpasture's attention to detail in handling tissues and microscopy, skills that are the *sine qua non* of experts. Cytoplasmic structures called mitochondria had been discovered in 1890 in virtually all cells, but their function was unknown. Surprisingly, in 1909 it was postulated that mitochondria tended to disappear or were absent from the cells in malignant tumors, suggesting that normal cells could be distinguished from malignant cells by the presence of mitochondria in the former. When a follow-up study in 1910 failed to confirm the initial observation, Dr. Goodpasture recognized that the discordance in results might be related to technical differences in the ways tissues had been handled after removal.

After finding the ideal fixative and staining technique for mitochondria in various tissues, he then sampled fourteen benign tumors and twenty-one malignant tumors of various types, all fixed within five minutes after removal and stained uniformly. By thus minimizing technical factors in tissue processing, he showed convincingly that the number and appearance of mitochondria might vary somewhat from those of normal tissue, but that the differences were not of sufficient magnitude to be of diagnostic value. This is one of several papers in which attention to detail and rigorous microscopy, cornerstones of good research in those days, further established his credibility as an investigator. This study on mitochondria, his subsequent studies of cholera (in 1922) and the appearance of viral inclusions (in 1924) are examples of significant contributions stemming from mastery of technique.

Fig. 2-12: Lieutenant Junior Grade Goodpasture in naval uniform, circa 1918.

The autopsy study of influenza at the Chelsea Hospital was thrust upon him by circumstances of being in the Navy when the influenza epidemic hit the New England area. In World War I, he served in the Navy from 1918 to 1919 as a lieutenant in the Medical Corps, with duty at the Chelsea Naval Hospital near Boston (Fig. 2-12). This was the firestorm period of the influenza pandemic, and Dr. Goodpasture was responsible for autopsying many of its victims. Very few service personnel have made such good use of their time in terms of investigating fundamental problems in medicine.[44]

These were his recollections of that pandemic, as written in 1957 in an unpublished summary titled *Path. of Influenza* 1918–57:[45]

My interest in influenza began on the morning of Aug. 26, 1918 when 10 sailors from the Navy Yard at Commonwealth Pier in Boston were sent to the Laboratory of the Chelsea Naval Hospital located near the Charleston Navy Yard on the edge of the city. These sailors had recently landed from Europe and had been given shore leave in Boston on arrival.

I was at that time a naval officer in the laboratory of Chelsea Naval Hospital, and it fell to my lot to examine these sailors who had been suddenly attacked by a febrile illness. Throats were examined and cultures taken.

Two days later Aug 28 I was ill with "flu." My infection was mild and in ten days I was back at work and by that time there was much for a pathologist to do, for the sailors had already begun to die in appalling numbers of a virulent pneumonitis. The fall epidemic of influenza in the USA had begun and was spreading rapidly west and south.

At first none of us at the hospital realized what we were dealing with. We had heard and read about what was at the time usually called Spanish "flu," erupting here and there in Europe since early spring. And there had been some outbreaks of clinical influenza in army camps in the U.S. early in the year, nothing, it seemed, to compare in severity with this, and its accompanying high mortality. It soon became manifest, however, that another great pandemic of influenza was upon us.

Until 1918 it was widely accepted that this suspected primary etiological agent of influenza and the bronchopneumonia which frequently accompanied it, was the small Gram negative bacillus discovered by Richard Pfeiffer in cases of influenza and described by him in 1893.

However as a result of my own studies of the pathology of influenzal pneumonia I came to the conclusion, and I think I was almost alone in this particular, that there were pulmonary lesions which could be considered to be the specific effects of a virus of influenza.

Although many bacterial agents had been isolated from the lungs of patients with influenza, the type of bacterium isolated was not consistent from city to city or over time. Because of these inconsistencies there was a suspicion, expressed even after the epidemic of 1889, that there was a *primary* lung-injuring process in influenza, with later superinfection by one of the numerous bacteria that had been isolated in various epidemics. Dr. Goodpasture noted that the pathologic anatomy of the lung lesions might provide evidence as to the causative agent, if cases could be found that were not superinfected.

Focusing on this possibility, Dr. Goodpasture found two cases at Chelsea in which careful bacterial studies were completely negative. The first of these had a typical clinical course for influenza, dying on the seventh day of illness with edematous and hemorrhagic lungs. Microscopic sections showed injury and destruction of alveolar walls with extensive fibrin deposition (hyaline membranes) in the portion of the airways called alveolar ducts. These lesions were noted by Dr. Goodpasture as typical of those found in all influenza cases. The second case was "unusual," the only "instance of its kind observed by us," and one that had not been described by others. This eighteen-year-old man had an illness of a month with right lower lobe consolidation, anemia, short remissions and massive hemoptysis (expectoration of blood)—all features that are decidedly atypical for influenza.

At autopsy, the typical hyaline membranes expected in influenza were present, but in addition there was massive intra-alveolar hemorrhage in areas of subacute inflammation with healing. The spleen and kidney were also affected, additional features that are not usually seen in influenza. The spleen contained numerous foci of necrosis, especially in the white pulp (lymphocytic tissue). In kidney sections there was inflammation of glomeruli (the filtering unit in kidneys). Dr. Goodpasture interpreted the lung findings in these two carefully selected cases[46] to mean that influenza was a "distinct disease, recognizable clinically only by its epidemic proportions and extreme infectiousness, characterized pathologically by a peculiar lesion in the lung, and caused by an unknown virus which gains entrance through the respiratory tract."[47]

This paper is remarkable for several reasons, the chief being that the author, barely six years out of medical school, showed impressive maturity in judgment and confidence in his skills in pathology. In terms of the latter, Dr. Goodpasture correctly interpreted the significance of the pathologic changes in the lung, and by painstaking technique was assured bacterial studies were actually negative. It is even more impressive that he recognized that the critical clue as to the cause of influenza might be found in the very rare case *without* bacterial superinfection rather than in the multitude of infected cases.

This study is also of historical interest in that it is the basis of the designation of certain coincident lung and kidney diseases as the Goodpasture syndrome.[48] As the 1919 paper did not mention kidney disease in its title, the proponents of Goodpasture's name must have had a formidable (more likely a fortuitous) knowledge of the literature. It is perhaps of interest that Sir Macfarlane Burnet may be responsible for this eponymic adventure, as it was initiated in Australia, and he was aware of the details of the 1919 paper.[49]

Dr. Goodpasture[50] stated that the use of his name for this syndrome was inappropriate, in that he was attempting to discern the cause of influenza rather than to establish a link between lung and kidney disease. It is difficult to be certain of the diagnosis in the second case, the "unusual" one, even after reviewing his description of the pathology. Although it could be the first reported case of "Goodpasture syndrome," the vasculitic component is more suggestive of Wegener's granulomatosis (another auto-immune disorder that differs from Goodpasture syndrome in cause and treatment). In order to establish the diagnosis, attempts have been made to find the sections from this case at Chelsea Hospital[51] and at the Armed Forces Institute of Pathology to no avail. Even if the sections were available for review, and the diagnosis of Wegener's granulomatosis were established by experts, the name of Goodpasture seems to be embedded in the medical literature for certain types of lung and kidney disease. In this case, good intentions—recognizing Dr. Goodpasture—paved the road to inaccuracy and inappropriateness.[52]

In 1921–22, while professor of pathology at the University of the Philippines, Dr. Goodpasture studied a series of cases of cholera at the San Lazaro Hospital in Manila. Taking special care to begin autopsies as soon as possible, and exerting "utmost care" in preserving the intestinal mucosa, he demonstrated that some patients died from cholera with intestines "anatomically intact except for edema."[53] Many of the mucosal changes described by others were attributed by Dr. Goodpasture to peri-mortem changes associated with shock and dehydration. He concluded that the causative organism (*Vibrio cholerae*) was not an invader of tissue as were bacteria in other infectious diarrheal diseases.

Instead, he postulated that a toxin might be produced and absorbed through intact mucosa. His close friend and colleague Watson Sellards had previously suggested this possibility, in view of the facts that cholera had an abrupt onset and was not associated with fever, conditions favoring a "chemical intoxication." This conclusion is correct. Subsequently it has been shown that *V. cholerae* are not invasive and that their harmful effects come from an enterotoxin that causes the secretion into the small intestine of massive amounts of water and electrolytes.

To appreciate the significance of this work, it is necessary to recognize that most of the bacterial diseases producing diarrhea are associated with ulcers and superficial inflammation at the site of bacterial entry into the intestine wall. Lesions of this type had been mistakenly described in cholera by others, but Dr. Goodpasture established that they were artifactual by the simple expedient of meticulous attention to details, these being immediate autopsies and careful fixation of the bowel. He failed to identify the toxin released by v. cholerae; a companion paper[54] postulated that a poisonous substance was present in intestinal contents, but he probably ran out of time before pursuing this problem to resolution as he was wont to do.

The basis for the close friendship of Dr. Watson Sellards with the Goodpasture family may be traced back to their joint sojourn in the Philippines. A. McGehee Harvey notes in his vignette about Watson Sellards that "Sellards spent the winter of 1921–22 working with Ernest W. Goodpasture in the Philippines. They were interested in the investigation of three diseases, amebic dysentery, Tsutsugamushi fever [scrub typhus, a rickettsial disease], and yaws. The study of yaws turned out to be particularly interesting as the disease proved susceptible to intravenous injections of arsenic (salvarsan)."[55]

Publications While at Harvard and Chelsea

1916 "Double primary abdominal pregnancy." *J Med Res*, 34(3):259–61.

1917 "Crystalline hyalin." *J Med Res*, 35(3):259–64.

"A contribution to the study of pancreas intoxication." *J Exp Med*, 25(2):277–83.

"An acid polychrome-methylene blue solution for routine and special staining." *J Am Med Assoc*. 69:998.

1918 "An anatomical study of senescence in dogs, with especial reference to the relation of cellular changes of age to tumors." *J Med Res*, 38(2):127–90.

"Observations on mitochondria of tumors." *J Med Res*, 38(2):213–24.

With Victor C. Jacobson. "Occlusion of the entire inferior vena cava by hypernephroma, with thrombosis of the hepatic vein and its branches." *Arch Internal Med*, 22:86–95.

1919 With F. L. Burnett. "The pathology of pneumonia accompanying influenza." *United States Naval Medical Bulletin*, 13(2):177–97.

"Bronchopneumonia due to hemolytic streptococci following influenza." *J Am Med Assoc*, 72:724–25.

"A peroxidase reaction with sodium nitroprusside and benzidine in blood smears and tissues." *J Lab Clin Med*, 4:442.

"The significance of certain pulmonary lesions in relation to the etiology of influenza." *Am J of Med Sciences*, 158(6):863.

1921 With Fritz B. Talbot. "Concerning the nature of 'protozoan-like' cells in certain lesions of infancy." *Am J Diseases Children*, 21:415–25.

"Myocardial necrosis in hyperthyroidism." *J Am Med Assoc*, 76:1545–51.

"The influence of thyroid products on the production of myocardial necrosis." *J Exp Med*, 34(4):407–23.

Publications While at University of the Philippines

1923 With Andrew Watson Sellards and Walfrido de Leon. "Investigations concerning yaws." *Philippine J Sci*, 22(3):219–89.

"Histopathology of the intestine in cholera." *Philippine J Sci*, 22(4):413–21.

"Complement fixation in treated and untreated leprosy." *Philippine J Sci*, 22(4):425–37.

"A poisonous constituent in cholera stools." *Philippine J Sci*, 22(4):439–45.

Personal Life at Harvard and Chelsea

Sarah and Ernest made many friends at Harvard and had family in the area as well. This letter was written by him on 10/14/18:[56]

My dear Mamma:

I have just finished writing up a lot of notes, and Sarah has finished a letter home. We are sitting here beside our oil-stove in the little back room trying to keep warm and awake. It is somewhat past our regular bedtime, but I want to send you a line before it is postponed again.

Here lately I have been pretty busy at nights working up the pathology of our influenza epidemic for publication. Yesterday though was my Sunday off, and we took a real holiday. Took a walk out into the country which is beautiful now in its many colors. The New England [word not legible] is one redeeming period in the otherwise unbeauteous seasons. The walking there Sundays is good too, since the roads are free of autos, and the pedestrian feels reasonably safe.

The fourth Liberty Loan Drive is on now in full, as you doubtless know if you take the [Clarksville] *Leaf Chronicle* as we do. We have bought $350 worth this time and almost $100 in war saving stamps. . . .

I wanted to write to little Sookie, but I'm getting so sleepy, guess I'll have to call it off for the present. Wish she would call off the counts [possible administrative work] and write to me all about herself and Karl [Dr. Karl Martzloff, his future brother-in-law. Sook and Karl married in 1923]. If Karl gets sent across she'll have to come up and give us that promised visit.

Don't get the influenza and if you or any of you get it *go to bed* immediately and stay there until entirely free of fever—*by the thermometer*. This epidemic isn't to be monkeyed with. For influenza, go to bed. 10 grains of Dover's powders at night. Eat plenty of soft nourishing food. With much love to all, Doc.

Fig. 2-13: Mother and daughter in Reading, near Boston, 1919.

There must have been great excitement in Montgomery County and in Reading when it became apparent that Sarah was pregnant. Their daughter Sarah was born on March 12, 1919. (Fig. 2-13) Owing to the length of her last name, Sarah was not given a middle name.

Personal life in Philippines

The Goodpastures embarked, presumably from Boston or New York, on the SS *Ecuador*, and occupied rooms forty and forty-one on the main deck. They landed in the port of Manila on July 27, 1921, and rented Judge Street's home in Manila (at number five Cortibetorte) (Figs. 2-14 and 2-15). In 1922, they returned via Hong Kong to Europe. The two Sarahs departed June 13, 1922, for Hong Kong to await the arrival of Dr. Goodpasture, who presumably left shortly after June 30.[57] They cruised on SS *Hanazaki Mani* from Hong Kong to Marseilles. A side trip to Cairo was made during this voyage, as we have a picture of a camel-borne Tennessean amongst a host of Japanese on a visit to the Pyramids (Fig. 2-16). From Marseilles, the Goodpasture family transited somehow to Liverpool, where they started the last leg of their journey back to the States.

TOP: Fig. 2-14: Dr. Goodpasture and Sarah in the Philippines, circa 1921.

BOTTOM: Fig. 2-15: The two Sarahs and friends in the Philippines, circa 1922.

On arrival at the Singer Institute, Dr. Goodpasture recounted on September 16 the last portion of their trip back to the United States:[58]

My dear Dad:

No doubt by this time you have heard from Clarksville of our safe arrival in Boston. In spite of the thousands of Americans who were falling over each other to get transportation home, this being the end of the tourist season, we succeeded in getting a freighter from Liverpool bound for Boston. It was a new ship built to accommodate 12 passengers. As it turned out we were very fortunate, the weather was good, our cabin comfortable and the other passengers agreeable. Besides we got through customs with all our oriental collection without any trouble and without having to pay any duty. I don't know whether we'd have been this lucky in the port of New York on a more pretentious steamer.

But we landed safely and all well last Wednesday. Several of our Reading friends came aboard the ship to welcome us and took us out to Reading for the night. The next day Thursday we moved our bag and baggage to cousin Lula's out in Dorchester where Sarah will make headquarters while getting our possessions together preparatory to moving to Pittsburgh. Thursday afternoon I left for Pittsburgh and arrived here yesterday, Friday morning. . . . The laboratory is everything I could wish, and tho I have had little opportunity to look for a place to live from what I have seen we can find a comfortable home. . . . I hope to be able to go down [to Clarksville] with her [Sarah] at least for a few days to see you all and think I can arrange to do so.

Your granddaughter is well and lively as a cricket. She entertained the passengers on board ship by showing them how she was going to hug and kiss her grandmothers and granddaddy. Only she insists on having two granddaddies, and I'm afraid you'll have to do double duty. She knows all about how she's going to feed the chickens and turkeys with Grandma Jenny and take care of the cows and sheep with Uncle Rid and help put her Paris coat on Aunt Mat. Altogether she's a great girl . . . With lots of love to you and hoping to see you soon, I am, affectionately, Doc.

Fig. 2-16: This picture of the Pyramids has the date August 22, 1922, in Dr. Goodpasture's hand on the back. It shows a group of Japanese tourists. Dr. Goodpasture is second from right in back row, but the Sarahs are not shown.

~

EPILOGUE

Sixty-eight years previously, at his inaugural address at the University of Lille on December 7, 1854, Louis Pasteur stated: "In the fields of observation chance favors only the prepared mind." Luck helps, too. In four months after moving to the Singer Research Institute, Dr. Goodpasture was fortunate to find an unusual virus and also his seminal collaborator Oscar Teague. Their studies on this unusual virus (from a fever blister) established his credentials as a scientist and virologist. Fever blisters are common complications of underlying febrile illnesses. The virus they isolated in February 1923 from a mouth blister in a patient

Fig. 2-17: The portrait of Pasteur that hung in Dr. Goodpasture's office. It is now located in Eskind Library, Special Collections.

with pneumonia was unusual in that it readily spread in the rabbit from the cornea to the brain. These two scientists took full advantage of their preparation and luck. Their collaboration made it possible for Dr. Goodpasture to become professor of pathology at Vanderbilt a year after their studies began. It is perhaps for this combination of chance and good fortune that a portrait of Pasteur (Fig. 2-17), and a picture of Oscar Teague,[59] hung in his office at Vanderbilt.

Chapter Three

SCIENTIST

R eaders may, in a few pages, begin to wonder why this chapter is so detailed. It is so because this chapter is the best opportunity to display the scope of Dr. Goodpasture's work and his competence as a researcher. His research was successful because he knew how to choose important problems and then had the force of will to hammer away at the problem, detail by detail, until the truth was revealed. Reading about these details is probably the best way to appreciate fully Dr. Goodpasture's accomplishments. This introductory paragraph is not intended as a forewarning; it is more of an advisory to proceed slowly. The sequence of presentation of his research may also be a concern to those expecting strict adherence to chronology in biographies. His most significant discovery was the development of the embryonated egg technique; it therefore has pride of place although occurring in mid-career. His discovery of the cause of mumps was also a *tour de force* that apparently gave him particular pleasure; it is covered last to emphasize its significance for Dr. Goodpasture. In between are descriptions of research on herpetic encephalitis, an early collaboration with Oscar Teague that stimulated Dr. Goodpasture's interest in viral diseases, and research on fowlpox inclusions. The latter was significant in demonstrating for the first time that living virus was present in some inclusions, work of great importance in terms of viral biology.

—

EMBRYONATED EGG TECHNIQUE

Background

Viruses are the smallest living organisms and use their small size to advantage by subjugating the intrinsic workings of host cells to viral propagation and transmission. Subjugation is effected by specific mechanisms of attachment to the host cell, followed by "forced" entry and pirating of the cellular metabolism, the latter enabling viral multiplication followed by transmission internally to other tissues or externally to another host.

Various viral species parasitize virtually all life-forms, including bacteria; viruses may coexist in mutual harmony with the host or may be pathogenic (capable of producing disease). The pathogenic types have caused some of the plagues that have been of sufficient magnitude and severity to shape history, namely influenza, yellow fever, smallpox, and poliomyelitis.

The small size of viruses contributed to their delayed discovery, as they were detected long after protozoa, fungi, and bacteria had been found. These agents are considerably larger and therefore easily seen by microscopy. Furthermore, most bacteria and all fungi are readily grown in pure culture on artificial media. In contrast, discrete viral particles were not visualized until electron microscopy was available in the mid-1940s, and viruses require living cells for culture. The currently used tissue culture techniques were not standardized until the 1948–55 period when different cell types could be grown and optimal culture media were developed; antibiotics came into general use in this period, greatly facilitating the use of tissue culture by inhibiting superinfection of culture media by bacteria or fungi.

Since tissue cultures were not readily available for viral isolation and propagation before 1955, it was necessary to study viruses by more laborious techniques. One of these was to expose various living tissues to infectious material that had been collected so as to minimize bacterial contaminants or filtered to exclude bacteria. Such infectious material might come from animals or plants. The resultant damage to the experimental tissue was evaluated by microscopy, with structures called inclusions being particularly helpful as an indicator of viral presence. Inclusions varied in location, appearance, and type of cell affected, variations that might be used by an experienced microscopist to identify or speciate the virus. This method of study was a cumbersome process that was very difficult to standardize even within a single laboratory; therefore, the process was frequently subject to misinterpretation and experimental misadventure. The net effect was that progress in diagnosing and understanding viral diseases, as well as in vaccine development for their prevention, proceeded at a snail's pace until well into the 1930s.

It was for these reasons that Dr. Goodpasture announced in 1928[1] what he termed the "great desideratum" [something desirable or essential] of developing culture techniques for viruses. His desideratum specified artificial media, but viral biology prohibits lifeless media for culture of viruses. At that time the best culture medium proved to be the embryonated egg. Eggs were readily available, cheap, compact, tolerated manipulations, and were subsequently proven to be susceptible to many viral agents. Eggs were good culture media for viruses because they contained the three basic tissue types, one of which might be preferred by a specific virus. With reasonable care to exclude bacteria and fungi, it was possible to transfer virus-containing infectious material to embryonated eggs from either experimental animals or human hosts. The embryonated egg technique developed by Dr. Goodpasture in 1931 was greeted with such great enthusiasm by viral researchers around the world that it has been judged a landmark event in animal virus research.[2] A review article on cultivation of viruses in 1939 described thirty different viruses that had been studied since 1931, with successful cultivation in the egg of twenty-one.[3] Monographs[4] and chapters in standard texts[5] devoted to culturing viruses in embryonated eggs further attest to the significance of this method. In Sir Macfarlane Burnet's analysis,[6] the chick embryo technique showed "that a new approach to virology had been opened at Vanderbilt which for another ten or twelve years was to represent the mainstream of virus research. Then, except for specialized applications, it rapidly disappeared. The chick embryo was displaced probably forever by the tissue culture techniques." These rumors of the demise of embryonated eggs as an investigative technique proved premature. There have been 117 citations in the medical literature since 1990 on this method.[7] We should all be gratified to learn that viruses as well as other infectious agents are still being grown and studied using this technique.

Thomas Francis Jr., in his biographical memoir for the American Philosophical Society, supplied a balanced analysis of the use and value of the chick embryo technique:[8]

> Some have considered the result primarily the demonstration of a technic for growing viruses. Goodpasture, however, recognized that a neatly packaged, sterile, complete animal with its corporate organs and varied tissues, equivalent to a wide variety of hosts, offered a rich medium for study of the varied stages of pathogenesis, particularly the incubation periods of a variety of infections. In fact, the specificity of virus-cell relationships and the meaning of the intracellular state were always in his mind along with the concept of cellular immunity in resistance to viral infection.

We may never know what led Dr. Goodpasture to investigate this particular technique, as the laboratory notebooks from that period have apparently been lost and his publications do not describe precisely the thought processes or work leading up to the use of embryonated eggs. In 1933[9] he wrote that the chick embryo technique arose from a need to obtain fowlpox virus in quantity, specifically:

Our interest in this technic was aroused as a result of a study of one of the virus diseases, namely, fowl-pox. We were trying to obtain the virus in quantity uncontaminated by ordinary bacteria. By using minute amounts of uncontaminated virus Dr. Woodruff succeeded regularly in infecting the chorio-allantoic membrane. The lesion was extensive and typical of the disease and usually uncontaminated by bacteria.

A complete summary of the work on chick embryos was given by Dr. Goodpasture in the Leo Loeb Lecture on March 24, 1938, at Washington University School of Medicine.[10] In the Loeb Lecture, Dr. Goodpasture began by reviewing embryological experiments dating back to 1749, complete by 1815 with cover-glasses placed over apertures in the egg shell (a practice followed more than one hundred years later by Dr. Goodpasture and associates). The first report on infection in embryos was published in 1906, when blood infected with bacteria was injected by needle into egg albumen. In 1911 Rous and Murphy found that a neoplasm of fowls (now known as Rous sarcoma) would grow on the chorioallantois either when small bits were injected via needle or, remarkably, if a cell-free filtrate was used instead.[11] By 1920, there were a few experiments using the avian pest virus injected into the embryo, and in 1929 vaccinia was passed for a short time by yolk sac injections.

Before 1931 chick embryos had therefore been used to study embryology, infections and tumors. The scientific rationale for Dr. Goodpasture's use of chick embryos is clearly laid out in his 1938 article: namely, that viruses grow only in the presence of viable cells and that most viruses affect only certain cell types (cytotropism). This specific feature of viruses is exemplified by the dog wart virus that attacks only the squamous epithelium in the mouth of dogs, not squamous epithelium elsewhere in the dog and not squamous epithelium in other animals. Because the chorioallantoic membrane of chick embryos is the first structure presented when the egg shell with its membrane is removed, and because the chorioallantois contains all three cell types, this membrane allowed direct inoculation of virus on a maximally susceptible single tissue that was readily accessible for study. Dr. Goodpasture's account reads:[12]

> With these facts in mind Dr. Woodruff and I, a few years ago, began our experiment with fowlpox in the embryo by making a window in the shell and applying the fowlpox virus, which is primarily epitheliotropic, directly to the presenting ectodermal surface [from which the epithelium is derived] of the chorioallantois. As a result characteristic lesions developed locally and they were subsequently easily located and studied.

Whatever the genesis of this breakthrough in virology, Dr. Goodpasture immediately recognized the applicability of embryonated eggs to a broad range of questions, and thereafter relegated studies of fowlpox to a much more minor role. There is another comment of interest on the development of the chick embryo technique in the introduction to the Leo Loeb Lecture:

> The method of cultivating bacteria in pure strain on artificial media, especially solid media, lay at the very foundation of the bacteriological period of medicine. That method, as have so many important technological contributions, required the gift of ingenuity with which Pasteur and Koch were richly endowed. The method of tissue culture, leading to such far reaching explorations into the realm of cytology, is of a similar category of scientific fertility.
>
> It is possible, however, for experimenters to find at times methods of great potential usefulness, almost by chance, through the more clumsy procedure of trial or, as Claud Bernard expressed it, an experiment to see, combined with fortunate coincidence. In biological work I believe this is not infrequently the case.

The disclaimer "almost by chance" hardly seems applicable to Dr. Goodpasture's approach to investigation, but the "fortunate coincidence" in this case was having the world's expert on fowlpox open an embryonated egg sometime in 1930 and see the possibilities therein.

Finally, in a letter to Alfred Blalock in 1955[13] Dr. Goodpasture made the following comments:

> As to your inquiry [as to how Dr. Goodpasture came upon the use of the chick embryo], I feel that in reply to such a question it would be easy for one, not knowing the answer, to indulge in a good deal of speculation. Personally I cannot attribute our use and development of the chick embryo technique to accident, design or intuition, but rather to a concatenation of ideas attributable to a continuity of thought along a particular line of research for a prolonged period. A conjunction of ideas which seems so obvious once achieved is for most of us extraordinarily difficult (for the more intuitive the less difficult) and comes about only as the result of long and continuous pondering and experimenting.
>
> As I see it now there were four chief lines of thought that led to the use of chick embryos in our work—(a) a long research experience with a disease of chickens, fowl-pox, (b) a firm conviction from much evidence that viruses multiply only in living, especially in young cells and are often quite selective with respect to their preferences, (c) a knowledge that chick embryos had been previously used experimentally for studying infections and grafting tumors including the so-called Rous Sarcoma which appeared to be due to a virus, (d) an obvious and pressing need to have at our disposal large quantities of fowl-pox virus free from contamination by other microorganisms or viruses. With the first three converging on the fourth it is surprising that we did not think of using the embryo earlier for it presents, as we knew, an ectodermal surface of its membranes when the shell is removed. As one reviews past experiences it becomes a matter of great surprise, and often of regret, that incapacity to make quite obvious association of ideas, is the chief impediment to progress of one sort or another.

Another possible precedent for the egg embryo technique was brought out in an interview with J. D. Ratcliff in 1944.[14] Therein Dr. Goodpasture was quoted as remembering that another scientist at Hopkins had attempted unsuccessfully to grow the microbe of tuberculosis in eggs. This comment probably refers to one of Dr.

Goodpasture's classmates at Hopkins, Dr. Holland Newton Stevenson, who had several publications in 1917 and 1918 on tumor immunity in which embryonated eggs were used.[15] There was another interesting exchange of letters about the technique involving the writer Greer Williams, author of *Microbe Hunters*. Alice Woodruff wrote Mr. Williams on December 16, 1958, stating "you are kind in your words of praise about the virus culture work, but I would be embarrassed if you give me too much prominence in the story for I was active in the work such a short time and was only carrying out Dr. Goodpasture's suggestions." She sent a copy of her letter to Dr. Goodpasture, expressing concern about the enthusiasm of Mr. Williams. Dr. Goodpasture's response is dated December 22, 1958. After a cordial invitation for the Woodruffs to visit Nashville, Dr. Goodpasture wrote:[16]

> As to Mr. Williams—I saw him about a year ago and he sent me a draft of his chapter on the chick embryo work. It was written in such journalistic style and seemed so personal I was not able to approve it and decided to let him develop the subject more objectively and in his own way as I did not feel very congenial with his approach. It was somewhat embarrassing to feel that I was contributing to and in a sense promoting a eulogy (or obituary) to myself. The only pleasure I have derived from Mr. Williams' interest has been the opportunity it has given me of recalling more vividly happy days of yore when we were all working together in the laboratory at Vanderbilt.

In summary, embryonated eggs had been used for many different studies, but none approached a systematic exploitation of the technique. The word fallow summarizes best the status of fertile eggs as a method in virology in 1930; it is particularly appropriate that after the ground had been plowed, seed-planting and harvesting awaited a Tennessee farmer-*cum*-master investigator in virology. Once the technique was established, various viral and bacterial infections were studied to determine their pathogenesis; viruses were grown in order to test and produce vaccines; and viruses were passaged repeatedly to study their mutability. The susceptibility of specific tissues such as skin to viral infection was studied by grafting human and chicken skin on chorioallantoic membranes. Such skin grafts also afforded opportunities to evaluate immunity,[17] as one might determine if immunity were due to local or to circulating factors by grafting chicken skin from control and immune chickens onto membranes. Human placental membranes were also engrafted, in order to study their susceptibility to viral infection.

Adaptation of the egg embryo technique to the study of engrafted skin and human placental membranes is an interesting story in its own right, opening several fields of investigation. Previous studies had shown that grafts from other species were tolerated by chick embryos, as Murphy had shown in 1914[18] that certain malignant tumors of rat and mouse would grow on the chick chorioallantoic membrane. The decision by Goodpasture and Anderson to try human skin was based on the premise that certain viruses might infect such grafts, although chick tissues were not susceptible to them.[19] When they showed that human skin could not be infected with chicken pox or easily with herpes zoster, they then wondered if embryonic tissues such as placental membranes might be more susceptible. A *magnum opus* entitled "Virus Infection of the Mammalian Fetus"[20] evolved from these experiments. This paper was given on the occasion of the fiftieth anniversary of the University of Chicago in September 1941, when Dr. Goodpasture received an honorary doctor of science degree. He explored in depth the paradox that certain chick and mammalian embryonic tissues showed increased susceptibility to infection as compared to adult tissues, yet active infections in mothers were rarely transmitted to the fetus. For example, in the great contagions of smallpox, measles, and chicken pox there were few authenticated cases of infection of neonates despite active infection in the mothers. Here is Dr. Goodpasture's analysis:

> The relative infrequency of infection of the fetus from the maternal disease is indicative of a rather effective barrier between the susceptible tissues of the embryo and the virus- or germ-bearing cells of the mother. In the case of infective agents carried by the blood stream the determinative barrier in all probability is placental.

Grafts of human placental membranes were easily established, in which the two placental layers (amnion and chorion) were grown side by side. Interestingly, grafts of amnion but not chorion were readily infected with vaccinia, smallpox, and herpes simplex, as well as with an abortion-producing viral infection of mares that had not been previously propagated in human tissues. It is undoubtedly significant that chorion is the part of the placenta exposed to maternal blood flow *in vivo*; therefore it has intrinsic resistance to viruses. This important paper had these concluding paragraphs:

> Owing to the obvious importance of the placental union in determining whether or not infection of the fetus takes place, it is rather surprising to find so little knowledge concerning placental infection, and the relative specific resistance of placental and fetal membranes.
>
> Our experimental observations concerning the inoculation of human fetal membranes grafted on the chorioallantois of chick embryos indicate that the human chorionic epithelium is naturally a resistant membrane to a number of viruses, and the relative rarity of fetal infection by the active agents of the great contagions leads one to conclude that it is resistant to others which it was not practicable for us to test.

In sections below, the major studies by Dr. Goodpasture and associates are described and briefly discussed. Publications on the embryonated egg method by the Vanderbilt group are listed by year to facilitate understanding of their significance and the evolution of subject matter over time.

Publications by the Vanderbilt Group on the Embryonated Egg Technique

1931   With Alice M. Woodruff. "The susceptibility of the chorio-allantoic membrane of chick embryos to infection with the fowl-pox virus." *Am J Pathol*, 7:209–22.

With Alice M. Woodruff and G. J. Buddingh. "The cultivation of vaccine and other viruses in the chorio-allantoic membrane of chick embryos." *Science*, 74:371–72.

1932   With Alice M. Woodruff and G. J. Buddingh. "Vaccinal infection of the chorio-allantoic membrane of the chick embryo." *Am J Pathol*, 8:271–81.

1933   "Use of embryo chick in investigation of certain pathological problems." *Southern Med J*, 26:418–20.

With G. J. Buddingh. "Human immunization with a dermal vaccine cultivated on the membranes of chick embryos." *Science*, 78:484–85.

1934   With G. J. Buddingh. "Immunisation de l'homme par un vaccin dermique, cultive' sur les membranes de l'embryon de poulet." *Bulletin de l'Office international d'hygiene publique*, 26:1226–32.

1935   With G. John Buddingh. "The preparation of antismallpox vaccine by culture of the virus in the chorio-allantoic membrane of chick embryos and its use in human immunization." *Am J Hyg*, 21:319–60.

1937   "Vaccinia." Proceedings of the Institute of Medicine of Chicago, No. 11, Volume 11, pp. 206–20. Thirteenth Ludvig Hektoen Lecture of the Frank Billings Foundation.

With Katherine Anderson. "The problem of infection as presented by bacterial invasion of chorio-allantoic membrane of chick embryos." *Am J Pathol*, 13:149–74.

With Mae Gallavan. "Infection of chick embryos with H. pertussis reproducing pulmonary lesions of whooping cough." *Am J Pathol*, 13:927–38.

1938   With Alice Polk and G. J. Buddingh. "An experimental study of complement and hemolytic amboceptor introduced into chick embryos." *Am J Pathol*, 14:71–86.

"Some uses of the chick embryo for the study of infection and immunity." *Am J Hyg*, 28:111–29.

With Beverly Douglas and Katherine Anderson. "A study of human skin grafted upon the chorio-allantois of chick embryos." *J Exp Med*, 68:891–904.

1939   "Virus infection of the chick embryo." *Annals of Internal Medicine*, 13:1–11.

"Virus and bacterial infection of the chick embryo" (abstract and discussion). *Arch Pathol*, 28:606–9.

1940　With Katherine Anderson. "Immunity to fowl-pox studied by means of skin grafts on chorioallantois of chick embryo." *Arch Pathol*, 30:212–25.

"The developing egg as a culture medium." *J Lab Clin Med*, 26:242–49.

1942　With Katherine Anderson. "Virus infection of human fetal membranes grafted on the chorioallantois of chick embryos." *Am J Pathol*, 18:563–75.

1945　With Katherine Anderson and W. A. DeMonbreun. "An etiologic consideration of Donovania granulomatis cultivated from granuloma inguinale (three cases) in embryonic yolk." *J Exp Med*, 81:25–40.

With Katherine Anderson and W. A. DeMonbreun. "Immunologic relationships of Donovania granulomatis to granuloma inguinale." *J Exp Med*, 81:41–50.

With Katherine Anderson and W. A. DeMonbreun. "An experimental investigation of the etiology and immunology of granuloma inguinale." *American Journal of Syphilis, Gonorrhea and Venereal Diseases*, 29:165–73.

1959　"Cytoplasmic inclusions resembling Guarnieri bodies, and other phenomena induced by mutants of the virus of fowl-pox." *Am J Pathol*, 35:213–31.

Development of Embryonated Egg Technique

Before fowlpox could be inoculated onto the chorioallantoic membranes it was necessary to obtain abundant viral material free of bacterial and fungal contaminants. Filtering to remove bacteria was an option but resulted in considerable dilution of the infectious agent. Several methods were explored. As bacterial superinfection of fowlpox lesions on chickens usually occurred after seven days, the preferred method involved excision of six day-old lesions that had been bathed in 95 percent alcohol; after washing carefully and culturing to insure there were no bacteria, small pieces of lesions were inoculated into eggs. Several other methods were tried, including picking out single inclusions with a microdissection apparatus and prolonged digestion in 1 percent potassium hydroxide to kill bacteria and fungi. The former technique was laborious and the latter caused a reduction in viral infectiousness. Once a suitable source of uncontaminated virus had been found, techniques for opening the egg shell, observing the site

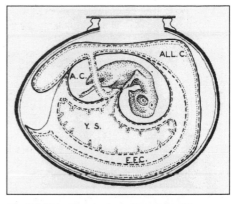

Fig. 3-1: This diagram shows the relationship between the shell, its membrane, the chorioallantois (membrane above "ALL.C." at top of diagram), and the embryo. From Katherine Anderson's thesis.

of inoculation on the chorioallantois, and preserving sterility were then developed.

The technique described in 1931 initially involved cleansing the egg surface around the aperture site by bathing in alcohol and brisk flaming (!) to achieve surface sterility; then a 7–10 mm square window was made by "cutting and scraping" with the points of small sharp scissors. The shell was removed and the underlying shell membrane was cut away with sterile precautions to expose the chorioallantoic membrane (Fig. 3-1). Readers attempting such experiments at home will, if inventive, quickly turn to a nail file for help, since a few aborted scraping efforts suggest that thirty minutes might have been required to prepare one egg. By 1933, experience with the technique had led to several modifications including the important step of mechanical grinding of the shell with a thin emory wheel mounted on a flexible shaft and powered by a small motor with speed control. The latter two components were standard dental equipment (Fig. 3-2). Fertile eggs were warmed in an ordinary bacteriological incubator, with moisture from water in shallow pans. After the Vanderbilt group began to use large numbers of eggs, a dedicated egg incubator was purchased. Fertile eggs were readily available in Nashville from a local hatchery at "a little above market price," a comment that suggests there may

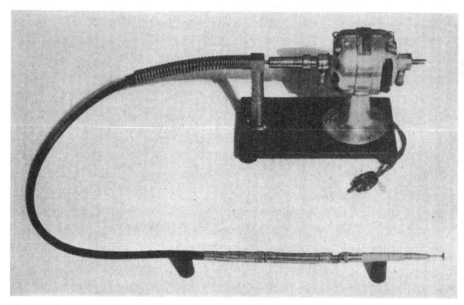

Fig. 3-2: The grinding device used by Dr. Goodpasture and associates to prepare eggs. Such an apparatus is preserved in Special Collections section of Vanderbilt's Eskind Library. From EWG and Buddingh, *Am J Hygiene* 1935.

have been bargaining by Goodpasture the farmer with the supplier. The percentage of fertile eggs and the vitality of embryos were lowest during the summer months, so that egg work was routinely suspended in July and August. After incubating six to twelve days, the eggs were candled [back-lit] in order to outline with wax pencil the air sac and membranes. The outline of windows was cut in the shell as described above, leaving the square of shell in place and the underlying shell membrane intact. After coating this area thinly with melted paraffin, the egg might be replaced in the incubator until time for inoculation. At that time the shell was lifted, exposing the shell membrane. After coating with paraffin to fix loose particles of shell as well as ambient bacteria and fungi, this membrane was then perforated with a spear-point needle, cut with fine scissors, folded back, and detached.

The chorioallantoic membrane was thus exposed and could be inoculated by a drop of emulsion prepared from infected material or a small fragment of infected tissue. A ring of warm vaseline and paraffin was expressed by syringe onto the shell around the window

(Fig. 3-3) and a coverglass pressed into place. Eggs were incubated without turning, the progress of the lesion thus being visible through the coverglass (moisture condensed on the underside could be evaporated by gentle heating).

Generally embryos had to survive at least four days for lesions to develop (Fig. 3-4) or for viral propagation to occur. Membranes could be harvested under sterile precautions for microscopy or as a source of virus. Although some chicks hatched after these manipulations, most experiments were terminated at four days or so when membranes or other embryonic tissues were harvested.

The studies with skin and placental grafts required considerable operative dexterity. Human skin was obtained from the margins of operative specimens, which perforce had been shaved, washed, and subsequently bathed in alcohol and iodine.[21] Squares 0.5–1 cm in size were spread on a smooth metal surface with the epithelial surface against the metal. If necessary, specimens were dissected to remove attached fat and connective tissue. The raw underside of the graft was laid upon chorioallantoic membranes per routine. Precautions that ensured success included strict sterile technique and preparation of thin grafts that had been carefully flattened on the metal surface so they were uniformly cohesive when applied to the membrane. The underside (vascularized surface) of grafts was directly placed on the membrane. Coverslips were then affixed with paraffin and the egg returned to the incubator. Grafts usually remained smooth and flat for twenty-four to forty-eight hours, after which they became slightly wrinkled; viable grafts were firm and glistening, while those that did not take became boggy, dull, and yellow. At appropriate intervals after inoculation with test materials, grafts and attached egg

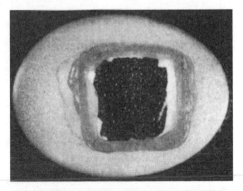

Fig. 3-3: The window has been removed and the opening ringed with paraffin preparatory to covering with a coverglass. The coverglass could be removed later if necessary for observation or manipulations. From EWG and Buddingh, *Am J Hygiene* 1935.

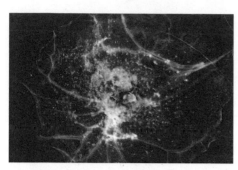

Fig. 3-4: Excised chorioallantoic membrane showing scattered opacities from viral growth and associated inflammation. This preparation by Katherine Anderson, from her thesis.

membranes were removed for histologic evaluation.

Placental membranes were obtained by dissecting fresh placentas on sterile cork boards. There are two membrane layers in the placenta—the chorion and the amnion; chorion and amnion squares were flattened on the metal applicator with the vascularized surface upward. After preparation, 1 cm squares were then flipped over onto the chick membrane. Engraftment of placental tissues was readily achieved, and bacterial contamination was rarely observed.[22]

Recognizing that many readers may be surfeited by this detailed description of the chick embryo technique, perhaps we should be reminded that it was the most important technique in virology for ten to twelve years. It was the basis for development of very effective vaccines against several deadly viruses. Dr. Goodpasture's reputation as a medical scientist was largely based on this work.

Application to Study of Vaccinia (Cowpox) and Other Viruses

The technique paper described above was submitted on March 7, 1931, and used fowlpox as the test virus. It concluded with the observation[23] that the study of other viral infections, "e.g. vaccinia, might prove advantageous." No specific reasons were given for their subsequent choice of vaccinia, but it certainly proved to be advantageous, with a paper in *Science* in October 1931, on cultivation of that virus[24] and a much more detailed paper on the same topic submitted to the *American Journal of Pathology* on February 3, 1932.[25] The team of Goodpasture, Alice Woodruff, and Buddingh had a very busy spring and fall, whether or not the laboratory was down in July and August because of infertility of eggs.

The Goodpasture group ultimately grew the viruses of fowlpox, vaccinia, rabies, smallpox, and herpes simplex in chick embryos. They were not able to grow the measles virus. Success with herpes was noteworthy, as neither adult nor young chickens are susceptible to that virus. Similarly, for reasons that are not clear, vaccinia grew rapidly in embryos but was only slightly pathogenic for adult chickens. With several viruses available for study, vaccinia was the agent studied in detail, probably with an eye on its potential use as a vaccinating agent.

The virus used was supplied by Dr. T. M. Rivers, a colleague then at the Rockefeller Institute for Medical Research. A bit of infected tissue the size of a pinhead was placed upon the exposed chorioallantoic membrane. Within twenty-four hours, the membrane became thicker and grayer around the inoculum, progressing by forty-eight hours to a 1 cm lesion flecked with small hemorrhages. The advancing margin of this lesion showed the most distinctive histological changes. The period of forty-eight hours proved to be ideal for harvesting membranes in vaccinia, since embryos routinely died by ninety-six hours. Viral yields were also maximal at forty-eight to seventy-two hours.

Histologic sections of affected membranes revealed edema, hemorrhage, and acute inflammation, with extensive necrosis of epithelium and plugging of capillaries by endothelial nodules. Older lesions showed marked degenerative changes, but at the edge of the advancing gross lesion the specific inclusion bodies of vaccinia were readily seen in all cell types. By several manipulations, vaccinia inclusions were shown to contain elementary bodies.[26] Therefore the Vanderbilt group was the first to show that vaccinia, like fowlpox, had inclusions containing elementary bodies. The more important discovery was that virtually unlimited quantities of pristine vaccinia virus were readily obtainable using the embryonated egg technique, a fact of great significance in the later vaccine studies.

Human skin grafts were successfully inoculated with the viruses of herpes simplex, smallpox, and vaccinia; after numerous failures with zoster, Goodpasture and Anderson were successful in one case when they happened to obtain the skin graft and vesicular fluid on the same

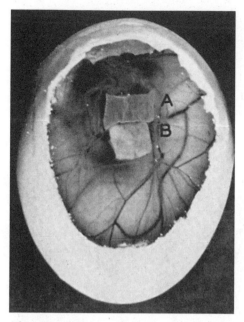

Fig. 3-5: Explants of amnion and chorion growing side by side on chorioallantoic membrane. From EWG and Anderson, *Am J of Path* 1942.

day.[27] They were never able to grow the virus of chicken pox. No information of particular biological significance was obtained from these studies, in contrast to that using skin from fowls. (See Application of Technique—immunity section below.)

Grafts of human placental membranes were of interest as the Vanderbilt group was able to successfully engraft the two components of the placenta, allowing them to be studied separately (Fig. 3-5). It was of particular interest that chorion, the part of the placenta exposed to maternal blood *in situ*, was resistant to viral infection while amnion was much more susceptible. This was the beginning of a much-needed study on the pathogenesis of intrauterine viral infections. The technique of placental grafts was also used in 1942 to study the recently discovered virus responsible for several outbreaks of abortion in mares. At this point we should not be surprised at the range of interest of the Goodpasture laboratory. The discoverers of the mare abortion virus were unable to establish a laboratory model for the disease and probably turned to the experts in virology at Vanderbilt for help. The virus of mare abortion was an important cause of loss to breeders, but it is presumably not of concern in human pregnancies. The virus of mare abortion affected human amniotic tissues that had been engrafted on eggs, but did not affect the chorionic grafts. This result is presumably yet another indication of the specificity of viral cytotropism. We are left to ask why the virus of mare abortion affects human placental grafts but (thankfully) not human placentas *in vivo*.

Application: Vaccine Production

It is surprising that immunization against smallpox was not standardized before 1935, considering the major importance of effective immunization for public health. The problems as summarized by Goodpasture and Buddingh included:[28] the methods of inoculation had not changed appreciably or consistently for 136 years; bacteria inevitably contaminated the vaccines as they were prepared from skin lesions of calves; pathogenicity of the vaccine for human subjects was not standardized and vaccines available varied greatly in potency.

Techniques for cultivating vaccinia virus at Vanderbilt had evolved by 1935 to industrial proportions (Figs. 3-6 and 3-7). A three-hundred-egg incubator was purchased from Sears-Roebuck and Company in order to inoculate fertile eggs on the fourteenth day of incubation in lots of sixty, three times a week. On the thirteenth day eggs were candled to mark the

TOP: Fig. 3-6: Dr. Buddingh at work in 1932.
BOTTOM: Fig. 3-7: The factory was still in operation in 1950. The expert technician Marguerite Snyder is preparing eggs for study in this case and not for vaccine production.

position of the embryo and then washed gently; a triangular window was cut through the eggshell, avoiding injury to the shell membrane, and the surface was covered with melted paraffin. Eggs so prepared were returned to the incubator at 37°C until the next day. For inoculation, melted paraffin was again layered over the window outline; the shell membrane was cut along two sides of the triangle, so the shell with its membrane could be carefully lifted away from the chorioallantoic membrane, onto which bits of infected tissue were rubbed lightly (Fig. 3-8). The shell flap was then closed and sealed with paraffin to allow continued incubation.

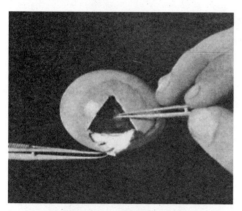

TOP: Fig. 3-8: Innoculation of prepared egg with infected material. From EWG and Buddingh, *Am J Hygiene* 1935.
BOTTOM: Fig. 3-9: Egg showing an ellipse of shell has been removed preparatory to harvesting the membrane. In these experiments, fowlpox was being studied rather than vaccinia. From EWG, *Am J Pathol* 1959.

For harvesting, the shell over the membrane was removed in one piece (Fig. 3-9), and the ellipse of infected membrane was excised, cultured, and stored at 0°C until bacterial sterility was confirmed. Uncontaminated lesions were ground while frozen to a finely divided state in a chilled mortar and pestle; sterile 50 percent neutral glycerin[29] in saline was added, and the glycerinated vaccine was stored at 0°C. Each step of this procedure was carried out in conditions that reduced the likelihood of infection; bacteria causing tetanus and tuberculosis were a particular concern. Lest the virus lose its potency, a regular process of maintaining seed virus of high potency (that with the largest numbers of elementary bodies) was repeated at intervals of two to three weeks.

Potency of freshly prepared vaccine was tested by placing 1–100 to 1–10,000 dilutions of each lot on shaved, lightly scarified flank skin of adult rabbits. Dilutions of 1–1,000 were expected to produce confluent eruptions over at least 90 percent of the vaccinated area within five to seven days, while the 1–3,000 dilution produced confluence of 70–80 percent. A table in the 1935 paper indicates the volume of vaccine produced. Twenty-one lots were evaluated for potency in rabbits, each lot representing the one hundredth passage of virus, and each lot coming from ten egg membranes. "Numerous other lots of vaccine prepared from other generations of the virus were tested with excellent results."[30]

Glycerinated virus could be stored at 0°C for twelve months without loss of potency, but after two years there was a considerable decrease in potency. Storage at 25°C and 37°C inactivated the virus within eighteen to twenty-one days.

This locally prepared chick vaccine was first tested against the standard calf-derived vaccine obtained from the New York City Health Board Laboratory. Twelve rabbits were inoculated with chick vaccine and twelve with calf vaccine. Comparable lesions developed in both groups, and revaccination with the same preparation showed comparable degrees of immunity from twenty-one to eighty-six days after the first inoculation; in both groups immunity was judged to be only partial. Similar experiments were performed with monkeys (M. rhesus), fourteen of which received various types of primary vaccination followed by tests for immunity twelve weeks later; the chick vaccine was found to be comparable to that of the calf in potency and safety. Human trials were next.

A pilot experiment involved eighteen persons, three to thirty-five years of age, who were assumed to be non-immune as they had no history of vaccination and did not have vaccination scars. These subjects, having received vaccine by a single scratch over the shoulder, were "carefully observed from day-to-day for thirteen days" in terms of the appearance of the scratch site, pain, malaise, enlargement of axillary nodes, and fever. That this study was carried through to human trials by the Vanderbilt Department of Pathology is a testament to Goodpasture and Buddingh's careful groundwork.

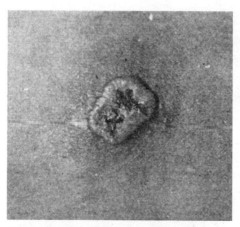

Fig. 3-10: Vaccination lesion in subject of trials of efficacy of vaccine prepared from embryonated eggs. From EWG and Buddingh, *Am J Hyg* 1935.

Even so, there may have been anxiety and then relief as they "carefully observed" that the lesions following chick vaccine were somewhat smaller and caused less discomfort than the calf vaccine (Fig. 3-10). The resultant scars were also thinner. Revaccination showed no difference in immunity at nine weeks up to one year after primary vaccination. They were now ready for field trials.

In cooperation with the Tennessee State Board of Health and local county health agencies, chick vaccine was tested in all non-immune children and young adults aged four to twenty years, from grammar schools and high schools, who were "available at the time."[31] They vaccinated 1,074 individuals with a success rate of 94.4 percent and no complications. The various state agencies agreed that the results compared favorably with those obtained with good quality calf vaccine.

In discussing these results, the authors stated that at the outset their intention was to improve the quality of smallpox vaccine. Vaccine virus had been cultivated for over two years by more than 160 successive egg passages without exhibiting alteration in potency for rabbit, monkey, or man. This stability was one of the most remarkable results of the investigation and was attributed to regular harvesting of eggs at forty-eight to seventy-two hours. At seventy-two hours the lesions contained the largest numbers of elementary bodies and were most infectious when titrated. Also the lesions had not developed a significant inflammatory reaction, which presumably reduced viral load. The authors concluded that repeated passage through embryonic tissue such as the chick maintained the original qualities of the vaccine virus and that it was not necessary to pass the virus back through rabbit or man to maintain a high quality immunizing agent as was the case with calf-derived virus. In conclusion, they believed "that the product derived from a proper observance of the method as outlined will be a distinct improvement upon the anti-smallpox vaccine at present in general use."[32] This was an unusually strong statement for Dr. Goodpasture to place in print and reflected the confidence he had in the soundness of the work and its potential usefulness in prevention of disease. This project was an impressive demonstration of the capability of Dr. Goodpasture's laboratory to move from basic research to production of a vaccine that had been fully tested in the field, all within three years.[33]

Application—Study of Bacterial Infections

Whooping cough

The study by Gallavan and Goodpasture in 1937[34] on pertussis (whooping cough) focused on the precise relationship between the causative bacteria and their preferential damage to certain cells in the host. The histopathologic changes in eleven autopsy cases of pertussis in the Vanderbilt Hospital files were analyzed as a prelude to the study of this infection in chick embryos. Analysis of the human material showed that injury and associated inflammatory reaction in the middle and basal layers of the bronchial epithelium was "no doubt a specific lesion" of pertussis. In addition, as found by others, small Gram-negative pertussis bacilli were noted among the cilia of the respiratory tract and nasopharynx.

A strain of the causative agent[35] was maintained on artificial media. A loopful (that amount held in a platinum loop) of a twenty-hour culture was transferred to the chorioallantoic membranes of six eleven-day chick embryos, causing hemorrhage and an acute inflammatory reaction in which a few bacilli were found singly and in clumps. More significantly, when the amniotic sacs of seven thirteen-day embryos were inoculated with 0.1 ml of fluid containing 100 million organisms, the surviving embryos had lesions of the ciliated epithelium of the trachea and bronchi in which there were numerous well-preserved bacteria. This experiment corroborated previous work on animals and man in which the disease had been induced by respiratory tract inoculations. Amniotic fluid in chick embryos (and humans) moves in and out of the respiratory tract; thus the embryonic respiratory epithelium was bathed with bacteria after amniotic inoculations. The authors were impressed with the specific localization of bacteria in ciliated epithelium. Necrosis of epithelium was particularly marked under infected ciliated cells, indicating that a toxic product produced by the bacteria acted locally. It was concluded that *B. pertussis* alone could produce the pathologic picture of pertussis and that there was no support for alternate possibilities of coinfection by *B. pertussis* and virus in whooping cough. This alone was a significant finding, but more interesting was the demonstration that ciliated surfaces in the chick constituted an optimum environment for parasitization, just as in the human. Chick bronchial epithelium could be infected only after day fifteen, when cilia appeared. Thus the conclusion by Dr. Goodpasture: the "environment for a particular microorganism may vary from time to time in the development of the embryo and in the human host."[36]

Granuloma inguinale

The specific bacterium causing granuloma inguinale (*Donovanosis*) was not identified until 1943, although the intracellular "parasites" responsible had been seen by Donovan in 1905. Identification was achieved by Katherine Anderson using the chick embryo technique, after animal studies by DeMonbreun and Goodpasture in 1931 had failed. We may only speculate as to why Dr. Goodpasture's group put so much effort into identification of the responsible agent. This chronic disease was disfiguring and unpleasant, producing persistent sores and inflammatory masses in the genitalia and inguinal areas. As a venereal disease, it ranked far behind gonorrhea and syphilis in morbidity and per se did not cause death. Yet DeMonbreun and Goodpasture in 1931 made an all-out effort to identify the responsible agent. They found that the Donovan organism could not be cultivated on a number of artificial media nor could infection be induced in guinea pigs, rabbits, kittens, dogs, or rats. In monkeys, infections were temporary and healed without ulceration. Other investigators had reproduced experimental lesions in human volunteers resembling *Donovanosis* on clinical and histopathologic grounds. Approximately ten years later, when the chick embryo technique was developed, the Goodpasture group returned to the problem of identifying the causative agent, even after it had been reported that the organism would not grow on the chick chorioallantoic membrane. The solution did not come easily, even after Dr. Anderson discovered that embryonic yolk was suitable as a growth medium for the Donovan agent.

Why was so much effort expended on this relatively unimportant disease when there were other problems of apparently greater significance waiting to be studied? A central tenet of Dr. Goodpasture's investigative philosophy was that information of biologic significance might be obtained from the seemingly inexplicable relationships between living things. In this case, Gram-negative bacteria that were regularly demonstrated in the lesion could not be cultured nor were infections inducible in experimental animals, in sharp distinction to other bacterial diseases in which bacteria were readily cultivated on artificial media and produced lesions experimentally. It was this apparent paradox that probably interested him, resulting in the pursuit of the cause of *Donovanosis* a decade after failing initially.

The three patients successfully studied by Dr. Anderson were biopsied on October 26, 1942, February 12, 1943, and April 28, 1944. The slow pace was due to selection of patients only if there were large numbers of Donovan bodies in smears and if there was minimal superinfection (infection by surface contaminants). After scrubbing the ulcerated lesion with saline-soaked gauzes to remove superficial exudate (pus and debris), a small piece of tissue from the ulcer bed was minced into pin-head sized fragments. These were smeared over six agar slants to determine if contaminating bacteria were present. Two of the six slants showed no bacterial growth after ninety-six hours of incubation but nevertheless contained viable-appearing Gram-negative bacilli that resembled the Donovan organisms. Washings from these two slants were pooled and 0.5–1 ml

Fig. 3-11: Katherine Anderson at work in the laboratory, circa 1935. She is checking culture results.

was inoculated into the yolk sacs of six eight-day embryos. Two embryos died three days later and smears of yolk showed no bacteria. The remaining four embryos were harvested eight days later, revealing abundant encapsulated and unencapsulated Gram-negative bacilli that were "indistinguishable from Donovan bodies." That finding must have occasioned a Eureka or two!

Once established, the strain was maintained for a year and a half by yolk to yolk passage in eight-day embryos; the encapsulated form of the organism closely resembled the Donovan body. Two key lessons were learned from this experience: that the Donovan organism could *survive* four days in culture on agar, although during this time it did not grow and produce visible colonies, and secondly that the Donovan organism readily grew in yolk of egg embryos. The initial culture step allowed Dr. Anderson (Fig. 3-11) to choose for egg inoculation only those pieces of tissue that were not superinfected with extraneous bacteria. She then successfully studied two subsequent patients. In both cases multiple bits of biopsy tissue had to be minced and cultured to find the few bits with abundant Donovan organisms that were not also overgrown with other bacteria.

Extensive studies were then undertaken with the yolk-passaged Donovan organisms. They would not grow on artificial media, although many different types were tested, nor were lesions inducible in mice, rabbits, dogs, or monkeys. Organisms would not grow in yolk of *unfertilized* eggs. However, yolk from four- to five-day embryos in test tubes maintained growth *if* embryonic chick heart was added. These results showed that special conditions "existing so far as is at present known only in human tissues and developing embryos" are necessary for the multiplication and that "some factor, perhaps furnished by living cells, provides the required conditions."[37] The human cell supporting multiplication was shown to be a monocyte thirty-one years later,[38] a possibility predicted by Dr. Anderson from the appearance of the lesion in humans. That the bacterial agent in embryonic yolk was responsible for *Donovanosis* was proven by skin tests of infected individuals with antigenic material from yolk-cultured Donovan organisms.[39]

These studies with bacteria are not as well-known as those with viruses, but they are important in illustrating the range of competence of the Vanderbilt group. With pertussis, Dr. Goodpasture extended the concept of cytotropism to bacteria by showing that specific tissues are susceptible to bacterial infections, a situation analogous to the specific tissue preferences of most viruses. With *Donovanosis*, the determination to find the causative agent might be characterized as dogged. Even so, their success was due to the combination of exploring all possibilities (injecting yolk sac after others had shown no growth on the chorioallantois) and remarkable attention to detail (showing that Donovan bacilli *survived* in cultures although they would not grow). It is impressive that to study this bacterial infection they chose as the inoculum bits of tissue that were "sterile" on routine media but were shown to contain Donovan organisms when smeared. Thus they found a bacterium that is like a virus in its need for living cells to propagate.

Application of Technique—Mutability of Viruses

Dr. Goodpasture's interest in the ability of viruses (and other infectious agents) to change in their disease-producing capacities spanned his investigative career. In 1923 with Oscar Teague he used a spontaneously mutated herpes simplex virus as an experimental tool to explore viral movement from the exterior to the central nervous system. These studies with Teague did not concentrate on the mechanism of mutation, but in 1938 Katherine Anderson worked on this phenomenon for her doctorate in pathology under Dr. Goodpasture's mentorship. The neurotropic strain of herpes used by Goodpasture and Teague was unusual in that it regularly produced encephalitis after corneal inoculations in rabbits. When placed on the chorioallantoic membranes of chick embryos by Anderson, initially this strain rarely spread to involve the heart or brain of embryos; however, after twenty passages, necrotic areas were routinely seen in the heart and other organs. By the seventy-fifth passage virulence for chick embryos had increased to the point that embryos rarely survived ninety-six hours. As virulence for the chick embryo increased, the effects on the rabbit decreased so that corneal inoculations caused minimal changes and no longer progressed to encephalitis. The strain that was virulent for chicks and of reduced virulence for rabbits still protected rabbits against encephalitis when they were challenged with the original virus.

Toward the end of his career, Dr. Goodpasture focused his laboratory investigations almost exclusively on mutation, giving lectures on mutation of fowlpox at Vanderbilt University at the Alpha Omega Alpha lecture on May 1954 and elsewhere.[40] A publication followed in 1959.[41] These lectures and the publication dealt with studies on his favorite warhorse of viruses, fowlpox. Noting that many viruses undergo recognizable changes under laboratory conditions of propagation, fowlpox in contrast was deemed to be extraordinarily stable until Buddingh found a mutation in an old laboratory strain.[42] This strain upon injection into the brains of baby chicks induced encephalitis and death in several days; sections showed infection and hyperplasia of endothelial and epithelial cells of the choroid plexus (a vascular structure in the brain). When transplanted back onto chorioallantoic membranes, infected epithelial cells dissociated and floated off the membranes, producing a white exudate. As the mutant strain used by Buddingh had been discarded, Dr. Goodpasture repeated these experiments with several stock strains of fowlpox as well as two recently isolated field (organisms found in the barnyard or in the wild) strains from chickens and a recently isolated field strain from a turkey. Although encephalitis and endothelial infection were not seen, other unusual phenomena were found. We should follow the course of these experiments[43] because they provide insights into Dr. Goodpasture's thoroughness in the laboratory, because he provides the code by which he kept track of the various ways the virus was handled, and because the results are interesting.

Beginning with a field strain of fowlpox (henceforth labeled DV for virus supplied by Dr. E. R. Doll of the University of Kentucky), infection was established as usual on the plucked scalps of two-day chicks. A bacteria-free strain was established by inoculating chorioallantoic membranes (now DVM, with M for membrane) with 0.1 ml of a 1:1000 suspension of infected epithelium. After passage through eight generations on chick membranes, DVM8 was inoculated intracerebrally (now the strain is DVM8C1—C for cerebral), and virus was recovered by placing brain tissue on chorioallantoic membranes. Although virus was present in the brain tissue, it did not produce encephalitis. Material from this passage was injected into the occipital bone because Buddingh had reported bone cells were accidentally infected by his mutant and Dr. Goodpasture was attempting to repeat this happenstance situation. A chick injected at the base of the skull was etherized and the bone removed; after grinding with saline, suspensions were placed on twelve-day chorioallantoic membranes (the code for the strain has now become DVM8C1M1B1M1—the B for bone) and DVM8C1M1B1M2 after the second membrane passage.

Surprisingly, this virus after subsequent manipulations produced dissociation of epithelium in a manner similar to that observed by Buddingh but in contrast did not produce endothelial lesions. However, there were two other remarkable lesions resulting from infection with this mutant: basophilic (blue-staining) inclusions resembling the inclusions of vaccinia (Guarnieri bodies), and hyperplasia of renal epithelium simulating a neoplasm. The basophilic inclusions were unique in Dr. Goodpasture's experience with fowlpox and coexisted in some cells with the eosinophilic inclusions expected in fowlpox. Once the possibility of coinfection by two viruses was ruled out, the blue inclusions caused Dr. Goodpasture to speculate that these animal viruses (fowlpox and vaccinia/cowpox) had a common ancestor. The adenomatous hyperplasia in the kidney and the epithelial dissociation suggested the invasive character of cancer cells, raising the possibility of cancer production by this mutant virus. Dr. Goodpasture speculated that there might be one or more fowlpox mutants involved in producing these changes, the unusual inclusions and the abnormal epithelium. He concluded[44] that these variations opened for animal viruses opportunities to explore the genetic factors responsible for viral behavior similar to those exploited so usefully by Delbruck and Luria with bacteriophage mutants.[45]

Dr. Goodpasture recognized that changes in viral behavior might be on a genetic basis[46] although there were no chromosomes in bacteria and presumably none in viruses. The significance of mutations was stated more presciently by Macfarlane Burnet[47] shortly after the demonstration by Avery and colleagues[48] that DNA was responsible for heredity:

> That heritable variations in bacteria and viruses arise by a process of discontinuous mutation essentially similar to gene mutation in higher forms and that the mass transformation of a strain as observed in practice is the result of selective survival and overgrowth of one or more mutant types.

Application of Technique—Studies on Immunity

From 1938 to 1942, when these studies took place, the understanding of immunity was extremely fragmentary and superficial, although infections had been successfully prevented or minimized for centuries by artificial induction of immunity. Dr. Goodpasture attributed our overall ignorance about specific mechanisms of immunity in part to the fact that:[49]

> there are few infectious diseases of man that can be induced in experimental animals with sufficient exactitude and constancy, amidst conditions simulating those under which they make their appearance naturally, to enable the investigator to translate his experimental data in terms of spontaneously occurring disease. This difficulty has tended to divert the attention of investigators away from studies of pathogenesis—that is, the mechanism of infection, without a knowledge of which specific immunity

cannot be fully understood . . . To understand the mechanisms of defense one should be able to watch the varying tide of battle between the active agent and the host, and to appreciate more intimately the tactics of the latter as it succeeds in gaining and maintaining the upper hand.

With these guiding principles, the Goodpasture laboratory had undertaken a large group of studies: to determine which bacterial and viral infections might be induced in the chick embryo, to determine how closely these infections resembled the natural process, and to describe some of the basic immune mechanisms in the chick.[50]

Inability to study infections under controlled conditions was a problem, but investigators at that time also seriously underestimated the complexity of the immune apparatus. Not only were they unaware of the roles of lymphocytes and monocytes in immunity, they did not even know that there were *different* types of lymphocytes and monocytes or how these cells were stimulated and repressed. Further, they were ignorant about the complexity of immune mechanisms in the barrier tissues such as skin, gut, and respiratory tract. These statements should not be viewed as criticisms, as many of the nuances and some of the fundamentals about immunity are just emerging fifty years later. Fifty years from now historians may be making similar observations about our ignorance, as this is a very complicated field.

In their experiments on immunity, Dr. Goodpasture and associates chose to exploit a basic characteristic of viral infections—cytotropism—to determine if normal skin or human placental membranes grafted on chick chorioallantoic membranes acquired susceptibility or resistance to virus and if skin from immune individuals would become susceptible when grafted. These experiments would specifically address whether certain cells had an innate capacity to resist infection and if immunity is retained when tissues were transferred to another host.

Immunity to fowlpox was studied first.[51] Six adult domestic cocks were infected with fowlpox, resulting in typical lesions. Reinoculations were made for four months until complete cutaneous immunity was established; that is, exposure to fresh virus did not result in new skin lesions. Thin pieces of defeathered breast skin from immune and normal cocks were excised after careful washing, iodination, and rewashing. These pieces were spread, raw surface down, on chorioallantoic membranes of eleven-day embryos. Pieces of skin from normal and immune cocks were often grafted side by side in the same embryo for purposes of control. After three to four days, each graft was delicately snipped with scissors and rubbed with fowlpox-infected material. As ninety-six hours was required for development of diagnostic cytoplasmic inclusions, grafts were sectioned microscopically at that time. Histopathologic examination of the side-by-side pieces of skin from normal and immune cocks showed identical involvement by fowlpox.

Immunity therefore was not innate in the tissue but was dependent upon a circulating factor, probably in the serum. This presumed humoral factor was elusive and was not pinned down by subsequent experiments in which injections of immune serum did not reduce fowlpox lesions on skin grafts. Failure to demonstrate a humoral factor might have been related to limitations on the amount of serum (0.5 ml) that chick embryos tolerated. The likelihood of a circulating factor was increased when it was shown that skin from immune cocks, grafted and then removed from membranes, regained immunity when it was replaced in the immune host from which it had been originally removed.

Studies on Fowlpox Inclusions

Background

The development of the embryonated egg technique was Dr. Goodpasture's most significant research accomplishment. The pathway of investigations leading to this major discovery began with his decision to study fowlpox, first the appearance of the fowlpox inclusion (1928), then the nature of the inclusion (1929–30), and then its growth in embryonated eggs (1931). In all likelihood, the decision about fowlpox was made in 1924–25, during his sabbatical year in Vienna. Just before departure for Vienna, on July 12, 1924, he submitted four papers on herpetic encephalitis to the *American Journal of Pathology*. These publications summarized his collaborations with Oscar Teague on the transmission of herpes virus in rabbits from the portal of entry to the brain, work that confirmed his interest in virology as well as his competence as an investigator. While in Vienna, he extended these studies to rabies and showed that similar mechanisms of axonal (nerve sheath) transport were also operative in that disease.[52]

His studies of herpes and rabies highlighted the importance of viral inclusions as a marker of viral diseases. The focus of his research efforts shifted to a detailed study of inclusions as he recognized that the appearance of inclusions was much more specific than filterability as indicators of the presence of specific viruses. Undertaking a detailed study of inclusions, he published papers on inclusions in herpes (1925), rabies (1925), molluscum contagiosum, a viral infection of skin (1927), and fowlpox (1928), showing that in each disease the appearance of inclusions was virtually diagnostic when examined by an expert. Having mastered the recognition of inclusions, he then chose to concentrate on the fowlpox inclusion in order to understand its relationship to the fowlpox virus. His reasons for concentrating on fowlpox inclusions were enunciated in part in the chapter on "Virus Disease of Fowls" in *Filterable Viruses* edited by Rivers and published in 1928:[53]

> It is particularly adaptable to investigations of the significance of specific cellular inclusions and their relation to the nature and behavior of viruses, to studies of intracellular parasitism and immunity, and to efforts toward that great desideratum, successful cultivation of the active agent on artificial media.

Additional details justifying the selection of fowlpox were cited in the Harvey Lectures in 1929:[54]

> If one were desirous of studying the significance of cellular inclusions in relationship with minute particles in the cell it affects, he would certainly

choose for his material a virus disease in which cellular inclusions and visible granules are a paramount feature.

Such considerations as these have led us in the Department of Pathology at Vanderbilt University to select for etiological studies a member of the pox-group of vertebrate virus diseases, one which is easily transmissible in series, with accessible lesions presenting distinct cyto-plasmic inclusions, and in the lesions of which minute structures resembling tiny microorganisms were long since demonstrated in smear preparations by Borrel. The virus is filterable and it reproduces itself at the site of the specific lesion. It is infectious to the tissue in which spontaneous lesions occur and it causes a lesion locally by direct inoculation. It has an unquestionable specific relationship with the squamous epithelial cells which constitute the chief bulk of the lesion, in that it induces an enormous hyperplasia of these cells which come to contain specific inclusions. This disease, fowl-pox, conforms then in every way to our previously suggested definition of a filterable cytotropic virus disease.

The change to fowlpox represented a significant break from the work on herpetic encephalitis and rabies in that he moved from mammal to fowl as an experimental animal and he began work on a problem related to the nature of viral inclusions rather than studying mechanisms of viral transport. Studying fowlpox, or for that matter fowls, seems very old-fashioned in these times when biologists overwhelmingly favor tissue culture and mice. To understand this choice, it might be helpful to know that in 1925 many biologists were thinly disguised naturalists who were often interested in several life-forms other than those in their area of expertise. In contrast to most modern biologists, they had actually seen chickens "on the hoof" and might well have been aware that fowlpox had been known since pocks were recognized as human afflictions. Fowlpox was extensively studied from the seventeenth into the twentieth centuries because the lesions in fowls had an alarming resemblance to that devastator of civilizations and cultures—smallpox. It was naturally concluded that humans might contract that pox from fowls. This fear was not put to rest until the 1890s when the inclusions of fowlpox were shown to be different in appearance from those of smallpox, and the restricted host range of various poxes had been established. By 1925, fowlpox was of limited interest to human biologists, and Dr. Goodpasture, having chosen to study this disease for reasons given above, quickly became the acknowledged expert. Such a loyal Tennessean could have hardly wished for more than that the disease "sorehead" (fowlpox) (Fig. 3-12) would revolutionize the

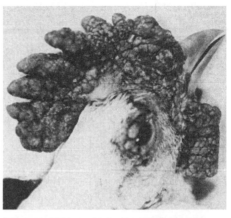

Fig. 3-12: Chicken with fowlpox induced in the laboratory by injection of virus. From EWG in Rivers's *Filterable Viruses* 1928 text.

study of viral diseases and the production of vaccines around the world. By finding this new challenge in the laboratory, Dr. Goodpasture would ultimately bring great credit to himself, his department, and his university.

Publications by the Vanderbilt Group on Fowlpox

1928 "Virus diseases of fowls as exemplified by contagious epithelioma (fowl-pox) of chickens and pigeons." In *Filterable Viruses*, ed. by T. M. Rivers, pp. 235–70. Baltimore, The Williams and Wilkins Company.

"The pathology of certain virus diseases." *Southern Med J*, 21:535–39.

"The pathology of certain virus diseases." *Science*, 67:591–93.

1929 "Cellular inclusions and the etiology of virus diseases." *Arch Pathol*, 7:114–32.

With Alice M. Woodruff and C. Eugene Woodruff. "Fowl-pox. II. The nature of the virus as indicated by further morphological data, and by experiments with certain chemicals." *Am J Physiol*, 90:560–61.

"Etiological problems in the study of filterable virus diseases." Harvey Lectures, 25:77–102, 1929–30.

"With C. Eugene Woodruff. The infectivity of isolated inclusion bodies of fowl-pox." *Am J Pathol*, 5:1–9.

1930	With Alice M. Woodruff. "The nature of fowl-pox virus as indicated by its reaction to treatment with potassium hydroxide and other chemicals." *Am J Pathol*, 6:699–711.

With C. E. Woodruff. "The relation of the virus of fowlpox to the specific cellular inclusions of the disease." *Am J Pathol*, 6:713–20.

1931	With C. E. Woodruff. "A comparison of the inclusion bodies of fowl-pox and molluscum contagiosum." *Am J Pathol*, 7:1–7.

With Alice M. Woodruff. "The susceptibility of the chorioallantoic membrane of chick embryos to infection with the fowlpox virus." *Am J Pathol*, 7:209–22.

1959	"Cytoplasmic inclusions resembling Guarnieri bodies, and other phenomena induced by mutants of the virus of fowlpox." *Am J Pathol*, 35(2):213–31.

Nature of Fowlpox Inclusions

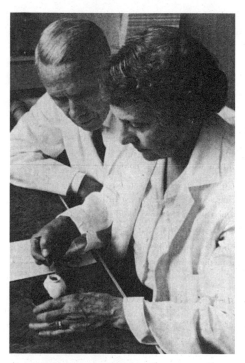

Fig. 3-13: The Woodruffs at work on embryonated eggs, circa 1933.

Dr. Goodpasture worked on fowlpox inclusions for about three years, in collaboration with Alice Miles Woodruff, Ph.D., and C. Eugene Woodruff, M.D. (Fig. 3-13). They obtained from Dr. Beaudette of the New Jersey Agricultural Experiment Station a field-strain of virus derived from a case of barnyard fowlpox. The disease was easily established by passage on scarified skin of susceptible chickens, and inclusions developed as expected in affected epithelium. When compressed under a coverglass, inclusions were seen to be myriads of minute bodies measuring about 0.5 microns that were "agglutinated by a viscous material."[55] These inclusions could be made to shrink in hypertonic salt solutions and would expand in hypotonic solutions like distilled water. In the latter state, the minute bodies danced with Brownian movement and were filterable after being freed by disruption of the inclusion bodies.

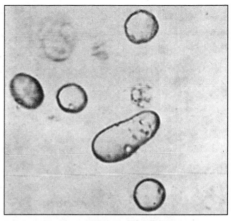

Fig. 3-14: Isolated inclusion bodies after digestion of encasing material by trypsin. Woodruff and EWG, *Am J Pathol* 1929.

The next step was to determine if individual inclusion bodies were infectious. Using a 1 percent solution of the proteolytic enzyme trypsin, the cellular material of a fowlpox lesion could be digested, leaving the inclusion bodies free as round or oval structures 2–50 microns in diameter. They were refractile, easily settled in liquids, and resembled "miniature white potatoes" under high magnification (Fig. 3-14). After washing in saline, the infectivity of inclusions was tested. Fowlpox lends itself ideally to such tests because the inclusions are large and because the precise inoculation site may be prepared by plucking a feather, leaving an epithelial-lined space ready for insertion of test material. A micro-dissection apparatus was used to pick up single inclusions. After defeathering, the skin of the right breast received the test material; supernatant fluid free of inclusions was inoculated as control on the left side. Following sixteen injections of single inclusions, seven chickens developed fowlpox lesions and nine did not; all of the controls injections were negative. The failure of nine chickens to develop lesions was attributed to unintended failure to place infectious material in the follicle, presumably because single inclusions stuck in the glass pipette and were thereby not inoculated.

The next project involved disruption of individual inclusions and tests of the infectivity of their contents. C. Eugene Woodruff and Goodpasture, having noted that inclusions became quite swollen in distilled water, observed that the inclusions disrupted abruptly if allowed to dry.[56] Single inclusions could be isolated, and allowed to disrupt, freeing thousands of minute structures called elementary bodies onto a glass slide.[57] The fowlpox elementary bodies had been named Borrel bodies after their discoverer. In a moist chamber of the micro-dissection apparatus, the fine point of a glass rod was placed on the Borrel bodies, accumulating a few of them on the glass point. The glass tip of the latter was broken off and carefully placed, glass and all, in a defeathered follicle. In all, 135 inoculations were made, producing fifty-two fowlpox lesions. Control inoculations (with glass tips containing the water used to wash inclusions) were uniformly negative. These experiments showed conclusively that Borrel bodies formed the major constituent of inclusions and "represent the actual virus of fowlpox." With this work, the Goodpasture laboratory established the infectious nature of viral elementary bodies and showed that some inclusions contained thousands of these bodies. This study represented a major advance into the nature of viral inclusions and thus into the nature of viral diseases by demonstrating that the histopathologic marker of fowlpox and presumably of other viral diseases, the inclusion body, contained infectious viral particles.

HERPETIC ENCEPHALITIS

Background

The collaboration of Teague and Goodpasture on herpes infections began in the fall of 1922[58] and continued for approximately nine months. By August 21, 1923, they had performed numerous experiments and submitted two manuscripts to the

Journal of Medical Research, titled "Experimental Production of Herpetic Lesions in Organs and Tissues of the Rabbit" and "Transmission of the Virus of Herpes Febrilis along Nerves in Experimentally Infected Rabbits." A third manuscript on experimental herpes zoster was submitted to the same journal on October 30, 1923.

It is to this collaboration of approximately nine months that Dr. Goodpasture attributed his interest in investigating viral diseases.[59] For this reason it is particu-

Fig. 3-15: Dr. Oscar Teague as shown in the photograph inscribed to Dr. Goodpasture and kept in his office throughout his Vanderbilt tenure.

larly interesting that neither Teague nor Goodpasture came to the Singer Research Institute with previous experience in the laboratory investigation of viral diseases. Dr. Goodpasture had written on autopsy findings in influenza[60] and about a child with presumed immunodeficiency,[61] in which publication the illustrations show what we now recognize as the viral disease cytomegalia. Although he coined the term cytomegalia, Dr. Goodpasture did not recognize the viral nature of this process. Dr. Teague (Fig. 3-15) was eight years older than Dr. Goodpasture and had published extensively about infectious diseases; all of his publications dealt with bacterial infections.[62] However, Esmond Long states in his *Biographical Memoir* that Teague had worked with Professor Lipschutz in Vienna the previous summer on herpetic infections of the eye in rabbits. This very effective collaboration at Singer Research Institute was tragically terminated on September 22, 1923, when Oscar Teague was accidentally killed in a car accident.

They obtained the virus used in their studies of herpetic encephalitis from a "fever blister" that appeared February 7,

1923, on the mouth of a patient with pneumonia.[63] Rabbits were known to be susceptible to this virus; corneal inoculations of material from the mouth lesion produced the expected inflammation of their cornea and conjunctiva, followed in four to six days with the unexpected clinical and pathologic evidence of encephalitis. This strain of herpes was then proven to be unusually neurotropic, with virtually all rabbits developing central nervous system lesions, regardless of the route of injection. After exploring the pathologic manifestations of herpes, particularly the precise nature of the inclusions that indicated the presence of the virus, they turned to tracking the anatomic pathway of the virus from the eye and other peripheral sites to the central nervous system. At this time the precise mode of transmission of virus from portal of entry to the brain or spinal cord had not been studied, although it was clearly of importance in diseases such as rabies and poliomyelitis.

Publications on Herpetic Encephalitis

1923   With Oscar Teague. "The occurrence of intranuclear inclusion bodies in certain tissues of the rabbit inoculated directly with the virus of herpes labialis." *Proc Soc Exp Biol Med*, 20:400.

With Oscar Teague. "The transmission of the virus of herpes febrilis along sensory nerves with resulting unilateral lesions in the central nervous system in the rabbit." *Proc Soc Exp Biol Med*, 20:545–47.

With Oscar Teague. "Experimental herpes zoster." *J Am Med Assoc*, 81:377–78.

With Oscar Teague. "Experimental production of herpetic lesions in organs and tissues of the rabbit." *J Med Res*, 44:121–28.

With Oscar Teague. "Transmission of the virus of herpes febrilis along nerves in experimentally infected rabbits." *J Med Res*, 44:139–84.

With Oscar Teague. "Experimental herpes zoster." *J Med Res*, 44:185–200.

With Robert H. McClellan. "A method of demonstrating experimental gross lesions of the central nervous system." *J Med Res*, 44:201–6.

1924   "Spontaneous encephalitis in rabbits." *Journal of Infectious Diseases*, 34:428–32.

1925   "Intranuclear inclusions in experimental herpetic lesions of rabbits." *Am J Pathol*, 1:1–9.

"The axis-cylinders of peripheral nerves as portals of entry to the central nervous system for the virus of herpes simplex in experimentally infected rabbits." *Am J Pathol*, 1:11–28.

"The pathways of infection of the central nervous system in herpetic encephalitis of rabbits contracted by contact; with a comparative comment on medullary lesions in a case of human poliomyelitis." *Am J Pathol*, 1:29–46.

"Certain factors determining the incidence and severity of herpetic encephalitis in rabbits." *Am J Pathol*, 1:47–55.

Transmission of Herpes Along Nerves in Experimentally Infected Rabbits

Recognizing that 25 percent of rabbits had "spontaneous encephalitis," the authors regarded only those lesions as herpetic (and thus a result of the experiment) that were acute and that contained typical intranuclear inclusions. They then varied injection sites in several sets of experiments in order to track the virus along sensory or motor nerves. These experiments must have occasioned a crash course in the anatomy of the rabbit nervous system, as the relevant nerves had to be carefully dissected and sectioned, along with the entire spinal cord and brain.

When rabbits were inoculated in the cornea of the right eye, the virus was tracked (by its inclusions) along sensory fibers of the right fifth cranial nerve until it reached the central nervous system; there it affected the hind-brain on the right side (Fig. 3-16), corresponding to the distribution of the sensory fibers of the fifth cranial nerve. Injection of herpes virus into the right jaw muscle caused infection and destruction in the motor nucleus of the fifth cranial

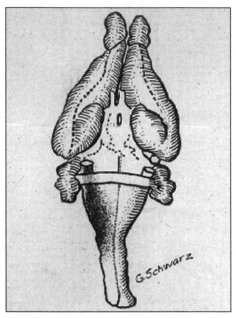

Fig. 3-16: The distribution of infection is apparent in this removed brain by the concentration of a dye trypan blue on the left side at the site of injury. From EWG and McMillan, *J Med Res* 1923.

nerve, with unilateral encephalitis in the appropriate sections of the hind-brain. They concluded:[64]

> We have been able to prove conclusively that the virus of herpes febrilis can pass from a peripheral site of inoculation along corresponding nerves to spinal cord or brain, and produce at the site of entrance and along the central distribution of these nerves an acute herpetic lesion demonstrable grossly and histologically to be directly related to the nerve along which it passed. The transmission of the virus may be along sensory, motor or sympathetic fibers, depending on the nerve supply to the inoculated area.

These experiments were important in establishing Dr. Goodpasture's interest in virology, but their greater significance lies in their establishing his competence as an investigator. The difficulties of viral research in this period are indicated by this comment in *A History of Virology*:[65]

> Goodpasture (1929) deduced that herpes virus must travel intra-axonally on the basis of histological evidence following different routes of inoculation. About thirty years later this generally accepted notion was questioned because of conceptual difficulties; it was hard to imagine axonal movements in view of the then current concepts on axoplasm. Other routes were suggested and a great deal of work was done (e.g., Payling Wright, 1953; Johnson, 1964), culminating in the conviction that Goodpasture had been correct after all (reviewed by Kristensson, 1978).

Recent work on neurites of cultured neurons suggests that virus may travel as a part of its multiplication cycle. Infection of the termini shows that virus loses its envelope as visualized in the electron microscope, and passes centripetally as a nucleocapsid (presumably by axonal flow) to the nucleus where multiplication occurs.

MUMPS

Background

The experiments on mumps by Johnson and Goodpasture were begun on January 25, 1933,[66] and reported in 1934, 1935, and 1936. During this time Dr. Goodpasture was investigating various applications of the chick embryo technique, including the development of a vaccination program against smallpox, the cause of granuloma inguinale (*Donovanosis*), and the nature of contagious lymphoma in dogs. Nevertheless, by August 1933 Johnson and Goodpasture submitted their first report to the *Journal of Experimental Medicine*[67] describing the isolation of the causative agent of mumps in monkeys with repeated passage of the virus in monkeys and reproduction of the clinical illness. It then remained to prove that the infectious agent that had been passed in monkeys was the causative agent of human mumps, a fact established in successful field trials that were analyzed and submitted for publication by July 13, 1934.[68] Then the follow-up papers dealing with immunity in monkeys and histopathologic changes in affected parotid glands were published in 1936.

The success of these experiments in proving that mumps was a viral infection was "one of his proudest achievements."[69] This disease had been clearly described by Hippocrates and had produced well-defined clinical manifestations since antiquity; it had been investigated repeatedly since 1908 to find the cause, but before 1933 no one had unquestionably induced mumps experimentally or clearly demonstrated the causative agent. One of the problems in finding the cause was that mumps rarely produced death, so that saliva from patients with mumps was the main source of infectious material. Histopathologic findings were also incomplete as there had been only a few biopsies of swollen glands and painful testes.[70] Since 1908 various experimental animals had been used, including rabbits, monkeys, and cats. Filtered saliva had been injected into parotid glands, testes, the brain, as well as into the lumen of the duct coming from the parotid (Stensen's duct) without establishing the viral nature of this disease.[71] Humans are the only known natural host for the mumps virus, and the carrier state is not known to exist.[72] Owing to the absence of a carrier state, and to the licensure of mumps vaccine in 1967, one would anticipate eradication of the disease in the near future.

Publications by the Vanderbilt Group on Mumps

1934   With Claud D. Johnson. "An investigation of the etiology of mumps." *Jour Exp Med,* 59:1–19.

1935   With Claud D. Johnson. "The etiology of mumps." *Am J Hyg,* 21(1):46–57.

1936   With Claud D. Johnson. "Experimental immunity to the virus of mumps in monkeys." *Am J Hyg,* 23(2):329–39.

With C. D. Johnson. "The histopathology of experimental mumps in the monkey." *Macacus rhesus. Am J Pathol,* 12(4):495–510.

Discovery of the Cause of Mumps

Experiments began on January 25, 1933, when saliva was collected from a medical student during the first twenty-four hours of parotid swelling.[73] Some preparations must have been made to have obtained this sample so quickly after symptoms began and to have monkeys available for tests. Perhaps there had been several local cases previously, so Doctors Goodpasture and Johnson were ready when the medical student became symptomatic. The rationale for their approach is clearly given in their first paper:[74]

In planning an experimental investigation of mumps we have been guided by the following assumptions: that monkeys would more likely be a susceptible host than lower animals; that the active agent should come in direct contact with the parenchymal cells of the parotid gland, preferably attended by some injury; and that the causative agent is in the saliva at least in the first stages of the disease.

They were right on all counts! Patients with the symptoms and signs of mumps rinsed their mouths thoroughly with saline and then expectorated for about two hours into sterile glass bottles. The medical student seen on January 25 had been exposed over the Christmas holidays while at his home in Pennsylvania. Two months after that first case, there was an epidemic in the Tennessee Industrial School in Nashville, and saliva was collected from several people there. Material was also collected from a case in southeast Alabama where there had been an epidemic. Altogether fresh saliva from six cases was used to inoculate monkeys. Four of these specimens induced parotitis, while the two that did not were from patients in the third or later day of illness.

Monkeys were anesthetized with ether "to relax the muscles of the cheek," and the sides of the face were shaved. The opening of Stensen's duct (the duct draining the parotid gland into the mouth) was exposed and cannulated with a small blunt-tipped needle attached to a 10 ml syringe. Two milliliters

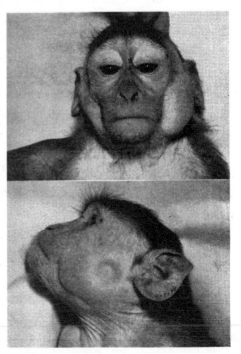

Fig. 3-17: Monkey with bilateral swelling of parotid glands after injection of mumps virus. The overlying tissue is edematous due to inflammation and may be pitted with pressure. From EWG and Johnson, *J Exp Med* 1934.

(about one-quarter of a teaspoon) of control or test saliva were injected under moderate pressure, causing the parotid to enlarge visibly. The saliva injected was undiluted, fresh, and unfiltered. Injected glands usually returned to normal size ninety-six hours later, but by the seventh day most monkeys receiving saliva from patients with mumps became febrile and had striking enlargement of the parotid glands (Fig. 3-17) with edema over the gland. Monkeys were sacrificed at this time, and the parotids were excised under sterile precautions. Glands were weighed, sectioned, cultured, and frozen for two to seven days until cultures for bacteria were shown to be negative. Then frozen pieces of gland were ground to create an emulsion along with sedimentable debris, which was discarded. If cultures of emulsion were negative, 2 ml were injected into Stensen's duct of another monkey to achieve the next passage. By the fourth passage, animals developed higher fevers and had exceptionally tender parotids and more edema. These animals seemed drowsy at times but were nervous and excitable at other times.

The isolated virus was then characterized. As a prelude to this work, each gland removed was rigorously cultured for bacteria and for leptospira (another infectious agent suspected to produce mumps). Smears and sections stained for bacteria and spirochetes were negative, as were dark-field examinations for spirochetes. Emulsions of glands were passed through a filter that retained bacteria added as a control. The virus, as expected, resisted freezing, drying, and glycerination.

Histopathologic changes of experimental mumps were reported after a detailed review of the literature on mumps in humans.[75] Because mortality is low, the histopathologic changes associated with human mumps had been studied in only a few cases. Most of these were single-case reports, and they indicated that parotid glands had been sectioned at different times after illnesses began. The pathologic picture described in reports from 1909 to 1936 was that of a protein-rich edema fluid and exudate in the interstices of the gland, hemorrhage with leukocytic (white-cell) infiltrate in the ducts, and early death of the glandular epithelium. Johnson and Goodpasture reported on the histopathologic changes in the parotid glands of "many" monkeys observed over a two-year period. The earliest lesions in the parotid were near the central portions of the lobules with degenerative changes as well as death of glandular epithelial cells. Collections of lymphocytes and mononuclear cells were then noted, the latter phagocytizing and removing debris. Both of these types of white cells are often present in viral infections. After the initial more centrally placed process (perhaps related to the artificial injection process), a second crop of lesions appeared throughout the gland, exhibiting in stages degeneration, cell death, and resolution. Severe edema of the gland and adjacent soft tissue was noted at the height of the inflammatory process. Inclusions were described in the affected epithelial cells. The authors concluded that "similar lesions in all probability underlie the pathology of mumps in the human."[76] Testicular sections were apparently not made nor were clinical changes described in the scrota of these monkeys.

Doctors Johnson and Goodpasture had the methods to solve one remaining question, and that dealt with the issue of immunity. Was the agent they had recovered from patients and passaged experimentally capable of producing mumps in normal volunteers, and were immune individuals susceptible? Because mumps is a very mild infectious disease without significant complications, the authors believed it was safe to conduct a field trial. Two milliliters of the diluted emulsion prepared from parotid glands was sprayed into the mouths of seventeen volunteers, aiming the spray at the opening of Stensen's duct. Then small cotton plugs immersed in the emulsion were placed over the openings of the ducts for fifteen minutes. The four volunteers with a recent history of mumps showed no ill effects. Of the thirteen supposedly susceptible volunteers, six developed definite parotid swelling on one or both sides. All recovered shortly and there were no complications.[77] The absence of mumps in the community and the geographic isolation of the volunteers insured against community-acquired mumps coincident with this experiment. Volunteer number sixteen is of interest; she developed bilateral parotid swelling and fever twenty-three days after exposure to emulsion. Saliva collected from this volunteer, when injected into two monkeys, produced typical changes of mumps parotitis in one of the two.

Monkeys were also shown to develop immunity to mumps virus.[78] After passing the virus thirty-five times in monkeys during three years, and after studying approximately 150 monkeys, the authors found that monkeys with bilateral or unilateral parotitis were invariably immune when reexposed to infectious emulsions. Immunity was not consistently produced after subcutaneous, intramuscular, or intravenous administration of mumps virus. The authors concluded that monkeys were relatively resistant to mumps as compared to humans and that it would be difficult to demonstrate subtle changes in immunity experimentally in the monkey.

Dr. Goodpasture had every right to be proud of this study. It is a model of careful experimental design and focused research. He overcame the considerable difficulties of imprecise histopathologic criteria for diagnosis of mumps parotitis and limited susceptibility of experimental animals to mumps. Then having passed the virus successfully, he proved by field trials in susceptible and immune volunteers that the mumps virus had been isolated. This work was soon confirmed in several laboratories.[79] It is interesting that there were no reported efforts to pass the infected material from monkey parotid to embryonated egg in the Goodpasture laboratory. Unsuccessful attempts were almost certainly made, as Dr. Goodpasture states that mumps virus (amongst others) "resists cultivation in the chick embryo."[80] From Habel's work, it proved necessary to isolate the virus in monkey parotid first before successful passage in chick embryos.[81]

Chapter Four

CHAIRMAN

T he greatest academic responsibility given to a faculty member is to be appointed chairman or head of a university department. Such an appointment reflects enormous trust by the university in the academic potential, leadership capacity, and good judgment of the appointee as most universities interact with the faculty-at-large through chairmen. Furthermore, the chairmen insure that the faculty properly carry out the educational, research, and service roles of the university. In these functions, chairmen prepare (and adhere to) budgets, recruit new faculty, energize or remove current faculty, oversee the educational activities of the department, and direct the departmental research program. Chairmen currently jockey with each other to obtain space, funding, and access to students; in olden days there was apparently much less room or need for maneuvering. Chairmen are also responsible for the official interactions between their own departments and the other components of the institution. In this role they serve on committees that have advisory or managerial capacities which cut across departmental lines. Finally, chairmen as faculty in a university may assume leadership functions on the campus as a whole, may help in the

Fig. 4-1: Singer Research Institute, circa 1915.

actions and relationships among its schools, or may facilitate development of interactive programs with the community.

Dr. Goodpasture was appointed professor of pathology at
Vanderbilt in 1924. As the only professor of pathology, he had the
responsibilities of chairman as described in the preceding section. Dr.
Goodpasture had comparable responsibilities at Singer Research
Institute, where his title was director of laboratories. The position at
Singer was held for twenty-one months during 1922–24. His success
there was probably responsible for his subsequent appointment at
Vanderbilt, where he was chairman[1] for thirty-one years. His appoint-
ment at Vanderbilt was critical in guaranteeing the success of the
reorganization plan of the medical school.

<hr />

WILLIAM H. SINGER MEMORIAL RESEARCH LABORATORY 1922–24

The William H. Singer Memorial Research Laboratory was
constructed in 1915; the fully equipped building was then

bequeathed to the Board of Trustees of the Allegheny General Hospital in Pittsburgh to be used as a research laboratory for the study of medical and surgical problems as well as to provide routine laboratory work for the hospital. The Governing Board of the laboratory was made up of three members of the Board of Trustees and three members from the medical staff of the Allegheny General Hospital. The building (Fig. 4-1) was free-standing, containing approximately twenty-eight thousand square feet in three stories and a basement. The first floor housed a museum, library, filing space, and chemistry laboratory, while the second floor contained the director's office, surgical pathology laboratory, technicians' rooms, autopsy room, bacteriology/serology laboratories, and four rooms for research. On the third floor were located animal quarters, research laboratories, and utilities, while the basement contained the photographic department, storage rooms, library stacks, sterilizing room, media preparation room, a shop, and the morgue.[2]

On February 14, 1921, Samuel R. Haythorn, M.D., submitted his resignation as director of the Singer Laboratory, stating that he planned to assume the directorship of the pathology department at the University of Pittsburgh.[3] The board of managers, in their next meeting on April 7, 1921, considered two competing applications for the directorship. The first was a communication from Dr. L. D. Felton,[4] who proposed a budget of $35,000 for the first two years and of $57,500 per year for the three succeeding years. The second was a letter from Dr. E. W. Goodpasture, in which a plan was presented for conducting the laboratory's affairs with an annual budget of $45,000. Dr. Goodpasture had probably been recommended by Dr. Haythorn, as they had both trained under F. B. Mallory in Boston.[5] In the general discussion that followed,[6] Dr. Felton's plan was rejected "largely for the reason" that there was little if any prospect of being able to meet his budget as proposed for years three to five. After the January 12, 1922, meeting, the board of managers sent a cablegram to Dr. Goodpasture (who was in Manila) notifying him that his proposition had been accepted. These arrangements were finalized by April 12, 1922, and Dr.

Goodpasture was appointed as director for one year beginning September 1, 1922. His responsibilities included: providing expert supervision of the routine work of Allegheny General Hospital in pathology, bacteriology, serology, and biochemistry, while promoting investigative work in these subjects; choosing the personnel of the laboratory, giving preference to men capable of conducting independent investigations; and reporting periodically to the board of managers on his actions for their approval. The salary of the director was to be $8,000 per year, while the budget of the laboratory was $45,000 per year. Thus the board, apparently for the difference in budgets of $12,500 per year, chose in Dr. Goodpasture the director who turned out to be the more productive scientist.

The Singer Memorial Research Laboratory with a budget of forty-five thousand dollars employed, in addition to the director, three doctors of philosophy, three assistants, two technicians, a stenographer, a record clerk, a caretaker of animals, two janitors, and a dishwasher.[7] Dr. Goodpasture presumably had precise guidance from Dr. Haythorn as to the resources and the mood of the board in order to estimate a budget of forty-five thousand dollars, but the only extant letter from Dr. Haythorn about finances is dated May 16, 1922, a month after Dr. Goodpasture's appointment.[8] However, a visit to the Singer laboratory had been arranged in the spring of 1921, during which Doctors Haythorn and Goodpasture obviously discussed the budget in some detail.

Dr. Goodpasture assumed charge in September, and it was evident that there was a new hand on the tiller by the meeting of the board on November 6, 1922.[9] His nine-page report provided recommendations for immediate improvements as well as a detailed analysis of personnel, equipment, routine work, research, financial status, and budget. An animal caretaker/ autopsy assistant, who had previously worked with Dr. Goodpasture at Harvard, had been hired, and Dr. Oscar Teague had been appointed as serologist, effective October 1. The building was described as "well-planned and excellently constructed," needing only renovation of the animal quarters in which walls and ceiling were washed, cages repaired and rearranged, and the operating room and preparation room "restored to the use of the staff." The outstanding need was improvement in the library facilities because medical libraries in that city were divided among various departments and usually closed at 5:00 P.M. It was the director's judgment that the museum should be closed and the space used for an "active, productive" library. Definition of the institute's research status began with the observation that the Singer Institute had been created to foster medical research and ended with the notification that the new director "proposes to use every means at his disposal to support and encourage such an interest." In terms of the budget, the director recommended a modest increase in laboratory supplies (from $2,151 to $2,584), an increase in animal purchases (from $309 to $500), and a large increase in library funds (from $324 to $1,000). In addition to Oscar Teague, he recommended that a biochemist and assistant serologist be hired with salaries of $5,000 and $1,800 per year, respectively. In closing this detailed report, the director welcomed frequent meetings of the board and the "interest and advice of individual members at all times." He concluded by expressing "his appreciation of the high standard that has been set in the conduct of the Singer Laboratory by the Board of Managers and by the previous director, Dr. Samuel R. Haythorn. It will be his endeavor to continue the high type of work which has characterized the previous administration and to increase the usefulness of the laboratory in proportion to the added means at his disposal."

By January 11, 1923,[10] Dr. Ann Kuttner had been recruited as an assistant in serology. She had received a Ph.D. in bacteriology from Columbia and had worked for two years as the chief assistant to Dr. Hans Zinsser, a leading bacteriologist. The report of July 11, 1923, contained a description of the investigations with Oscar Teague of the spread of herpes and a demonstration with Dr. McClellan of the gross lesions in the central nervous system induced by herpes. An estimate of $19,766 to complete the biochemistry laboratory was submitted for authorization by the board. The budget was balanced, with expenditures of $37,790 in salaries and $7,210 in supplies totaling $45,000. On October 8, 1923, the director had the sad task of reporting the death of Dr. Oscar Teague on September 25. The biochemistry laboratory had been built and was to be equipped for $3,000. Dr. Goodpasture's last appointments at Singer were Dr. George A. Robinson as bacteriologist and successor to Dr. Teague and Dr. Dorsey Brannan as assistant pathologist. In June 1924, Dr. Goodpasture resigned to accept the position as professor of pathology at Vanderbilt University.

Twenty-eight years later, Dr. Goodpasture summarized the importance of his tenure at Singer Research Institute in a speech delivered at the institute on the role of research in general pathology laboratories:[11]

Coming to the Singer Laboratory was a pleasant episode in my life, a momentous one too, and my sojourn of two years will always be memorable. Previously I had engaged in research only in laboratories of universities in this country, and in the Philippine Islands, where at the College of Medicine and Surgery in Manila I received the cablegram offering me the position which brought me to Pittsburgh. Before leaving the United States for a year in the tropics I had visited the original Singer Memorial Laboratory at the invitation of Dr. Samuel R. Haythorn who was for many years its distinguished director.

Because of my academic interest in investigative work, the word *Research* in the title, William H. Singer Memorial Research Laboratory, appealed to me and already the excellent accomplishments of its Staff were convincing evidence of the genuineness of its meaning. . . .

I was very fortunate in fact to be able to join that Staff, and I consider my experience here as probably the most profitable of my professional life. That this turn of events proved especially fortunate for me was due not only to the advantageous conditions afforded by the Laboratory and by members of its previous Staff but to the fact that I was soon joined here by Dr. Oscar Teague, one of our great American bacteriologists, to whom I owe a debt of gratitude for introducing me to the subject of viruses—a new subject at the time and one within the competence of only a few investigators. Dr. Teague had just returned from a summer in Europe where he had gone to gather the latest developments from laboratories there. . . .

Dr. Goodpasture's tenure at the Singer Institute was only twenty-one months, but during this time his candidacy for the Vanderbilt professorship improved markedly. The factors that changed were his age, from thirty-six to thirty-eight, number and quality of research publications, and demonstration of administrative abilities. He had peaked in these crucial factors at the optimal time, just when the number one choice (Wade Brown) became unavailable. This was an outcome that hardly could have been predicted on Dr. Goodpasture's arrival at the Singer Institute in September 1922, nor was it predictable that the all-important research with Oscar Teague would be so productive.[12] It is difficult for us now to imagine a Vanderbilt without Dr. Goodpasture or to place him in any other academic setting, but it was a close call.

VANDERBILT UNIVERSITY SCHOOL OF MEDICINE 1924–55

Medical School History

September 15, 1925, was a red-letter day in the history of Vanderbilt Medical School, as this was the day the recently constructed hospital and medical school opened on the main (west) campus.[13] It was in many ways a banner year for Vanderbilt University, as it marked the fiftieth year of its holding classes; the semicentennial celebration held from October 15–18 attracted delegates representing 167 American universities and colleges, nine foreign universities, as well as twenty-six national foundations and societies. Distinguished guests participating in the medical program included William H. Welch, Simon Flexner, and Abraham Flexner; the latter two and several other guests were actually housed for the celebration in the new hospital.

The 1925 version of Vanderbilt Medical School (Fig. 4-2) was created by the interaction of a handful of people. Chancellor Kirkland (Fig. 4-3) was the instigator, chief fund-raiser, and truly indispensable man in getting the project underway. Wallace Buttrick and Abraham Flexner through their positions on the Rockefeller General Education Board initially steered 5.5 million dollars into the enterprise, and Henry Pritchett through the Carnegie Foundation similarly dispensed 2.5 million dollars. G. Canby Robinson as dean was responsible for overseeing construction as well as for the detailed planning, recruitment of personnel, and development of programs. In particular, Kirkland, Flexner, and Buttrick attained a formidable working partnership, the former putting Vanderbilt in rare company indeed through his vision and energy. There is abundant evidence that these three professionals were close friends and had a common vision. The Flexner/Kirkland friendship may well have been cemented by the close approximation of their summer homes.[14] The depth of Abraham Flexner's respect for Chancellor Kirkland, and for Vanderbilt

Fig. 4-2: The recently constructed Vanderbilt Medical School and Hospital, 1925. The new nursing school is also shown.

University, is indicated by the fact that Vanderbilt was chosen as the only site for the lecture-ship established by Mr. Bernard Flexner in his brother's honor. Abraham Flexner is reported by Chancellor Kirkland[15] to have said: "My work at Vanderbilt University is perhaps more satisfactory than at any other place, and I believe I will ask you [Bernard Flexner] to offer it to the trustees of Vanderbilt University." Wallace Buttrick was equally respected; his name was placed on the biology building by the Board of Trust to commemorate his role (and that of the Rockefeller General Education Board) in the development of Vanderbilt.

Fig. 4-3: Chancellor Kirkland.

In broad outline, the key steps in this extraordinary commitment by the university and funding agencies to reorganize the medical school and hospital included:

- The Flexner report, citing Vanderbilt as the most promising institution for medical education in this area.
- The decision by Dean G. Canby Robinson that the future of Vanderbilt Medical School was brighter on Nashville's western side with the undergraduate campus rather than on the southern campus adjacent to Nashville General Hospital (the city's hospital, previously used by Vanderbilt medical students). Robinson was able to convince Kirkland and Flexner that this move was in the best interests of the university, although it was much more expensive and involved desertion of hospital facilities then under construction—the Galloway Hospital. Incidentally, the 1925 catalogue of the medical school[16] contains the statement that the proposition

for placing the medical school on the main campus had been considered many times but had not been pursued "because of lack of means."

- The resignation of the south campus medical school faculty, who were all essentially part-time. The resignation was an implied or stated condition of the funding agencies and enabled recruitment of a full-time as well as nationally recognized faculty.
- Construction of the medical plant that began on October 22, 1923, and was completed in July 1925.
- Provision of $8 million by the Carnegie and Rockefeller Foundations. Approximately $3 million was used for construction, and $5 million was placed into endowment.

There was great excitement on the Vanderbilt campus when the General Education Board announced on Thanksgiving eve 1919 the following gifts for medical education: Vanderbilt had been given $4 million, Johns Hopkins Medical School $2,210,874.11, Washington University in St. Louis $1 million, and Yale University Medical School $582,000. The board gave the following reasons for its generosity to Vanderbilt:[17]

1. Not a single medical school in the entire South possesses the facilities or the personnel needed to train men to meet existing conditions or to carry out the research by means of which unsolved health problems may be ultimately mastered.
2. The strategic point for the development of such a school is Nashville, because it is situated well in the heart of the South.
3. Vanderbilt University has played a leading part in creating and maintaining scholarly standards in the South; and, finally, and perhaps most important of all, the Chancellor of Vanderbilt University, Dr. Kirkland, has the vision, energy and leadership which are required in the launching and development of an enterprise involving the establishment of a modern School of Medicine.

Whether Vanderbilt deserved such a favorable analysis might be debated, but Chancellor Kirkland certainly was chiefly responsible for the showcasing of the reorganized medical school to the academic world in those heady days in October 1925. However, it was G. Canby Robinson who permanently put Vanderbilt Medical School on a special path through his particular blend of idealism and aggressiveness.[18] A contemporaneous statement by Canby Robinson provides his rationale for its reorganization:[19]

> At the outset certain principles of organization were adopted. The medical school was to be constructed to accommodate a relatively small number of students, the classes being limited to fifty. The construction was to be such as to encourage a close coordination of the laboratory [that is, basic sciences] and clinical departments of the school, and ample facilities for research, in the clinical as well as in the laboratory departments of the school, were to be provided with the idea of giving a true university spirit to the entire school. In order to carry out these principles, plans were drawn to accommodate all activities of the school and hospital with the exception of the power plant and the School of Nursing, in a single building. This building was so located that the laboratories and the general student activities are conducted in the northern portion of the building adjoining the other schools and buildings of the university, while the hospital wards extend toward the south, and are separated from the main activities of the university campus.

This factual and somewhat bland summary does not reflect the drama, maneuvering behind the scenes, and at least one fractious interaction between Chancellor Kirkland and Dean Robinson, who, after his appointment in 1920, did not reside in Nashville until 1924. In 1923 he even served as acting head of medicine at Hopkins! The relationship between Dr. Robinson and Chancellor Kirkland was somewhat unusual from its beginning:[20] Dr. Robinson was essentially handpicked by Flexner; the General Education Board participated in negotiations with Dr. Robinson as to his salary; and Dr. Robinson submitted his reorganization plan for the medical school on the west campus *simultaneously* to the General Education Board and to Chancellor Kirkland. This plan had been requested by Flexner and Buttrick but should have been cleared first with Chancellor Kirkland; its content and manner of submission seriously stressed the complex working relationship between all parties involved. The reorganization proposed by Robinson[21] was drastically different from the program that he had been hired to develop as well as much more expensive; worse, protocol had been violated in terms of the fundamental relationship of chancellor to dean by this academic ménage à trois. Unusually harsh words appear in several follow-up documents, and undoubtedly we are witness only to portions of this controversy. Chancellor Kirkland, who had worked very hard from 1917 to 1919 to obtain the $4 million in hand, did not feel he could turn to the General Education Board for that much again.[22] Further, Chancellor Kirkland was distressed at the prospect of abandoning the buildings on the south campus where the Galloway Hospital was then under construction. He knew his medical school faculty would condemn such a move.[23] There was the additional problem that the Galloway Hospital project was partially subscribed by the Methodist Church. The chancellor certainly hoped to avoid reopening the wounds from recent battles with that organization. The Galloway Hospital was left unfinished, and feelings of resentment were not assuaged by placing its name on the west campus hospital when it was constructed.[24] Flexner, for his part, stated that Dr. Robinson's report had been "embarrassing," that the questions raised in it should have been first addressed to Chancellor Kirkland, and that his advice was to take the bird in hand,[25] that is, the money available for development of the medical school near Nashville General Hospital. In turn, Dr. Robinson was distressed that the chancellor "seemed to think his report contained extravagant and idealistic fantasies,"[26] and that he had "hypnotized" himself in the preparation of the report. The most significant outcome of these multilateral bruises was that Dr. Robinson threw down the gauntlet to the chancellor and the General Education Board. He maintained that the board should spend its funds for a model school, not a patched-up compromise on the south campus,[27] and that a large unified building would establish a harmonious interaction among students, faculty, and patients on the one hand and between the medical school and university on the other. To the chancellor, his reply was "sharp," noting that his "faith, hope, and enthusiasm were severely strained by the manner in which my plan of reorganization was received," and that the controversy "has made me feel I am not the proper person for the work which is before you."[28]

The eminent good sense of Dr. Robinson's plan ultimately carried the day. After an outside study or two, plus some cooling of passions on all sides, the General Education Board and Carnegie Foundation each contributed an additional $1.5 million, thus enabling construction on the main campus to proceed and permanently putting an end to the south campus as a medical school site. Perhaps there is a lesson here for idealistic administrators. Robinson had done his homework thoroughly, and his thirty-two page report on reorganization was ultimately reflected in the structure as well as *modus operandi* of the completed school and hospital.

With this background in mind, it would be particularly interesting to know Chancellor Kirkland's private reaction to the news that Dr. Robinson had chosen to leave Vanderbilt to accept the directorship of the New York Hospital-Cornell Medical College Association after only three years in Nashville. Paul Conkin's conclusion is that this move caused "delight" in Kirkland.[29] Serious negotiations about this recruitment began in October 1926, with a decision by Dr. Robinson to accept on July 1, 1927. Officials at the two university medical centers then agreed to a sharing plan of one year's duration, with Dr. Robinson remaining at Vanderbilt while "cooperating in the architectural and other planning in New York as needed."[30] The necessary adjustments at Vanderbilt were the appointments of Waller Leathers as associate dean in preparation for the deanship, of John Youmans as associate professor in medicine, and later of Sidney Burwell as professor of medicine and chairman.

When G. Canby Robinson left Nashville in June 1928, the faculty of Vanderbilt Medical School adopted a resolution setting forth the accomplishments of the school in the previous three years. As subsequently quoted by Robinson in his book *Adventures in Medical Education*,[31] this resolution is particularly significant as an expression by those who had participated in the initiation of the new program, at a time when they were surely wondering what the change in leadership would bring:

> The plans provided for the construction of the medical school and hospital were developed so that there would be a coordination between the teaching of preclinical and clinical subjects. It was a fundamental conception of the plan that the laboratories for anatomy, physiology, biochemistry, bacteriology, pathology, and pharmacology should be related to the hospital, so as to afford opportunity for the members of these departments and the teachers of clinical subjects to correlate their instruction. This was to enable the students to apply better, in the wards of the hospital, the information obtained in the preclinical subjects.
>
> The building which has been provided for this purpose is regarded as a conspicuous success. The close coordination of all departments of the medical school and hospital is sure to prove an important factor in the future of medical education. The fact that the students spend all of their time in one great building, housing not only all the facilities of their entire course but also a hospital and out-patient department and laboratories for research, creates a new condition in medical education which is of distinct value. The students are thrown into close contact with the faculty as a whole; they obtain a grasp early in their course of the ultimate aim of medical education; they see the coordination of the laboratories and hospital wards and soon learn to appreciate their mutual dependence. The students are also exposed to the spirit of research and are afforded opportunity to catch the spirit, which it is hoped they will carry into their future work.

There are actually two more paragraphs in this resolution of the executive faculty, not included by Dr. Robinson in his memoir apparently because they gave him sole credit for the new school; here are the additional paragraphs from the original *Executive Faculty Minutes* of November 8, 1928:[32]

The creation of the plan by which these ideals could be better carried out originated with Doctor G. Canby Robinson who on July 1, 1920 assumed responsibility as Dean of Vanderbilt Medical School. During the years that followed, until the opening of the new Vanderbilt Medical School and Hospital on September 15, 1925, he supervised the construction of the plant for teaching medicine in Vanderbilt University and reorganized the faculty in such a way as to carry out the plan and promote the ideals above indicated. The reorganization of the faculty has resulted in bringing together a group of new men to be associated with those who have previously been members of the faculty, and in creating in the most gratifying way a harmonious teaching staff. All of this has been a task of large magnitude which could only have been accomplished in the time available by a spirit of industry, cooperation and enthusiasm. In large measure credit for the remarkable results that have been attained in the building of the new medical school of Vanderbilt University and the reorganization of the faculty must be attributed to the forethought, wisdom and splendid scientific leadership of Dr. Robinson. His untiring effort, fine spirit, cooperative attitude, intelligent interest and inspirational qualities have been the predominant factors in providing at Vanderbilt University a medical school which meets in an admirable way the modern ideals in medical education.

As a faculty we wish to express our affectionate regard and high esteem for Dr. Robinson as a wise and scholarly leader. We shall follow with deep interest the building of the Cornell Medical Center, of which he has been made Director, as another great opportunity for the advancement of medical education.

This resolution was prepared by Doctors Garrey, Cunningham, and Leathers. The medical faculty was clearly unaware of the key role played by Chancellor Kirkland in the whole process; otherwise, they hardly would have read this resolution in his presence. Chancellor Kirkland routinely attended executive faculty meetings, and at this meeting graciously moved acceptance of the resolution, since he "thought that the statement, as read, was very appropriate."[33] Privately, he must have wondered if Dean Robinson had spawned a hotbed of poorly informed and unappreciative faculty that would continue to bedevil him, and might also have wondered why a resolution or two had not come his way. Dr. Robinson replied to this resolution on November 21, 1928; his letter included a rather small olive branch to set the record straight vis-à-vis Chancellor Kirkland's role:[34]

> In leaving the Vanderbilt University, I have left behind many things that I shall always cherish. Nothing, however, has been left behind with so much regret as the stimulating, helpful and sympathetic personal relations that I have had with each member of the executive faculty. The wise counsel and the clear penetrating analysis of problems by Chancellor Kirkland have taught me much, and the intimate intellectual association with each one has been of the greatest value.

An analysis of Vanderbilt University Medical School forty years later was provided by Dean Youmans in an address to the medical alumni reunion on June 5, 1965, under the title "Vanderbilt—Yesterday, Today and Tomorrow."[35]

> The general architectural nature of the original new plant, with particular respect to function, was the result of Dr. Robinson's ideas. Pencilled sketches of his have been preserved and have been on display in the library at times [Fig. 4-4]. The distinctive features as seen then were the unitary construction of medical school and hospital with departments, wards, outpatient, library, and administrative space, all designed from a functional point of view. . . .
>
> All in all, the plan was a success. It did provide for close relationship of functions and personnel and contributed greatly in my opinion to the closely knit, integrated and coordinated mechanism or organization in medical teaching, as well as medical care and research, for which it was designed and for which it represented a new concept.

In addition to these recollections and memoirs, there have been five histories of local origin dealing, at least in part, with

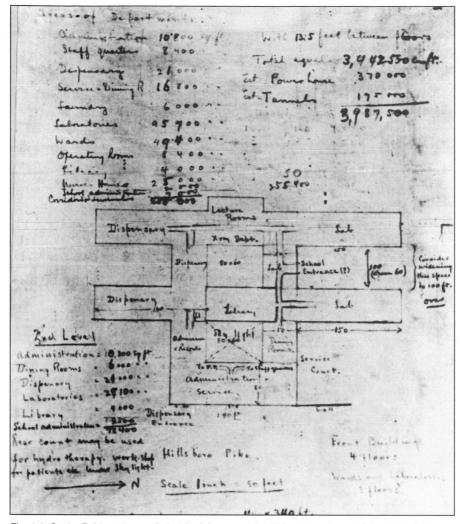

Fig. 4-4: Canby Robinson's pencil sketch of the reorganized Vanderbilt Medical School, faithfully reproduced in the finished structure.

Vanderbilt Medical School: that of Edwin Mims (*History of Vanderbilt University*, Vanderbilt University Press, 1946); those of Rudolph Kampmeier (*Recollections: The Department of Medicine Vanderbilt University School of Medicine 1925–1959*, Vanderbilt University Press, 1980, and *The Making of a Clinical Teacher*, Private Printing 1985/VUMC Archives); that of Paul Conkin (*Gone with the Ivy: A Biography of Vanderbilt University*, University of

Tennessee Press, 1985); and that of Timothy Jacobson (*Making Medical Doctors: Science and Medicine at Vanderbilt since Flexner*, University of Alabama Press, 1987). All five presumably had as common source material the papers of Kirkland and Robinson that are archived at Vanderbilt, while the papers of Deans Leathers, Goodpasture, and Youmans were also available to Kampmeier, Conkin, and Jacobson. It is not surprising that these histories reached the same conclusions: that the placing of the hospital and medical school on the main university grounds was felicitous in effect; that the building design, coupled with facilitation of communication between preclinical and clinical faculty, was key to creating the harmonious and collegial atmosphere for which Vanderbilt was (and is) known. Other factors that must have played a role in this successful outcome were the relatively small size of the first faculty (there were nineteen professors, associate professors, and assistant professors recruited by 1925), as well as the common education and training of most of these faculty at the two

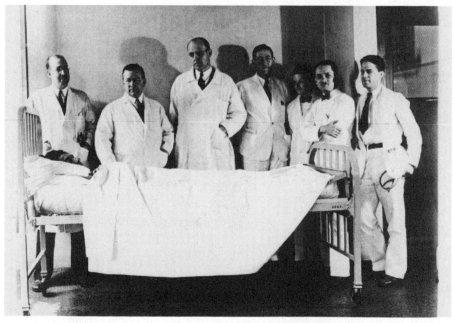

Fig. 4-5: Dr. Robinson on rounds in 1928, shortly before leaving for Cornell, with Dr. Burwell on his right and Dr. Morgan on his left.

premier medical schools Hopkins and Harvard. Finally, Robinson, as the chief administrative officer, was also down in the trenches as the chief of medicine (Fig. 4-5). He apparently not only imparted a sense of mission to the faculty but had also placed them in an unusually stimulating environment in which they were expected to teach, do research, and care for the sick without the encumbrances they had experienced in other settings.

Medical School Environment

Each of these cited references has a common theme—that Robinson's architectural venture with placement of students and faculty under one roof on the main campus was novel and successful—as well as a slightly different perspective. They have been quoted in some detail in order to understand why the medical school achieved instant success and why it provided such a congenial environment for Dr. Goodpasture. It was anticipated that more direct insight into these matters from Dr. Goodpasture's perspective would be found in the Goodpasture correspondence. However, there are no letters or other communications extant about this early period from Dr. Goodpasture to his many friends, colleagues, or family, although it would be natural and expected for him to let people know how the new job at Vanderbilt was progressing. His views would have been interesting, but his actions (in conducting a very active research program, in training younger colleagues, and in refusing offers to move) speak louder than words in showing his contentment with being at Vanderbilt Medical School. Some of his speeches (cited below in this chapter) are also relevant to this point, as they clearly state his view that university medical centers in general and, by inference, Vanderbilt in particular were key institutions in maintaining social welfare.[36]

One factor contributing to the collegiality at Vanderbilt was the then-simple fact that faculty could gather almost daily for lunch in the doctors' dining room, now part of Department of Surgery space on the second floor of Medical Center North, T corridor. Approximately eight hundred square feet were set aside for dining.

There was an adjacent kitchen that served the doctors' dining room and a separate nurses' dining room. As witness to the enlightenment of Dr. Robinson and the architects, the nurses' space was more favorably located and was more spacious by four hundred square feet. Lunch cost fifty cents. This facility was of such importance that it received equal billing with the faculty in Rudolph Kampmeier's book, *Recollections*. His curious apposition of words in the chapter entitled "The Dining Room and the Core Faculty of the School" (page 37) is justified in the accompanying text:

> The dining room was the focal point and probably the most important spot in the individual growth of the Vanderbilt faculty and graduates. The importance of the dining room has been emphasized over and over by those familiar with the new school in its first couple of decades, summed up in a letter from Tinsley Harrison:
>
> "The great virtue of the place was in its smallness. Interns, residents, and faculty members all ate in the single hospital dining room. There were no fixed places. One day I might have lunch at the same table with the Chairman of a preclinical department, or a junior full-time teacher and one or more interns and assistant residents. The next day there would be a different group."
>
> The dining room accommodated eight tables, each sitting six to eight persons. Although house staff in their comradeship usually congregated at two tables, it was not by assignment, and often they joined senior faculty at other tables.

Dr. Kampmeier then goes on to describe his interactions with the core faculty in the informal setting of the dining room. Chancellor Kirkland apparently was a frequent visitor, and this photograph of Chancellor Carmichael, Dean Leathers, Hugh Morgan, and Tinsley Harrison at lunch is in our archives (Fig. 4-6). The specifics of Robinson's interactions with Dean Leathers and other faculty after 1928 are also of interest in terms of giving insight into the ambiance of Vanderbilt Medical School. There are many letters in Dean Leathers's files from Dr. Robinson, even after the latter was forced to leave Cornell for a position of less responsibility at Hopkins. Interspersed telephone conversations and visits are also documented, so the record in aggregate clearly establishes that Dr. Robinson remained a close friend and enthusiastic supporter of Vanderbilt. Faculty appointments and news were routinely discussed, and the various machinations in obtaining General Education Board support for the enlargement of the hospital in 1935 show the extent and effectiveness of Dr. Robinson's continued participation in Vanderbilt affairs.

The memorandum that follows was written by Dr. Robinson after a visit to Nashville in April of 1930:[37]

> To the executive faculty of the Vanderbilt University Medical College, Nashville, Tennessee.
>
> As it has been impossible to express to each member of the faculty my thoughts regarding the medical school as I have seen it on my recent visit, I wish to express to the executive faculty as a whole my sincere enthusiasm for the progress that has been made in the work of the school since my departure.

Fig. 4-6: Doctors' dining room, with Doctors Morgan and Harrison and Dean Leathers in discussion with Chancellor Carmichael.

Fig. 4-7: Portrait of G. Canby Robinson presented to Vanderbilt in 1938, now hanging in 208 Light Hall.

It has been a matter of great gratification to see the enthusiastic and sincere spirit that pervades the whole institution and which certainly emanates primarily from the heads of the various departments. My visit was a memorable one and will also be one of the outstanding events of my life.

I wish to take this occasion to express my very warm congratulations to each member of the executive faculty and to say how keenly I appreciate the splendid spirit that has developed and is being carried on in the school. It was with a distinct feeling of pride that I saw the results of the undertaking in the initiation of which I had a part, but which has been brought to its present eminence by the loyal and intelligent cooperation of those who are directing the affairs of the school.

I want to express also my sense of personal gratitude for the great kindness and good-will that were shown to me by everyone and to assure you that my interest in the medical school and my keen desire for progress have in no sense lessened by my absence. May the future be as full of progress as have been the past two years.

The continuing goodwill between Dr. Robinson and the Vanderbilt faculty is also exemplified in the commissioning and presentation of his portrait to the school in June 1938. The Robinson portrait (Fig. 4-7), now hanging in a central position in 208 Light Hall, was presented officially to the university by Dr. Goodpasture, with whom the Robinson family stayed on their visit to Nashville.[38] The festivities were held at the Belle Meade Country Club; speakers included Doctors Morgan, Witt, Cullen, and Goodpasture, Dean Leathers, Chancellor Emeritus Kirkland, and Chancellor Carmichael, with Sidney Burwell presiding.[39] Chancellor Kirkland's remarks on this occasion have been preserved:[40]

> This was the greatest undertaking in the history of the university, comparable to its founding by Bishop McTyeire in 1874 or 1875. The success of these years of labor was due largely to the wisdom, patience, and determination of the new Dean whom we honor tonight. . . . The influence of those early years and of our first Dean will ever remain an important part of the history of the medical school of Vanderbilt University.

The four-year sojourn at Vanderbilt of G. Canby Robinson, as abbreviated as it was, may have been the highlight of the career of this idealistic and talented medical administrator. In his correspondence and written accounts of his life, Robinson turns repeatedly to the collegiality at Vanderbilt, as in his letter accepting the Goodpasture invitation for the portrait presentation: "we shall be very happy to be back where we know we are among friends without any doubt."[41] There is also a section in his book on *Adventures in Medical Education* titled the "Spirit of Vanderbilt."[42] The dining room is not specifically mentioned as a factor in the *esprit de corps*, but these were his recollections thirty years after the event:

> A fine spirit pervaded the medical school, and the members of the faculty were good friends, showing a remarkable cooperation in their work and in the school as a whole, and the spirit of comradeship extended to the members of the families of the faculty. Life was pleasant—happily industrious and stimulating, and everybody seemed to feel he was in the right place.

Institutions are often compared in terms of their spirit and accomplishments, but both features are notoriously difficult to document and quantitate. The various attestations given above seem genuine in relationship to the collegiality and interdisciplinary cooperation we treasure as part of our heritage. It is clear that these manifestations of goodwill, the executive faculty resolution, the portrait presentation, and most importantly the extensive correspondence between Leathers and Robinson, are all a litmus test of the mood and working conditions of the Vanderbilt faculty after 1928. The faculty understandably might have resented Robinson's departure for New York and the promised millions, while his recruits were doing the hard work in Nashville of making his dream a reality with far fewer resources. In fact, this dream was recognized as a unique opportunity, and the faculty was eternally grateful to him for the opportunity to be a part of Vanderbilt's ascendancy as a medical school.

Rank of Vanderbilt Medical School

What is the evidence that Vanderbilt Medical School had ascended to the first rank? Here is Mims's conclusion;[43] please be informed that Conkin[44] states that Mims may have hagiographic tendencies:

> Much space has been given to the development of the School of Medicine because it is the one school of the University that may be measured by the highest national standards. It is not only one of the best, if not the best in the South, but it is also one of the half-dozen best in the whole country.

Kampmeier in *Recollections* and in *The Making of a Clinical Teacher* puts it this way:[45]

> In these days of bigness it is important to recall the smallness of a reorganized old medical school which was to attain, while small, the swift recognition and prestige which even when it became a big school would not be surpassed . . . The esprit-de-corps of a select student body, a select house staff and a full-time faculty of second generation Oslerians, and a comparable volunteer faculty explains,

certainly for the medical department, the rapidity with which Vanderbilt was catapulted into national prominence so quickly after its reorganization in 1925.

Conkin in *Gone with the Ivy* has this analysis:

But the result [the equipped hospital and school] was universally admired, the first unified school and hospital in the country, a showplace for visitors from all parts of the country and even from foreign countries, and a widely copied model for other new medical schools [Universities of Rochester and Colorado] . . . What he [Robinson] hired were the best professors available in each field, from institutions all over the country (Fig. 4-8). He paid what he needed to get them. The result was a faculty that ranked among that of the four or five best schools in the country.[46]

Fig. 4-8: Recently appointed senior faculty in their first group photograph before the North Portico, the entrance to the medical school from the university. Burwell, Goodpasture, and Brooks are on the right side; Robinson is in the center in front of Morgan.

In those happy days before we were consistently ranked by such an authoritative judge as *U.S. News and World Report* as sixteenth or so[47] there were few guides as to the ranking of institutions. Youmans attempted to provide semiquantitative evidence in "Vanderbilt—Yesterday, Today and Tomorrow" by analyzing the faculty as well as graduates of the school in terms of their accomplishments and recruitment by other institutions. He obtained information in a manner that was not defined about graduates from 1925 to 1935: 60 percent of the 1935 graduates obtained residencies in university teaching hospitals; 25 percent of the 475 graduates in the first ten years had published papers; 40 percent of these graduates were in general practice and 40 percent in specialty work; of the original nineteen faculty at the rank of assistant professor or above, eight had left "presumably for greener and more prestigious fields"; in 1935, forty-two faculty had 142 publications including one book; seven of the original nineteen faculty were members of the prestigious Association of American Physicians by 1940. Dr. Youmans concluded that this information meant that "The first decade of the new school's existence rapidly established its firm position as one of the outstanding schools in this country."[48]

Before the flowering of medical schools west of the Mississippi, these various assessments are probably close to the mark. Certainly in this period Vanderbilt was the most prestigious *southern* medical school. Dr. Goodpasture had a major role in the success of the school, in part because the recently completed facilities and recently recruited faculty could hardly have been more to his liking had he been responsible for the buildings and recruitment.

Recruitment of Dr. Goodpasture

The recruitment of Dr. Goodpasture by Dean Robinson was consummated between February and April of 1924.[49] A letter to Dr. Goodpasture dated April 23 notified him that he was recommended for appointment as professor of pathology and authorized his European trip, including work in Vienna. A letter dated May 31 indicates Dr. Goodpasture had seen the building plans and had made suggestions "that seemed reasonable and simple." Although the selection of Dr. Goodpasture as chairman seems a natural choice in hindsight, he was actually Robinson's third choice.[50] The first, James Wesley Jobling, was professor of pathology on Vanderbilt's south campus, where he had an outstanding record.[51] The second was Wade Brown, a Hopkins graduate of 1907, designated "the man for the job" by Robinson in 1920.[52] Dr. Brown made a trip to Nashville on May 28, 1920, and remained the leading contender until 1923, when he received a lifetime appointment to the Rockefeller Institute.[53] Dr. Goodpasture was not mentioned as the first choice of either Doctors Whipple or Winternitz when they were asked to name candidates by Dr. Robinson;[54] Dr. Welch probably would have also been asked for recommendations, but there are no records of that presumed interaction. Two subsequent Nobel laureates, Rous and Whipple, were also asked to consider coming to Vanderbilt, but neither expressed interest.[55] Dr. Goodpasture surfaced as a serious contender in 1923 when Dr. Robinson mentioned him as a second choice if discussions with Wade Brown fell through. Dr. Goodpasture's candidacy progressed rapidly after an interview in Pittsburgh by Dr. Robinson in February 1924. They agreed in principle in early April 1924; on April 23 Dr. Goodpasture was recommended to the chancellor, to whom he sent a hand-written letter of acceptance dated May 1, 1924.[56]

In essence, timing was a key factor in the Goodpasture appointment. If Jobling had remained in Nashville, he would have been the only faculty member other than Lucius Burch[57] to be retained. The time required for the move to the west campus, with the attendant extensive construction, allowed Wade Brown to secure a tenured position at the Rockefeller Institute. In 1920, when Dr. Goodpasture's name was first mentioned by Max Souby, he was thirty-four and had fifteen publications that were somewhat heterogeneous in subject matter; it was a notable research output but not focused and authoritative. By 1923, Dr. Goodpasture had an additional fourteen publications, many focused on viral pathogenesis.

Fig. 4-9: Basic science wings of the recently completed medical school. Dr. Goodpasture's office was on the top floor, right, and overlooked part of the university campus. The North Portico is shown as originally designed, before the courtyard was enclosed by Learned Laboratory.

Also he had been made director of the Singer Institute and had turned down a proposal from Iowa for a professorship there. It is clear that the appointment at Singer Institute, with the opportunity to collaborate with Oscar Teague, made Dr. Goodpasture's selection at Vanderbilt possible.

Assumption of Responsibilities by Dr. Goodpasture

Dr. Goodpasture and his family docked in New York on July 27, 1925, finally on their way home after extensive training and study in Baltimore, Boston, Manila, Pittsburgh, and Vienna.[58] They would have taken the train (Pan-American via Louisville) to Nashville, coming as soon as possible because there was a prodigious amount of work to be done in preparation for the beginning of school in September. In addition, there were the usual personal arrangements attendant to settling in as a family after such a long absence. So it is likely that Dr. Goodpasture stepped on the

Vanderbilt campus for the first time as professor of the Department of Pathology one fine day in late July or early August 1925. We can only imagine how meaningful it was for him to walk down the freshly painted corridors into his department and to see the main campus from his office windows that opened to the north (Fig. 4-9). This privilege of being in a medical school on university grounds might be traced directly to the first sentence in Canby Robinson's reorganization plan of five years before in which he stated:[59] "Medical education, during the past thirty years, has rapidly developed from the status of vocational training based on the practice and customs of the profession to a position which allows it to take its place as an integral part of a true university." And so here this Tennessean stood, on his campus, in the office he would hold for the next thirty years, eminently prepared professionally for the responsibilities and opportunities of an academic life, and, even more importantly, prepared philosophically for life at Vanderbilt.

The word *spirit* appears repeatedly in Canby Robinson's writings; in the reorganization plan[60] we find "spirit of intellectual enthusiasm," "development of the scientific spirit," "fostered the same spirit." In this document he records his criteria for recruitment of faculty:[61]

> The success of the school is to depend on the initial group of men who are selected. They must enter into the undertaking with enthusiasm and with the feeling that it holds for them a worthy object for permanent interest and a life's work. They should be young men with a future rather than a past, who are plastic and receptive, and ready to take a full share in the development of the intellectual "team-work" on which the spirit and the life of the school will depend.

These words are timeless, as powerful now as they were in 1925 for Ernest William Goodpasture. Eighteen years later, when Dr. Goodpasture gave the baccalaureate address to the Vanderbilt seniors graduating in 1943, his speech was titled "The Spirit of Inquiry."[62] It was not necessary to remind the graduates that they were leaving for a world in conflict, but they did need to see the larger picture, and the place of universities in that picture. So we read:

> War and peace, peace and war, have ever been the alternating episodes in the long journey. Yet we trust, if we are naïve or very sanguine, that the alternation is not inevitable . . .
>
> At Commencement [in Bologna] candidates assembled in cap and gown at Coventus where a public examination was held. They went before the town beforehand inviting the public officials and friends to the ceremony and to the great banquet to follow. After they acquitted themselves satisfactorily at the examination and received the licentia at the hands of the Archdeacon, the magisterial biretta was placed upon their heads, and they were escorted in triumph through the city, surrounded by a mounted cavalcade preceded by the 3 University Pipers and the 4 University Trumpeters. Then followed the banquet which they themselves contributed. Later in Spain the graduating class was required to provide a bull-fight for the delectation of the university. It seems a pity that these delightful old university customs have in time been discarded, and only the austere cap and gown are left to connect us with so intriguing a past. . . .
>
> The old medieval universities favored international comity within their folds, and under the most hazardous and apparently insurmountable difficulties they dug the excavations and laid the very foundations for whatever of intellectual, political and religious freedom succeeding generations have enjoyed. Furthermore they established a self-propagating and a self-perpetuating institution for scholars and learners, that now finds its offspring in all lands on the face of the earth; and finally they and their successors not only retrieved and revived the older classical methods for purifying rational thought, but what has proved to be of far more importance they fostered the discovery of a new method upon which our modern science is based, namely the method of experiment and control. . . .
>
> To wear our caps and gowns on this commencement is too small a tribute to pay to their memory, and I would move that we declare a special holiday and provide a banquet and a bull-fight, at university

expense, to commemorate them for liberating the reason of man, and for exalting the individual human being from a degraded and pessimistic thraldom to a position of respect and dignity. . . .

So our civilization has preserved and pursued for seven hundred years these aspirations for liberation and cultivation of the individual mind. From them have sprung what knowledge we possess of the physical universe about us, with its great resources of power and wealth. . . .

In the search for common denominators, whose acceptance might bring the fundamental interests of the world closer together and inspire mankind to protect them with all their will and power, there is a challenge to every man, and every group and nation of men. We believe these formulas should be expressions of an ideal of individual liberty, and as students of science and students of life we should realize that underneath and supporting all of our chartered modes of freedom lies a many-sided spirit; and the facet of that spirit, to my mind, that would be essential to the maintenance and growth of liberty is the spirit of rational inquiry. To question ourselves, to question our universe, to question our gods, our devils and our destiny, and to listen sensitively and intelligently to spontaneous and induced revelations of truth, is the last bulwark of our hope at least to know a better world. Seek and ye shall find.

Toward the end of his life, in 1957, Dr. Goodpasture held to this theme in an address to the graduating class of Tulane Medical School when he was awarded an L.L.D.:[63]

But the university is the home of the medical school and the entire great edifice of learning will continue to profit by association with its science, its art and its humanity. . . . Medicine is the most universally acceptable example of what education and science can do in the interest of well being. . . . The university as conservator, educator, creative builder of knowledge, evaluator and disperser of the arts and science should, above all civil institutions, be respected, protected, supported and promoted in the interest of human culture.

Of all the tasks in a university, none is more demanding or more important than recruiting the right person at the right time. This

Fig. 4-10: Ernest William Goodpasture as young professor.

ability may have been Dr. Robinson's forte, but he also had a bit of luck. Although Vanderbilt Medical School exists as an institution in large part due to the guidance and scholastic principles of Chancellor Kirkland, our chancellor for forty-four years, its most special features are attributable to our peripatetic dean and professor of medicine, Dr. G. Canby Robinson, who was in Nashville for only four years. Of his appointments, that of Ernest William Goodpasture may well have been the crucial one, precisely matching the needs of Vanderbilt University with the philosophy and abilities of its professor of pathology (Fig. 4-10).

Responsibilities—Department of Pathology

The responsibilities of the department were summarized in the booklet on *Methods and Problems of Medical Education* published by the Rockefeller Foundation in 1929. The chapter by Dr. Goodpasture begins with a section titled Scope of Activities:

> The Department of Pathology of the Vanderbilt School of Medicine is designed primarily for the study and teaching of the morphologic aspects of disease both from a descriptive and an experimental approach. The undergraduate teaching consists of a curricular course in general and special pathology for second-year students, conducted during the first two trimesters of the year. In connection with this course during the second trimester, after the students have gained some knowledge of morbid anatomy, examples of particular

diseases or pathological processes which they have studied are demonstrated to the class by a member of the medical staff each week. Throughout the year a clinical-pathological conference is held weekly for the third- and fourth-year classes.

The staff of the department conducts the post-mortem examinations at the Vanderbilt and the Nashville General hospitals. The department is not responsible for, but has access to, the surgical pathologic material.[64] The Departments of Pathology and Bacteriology are separately conducted.

Opportunities for research are offered, particularly in the field of morphology, for the study of morbid processes experimentally induced or encountered in the routine post-mortem work. In the investigative work etiological aspects of disease have been particularly emphasized, and especially the causation of and the changes incident to those diseases which are due to filterable viruses.

Departmental space totaling forty-two hundred square feet was on the third floor, in the northern wing called then medical school Building "C," now the C corridor where pathology still resides (Fig. 4-11). The two offices at the end of the hall were

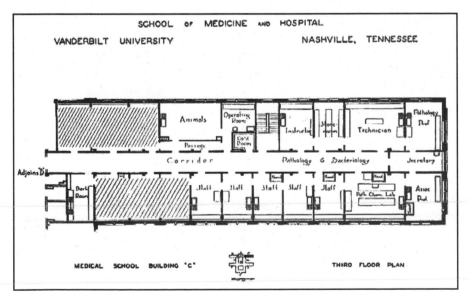

Fig. 4-11: Architect's drawing of pathology department space.

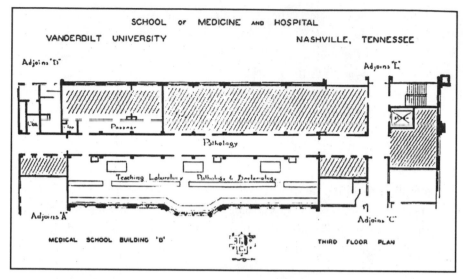

Fig. 4-12: Architect's drawing of teaching laboratory used by pathology and bacteriology.

equal in size and were occupied by the professor and associate professor, respectively. The departmental secretary had the intervening space as her office; this space is now the corridor into Learned Laboratory. There were five staff offices, one office for an instructor, laboratories for technicians, a storeroom, animal quarters, an operating room, a cold room, and a dark room for photography. The adjoining Medical School Building "B" (now T corridor, third floor) (Fig. 4-12) overlooked the courtyard above the medical school entrance and contained the teaching laboratory for both pathology and bacteriology. The autopsy room was located on the first floor in Clinical Laboratory Building "E"; it is now a research laboratory off the T corridor.

Education of medical students

Shortly before returning to the United States in 1925, Dr. Goodpasture was notified by Dr. Robinson that "we will have to start pathology this year in the beginning of the term, that is, in September."[65] A temporary schedule was enclosed, showing that pathology had been assigned the hours of 9:00 to 12:00 Monday through Saturday, 12:00 to 1:00 on Tuesday, Thursday, and

Saturday during the first trimester; in the second trimester, hours were 9:00 to 12:00 Tuesday, Thursday, and Saturday. Clinical pathological conferences for third- and fourth-year students were on Wednesdays at 3:30. The pathology department thus had 308 hours for instructing the second-year students. The final schedule as published in the July 1925 bulletin has classes beginning at 8:30 but is otherwise similar to that given in the missive from Dr. Robinson. It is poignant, even now, to see Dr. Goodpasture's scribbled calculations on this letter regarding the number of lectures this schedule required. Assuming twenty full weeks in the two trimesters, and five lectures a week, the grand total was one hundred! Such a number would daunt any teacher. Fortunately, he had recently recruited Arthur Wright to join the faculty, but even so, this reminder as to the amount of work to be done in preparation for teaching his first Vanderbilt class could have squelched any latent tendencies Dr. Goodpasture might have had for savoring the culture of Vienna.

Fig. 4-13: Class of 1929, during the anatomy course. Freshmen then usually wore tan coats and brought accessories for the picture.

Fig. 4-14: Four years later, the class of 1929 was the first to graduate from the reorganized Vanderbilt Medical School.

There is some information about the work required to prepare for the first class in 1925 (Figs. 4-13 and 4-14). Dr. Goodpasture's reports to the dean in 1926 and 1927 contain these accounts:[66]

> Dr. Wright and I arrived in Nashville to begin work early in August, and since September we have been assisted by Dr. Nunez, who volunteered to spend about half his time in the department. Our first job was to transfer supplies and apparatus from the Department of Pathology in the South Campus to the new medical school building and to install our equipment, which was accomplished early in September.
>
> As the course in pathology for the second year students began on September 24th, and as the materials on hand were not satisfactory for teaching purposes it became necessary to prepare in large part a loan collection of microscopic slides for class work. With materials which we had brought with us, and that acquired from the Vanderbilt Hospital and other sources we have made something over 10,000

microscopic preparations which with selected preparations from the old set have served as the basis for instruction in pathology this year. Work is being continued on the teaching collection with the idea of having ready for next Fall a complete loan collection of carefully selected and prepared slides and specimens illustrating the most important disease processes in both general and special pathology. . . .

It is a pleasure to state that everyone in the department seems contented in his work, and I am much indebted to each of them for cordial cooperation.

By 1927 additional work had been done to prepare for classes:

Much of the routine work of the laboratory has consisted in the completion of a loan collection of microscopic preparations for teaching purposes. Approximately 20,000 microscopic slides are now available for teaching, each student being provided with 300 preparations illustrative of various disease processes which form the basis of the course in pathology. Over 200 gross preparations have been prepared for demonstrative purposes. The teaching collection is constantly being added to and improved with the accumulation of desirable material.

The schedule for the pathology course had stabilized by 1928 and was followed for a number of years; it consisted of seventeen hours per week in the first trimester, thirteen hours per week in the second, totaling 330 hours of instruction exclusive of clinical pathological conferences. A surgical pathology course was taught to third-year students from 1:30 to 4:30 on Mondays by the Department of Surgery. Dr. Goodpasture described the pathology course in the early years in the Rockefeller Education Series, under the title Undergraduate Instruction in Pathologic Anatomy:[67]

In this department, undergraduate instruction in pathology is conceived as a discipline in the recognition and interpretation of the gross and microscopic changes brought about by disease. The student is taught that the material investigated, far from always being the end-product of

Fig. 4-15: Photograph of pathology teaching laboratory. There were two long benches running the length of the room. Stools (partially hidden under desk) were provided for microscopy.

disease, is more frequently a means of rendering accessible and visible many of the agencies and processes actually contributing to disturbance of function at a definite period. He is therefore encouraged to think of his material in terms of the function which it represents.

The course in general and special pathology is taught during the first and second trimesters of the second year by means of laboratory work, demonstrations, and lectures, occupying a total of three hundred and thirty hours in the curriculum (Fig. 4-15). The clinical pathological conferences occupy sixty-six hours. Therefore, there are scheduled three hundred and ninety-six hours of instruction.

The basis of the course in pathology for second-year medical students consists of a loan collection of approximately three hundred slides in each set. A complete set of slides is issued to each student on entering the course. This material has been collected with great care and prepared with the best of technique in order that the student may have the opportunity of studying good examples of pathologic processes by the method of histologic presentation. General pathology, the pathology of infectious diseases, and special pathology are treated systematically in the course by the use of the loan collection of slides, preserved gross specimens, fresh material from the autopsy room, and by the demonstration of experimental material. Considerable stress is placed upon the study of gross lesions. For this purpose fresh material from the autopsy is utilized so far as possible. This is supplemented by a large assortment of specimens preserved in formaldehyde unmounted, which the students may handle and section as well as observe. Mounted specimens are utilized only to illustrate lectures and demonstrations . . .

The paragraphs quoted above (edited slightly to remove redundant comments) are a comprehensive summary of the rationale and methods of instruction in the pathology course,[68] which for many students was their defining educational experience at Vanderbilt. However, this rather dry and detailed description is hardly the way most medical students would describe their own experience in that course. Firstly, it was the course in which Vanderbilt students began to study diseases and had to face the reality that diseases could result in death. Being on call for autopsies was somewhat unsettling for students with long-established routines and signified a transition from personal independence to the assumption of responsibility for patients. The dress code also changed abruptly, from casual to professional; sophomores were subject to inspection, in classes and out, to ensure that white coats were clean, that ties were in place, and that shoes had been polished.

The real shock, always recounted in later years with a knowing shake of the head and with a chuckle or two, was the terror inspired by Doctors Dawson or Shapiro, the two major assistants of Dr. Goodpasture. They ran the course from the late 1930s until the 1960s, and fortunately they were both not operational at full power at the same time, Dr. Dawson being the elder. Both teachers knew students on sight by the first day in class, when they instituted strict dress and behavior codes that by student testimonial lasted a lifetime. The extent of one's ignorance and general ineptness was subject to intense scrutiny at all times, as well as to public disclosure. Of course, veterans of the pathology course made freshmen fully aware of this educational trial by fire awaiting them as sophomores, in which the heretofore routine events of study and recitation seemingly assumed life and death significance. Veterans knowingly related various high-noon events and escapades, some of which had actually involved other classes but were passed down from year to year in Homeric fashion. The reality was often as bad as the expectations created by these frequently embellished stories. Almost everyone had a soul-shaking experience to pass on to the freshmen, or recount to an upper-classman, as students underwent overnight transition from upper-level biology majors to lowest-level physicians-in-training.

There was a positive side. Both Dr. Dawson and Dr. Shapiro were superb teachers, and they understood how to make basic concepts about disease understandable and unforgettable. Both had student interests and the educational process as their first priorities, a fact students initially intuited and ultimately recognized. On the day the course ended, both called students by their first names and proved to be effective student advocates. Later, after graduation, both were highly respected as teachers and treasured as colleagues. What was Dr. Goodpasture's role in this training ground for physicians? After the late thirties the course was managed from day to day by Dr. Dawson or Dr. Shapiro, who were responsible for the lectures, demonstrations, conferences, examinations, and discipline. Within their own agendas for orchestrating these various components of the course, there was the carefully sheltered Goodpasture component. Dr. Goodpasture's main participation in the class was to lecture at 11:00 A.M. on Tuesdays and Thursdays, lectures which were clearly marked as COMPULSORY in every student notebook. These lectures were an occasion when the class was put on display for the honored chief, as Dr. Dawson and Dr. Shapiro had enormous respect for Dr. Goodpasture (Fig. 4-16) and were determined that the students in turn show their respect by hard work and appropriate demeanor.

Through no intention of his own, Dr. Goodpasture was viewed by students as unapproachable and somewhat distant. Although students knew the barest particulars justifying his fame as a medical scientist, they saw in clearest detail the esteem, even veneration, in which he

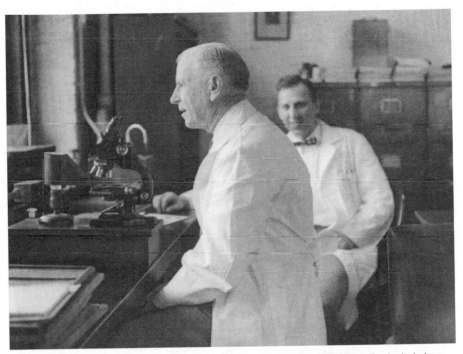

Fig. 4-16: Doctors Goodpasture and Shapiro discussing a case. Dr. Goodpasture's office had windows facing the campus to the north. His microscope was on the bench underneath these windows.

was held by Dr. Dawson and Dr. Shapiro, who were themselves regarded with equal measures of respect and fear by generations of students. So each Tuesday and Thursday, at 11:00, an attentive, spiffed-up class (along with the house officers in pathology) was presented to Dr. Goodpasture, with Dr. Dawson or Dr. Shapiro very much in attendance and in control at the back of the lecture hall. It is doubtful that Dr. Goodpasture was aware of the personal refurbishing each student had undergone, although he was at least partially responsible for the improvements.

The material presented in the pathology course evolved with new knowledge, but the basic format varied only slightly over the years. Dr. Dawson or Dr. Shapiro would present the essential information about disease processes (general pathology section, first trimester) and then cover the major diseases in specific organs (special pathology, second trimester). Approximately one hundred lectures were given each year, with seventy-five of these by Dr. Dawson or Dr. Shapiro, other faculty, and the house staff.[69] In 1953–54 Dr. Goodpasture gave twenty-four lectures, often emphasizing the historical aspects of pathology and medicine, on topics that had usually been covered by other faculty. His voice was soft and rather monotonous, and most judged his presentation less effective than the content warranted.[70] The students knew what he was saying was *very* important, in part because of the close attention paid by the authorities in the back of the room. In retrospect, his lectures were more sophisticated than his student audience.

In any case, the repetitive presentation of material in pathology reinforced its retention. For example, in 1953–54 Dr. Shapiro discussed inflammation in four lectures from October 8 to 13; Dr. Goodpasture covered this topic on October 13, while emphasizing the discoveries of Galen, Metchnikoff, J. Hunter, and Starling.[71] Infections of various types were presented by Doctors Shapiro, John Thomison, and Frank Womack in thirteen lectures beginning on October 14 before Dr. Goodpasture spoke on October 29 about basic concepts in infections, including portals of entry, natural history of infections, and parasitism.

In 1954, Dr. Goodpasture participated in a "teaching institute" and gave the following response about the cardinal objectives of undergraduate medical education:[72]

> By means of lectures, demonstrations and discussions to bring to students a scientific interpretation of the meaning of disease and the historical development of knowledge concerning it; by means of autopsies, gross and microscopic specimens and preparations to acquaint students with methods of acquiring and evaluating knowledge of morphological, etiological and other factors of disease; by personal example through observation, critical judgment, scholarly study and research to impress upon students the productivity and reliability of the scientific method and the necessity for acquiring self-reliance through its cultivation. As in all medical teaching the cardinal objective should be preparation of the student for self-instruction.

Performance of autopsies

The major responsibilities of the Department of Pathology from 1925 to 1955 were teaching the second-year course, research, and performance of autopsies. Laboratory tests other than autopsies were overseen by medicine and surgery, with the clinical laboratories initially managed by the Department of Medicine. It should be noted that urinalyses, white blood cell counts, red blood cell counts, cultures, and other relatively simple tests were routinely performed by medical students and resident staff, particularly at night and on weekends. Surgical pathology was staffed, managed, and taught by the Department of Surgery until the 1950s, when the pathology department assumed a greater role and finally took control of this laboratory.

Autopsies had an important role in every academic medical center in the period of Dr. Goodpasture's chairmanship and for at least one preceding century. Diagnoses were not established in many difficult cases until an autopsy was performed. The mechanism of disease production and how a disease caused manifestations in patients were often revealed by an autopsy. Analyses of autopsy material resulted in more precise classifications of diseases by establishing disease entities; many diseases that seemed homogeneous were shown to be mixtures of different entities. The great clinicians of the late 1800s and early 1900s, including William Osler, were experts in or were at least practiced in the performance of autopsies, and in the interpretation of gross as well as histopathologic changes. Autopsies then, and now, were useful as methods of instruction for second-year students, providing examples of the ravages of various diseases for discussion and study.

Autopsies were therefore a major part of the diagnostic and educational program in academic medical centers, as manifested by the number performed, the percentage of patients on whom autopsies were requested, and the extensive use of autopsy material in the education of the clinical services and students.

The performance of autopsies took precedence over other activities, and they were begun as soon as permission was obtained. The removal of organs, their examination, and processing of tissue for microscopy required two to three hours in routine cases. Abstracting the clinical record, interpretation of microscopic sections, literature searches and write-up of the cases might require an additional six to ten hours and was usually completed within a month to six weeks. The sign-out process involved presentation of the case in its entirety to a faculty member, who was responsible for reaching a final diagnosis, making clinical-pathological correlations, contacting the responsible physician and family, and editing the written report. Bound volumes of autopsy reports were once kept in the departmental library (with bound volumes of reprints) as important records of departmental activity, while the microscopic slides, tissue blocks, and illustrative materials were stored for future study. The organs, after fixation in formalin, might be used for several years in the pathology course for demonstrating classical lesions, as in cases of cancer, tuberculosis, or heart disease.

The Department of Pathology performed 58 autopsies from September 1925, until the first departmental report was written in April 1926, with 21 of these at the Nashville General Hospital. In 1927, there were 128 deaths in the hospital, with 72 autopsies equally divided between the medical and surgical services. There were an additional 43 examinations at Nashville General Hospital. In 1930, there were 240 deaths and 154 autopsies, yielding a rate of

Fig. 4-17: Autopsy room with infamous metal racks for students.

Table 4-1
Tabulation of Autopsy Records
for Vanderbilt Hospital, 1926–1939

Year	Deaths	Autopsies	Percentage
1926	149	87	58
1927	117	72	61
1928	171	96	56
1929	200	125	62
1930	240	154	64
1931	275	192	69
1932	213	139	65
1933	245	152	62
1934	284	184	64
1935	323	186	58
1936	318	190	59
1937	281	188	67
1938	296	170	58
1939	348	216	62

64 percent; these cases came equally from medicine, surgery, and pediatrics. In 1940, there were 318 deaths (125 on the medical service, 90 in pediatrics, 93 in surgery, 10 in obstetrics and gynecology), and 197 autopsies, giving a percentage of 61. The number of deaths, autopsies, and percentages were tabulated in 1940 (Table 4-1). The high percentage of autopsies during this period emphasizes the importance of the procedure as a departmental activity in improving patient care in the hospital and in education of medical students.

The autopsy room was located on the first floor, close to the morgue and the dissection rooms used in anatomy. It was an open room, thirty-by-thirty feet in dimension, lined by white tile and containing the autopsy table, stands for viewing (Fig. 4-17), a refrigerator, and shelves for supplies or storage. It was a little on the grim side in the best of circumstances. Regardless of its value in education and in providing much-needed information to patients' families and their physicians, there was no disguising its basic purpose. Death may be a blessing now for those with Alzheimer's disease, or extensive malignancy, or the debilitations of diabetes, but then many patients were young adults or children. Their presence represented a failure to diagnose or inability to treat many diseases that are now cured. Furthermore, there were unpleasant smells to which the students were not accustomed and unpleasant sights for which they were not prepared; freshmen had of course dealt recently with the smells and sights in anatomy's dissection rooms, but the autopsy was a much greater challenge.

So, now bring into this room, in the middle of the night, on about the third day of the pathology course, fifty or so medical students, assembled by custom *en masse* to view their first autopsy. They would have been rousted from their beds and would have hurriedly dressed as no one wished to straggle in last. They assembled on the tiers of metal stands provided for viewing, while the house staff and faculty put on gowns and gloves, or otherwise prepared for the autopsy. The first student pair on call during this time would be desperately trying to get their gear on correctly, and find a place to put their hands, and generally to remain unnoticed.

There was no mistaking the solemnity of the occasion or the importance Dr. Dawson or Dr. Shapiro attached to it, while they were being gowned and gloved by attendant house officers. No upper-class warnings or advice was adequate preparation for the pervasive and engulfing nervousness of the class as it assembled student by student for that first autopsy. Then, to add to the apprehension, some student on the third tier in the stands, scrunched in so identifying features were barely visible, or the absence of a tie was not noticed, would invariably be called on to answer some question about cancer, or strokes, or heart attacks. Worse yet, he or she might be called down from the protection of the herd to view a lesion close-up.

Most medical students at this moment were not considering matters of global significance; but in fact this is when they left their previous lives behind and stepped through a door into the world of medicine, with its demands, opportunities, and responsibilities.

Administration of Department

Dr. Goodpasture was head of the Department of Pathology for thirty-one years, thereby holding the record for longevity in terms of chairmanships in the medical school at Vanderbilt. He was thirty-eight when appointed; his last three years were served by permission of the Board of Trust, as he was sixty-five years old in 1952. The department mission and space were essentially unchanged during the three decades of his tenure, while there was considerable upheaval in our financial status (epitomized by the Great Depression of 1929–32) and in geopolitics (World War II lasted from 1939–46). The former caused a moderate reduction in endowment return, curtailing all department budgets from 1933 until about 1943. The latter, in terms of local effects, sharply reduced faculty numbers during the war, sharply increased student and faculty burdens by accelerating the course of instruction, and created major problems in personnel relocation after the war. Faculty remaining on the home front had to assume extraordinary responsibilities for the good, perhaps survival, of the school. For example, Dr. Kampmeier for two years was the only full-time faculty member in the Department of Medicine, and Dr. Goodpasture assumed the responsibilities of the deanship from 1945 to 1950 in addition to those of the Department of Pathology.

Committees of various types may be standing and thereby semipermanent, or they may be formed ad hoc to address specific issues. In either case they are advisory to the dean or a chief administrative officer and generally do not assume managerial roles. In some circumstances, committees are the workhorses of an institution in terms of acquiring and analyzing information needed to make or implement specific decisions. In other circumstances they have an educational role by facilitating the percolation of information through the faculty or by overseeing student instruction. In yet other circumstances they may function as a sounding board for advice and counsel when particularly difficult issues are presented to the administration. Finally, committees have been used to provide legitimacy and support in controversial matters; they have even been used for purposes such as procrastination and obfuscation. Deans, or other chief administrative officers, in giving committees their charge and in their actions on committee reports have a great influence on the outcome of academic affairs. The chairman is appointed by the dean when the committee is formed and likewise may influence the outcome through bias or controlling the agenda.

The committee with the greatest responsibility at Vanderbilt Medical School in the early years, and perhaps even now, is that of the executive faculty (called the advisory group for several years). It is responsible for overseeing the educational activities of the medical school, including promotions and the awarding of degrees; the executive faculty approves promotions and appointments and generally has an advisory function in relation to the dean. The executive faculty is composed of the chairmen or heads of departments and senior administrative officers. In addition to serving on this committee for thirty years, Dr. Goodpasture sat for many years on the Committee on Instruction, a committee presumably responsible for detailed curriculum planning and review; the Committee for Graduate Instruction (formed in 1931); the Promotions Committee for second-year students and for third-year students after 1934; the Committees on Graduation, on the Library, on Scientific Publications, on the School of Nursing, and the Hospital Committee of the Medical Faculty. He was also involved in search committees to replace faculty or administrative officers, as well as to find distinguished lecturers.

The intricacies of the financial affairs of the medical school and hospital are beyond the scope of this biography, although they are supremely pertinent in terms of the welfare of the institution, the quality and quantity of faculty, and the quality of students. Furthermore, very few people are ever in position to understand university finances in terms of the broad scope of total income, total expenses, and reserve or balance. With the admission that university finances seem particularly labyrinthine and murky to faculty members, it will nevertheless be useful for us to attempt to summarize the financial affairs of the 1925 Vanderbilt Medical School and Hospital at this remove in time of seventy-five years.

The figures given herein are derived from the yearly departmental reports sent from chairmen to the dean.[73] The medical school and hospital have separate budgets, although in Dr. Goodpasture's time they occupied the same facility and employed the same faculty. During most of his tenure, the medical school and hospital also had separate endowments, with the interest from the former covering personnel costs of the basic science faculty and staff as well as some expenses. This endowment also supported portions of the salaries of clinical faculty, the balance coming from patient charges. The cost of running the hospital, in terms of staff and supplies, was met by returns from the endowment for the hospital, supplemented by minimal patient charges. The rationale for this approach was that the hospital existed in order to provide patients for medical students and staff, with the patients available for teaching and clinical investigation. Patients were not "experimented on" by medical students, as often reputed in the community. Also in those idealistic times patients were not a source of income as expected now. Vanderbilt was truly a "not-for-profit" hospital, with the cost of running the hospital frequently exceeding resources.

The budgets for the Department of Pathology and the medical school from 1925 to 1955 are shown in Table 4-2; these data were obtained from the yearly departmental reports and from the dean's reports to the chancellor.[74] The salary of Dr. Goodpasture is in line with the salaries of other preclinical chairmen, as is the budget for the department. The pathology department consistently received about 7 percent of the medical school budget through the years.

Money for support of research was a pittance by modern standards, but very welcome to those with a five-figure budget. Research expenditures are not included in the amounts shown in Table 4-2. In the years shortly after 1925, research funds for the pathology department included the Pouch Fund;[75] the "Fluid Research Fund";[76] grants from International Health Division of the Rockefeller

Table 4-2
Dr. Goodpasture's Salary, Departmental and School Budgets by Year

Year	Salary	Dept. Budget	School Budget	Full-time Assistants†	Residents
1925	$7500	$20,000	$223,321	1	2
1926	7500	20,000	277,121	1	
1927	7500	20,000	284,000	1	1
1928	7500	21,410	330,864	1	2
1929	7500	22,375	360,477	1	2
1930	7500	24,475	379,577	2	2
1931	7500	25,675	375,370	2	2
1932	8000	41,600*	379,000	2	2
1933	8000	39,883*	374,250	3	2
1934	7700	36,692*	374,250	3	3
1935	7700	36,692*	347,843	2	2
1936	7700	36,692*	358,216	3	2
1937	8000	37,692*	368,754	4	3
1938	9000	36,562*	369,942	3	2
1939	9000	36,562*	387,258	3	2
1940	9000	36,562*	392,730	3	1
1941	10,000	38,490*	391,974	3	3
1942	10,000	38,790*	398,818	3	3
1943	10,000	38,290*	423,910	3	2
1944	10,000	43,020*	430,311	3	2
1945	8000+	41,095*	439,531	2	–
1946	8000+	41,095*	563,099	2	–
1947	8000+	40,500*	653,601	3	1
1948	8000+	39,475*	749,496	2	–
1949	8000+	38,500*	780,695	1	1
1950	12,000	42,535*	826,284	1	**
1951	12,000	44,500*	894,212	2	**
1952	12,000	50,200*	998,645	3	**
1953	12,000	–	1,414,420		
1954	12,000	57,240	1,349,644	3	**
1955	12,000	–	1,433,387		

*Includes bacteriology
**Residents no longer carried on departmental budget
+Had additional salary of $4,000 as dean
†Assistants listed if they were on departmental budget. Assistants are not shown if part-time or carried on other budgets. Students routinely took autopsy call, particularly during the 1940s.

Foundation, the Josiah Macy Jr. Foundation, and the John and Mary R. Markle Foundation. In 1936, for example, the department received two thousand dollars from the International Health Division to pay the salary of John Buddingh while he was working on vaccinia, a grant from the Fluid Research Fund, a grant from the Josiah Macy Jr. Foundation for the study of mumps, and a grant from the International Cancer Research Foundation for Dr. Robert Schrek to study cancer.

In the fiscal year ending April 30, 1940, the medical school was still suffering the lingering effects of the depression. The budget for the pathology department shows the personnel and their salaries.[77] Most of the technicians and dieners were longtime employees, and the secretary, Margaret E. McGovern was employed from 1925 to 1955.

- Professor, E. W. Goodpasture $9,000
- Associate Professor, R. C. Avery $4,275
- Assistant Professor, Jas. R. Dawson Jr. $3,750
- Assistant Professor, W. A. DeMonbreun $500
- Assistant Professor, G. J. Buddingh $2,400
- Instructor, W. J. Cromartie $1,800
- Assistant Resident Jack Adams $325
- Assistant Resident David K. Gotwald $325
- Technical Assistant, Katherine Anderson $900
- Technician, Mrs. Hans Geissberger $1,140
- Assistant Technician, Mrs. Edith Drain $900
- Secretary, Margaret E. McGovern $1,425
- Assistant Secretary, Alice Mitchell $900
- Autopsy Technician, William Gunter Jr. $1,425
- Assistant Autopsy Technician, Albert Gunter $1,200
- Diener-Technician, James Harris $924
- Diener, Charles Manlove $740
- Animal Attendant, Andrew Witherspoon $740
- Janitor, Sam Witherspoon $740

Supplies and equipment came to $3,153.18, yielding a total budget of $36,562.18; of this amount, $6,675 was for salaries of

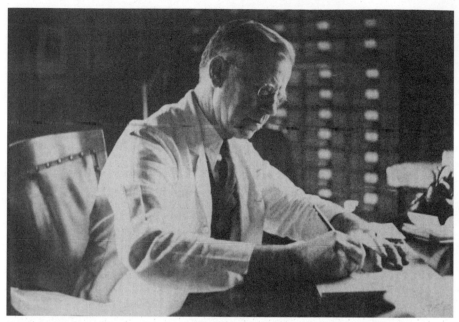

Fig. 4-18: Dr. Goodpasture at desk, circa 1950. His chair has been preserved in Eskind Library, Special Collections.

Doctors Avery and Buddingh, since bacteriology was merged administratively for several years with pathology. Please be reminded that the budget fifteen years earlier totaled $20,000.

Departments as the fundamental organizational units of faculty have at Vanderbilt traditionally had responsibilities for education, research, and service. The Department of Pathology excelled by all accounts in meeting its responsibilities in these three areas under Dr. Goodpasture's tenure, with the exception that after 1945 research productivity dropped, partly because in that year he became dean.

Dr. Goodpasture deserves full credit for the success of the department (Fig. 4-18). As its chief administrative officer he was highly respected for his idealism, collegiality, trustworthiness, and support of his staff. Dr. Goodpasture, through his impressive research accomplishments, led the department scientifically as well. He was designated as head of the department for the first time in the 1945–46 Vanderbilt Medical School Register, having previously been listed only as professor of pathology, at a time when there was only one professor.

This new designation reflected a comprehensive change in titles, presumably occasioned by the growth of the faculty and the anticipated presence of several full professors in each department. Dr. Shapiro later insisted that he should be called head rather than chairman, the latter term perhaps implying that the person in charge was not fully responsible. There was never any doubt as to who was in charge with either of these two.

Judging by the loyalty of the staff and the testament of employees, Dr. Goodpasture ran a happy and productive department (Figs. 4-19 and 4-20). The late 1930s may have been the golden years, in that the success of the embryonated egg technique in viral culture cast a warm glow on the department and the school. (See the color section for a handmade departmental Christmas greeting.) His department reports frequently refer to the stimulating and collegial atmosphere in the department, statements corroborated in letters from faculty who had moved elsewhere.

Fig. 4-19: Faculty and staff, Department of Pathology, 1937. From left, front row: Alice Mitchell (who married John Buddingh) in a flowered dress, Miss Margaret McGovern in center wearing a flower, Mae Gallavan and Katherine Anderson at far right. Back row: Unknown, Dr. DeMonbreun, Dr. Goodpasture, with Doctors Buddingh and Avery on the far right.

Resignation of Dr. Goodpasture

The last department report by Dr. Goodpasture was submitted on March 25, 1955, and bears these comments, in addition to the customary summary of department affairs:[78]

> On June 30, 1955 Dr. Goodpasture retires as professor of pathology and head of the department. It is my understanding that a successor has not yet been appointed, but Dr. Shapiro will be in interim charge of the department.
>
> This being the last annual report to be submitted by the writer I wish to take this opportunity to express to the Dean and to the Chancellor my deep sense of appreciation for the honor and privilege of serving Vanderbilt University and its School of Medicine for the past thirty years. In retiring I have a feeling of great gratification that the School of Medicine is in the hands of an Administration and Faculty who will carry it on to greater heights of service and distinction during the years to come.

Dean Youmans's response was inappropriately terse and formal:[79]

> It is with regret that I inform you of the termination of your active appointment, and personally and on behalf of the University I wish to express our thanks and appreciation for your long and valuable services.

The exchange of letters at this time between Dr. Goodpasture and Chancellor Branscomb is interesting in their mutual expressions of great respect. The series began with Dr. Goodpasture's letter notifying Chancellor Branscomb on April 29, 1955, that the appointment as scientific director at the Armed Forces Institute of Pathology had been consummated, effective July 1. This was from Chancellor Branscomb on May 6:[80]

> I am in receipt of your letter of April 29 telling me that you have resigned from the Vanderbilt Medical School to accept a position in Washington. The latter is important, and I know you will render a great service. I would not be honest, however, if I did not say to you that I

will feel bereft when you are no longer in the medical school, not only for myself, but for the students in that school.

I cannot say anything to you which would anything like express the enduring appreciation which Vanderbilt University holds for you. At the moment, I can't get beyond the fact that the Dean and his committee permitted you to resign. I don't like ostentatious separations either, but we can't let you leave without expressing to you what we think of you and what you have meant to this University.

This was Dr. Goodpasture's response on May 12:

I count my experiences at Vanderbilt among my many blessings and of course my leaving will be a sort of personal upheaval. Nevertheless Katherine and I feel that the new experiences awaiting us have much of interest and satisfaction in store.

There is no way that I could ever properly acknowledge, much less attempt to repay, my indebtedness to Vanderbilt University. The

Fig. 4-20: Faculty and house staff, Department of Pathology, 1955. From left: Doctors Gatling, Harwood, Randolph, Randall, Paplanus, Goodpasture, Collins, Shapiro, Humphries, Levitan, and Thomison.

preparation, the ideals, the liberal spirit, the friendships and the examples which I received as an undergraduate student are beyond all measure. Then the environment which the university made available to me for the past thirty years to cultivate whatever resources I might have had, has been so congenial that I doubt if anyone of my particular bent and temperament has ever been so fortunately situated. The understanding, the warmth of appreciation, the great liberality, and generosity of spirit are intangible values which I have received far beyond the bounds of merit.

Now, since we are dealing with personal values, I want to tell you that in my opinion you have been a tower of strength to the University in your capacity as Chancellor, and I am happy to have served under your administration. My warm feeling of friendship and high personal regard go out to you with good wishes for the future.

I hope you will not feel the need to take any further notice of my retirement; it would only place me further into debt to the University which already is beyond my capacity to think of repaying.

Chancellor Branscomb replied on May 27:

It was with keen regret that I received your letter resigning, of necessity, from two University committees.

The more I have learned as to how this matter was handled, the more indignant I have become. We have let one of our greatest assets get away from us, and while it may be that you will find the new experience a happy and stimulating one, and I trust that you will, I think we neglected our own interest and appeared indifferent to everything that you still mean to this University.

The chancellor was being somewhat disingenuous. He was aware that Dr. Goodpasture had already received a three-year extension from the dean and the Board of Trust and had been advised that the time had come to search for a new head of the pathology department.[81] Those issues aside, Dean Youmans surely was more collegial and appreciative than indicated by the record,[82] although the dean was in an awkward position. He had to deal on the one hand with Chancellor Branscomb's concerns that the medical school was limited in the financial package that might be offered candidates for the chairmanship,[83] and on the other with the retiring of the medical school's most distinguished faculty member. In the aggregate, the university seemed clumsy and heavy-handed in its send-off for Dr. Goodpasture.[84]

We do not know how Dr. Goodpasture said good-by to his department and university. Dr. and Mrs. Ernest William Goodpasture left their calling card[85] at the chancellor's home in late June, with these notes on the back of the card in their hands:

> We just called to tell you we will be looking forward to seeing you both in Washington. We're leaving tomorrow early. Have rented a furnished house for the summer & that will give us a chance to look for more permanent arrangements. Best wishes to you both, Ernest and Katherine.
>
> We want to give you both our love and we will look forward to seeing you before long. Ernest says probably sooner than you think.
>
> Katherine G.

Chancellor Branscomb wrote on July 5, expressing regret that he had been out of town, and closing:[86]

> May I add, dear Ernest, that you are not out of the Vanderbilt family. I shall cash in on this, I am sure, from time to time when I will need desperately some objective sagacious counsel.
>
> Thank you again for your thoughtfulness in calling in the midst of all your rush of getting away. We all appreciated it more than you know.

Department of Pathology Faculty and Staff

During Dr. Goodpasture's tenure, there were sequential periods during which at least one faculty member had major responsibility for the course in pathology and for supervising the autopsy service: Dr. Eugene Woodruff from 1927 to 1935, Dr. William

DeMonbreun from 1929 to 1938, Dr. James Dawson from 1938 to 1949, and Dr. John Shapiro from 1946 through 1955. These people deserve our focused attention because of their vital role in the department activities. Also included for special consideration are Dr. John Buddingh and Dr. Charles Randall because they had extensive collaborative research programs with Dr. Goodpasture and because they were chiefly responsible for the bacteriology laboratory from 1938 to 1952.[87] Dr. Buddingh was at Vanderbilt on the faculty from 1938 until 1948, and Dr. Randall was on the faculty from 1949 until 1957. Katherine Anderson is included because she participated actively in the department research program from 1932 until 1945. This is also a logical place to pay tribute to the department secretary throughout Dr. Goodpasture's tenure, Margaret McGovern.

C. Eugene Woodruff

Woodruff was born in 1900; he came to Vanderbilt in 1927, having graduated from Yale University Medical School in 1926 and having served on the house staff there for a year. He came into the department with his wife, Dr. Alice Miles Woodruff, who had earned a Ph.D. at Yale.[88] Dr. Woodruff initially inquired about a position at Vanderbilt in a letter dated November 28, 1926. Formal application for a position was made on December 14, and Dr. Woodruff was immediately accepted probably owing to a favorable recommendation from Dr. Winternitz at Yale. In February 1927, Dr. Goodpasture was offered the opportunity to set a summer wedding date for Dr. Woodruff and "the wonderful girl who is to be my wife." Dr. Goodpasture's reply has been lost, but it must have been tactful, as Dr. Woodruff replied on March 10: "Thank you for your letter and for your offer to cooperate in the plans which my fiancee and I will have to make."

At Vanderbilt, the Woodruffs were instrumental in the development of the embryonated egg technique for viral cultures. He was recommended strongly by Dr. Goodpasture in 1939 for a position at Washington University School of Medicine: "He is a good teacher, he has a very pleasant and agreeable personality and is well versed in Pathology. He has done and is doing very creditable research." In 1935, Dr. Woodruff became director of the pathological laboratory at the George H. Maybury Sanatorium at Northville, Michigan, where they remained for the duration of his career.

William DeMonbreun

Descended from one of Nashville's earliest settlers, W. A. DeMonbreun was born in 1899 and received his M.D. from Vanderbilt in 1927. After two years as a house officer, he was appointed instructor in 1929 and remained on the staff full-time until 1938, when he became director of the pathology laboratory at the Nashville General Hospital. Dr. DeMonbreun (Fig. 4-21) was judged thusly by Dr. Goodpasture in 1939:[89] "DeMonbreun is well trained in pathological anatomy, bacteriology and clinical pathology. He has done some good investigative work. He is a hard worker, accurate, conscientious, and reliable." This recommendation is an understatement in view of the importance of the landmark paper by DeMonbreun on histoplasmosis (a fungal infection). This paper was published in 1934 in the *American Journal of Tropical Medicine* and provided a complete description of the growth requirements and morphological features of this fungus. Dr. DeMonbreun's paper was the basis for most of the early studies on this infection. Histoplasmosis was subsequently proven, in important epidemiological studies by Doctors Christie and Peterson in the Department of Pediatrics, to cause widespread infections in the Ohio River valley. Because of these

Fig. 4-21: Dr. DeMonbreun, circa 1938.

studies and Dr. DeMonbreun's work, histoplasmosis is appropriately called "the Vanderbilt disease." In terms of research contributions from the Department of Pathology, this paper probably ranks in significance just below the studies of viral propagation in the embryonated egg and discovery of the viral causation of mumps. Dr. Goodpasture concurred in this judgment in a letter to Dean Youmans in 1950 about the significant contributions from his department in the previous twenty years or so and was equally laudatory in a letter written to Dr. DeMonbreun in 1957 about the history of histoplasmosis research: "As time goes on I am constantly more impressed by the superior and classical quality of your [Dr. DeMonbreun's] work in cultivating Histoplasma capsulatum, on your demonstration of its etiological role in Histoplasmosis, and your interpretation of the importance of this disease, which has been amply proved by subsequent discoveries."[90]

Dr. "De's" salary in his last year (1937) was $3,725; he had a large family, and it was reputed that his move to Nashville General was necessary for financial reasons. The pathology house staff rotated through the laboratory there for many years, and until the end of his career there was no diminution in his attention to detail. We were impressed by the careful, handwritten descriptions of all gross specimens, including normal appendices. Dr. DeMonbreun was awarded emeritus status in 1965 and died in Nashville on December 11, 1968.

James Dawson

Born in Birmingham, Alabama, in 1908, James Robertson Dawson Jr. received his B.A. and M.D. degrees from Vanderbilt, the latter in 1931, thereby becoming the fourth generation of physicians in the Dawson family. Early in his career, he fell under Dr. Goodpasture's influence, voluntarily working on the autopsy service in the summers and throughout the junior and senior years as his schedule permitted. It was to be expected that he would remain for a residency in pathology. Upon completing his residency in 1934, he became an assistant at the Rockefeller Institute for Medical

Research under Dr. Leslie Webster, and in 1935 joined Dr. Neill (formerly professor of bacteriology at Vanderbilt) at Cornell Medical School. Dr. Goodpasture advised Dr. Dawson to take the Cornell position in a letter that also defined the goals for an academic pathologist:[91]

When we returned from Clarksville Sunday evening I found your "special" [delivery] awaiting me, consequently the late hour of my telegram.

I had heard through Jimmy Neill that you would probably be offered a place on his staff if Alloway went to China, so I was not entirely taken unaware. It seems to me as far as I can judge, that the new opportunity is a good one, and that you would profit by accepting it. It would take you back to university work with teaching and under what should be congenial surroundings. It would give you a broader background of training for whatever work you may finally engage in.

There are two things which seem to me to be particularly important in the experience of preparation for an academic career. The one is to have in mind and in purpose the particular phase of academic work most congenial, and to weigh whatever move one may make in the light of furthering that special interest. The other is to choose a particular field of investigation as soon as possible and concentrate upon it with a view to making it a life-long pursuit. It is not always possible to find one's most delectable investigative province, and the only way it can be found is by continuous work, at first preferably under different environments.

If you should have in mind making a career of pathology, the object of the preliminary years would be to get the viewpoint of bacteriology and immunology and especially to become familiar with methods, and problems you would like to investigate. If investigative work seems to offer you satisfaction and the academic life appeals to you, it is my opinion that a university is the place to live and toil.

As you know a professiorate in pathology requires long experience in pathological anatomy including surgical pathology; for a knowledge of various lesions is the result of accumulated experience, and as soon as possible you should begin the process of accumulation that can best be done in a laboratory of pathology where a diversity of material may be constantly scrutinized. But in conjunction with this, and as important or more so, is a constant and intensive program of investigation. This sometimes must be carried on at great disadvantage, although, fortunately, there are not so many hardships now as formerly. But you can never let up on investigation or you will lose interest, and it is almost impossible to bridge any considerable hiatus of investigative inactivity. So the two must go together, accumulation of experience and application to research. In bacteriology and immunology the importance of an accumulation of extensive knowledge of phenomena is not so important as in pathology, because the latter partakes more of clinical medicine.

In the Institute [Rockefeller] one cannot accumulate much pathological experience except in specific research, but is freer to follow lines of investigation. While the Institute might equip a man quite well for an academic post in bacteriology, immunology or chemistry, it does not train pathologists, except in research.

If you like bacteriology or immunology you can get better training for an academic post at a university by work in a university department, for there one keeps in touch with students and the teaching function is emphasized. But of course always there must be investigation.

I think it will be of great value to you if you go with Jimmy [Neill] to try yourself out in independent investigation. It will stretch your mind and imagination, and you can better determine your attitude toward an essential part of any academic medicine vocation.

Sarah joins me in best wishes to Margaret, and we are all looking forward to your visit this summer. After all it's fishing that counts.

Dr. Goodpasture was a strong supporter of Dr. Dawson, as evidenced by this letter to Dr. Stuart Graves at the University of Alabama in Tuscaloosa regarding a vacancy there:[92]

I regard Dr. Dawson as having an especially well rounded training and experience. He is an able young man, full of energy, a stimulating teacher and thoroughly competent in the fundamentals of Bacteriology, Pathology and Immunology. He is also capable of conducting independent research.

He is interested in making the teaching of Pathology and investigation his life's work, and I believe he has a good future and would like to see him return to the South under favorable conditions.

Although this prospect held some appeal, there was no follow-up from Dr. Graves.[93] Then in March 1938, Dr. Dawson was delighted to receive the following invitation from Dr. Goodpasture:[94]

When your letter came I was about to write you in regard to the situation here. On the first of February DeMonbreun went to the Nashville General Hospital as Director of their laboratories, and I feel sure he will do a good and much needed job there. He still retains his position on my staff, and will help us some with teaching, but his full time will practically be spent at the General Hospital.

His acceptance of this post leaves a vacancy on my staff, and I am looking for a man who has had some experience in pathological anatomy and is interested in having more. In fact I want some one who can take on much of the teaching of pathology, and in the next few years can become sufficiently experienced to assume most of the responsibility for this work. I am beginning to feel the need of a good teacher and an expert morbid anatomist on whom I can rely. From the standpoint of departmental routine this would be a first requirement, although there would be I believe ample time and encouragement for research, and I would naturally expect the incumbent of the position to be a productive investigator. I don't know how you feel now about returning to pathological anatomy, but I have been wondering whether you might be interested in this position.

The appointment would be that of an Assistant Professorship in the University and the salary would be $3,500.00 to begin with. The appointee would be in a favorable position for promotion to an Associate Professorship as his services became more valuable through experience, and as he demonstrates his ability to stand on his own feet. I want the appointment to begin July 1, 1938.

I may say that I would do all I could to make conditions as profitable and agreeable as circumstances permit.

Dr. Dawson replied immediately by accepting the position enthusiastically, with this one request: ". . . that I be given the same microscope I had before."[95]

Conditions here were agreeable, although hardly profitable in a financial sense. Although there were only two publications over the next eleven years, Dr. Dawson's other accomplishments were sufficient to obtain an appointment as chairman at the University of Minnesota in 1949. His departure was a great loss to Dr. Goodpasture, who at this time had assumed the deanship in addition to his departmental duties. The executive faculty was sufficiently moved to draft this resolution:[96]

> In accepting his resignation the Executive Faculty expressed its sense of loss in the departure of Doctor Dawson from our midst. His loyalty to Vanderbilt, his important contributions as a member of the Faculty of Medicine, and his friendly companionship will be greatly missed. The Faculty, however, in view of the recognition of his outstanding qualifications, as manifested by his appointment to so important a post, extends to him its cordial wishes for happiness and success in his new undertaking.

Dr. Goodpasture wrote this comment on the original: "This sounds too obituary but you know what we mean," and signed "Ernest."

It should have been no surprise to the University of Minnesota that Dr. Dawson's strengths were in teaching and diagnostic pathology and not in investigative work. In 1967, three years before Dr. Dawson left for the University of Mississippi, an associate wrote the following account under the title *Our Senior Educators*:[97]

> Dr. Dawson has a commitment to the concept that the chairman of a department should devote himself to the academic advancement of individuals at all levels at which the department functions. Thus he has presented the majority of the lectures to the medical students; and with the residents he has devoted a great deal of time to reviewing their autopsy material. Since a solid experience in autopsy pathology is essential for the mastery of pathology, this has provided a fundamental training few other

institutions offer. He likewise has made himself available for consultation and advice to his departmental colleagues. This has been done in an unhurried spirit of mutual exploration and with great wisdom and objectivity, so that the final result has reflected a combined effort in which Dr. Dawson's very profound intellectual capacities and extensive knowledge of medicine and pathology have made an important contribution.

Reading between the lines, this account suggests that Dr. Dawson continued to provide at Minnesota the devotion to teaching and expertise in anatomic pathology that characterized his Vanderbilt experience. His department was said to be "sturdily grounded in fundamentals," but there is not a word about research. There is some evidence that the absence of research contributions affected his standing at Minnesota with other departments, so that there were mixed reviews of his potential when Dr. Goodpasture resigned in 1955 and Dr. Dawson was being considered as his replacement.

The view of the matter from Dr. Goodpasture's side was reflected in a letter to Dr. Dawson dated 5/17/55:[98]

> Your good letter is the nicest thing that has happened to me since this retirement virus began to take affect. . . . As to the situation here I do not know very much except that a committee was appointed last fall to make recommendations. I do not know who are on the committee with two exceptions. I haven't been consulted by the committee but one member asked my opinion and I recommended you. But I judge nothing has come of it. John [Shapiro] has agreed to carry on in the interim. I wish you could come back. . . . Thank you Jim for your affectionate interest and Katherine joins me in love for you all. You will never know Jim what a comfort you were to me during sad and difficult days and always.
>
> Ernest

His return here was not to be. The search committee[99] considered seventy-five or so names and narrowed their search to Morgan Berthrong and John Shapiro, with the former withdrawing on February 13, 1956. The only written comments are that consideration of Dr. Dawson's candidacy was "deferred"[100] and he was not mentioned in the minutes thereafter.

There are very few letters from Dr. Dawson in the Goodpasture papers after 1954. In 1970, he resigned as chairman at Minnesota to become professor of pathology at the University of Mississippi, this by invitation of Dr. Joel Brunson, a former student. Dr. Dawson had six very effective years there as a teacher and consultant before retiring in 1976. He had a massive stroke and died on March 18, 1986, in Jackson, but he is buried in Calvary Cemetery in Nashville.

There are several other aspects of this story that are relevant to our understanding of Jim Dawson and of his relationship to Vanderbilt. In 1997, his widow, Margaret Geny Dawson, stated that there were few memorabilia from the Vanderbilt days—other than a single picture. This picture had remained on their bedroom wall all the years in Minnesota and in Mississippi; for that reason, Margaret had kept it in her bedroom when she returned to Nashville following Dr. Dawson's death. It turned out to be the composite of the entire Vanderbilt Medical School class of 1949, his last class in Nashville.

Although there are rumors that Dr. Dawson was somewhat chauvinistic about "women doctors," there was no mistaking his pride when he brought his granddaughter Alice Clark to interview in 1985 for admission to Vanderbilt Medical School. He died in March of her sophomore year at Vanderbilt and was not to know that she became a pathologist or that she has remained in academic medicine and is the course director of Pathology 501, the descendant of the course for which he was responsible fifty to sixty years ago. Finally, the Dawsons' first son (born in June 1935) bears the name Ernest William. Here is Dr. Goodpasture's response when informed of this honor:[101]

> The greatest compliment I have ever received is your and Margaret's willingness to name your first-born for me. Only once before have I been honored with a namesake, the fourth son of the Long family living on our farm in Montgomery Co., but as the three elder brothers were Geo. Washington, Ananias and Jesse James, respectively, I have always felt that little Ernest had an insuperable handicap to begin with. Although young

Dawson hasn't any such precedents to contend with, it is my opinion that he should have some say in the matter, and perhaps that frown is his expression of displeasure in the lack of opportunity to vote for James R. III, or a registration of opposition to the intent of his parents.

However that's between you and him, and I hereby accept him as my first grandson regardless of name, and fully expect him to be a better man than his father and grandpa combined. . . .

The two Sarahs and all the staff join me in expressions of love and best wishes for you and Margaret and *our* boy.

Outside of Vanderbilt, Dr. Dawson is best known for his work on subacute inclusion body encephalitis, a rare type of encephalitis characterized by distinctive nuclear inclusions resembling those seen in herpetic infections. He reported two cases with careful descriptions of the histopathologic changes and extensive efforts to reproduce the disease in experimental animals. Twenty-five years later, in a letter to Webb Haymaker, Dr. Dawson stated: "I would like to make it quite clear that if it had not been for Dr.

Fig. 4-22: Dr. Dawson at his desk, circa 1948.

Goodpasture, I would not have known that the inclusions were really important and that they should be reported."[102]

Inside Vanderbilt, he was known as a teacher, expert pathologist, and trusted colleague. The students called him "Lean Dog" or "Mad Dog," the latter a double or triple entendre referring in part to his work on rabies. Lean he was (Fig. 4-22), intent on his responsibilities in the department, in which he gave most of the lectures in the second-year course, supervised the autopsy service, and routinely was the principal from pathology in the clinical-pathological conferences. Other notables of his stature and rank on the Vanderbilt faculty during this period were Tinsley Harrison in Medicine, Alfred Blalock in Surgery, and Katie Dodd in Pediatrics. All of these faculty were destined for acclaim and professional recognition after leaving Vanderbilt, having made a permanent imprint on their first academic home.

It is in this academic home that we find Dr. Dawson's preeminent legacy in the year 2002; the course in pathology is remembered and treasured by virtually all students because of its high expectations, as well as for its effective introduction of the study of disease. Just as we can trace the tradition of collegiality at Vanderbilt to the plans of G. Canby Robinson, so can we trace the reputation and accomplishments of Pathology 501 to Jim Dawson.

John Shapiro

John Lawton Shapiro was born in Theta, Tennessee, in 1915; Theta is located halfway between Franklin and Columbia and remains rural in ambiance. His father ran a feed store and sold chickens on the side. His father and mother had a strong sense of values and a work ethic passed down in full measure to their son. They moved to Nashville in 1921. John attended Hume-Fogg High School and Vanderbilt University, excelling in academics and sports at both institutions. He was elected to Phi Beta Kappa at Vanderbilt, and received his M.D. degree in 1941.

John Shapiro originally intended to be a surgeon, but these plans were changed by a badly infected shrapnel wound received while he was serving as a medical officer in the Fifth Army (142nd Infantry) in the Italian campaign. After this injury, and prolonged rehabilitation, he was left with a stiff leg and a profound disdain for inept leadership.

Pathology was chosen as an alternate career. It was fortunate for Vanderbilt that he returned to his alma mater for training, which he began as a resident in pathology in 1946. His promotion record is interesting as an indicator of his value to the medical school. He held the standard coappointments as chief resident and instructor in 1950, was assistant professor of pathology from 1951 to 1952, associate professor from 1953 to 1955 (Fig. 4-23), acting chairman from 1955 to 1956, professor and head of the department from 1956 to 1971. When promoted to associate professor, he had three publications, two on arteritis (inflammation of arteries, often auto-immune in cause) and the other on Rocky Mountain Spotted Fever.

Between 1953 and 1956, when he was made head of the department, there were four more publications, two of which were case reports, one other an analysis of lung scar carcinomas, and the last a report of granulomatous lesions produced by injections of a material used in skin testing for tuberculosis.

These unusually rapid promotions are obviously attributable to factors other than the quality or quantity of publications. These factors included a "shining integrity,"[103] unparalleled loyalty to the medical school and university, and exceptional effectiveness as a teacher. Here is a portion of

Fig. 4-23: Dr. Shapiro shortly after becoming a faculty member in the pathology department.

Chancellor Branscomb's tribute at the memorial service for Dr. Shapiro in 1983:[104]

> John Shapiro was a unique and unforgettable individual. One of the good things about academic life is that it permits and probably encourages individuality and difference. We cannot claim any credit for John Shapiro, however. He would have been the same unique person in any environment.
>
> Watching John from across the campus with steadily increasing appreciation and regard, he seemed to me to possess qualities rarely found together in such strength. He was strong, but also gentle. He could be demanding, but he also had a sense of humor. He had high standards to which he held himself and others. Whatever he undertook, he committed himself to it without reservation, with, I think I might say, a kind of devotion, a devotion that made the daily tasks less daily because it gave them meaning and value. With these qualities went also a great sensitivity to the needs of others, to their struggles and suffering. And he had great team spirit. "Chancellors and Deans," as a colleague once wrote, "knew him as a source of loyalty, temperate opinion, accurate information, and wise counsel."

Fig. 4-24: Dr. Shapiro as head of the department in 1956.

As head of the department (Fig. 4-24), Dr. Shapiro instituted several programs that were badly needed for the development of the department as a service and research unit. He established at Vanderbilt one of the first cytopathology laboratories in the state and perhaps in the South. Cytopathology in 1956 seemed a poor stepchild of anatomic pathology but became an important part of cancer prevention and is now a discipline unto itself. The development of the cytopathology laboratory and the associated school for technologists has been recounted by Dr. Lily Mauricio. The details are of interest as they provide insight into Dr. Shapiro's effectiveness as head of the department:[105]

> In 1968, when I [Dr. Mauricio] started my residency in pathology at Vanderbilt, Dr. Shapiro was chairman of the department and titular head of cytology. . . . Cytology was a "step child" that no one really knew anything about. . . .
>
> The Clinical Laboratory Improvement Act of 1968 (CLIA) ruled that all pap [for Georges Papanicolaou, originator of cytology techniques] smears shall be screened by certified cytotechnologists, all atypical . . . suspicious or malignant smears shall be interpreted by pathologists, and 10 percent of "negative" pap smears shall be reviewed by pathologists as part of Quality Assurance.
>
> Buoyed by this new federal regulation, Dr. Shapiro . . . predicted that all of the "pap mills" will close down, cytology business at VUH will increase and cytology will be a major discipline in Anatomic Pathology. . . . He sought and obtained accreditation for a Cytotechnology School at VUH, a twelve-month course offered for high school graduates. . . . The only other accredited school at the time was UT Memphis. Dr. Shapiro strongly felt that certified cytotechnologists were needed in our academic setting to work with residents and to infuse the open market of private practice pathology with qualified graduates from our school. In the next twenty years, a substantial portion of graduates from our school and cytotechnologists who trained with our program were active in practice in all the major pathology groups.

Dr. Shapiro was a strong proponent for bringing a forensic pathology laboratory to Metro Nashville, a need he recognized as a citizen and as a physician. He brought the surgical pathology laboratory into the department where it belonged and thereby greatly strengthened pathology's residency training program.

Dr. Shapiro activated the M.D./Ph.D. program in pathology, enabling students doing research in the department to earn doctorates of philosophy and obtain an M.D. degree.[106] Doctors Mary

Phillips Gray and Virgil LeQuire were recruited from anatomy to establish the necessary research laboratories. He offered the expert services of the department to community hospitals in order to improve the quality of pathology in the region. All the while, he was probably the most effective teacher at Vanderbilt, and pathology was the course defining the educational process. It is interesting that he was never given a nickname by his students. The class of 1967, cloaked in the safety of a song at Cadaver Ball, made a half-hearted attempt with "Big John," but it did not take.

In short, Dr. Shapiro brought balance to the department, matching its teaching success with comparable achievements in service. The research program albeit small had a distinguished record in graduating students who are now leaders in academic medicine.

Chancellor Branscomb had these comments about Dr. Shapiro's retirement:[107] "John's last serious undertaking mirrors the character of the man. When he retired he found himself with time and an ample supply of energy. 'I found out by sitting,' he

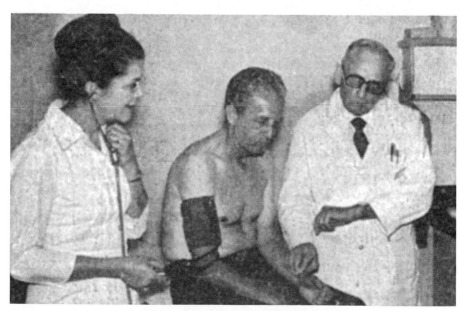

Fig. 4-25: After retirement, Dr. Shapiro worked as a volunteer in the Union Rescue Mission for the homeless.

said, 'that I can't sit.'" He proposed to the Nashville Union Rescue Mission (an institution to help the homeless and the defeated of society) that he establish for them a medical clinic. "The good Lord brought us together," was the comment of the Reverend Mr. Riesner, who directed the clinic. John volunteered his services, recruited volunteer nurses, talked local pharmacists into donating a supply of drugs, and started his clinic (Fig. 4-25). At first it operated in the kitchen of the Mission, then moved to a room built for the purpose. He ran the clinic three days per week, providing primary care for some forty patients per day.

What is the legacy of Dr. Shapiro? For a man with such a well-developed sense of humor, a man with such a strong sense of perspective, and a man so widely experienced in the frailties and foibles of humankind, it is somewhat surprising that Dr. Shapiro could take, and vigorously defend, hard-line positions on issues that at the least seemed debatable to the rest of us. Yet it was often the case that his was the only dissenting vote, his the only voice raised against an ill-conceived plan or perceived wrong. Some battles were probably not worth winning but nevertheless drew his full energy and attention. His conversations, exhortations, and explicatory comments were often laced with rather pithy challenges: "Fish or cut bait," "No shady deals," or "To the barricades." Students and residents might feel these comments were focused on straightening them out, but in fact they were applied up and down the line, to colleagues and superiors as well. Life was harder for him, for his friends, and for his family because he refused to back down when he felt steps were being taken to diminish the quality of student education or the integrity of the university.

John Shapiro was wholly committed to the educational process in its broadest sense. The imparting of information was just the beginning of the responsibilities he assumed; he was determined to shape the graduate in demeanor and ethos as well. One may well ask in these times when polish often seems more valuable than substance, if these are not the proper goals for a university and its medical school. Dr. Shapiro's legacy to this medical school and university was to demonstrate by example that loyalty, integrity, and commitment may be taught and learned.

John Buddingh

Born in 1904 in the Netherlands, he came to this country at age three with his parents. He was reared in Michigan, received his A.B. degree from Calvin College in Grand Rapids in 1929, and entered Vanderbilt Medical School in the fall of that year. In 1933, after completing the third year, John became a research associate in the Department of Pathology, a post he held for two years. After the M.D. degree was awarded in 1935, he entered the residency program in pathology and steadily progressed up the academic ladder at Vanderbilt, becoming professor of bacteriology in 1946. Fortunately there was time in 1941 to marry Alice Mitchell of Nashville, then an assistant secretary in the Department of Pathology. In 1948 he was named professor and head of the Department of Microbiology at Louisiana State University and senior visiting scientist in the Department of Pathology, positions he held until 1974. Dr. Buddingh died in New Orleans in 1976.

Fig. 4-26: Dr. Buddingh in laboratory. Typical laboratory equipment of the time is shown.

John was fortunate to take pathology and also get a full dose of Dr. Goodpasture's influence in 1931, just as the chick embryo technique was being announced. He had a paper in *Science* in 1931 and another in the *American Journal of Pathology* in 1932, both coauthored with Dr. Goodpasture and Alice Woodruff, on vaccinal infection of the chorioallantoic membranes; there were three more with Dr. Goodpasture by graduation in 1935. Then as an independent investigator (Fig. 4-26), with many collaborators, he published another thirty papers during his Vanderbilt tenure dealing with the effects of various viral and bacterial agents on the chick embryo. Perhaps his most impressive accomplishment during this period was the vigor and competence he brought to the use of chick embryos for the culture of vaccinia. Through this study the Vanderbilt group standardized this important vaccine and took it through successful field trials.

At Louisiana State University School of Medicine Dr. Buddingh excelled in the trilogy of teaching, research, and service.[108] Of all his accomplishments there, perhaps the one most reflective of his roots in Nashville was the custom of regularly having small groups of medical students and wives in the Buddingh home on Sunday evenings for coffee, guidance, and friendship.

Charles Randall

Born in Cedar Rapids, Iowa, in 1913, he obtained a B.S. degree in chemistry at the University of Kentucky in 1936 and an M.D. degree from Vanderbilt University in 1940. He served in the Army from 1941 to 1945, with the last three years as chief of the Bacteriology Service of the Fourth Medical Laboratory, which was stationed in North Africa and France. Dr. Randall returned to Vanderbilt in 1946 as a resident in pathology and then as a postdoctoral fellow in the laboratories of Doctors Goodpasture and Buddingh. In 1949 he joined the pathology faculty as instructor with rapid promotion up the professorial ladder to associate professor of bacteriology in 1952 and in 1955 to professor of microbiology and acting head of the recently established Department of Microbiology.

Fig. 4-27: Dr. Randall, circa 1955.

Dr. Randall became professor and chairman of the Department of Microbiology at the University of Mississippi in Jackson in 1957, a position he held until retirement in 1978. He was very successful in this position as an academician and remained productive in the laboratory. In particular, his group made significant contributions to understanding the biology of two viral diseases initially studied at Vanderbilt— equine abortion and fowlpox. These studies often reflected his early training in histopathology as well as in virology, as he is one of the few virologists to correlate morphologic changes in cultured cells with biochemical changes. Dr. and Mrs. Randall currently reside in Jackson, Mississippi.

In 1950, the recently developed technique of tissue culture was successfully brought to Vanderbilt by Dr. Randall (Fig. 4-27). Fifty years later he provided this description of the birth of tissue culture at Vanderbilt:[109]

Shortly after joining the faculty [in 1949], I approached Dr. Goodpasture with the idea of cultivating viruses in tissue culture, and in preparation for this effort, enrolling in a formal course taught at the hospital in Cooperstown, New York. It was known as a research oriented institution. Clinton VanZant Hahn was head of the pathology department there and a strong supporter of the enterprise.

Dr. Goodpasture, after learning the details, was my sponsor and a strong supporter of my ambition and he was kind enough to offer financial support for my maintenance at Cooperstown which extended over a period of several weeks. . . . The faculty comprised most of the leading exponents of the art. From my ancient memory those that I recall best were Dr. George Gey, Milton Earle, and John Hanks.

The laboratory work where we learned the techniques of tissue fragment culture, plasma clot and individual suspended cell culture, and staining techniques was conducted on standard lab benches. Each individual had the requisite equipment for the various exercises. After appropriate demonstrations, we prepared media and tissues, washed and sterilized glassware etc. Our success in obtaining appropriate culture was critical and repeated if necessary. Finally, each participant was required to give a seminar on the application of tissue culture to a proposed research project.

At Vanderbilt, in the Department of Pathology, with the partial aid of a research grant from the Grayson Foundation, a tissue culture lab was organized and graduate students were trained in the various techniques which they applied to individual thesis research. To mention a few students: Dorothy Turner, E. V. Bracken, Fred Ryden and Glenn Gentry.

Dr. Goodpasture lent strong support to our efforts and I recall his interest and enthusiasm in personally observing the results obtained by various tissue culture methods. [In a personal communication, Dr. Randall remembered that Dr. Goodpasture routinely checked on the progress of this laboratory, often enthusiastically commenting: "This is the future!"]

Katherine Anderson

Katherine's full name was Frances Katherine Anderson, the name by which she registered at Vanderbilt University in the fall of 1928. She came from Williamsport, Tennessee, a small community on the Duck River twelve miles to the west of Columbia. At Vanderbilt, an overall distinguished undergraduate record including grades of As in bacteriology, led

Fig. 4-28: Katherine Anderson in her laboratory, circa 1938.

to her election to Phi Beta Kappa as a junior. Majoring in biology with minors in mathematics and chemistry, she graduated magna cum laude, ranking eighth in a class of 168 with a grade point average of 2.522—when As were really As.

Katherine worked as an assistant in the Department of Pathology from 1932 to 1936. This may well have been her first paying job. During this time her assistance of Doctors Goodpasture and Buddingh was acknowledged in one of their publications on smallpox vaccine.

Katherine became a candidate for a Ph.D. in bacteriology under the tutelage of Dr. Goodpasture in September 1936 (Fig. 4-28). Her thesis was titled "Variation in Viruses" and dealt with the changes that occurred in viruses under natural and experimental conditions. Such changes were an important topic, key to an understanding of viral infection in general, to the development of vaccines, and to the establishment of methods for their diagnosis. After a thorough review of the literature, her thesis covered three years of experimental work in which she compared the pattern of infection of herpes virus in chick embryos and in rabbits. Detailed experiments were required to establish this pattern and to document a variation in the virus. As an example of her persistence, it was only after the virus had been passed twenty-five times that a change was detected in the viral effect in chick embryos and subsequently in rabbits. Katherine then showed how the altered strain

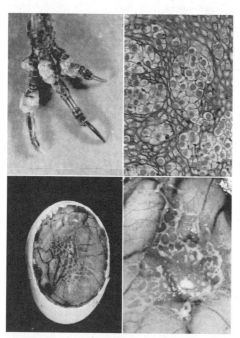

Fig. 4-29: Plate from the Goodpastures' last publication showing lesions (pocks) on foot of junco, lesions on chorioallantoic membrane, and microscopic of inclusions.

still produced immunity in rabbits and might be useful as a vaccine. The essence of this work was published in *Science* in 1939 in a paper carrying her name alone.

As a member of one of the premier pathology departments in the country, she was very productive. Fifteen papers were published from 1937 to 1945. Particularly notable were those in *Science* and the *Journal of Experimental Medicine* with Doctors DeMonbreun and Goodpasture on the cause of granuloma inguinale, a common infection of the time, in which Katherine was the first to isolate the agent. She also showed with Dr. DeMonbreun that dogs were natural hosts for histoplasmosis; this was at a time when histoplasmosis was first recognized as an important infection in this part of the country.

Katherine wrote no papers in the medical field in the years 1945–62, years during which she had assumed important new roles as Dr. Goodpasture's wife; they married five years after the death of Sarah Catlett Goodpasture. Now Katherine had responsibilities as wife of a distinguished chairman of pathology and a member of the Goodpasture family.

However, there was to be one more virology paper—their last—published in April 1962 in the *American Journal of Pathology*. It was titled "Isolation of a Wild Avian Pox Virus Inducing Both Cytoplasmic and Nuclear Inclusions" and was authored by Ernest W. Goodpasture and Katherine Anderson. The research team that was so productive in the 1940s was back in action. Their experiments began with a slate-colored junco trapped in Jackson, Mississippi, on January 17, 1960. Warty nodules on both feet were sampled before the bird was released in good condition. Their paper began with a brief statement outlining the significance of finding both cytoplasmic and nuclear inclusions in this infection.[110] Then we come to this sentence: "In the course of trapping and banding wild birds, a wintering slate-colored junco with warty nodules on all the toes of both feet, reminiscent of infection with fowlpox virus, was trapped in Jackson, Mississippi." It seems particularly appropriate that these two scientists with such complementary abilities should have trapped that particular bird shortly before they returned home to Nashville in the spring. Dr. Goodpasture and Katherine were able to pass the virus serially on chick membranes, and they initiated studies on the nature of the nuclear inclusions (Fig. 4-28). The analysis of this infection was almost completed in the three months remaining before Dr. Goodpasture died on September 20, 1960. A year later Katherine had this, their last paper, finished and accepted by the *American Journal of Pathology*. She cited Bill Cheatham's help in the preparation of this manuscript.

Fortunately, notebooks describing this joint research activity have been preserved. These are among the very few laboratory notebooks extant that were used by Dr. Goodpasture.[111] A two-ring notebook (labeled 8/27/60, Book 3) contains descriptions of experiments performed over the summer of 1960, including the last notes made by Dr. Goodpasture. In addition there are three small spiral notebooks, each costing fifteen cents, that are priceless in that they describe the daily conduct of their research in the winter of 1959 and 1960. Book number one is labeled Jackson, Mississippi, and bears Dr. Goodpasture's name; it contains daily notations about their research, speculations, and literature surveys. Book number two is labeled VU 1960; beginning on May 7 and continuing until August 30, 1960, various research activities at Vanderbilt were described. Both of these books contain marginal notes by Katherine in which specific information is given about handling of individual specimens. A third spiral notebook is unlabeled; in this book both Katherine and Dr. Goodpasture made entries. This third book has an extensive description by Katherine of the trapping of the junco and has many entries corresponding to those made by Dr. Goodpasture in book number one.

Katherine finished these experiments over the next two months. Her first note after Dr. Goodpasture's death was dated October 11, 1960, and the last experiment was dated November 5.

Margaret McGovern

Miss Margaret E. McGovern came to Vanderbilt in August or September of 1925 and was the chief secretary in the Department of

Fig. 4-30: Margaret McGovern, circa 1938.

Pathology for thirty years. She applied by letter on August 21, 1925:

Dr. Goodpasture, c/o Vanderbilt University, Medical Department, Nashville, Tennessee

Dear Sir: I heard today through a friend of mine that you needed a stenographer, and I hereby offer you my services. I am not a young woman, but my health is excellent. I have not been absent from my work for one day on account of illness. Yours very truly.

This letter[112] was unsigned and was not initialed, but the address of 610 Fatherland typed on the letter was Miss McGovern's address in 1925.[113]

She was thirty-one when she applied for a position in 1925. By 1930 she had moved closer to work, living at 1912 Grand Avenue. Her office was in the hallway adjacent to that of Dr. Goodpasture. With good spirit and competence, she (Fig. 4-30) managed virtually all of the departmental correspondence, filing, and typing of autopsy reports as the main secretary from 1925 until 1955.

Miss McGovern retired in 1955 and continued to live in the Nashville area until her death on January 15, 1986.[114]

Chapter Five

DEAN

D r. Goodpasture accepted the appointment as dean on July 1, 1945; he had also served as associate dean since February 1, 1943. The precise division of labor between dean and associate dean in 1943–45 is difficult to assess, and Dr. Goodpasture may have had only a backup role during these two years, as *Executive Faculty Minutes* and other major documents bear Dean Leathers's signature until June 30, 1945 (Fig. 5-1). Dr. Goodpasture's resignation as dean was accepted in January 1950, and the reins of office were handed to John Youmans in March 1950. During those seven years of responsibility in the dean's office, Dr. Goodpasture retained the title and duties as head and professor of pathology.

The rationale for his appointment as dean is partially documented. Chancellor Branscomb in his autobiography[1] states that Dr. Goodpasture "had been persuaded to accept the deanship as a service to the school," while Esmond Long concluded:[2]

> In Goodpasture's later years at Vanderbilt, the exigencies of time and
> circumstance forced him into administrative work. He had little love for
> this, in comparison with his feeling for teaching and research, but his

outstanding position on the Vanderbilt faculty and his own strong sense of loyalty to the school made it inevitable that he would accept the deanship at a critical time. . . . It was an unselfish labor with little obvious reward for one with Goodpasture's taste and talent for research, but one in which he felt a moral responsibility in the light of his long identification with the medical school.

There certainly was no more time for research. Three papers already in the pipeline on granuloma inguinale were published in 1945, but it was thirteen years before he published another research article. It is saddening to see the pictures of him as dean (Fig. 5-2) and to realize that there were no reasonable alternatives to his appointment. Conkin states without documentation that "Goodpasture was sick at heart from the endless strain of seeking money, from skimping on budgets, and from watching his ablest faculty leave for better paying jobs."[3] There may be some hyperbole in this analysis because Dr. Goodpasture's wry humor persists in correspondence. In a letter to Granville Bennett dated April 3, 1946, responding to an inquiry regarding the suitability of Tinsley Harrison as a candidate for the deanship at the University of Illinois, Dr. Goodpasture noted:[4] "Doctor Harrison during the past several years has had considerable experience in administering two schools of medicine, and judging from my own feelings at the present time I should think he would have had enough of it but you can never tell."

Conkin in *Gone with the Ivy* criticizes the university for the appointment of Dr. Goodpasture as dean:

> Why is hard to explain. He had rejected a deanship at the Johns Hopkins [actually, the Professorship in Pathology] in 1942 and already had the highest professorial salary at Vanderbilt ($11,000). He was, by the war, the most honored scientist in the South and a member of the National Academy of Sciences (an honor not yet achieved by anyone else in the College). Administrative duties now diverted him from his research and proved personally unrewarding. His talents clearly lay elsewhere. Once again, in an old pattern, Vanderbilt asked its ablest scholars and scientists to take on administrative duties.[5]

Fig. 5-1: Dean Leathers and his faculty in 1936. From left are Doctors Cunningham, Lamson, Goodpasture, Burch, C. S. Robinson, Garrey, Casparis, Leathers, Morgan, and Brooks.

Positions at the level of dean are filled now only after extensive searches and generation of numerous documents. There is no such correspondence in Chancellor Carmichael's papers and no evidence that a search committee was formed. Dr. Goodpasture's papers contain very little specific information about his rationale for assuming the responsibilities of dean, or his state of mind when he resigned from the deanship. There is this note on July 18, 1945, to his friend Sidney Burwell, then dean at Harvard:[6]

> Many thanks for your words of encouragement. All such are grate-fully received and deeply needed. The times are critical and the work is important. It would give me a great deal of satisfaction to be of help. It is not difficult for one to envision a constructive program but the impediments to execution are at the present largely beyond control; however, we hope for better times.

At the end of his tenure as dean, on March 3, 1950, Dr. Goodpasture wrote his good friend Sam Clark to thank him for his support and help:[7] "It has given me a sense of confidence and comfort to know that I could count on you at all times for an unbiased appraisal of problems which it was our duty to solve." This was Dr. Clark's reply:

> Your note expressing appreciation for my efforts as Associate Dean was a pleasant surprise. The privilege of working with you and having thereby a closer acquaintance with you has been an experience I value highly. To be along as you kept a straight course through many perplexing difficulties has been inspiring. You have accomplished so much as Dean, and have given so freely of your time and energies and wisdom, Vanderbilt will continue to be a better school because of your work. Thank you for letting me be near enough to see it, and to enjoy the association with you as a person as well.

Lest we judge the university too harshly in relationship to Dr. Goodpasture's appointment as dean, 1945–50 was a difficult period for universities and governments around the world. After all, there had been a war on, and most civil societies had been seriously disrupted by wartime exigencies. Basic research in this country was nonexistent and would obviously not recover for a decade or so. It appears from this distance in time that Dr. Goodpasture, after reviewing the future of research and his duties as a citizen and faculty member, put duty, loyalty, and university first. Furthermore, it is my perspective that he never regretted the decision.

Fig. 5-2: Dean Goodpasture is shown in his office in the pathology department. The large stack of papers is presumably his "in-box." The picture on his desk shows daughter Sarah and granddaugters Sarah and Susan. The picture on wall at left is of Jim Dawson. The etching of Pasteur partially visible to the right now hangs in Eskind Library, Special Collections.

RESPONSIBILITIES OF DEAN,
VANDERBILT SCHOOL OF MEDICINE

The current job description[8] for the dean of Vanderbilt University Medical Center states that the dean is the chief academic officer; that the dean is responsible for providing the leadership and vision to ensure integration and continued development of its missions; that the dean must have an earned M.D., have experience in administration and leadership, have demonstrated financial skills as well as scholarly achievements of national interest, and finally have made significant contributions to the medical literature.

There is a more detailed job description for the dean in the bylaws for the School of Medicine presented to the executive faculty by Chancellor Branscomb on March 9, 1962. In presenting this document, the chancellor commented that he had followed the "conclusions and, so far as possible, the wording of a report on this subject presented to the executive faculty by an ad hoc committee chaired by Doctor Shapiro."[9] That committee had been appointed to "explore expressed discontent concerning administrative relationships within the School of Medicine,"[10] a frank censure of Dean John Patterson's working relationships with the executive faculty. In Conkin's analysis, Dean Patterson administered efficiently but "ruled arbitrarily."[11] The ad hoc committee "after deliberation, had decided that the major problems were: the provision of means for expression of faculty opinion concerning policies of the school; clarification of administrative practices; and a definition of the composition of the executive faculty."

This committee offered operational bylaws for the School of Medicine that were accepted in large measure by the chancellor and Board of Trust. So, these bylaws written in 1962 provide the first detailed job description of the dean of Vanderbilt Medical School:[12]

Section V. THE APPOINTMENT AND DUTIES OF THE DEAN

The Dean is elected to his office by the Board of Trust of the university upon recommendation of the Chancellor. The Chancellor may seek the advice of a representative committee of the School of Medicine but the decision in this matter is his responsibility.

The Dean is the administrative head of the School. Among his duties are the following: a. He shall enforce all rules and regulations of the university and of the School of Medicine. b. He shall, with the assistance of the Faculty as indicated below, make recommendations to the Chancellor for appointments to the Faculty and promotions within it. c. He shall prepare the annual budget of the School, and be responsible to the Chancellor and the Board of Trust for all financial matters concerning the School. d. He shall assign space which is available for the use of the School of Medicine to the departments and divisions. e. He shall serve as the official channel of communication concerning the affairs of the School. f. He shall appoint all standing committees of the School. g. He shall appoint acting chairmen for departments when this becomes necessary. h. He shall recommend to the Chancellor such assistant Deans as may be necessary to discharge the duties of the Dean's Office.

In discharging his responsibilities, it is clearly recognized that the Dean may wish to seek advice and counsel from the faculty.

In clause b. in these bylaws there is a hook—the phrase "with the assistance of the Faculty as indicated below" actually meant that tenure appointments were to be made by a Committee on Tenure Appointments and Promotions, a committee constituted *by the chancellor and not the dean*.[13] Such an unusual arrangement severely limited the authority of the dean, so it is not surprising that Dean Patterson resigned shortly afterwards. However, these 1962 bylaws do provide a reasonable description of the duties of Dr. Goodpasture as dean, with the exception that he (and his predecessors) largely controlled the faculty appointment process (Table 5-1). He was aided and undoubtedly comforted during the deanship[14] by his good friend and confidante Sam Clark, who served as associate dean.

TROUBLED TIMES, 1945–50

It would be interesting to know if Dean Goodpasture attempted to sort the problems he faced into major and minor categories, or if he sorted problems by whether they were curable. In any case, he would have to contend with the following issues. World War II left university medical centers short of staff and seriously overworked. The pervasive and deleterious effects of inflation were just becoming apparent. Vanderbilt University was in the process of changing chancellors. The medical school and hospital had an archaic accounting system. Both medical school and hospital had been chronically underfunded for at least a decade. Staffing of support services (nursing, housecleaning, laboratory) in the hospital was particularly problematic. There had been inadequate maintenance of plant and equipment in the medical center for at least a decade. The administrative lines of responsibility between the chancellor and the dean of the medical school were not clear. The endowment provided the sole financial underpinning of the medical school and hospital, and no longer kept pace with needs and inflation. These were some of the major problems that he faced on July 1, 1945, and that persisted throughout his tenure.

Before we begin our analysis of these troubled times, a brief comment about the incompleteness of available records is in order. It is surprising that the official records of the university and the medical school, namely the minutes of the Board of Trust and those of the executive faculty, do not describe more precisely the problems and solutions under discussion. Unfortunately, these minutes leave much to the imagination, and we are dependent on correspondence for details, with the hope that crucial letters have not been lost or misfiled. Consider the *Executive Faculty Minutes* signed by Dr. Goodpasture on January 19, 1949. The subjects under discussion at this meeting were perhaps the weightiest and most distressing topics ever pondered by that

A CATALOGUE

—OF—

Tennesseana
Page 2

Americana
Page 5

Negro and Slavery
Page 15

Most of these Books we are offering at
reduction of from 20 to 50 per cent....

From the Second-hand Stock of

GOODPASTURE BOOK CO.

511 Church St., Nashville, Tenn.

We have catalogued only such books as we think will give
satisfaction. Prices do not include carriage.

Plate 1. Goodpasture Book Company catalogue.

Plate 2. Ernest in 1896.

Plate 3. Dr. Goodpasture circa 1958.

Plate 4. Ernest Goodpasture upon graduation from Vanderbilt in 1907.

Plate 5. Diploma from Johns Hopkins School of Medicine, 1912.

Plate 6. Osler's *Practice of Medicine* used at Hopkins by Ernest Goodpasture.

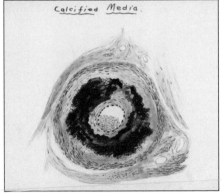

Plate 7. Sketch of atherosclerotic vessel prepared by Ernest Goodpasture while a second-year student at Hopkins.

Plate 8. Lieutenant Junior Grade Goodpasture in uniform at Chelsea Naval Hospital, circa 1918. While at Chelsea, Dr. Goodpasture was in the midst of the influenza pandemic.

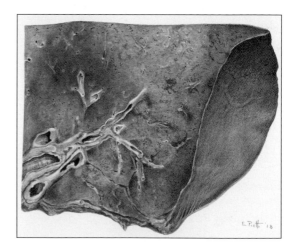

Plate 9. This drawing (from Burnet and Goodpasture, *U.S. Naval Bulletin*, 13:177–197, 1919) shows abnormalities in the lung caused by influenza. This disease was extensively studied during 1918 and 1919 by Dr. Goodpasture. His prediction that influenza was a viral infection was confirmed about ten years later.

Plate 10: Dinner menu and program for the last night on board ship when the Goodpastures were on their way home from Vienna in 1925.

Plate 11. This photograph of Dr. Goodpasture was taken around 1945.

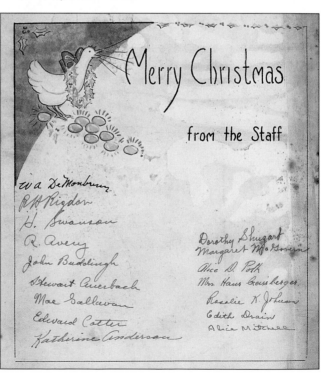

Plate 12. A hand-made Christmas card from the staff of the Vanderbilt Department of Pathology. This card probably dates from 1937 as it carries the names of faculty and staff shown in the picture of the department made in that year. See Figure 4-18.

Plate 13. Dr. Goodpasture as a young professor at Vanderbilt.

Goodpasture

THE JOURNAL

OF

EXPERIMENTAL MEDICINE

EDITED BY

SIMON FLEXNER, M.D.   PEYTON ROUS, M.D.

VOLUME 59, No. 1   JANUARY 1, 1934

Plate 14. The *Journal of Experimental Medicine*, front cover. This issue bearing his signature contained the article by Johnson and Goodpasture describing the discovery of the cause of mumps. This work was obviously treasured by him as this is the only such signed journal in his memorabilia.

Plate 15. Wisteria Cottage at Monteagle, as painted by Dr. Goodpasture.

Plate 16. Cabin, Basin Spring.

Plate 17. Creek, Basin Spring.

Plate 18. Naturalist and snapping turtle, somewhere in Tennessee. The chelonian ancestor of this snapping turtle (*Chelydra sepentina*) appeared in the fossil record in the Jurassic Period that extended from 135 to 195 million years ago. A drought or the search for new territory may have forced the migration that led to the roadside encounter of this snapper with an informed and cautious naturalist. Much older fossils from the 500 million year old Ordovician Period may be found in the limestone bed under Basin Spring.

Plate 19. Flowers, Basin Spring. After the last Ice Age, deciduous forests emerged in the central basin of Tennessee atop a floor of limestone, shale, and sandstone of earlier eras. It provided the humus that supports wildflowers at Basin Spring like this celandine poppy (*Stylophorum diphyllum*) above and white baneberry (*Actaea pachypoda*) below. The observation and study of the biodiversity and interdependence of the ecological systems of Basin Spring were a continuous source of pleasure for Katherine and Ernest Goodpasture. The legends for plates 21 and 22 were kindly provided by Dr. Joseph A. Little III, Dr. Goodpasture's grandson.

Plate 20. Portrait of Dr. Goodpasture painted by Martin Kellogg. Now in 208 Light Hall, Vanderbilt Medical Center.

Plate 21. Goodpasture home from 1922 to 1924 in Sewickley, Pennsylvania, as of 1997.

Plate 22. Goodpasture home at 408 Fairfax Avenue in Nashville, circa 1930.

Plate 23. Goodpasture headstone, Greenwood Cemetery, Clarksville, Tennessee. Site of graves of Sarah Catlett and Ernest William Goodpasture.

group: the future of the medical school and how the chronic financial crisis might be resolved. However, the *Executive Faculty Minutes* simply read as follows: "The Dean stated that the chief object of the meeting was to discuss the future policy with reference to the School of Medicine. A full discussion followed. There being no further business the meeting was adjourned." The subjects discussed become evident only through follow-up letters to Dr. Goodpasture from Doctors Sam

---

Table 5-1
Life of a Dean

COMMITTEE ASSIGNMENTS

Standing Committees
Executive Faculty
Dean's Committee, Veterans Administration Hospital
Admissions
Instruction
Scientific Publications
Hospital Committee of Medical Faculty
Medical Library
Nursing Services

Ad Hoc
1945 Search committee to replace Dr. Leathers, Preventive Medicine
Search committee to replace Dr. Burch, Obstetrics and Gynecology
Search committee to replace Dr. Garrey, Physiology
Committee to review affairs of the Department of Medicine
1947 Search committee to replace Dr. Millikan, Physiology

Clark, Lamson, Luton, and Pilcher,[15] letters that are covered in more detail in the section "Financial Crisis."

In the Board of Trust meeting of February 7, 1949, the proposal of Dean Goodpasture to abolish the undergraduate medical curriculum was deliberated and rejected. The discussion[16] was summarized in a letter as follows from Chancellor Branscomb to Dean Goodpasture: "The Board discussed at length your proposal for the establishment of a research institute. They were both interested and appreciative, and there were repeated expressions of admiration for the objectives and general tone in which you had stated this proposal. Every one wanted to do it. The Board, however, passed the following resolution: RESOLVED: That the Board of Trust appreciates the position taken by Dean Goodpasture; that it feels the research program which he has outlined represents an important contribution; that it believes, however, if possible such a program should be worked out in connection with a four-year medical school."

Imprecise Administrative Arrangements

Before there were vice-chancellors and we had only deans, as in 1945, the superintendent of Vanderbilt Hospital, Mr. Clarence Connell, reported directly to the chancellor.[17] It is paradoxical that one of the two major headaches for Dr. Goodpasture, the burgeoning hospital deficit, was on paper the hospital superintendent's problem. The second, the burgeoning deficit of the medical school, was unequivocally the problem of the dean. Both were equally difficult to remedy and had similar causes, as discussed below under "Financial Crisis." Together, these financial problems ultimately led to Dr. Goodpasture's resignation as dean in 1950. Mr. Connell was an engineer, retained from the time of hospital construction, who was not trained as a hospital administrator. He and Dr. Goodpasture were quickly in over their heads in terms of hospital management.

Tables of organization not withstanding, the dean was responsible for submitting the budgets of Vanderbilt Hospital,[18] and Dean Goodpasture was the chief target of the chancellor's concerns, directions, and interventions relating to affairs of the hospital and medical school. On January 5, 1948,[19] Chancellor Branscomb informed Dean Goodpasture (with a copy to Clarence Connell) that:

> The Board of Trust meets February 2. I am sure they will want to give a good deal of time to the problems of the School of Medicine. . . . The Trustees are sure to ask questions concerning the School of Medicine as regards enrollment, its financial condition, with reference to the budget adopted, the average census of the hospital, the financial condition of the latter, and they should be told of any important developments, such as the establishment of the Department of Psychiatry . . . Last year I spoke to you with reference to meeting with the Board of Trust and discussing our problems with them. Would you care to do this at the February meeting? If not, I certainly would be glad to have you appear in June.

Dean Goodpasture took his medicine in February, when he must have undergone a high-level grilling on these various topics. *The Board of Trust Minutes* of June 1948[20] are an example of the distress and storm flags that were flying during this period from Kirkland Hall (site of chancellor's office), and the close supervision [budgets were subject to review every ninety days and "strict budgetary control"] was a clear warning to Dean Goodpasture:

> The financial condition of the School of Medicine and the Medical Hospital continues to constitute the Number One financial problem of the administration. . . . Against this budget of $617,649.18 [for the year 1948–49] we have available estimated income of $447,021.28, leaving a contemplated deficit of $170,627.90. According to present estimates the only way to cover this deficit is by drawing on all available reserves of the Medical School and Hospital remaining. These should be just about sufficient to cover the deficit on June 30, 1949. It should be pointed out and emphasized that the budgetary operations of the medical school and hospital are undertaken for this year with the definite understanding that they will be subject to review every ninety days to determine if income realized is equaling estimated income and with a view to keeping expenditures under strict budgetary control.

The ambiguities of the command structure of the hospital were exacerbated in July 1948 when Dr. Henry Clark became director (not superintendent as was the case with Clarence Connell). Dr. Clark clearly reported directly to the chancellor, in terms of hospital reorganization,[21] concerning problems with personnel, including the hospital superintendent,[22] and concerning problems with faculty, including heads of departments.[23] Chancellor Branscomb defined[24] the duties of Dr. Clark as: "The Director will be responsible for the administration of the University Hospital. On matters of finance and over-all policies, especially as these may affect the relations of the University to the public, you would be responsible directly to the Chancellor's Office. In relation to Medical School policies, you would be responsible to the Dean of the Vanderbilt Medical School."

In practical terms, the closely integrated functions and problems of the medical school and hospital meant that Dean Goodpasture was assumed by the chancellor and the medical school faculty to be responsible for both organizations. However, Dr. Clark during his tenure routinely communicated directly to the chancellor on issues ranging from financial matters to hospital policies and personnel, the latter including medical school faculty. Between July 22 and November 8, 1948, there are eleven letters on file[25] from Dr. Clark to Chancellor Branscomb. Copies of most of these letters are present in Dean Goodpasture's files, and others were undoubtedly shared with him in the hospital committee, executive faculty meetings, or informally.

The command structure of the hospital was changed in 1962 to address some of these ambiguities. The 1962 bylaws state for the first time that there will be a Vice-Chancellor for Medical Affairs.[26] While Chancellor Branscomb did not precisely define the relationship between dean and vice-chancellor, the latter is now responsible for the joint operations of the medical school, nursing school, and hospital, and presumably had these same responsibilities in 1962 as well. The Shapiro Committee summarized the working relationships as follows: "Under the direction of the Chancellor of the University and the Vice Chancellor for Medical Affairs of the University, the Dean shall be the administrative head of the School of Medicine."[27]

Financial Crisis

Overview

Even fifty years later, the financial crisis of the medical school and hospital in the 1945–50 period is alarming (Table 5-2). The treasurer's report of the university for 1945[28] contains the first hint of impending trouble: "The School of Medicine also had a satisfactory surplus to carry into its reserve account. . . . Only the Hospital income, even though increased substantially over that of last year, was not sufficient to cover the heavy increase in expenses. It was necessary to take from the Hospital reserve account the sum of $90,069.05 to cover the deficit in its operations."

In 1946, the report noted that "The Hospital sustained a loss of $79,149.42 on the year's operation which was drawn from its reserve account. The loss was less than the budgeted deficit, but the heavy drain of the last two years has practically depleted the hospital reserve. The budget for the fiscal year ending June 30, 1947 carries a contemplated deficit of $150,121.01. The situation is quite alarming." By 1948, deficits had reduced the combined reserves by $281,000, leaving only $30,458. A special reserve fund, derived from income on $1.5 million donated by the General Education Board for completion of the "new" (D) wing of the hospital, was also reduced from $139,015 to $16,074. Combined, the deficits of the medical school and hospital in the three-year period of 1946–48 totaled more than $400,000, reducing the reserves at the end of the 1948 fiscal year to $46,522. The combined budgets for those years totaled approximately $5.3 million.

With this rate of loss, it is doubtful that the Board of Trust would have authorized covering additional deficits by expending endowment principal, or would have launched an emergency capital gifts campaign to save the medical school. The term *reserves*, for those not fiscally inclined, might be viewed as a savings account at the local bank, with the exception that this bank (Board of Trust) did not pay interest and would not tolerate overdrafts. By 1949, the operating loss of the medical school of $71,260 was covered by profit in the hospital of $108,515, and the hospital reserve received

Table 5-2
Budgets 1940, 1945–1952

Medical School Budgets 1940, 1945–1952

	1940	1945	1946	1947
Income	519,346	551,763	534,800	576,944
Expenses	519,218	533,599	563,099	653,601
Tuition	79,151	120,236	86,495	95,216
Endowment	288,581	311,805	315,167	312,489
Reserves*	6,580	214,679	197,010	120,716

Hospital Budgets 1940, 1945–1952

	1940	1945	1946	1947
Income	567,550	715,305	818,020	1,073,192
Expenses	655,834	805,374	897,169	1,131,581
Receipts-patients	208,646	426,119	518,870	785,468
Endowment	298,703	268,382	285,066	282,654
Reserves*	78,229	101,661	18,602	0
Balance, special fund**	139,015	139,015	139,015	93,341

*Reserves should be viewed as non-interest bearing savings account, derived from previous surpluses

the balance. Mr. A. B. Benedict as treasurer concluded on June 30, 1949: "The position of the School of Medicine and the Hospital is less critical at this time than it was a year ago due, as shown above, to the better results of the Hospital operation. If this experience can be continued, and it would seem that it might, we shall be much less concerned about the medical school set-up after the next year."

By 1950, the hospital was clearly running in the black, generating a surplus of $169,682 which was used to offset a continued deficit in the medical school of $114,269. At this point, the decision was

1948	1949	1950	1951	1952
659,063	709,435	712,015	964,182	1,075,103
749,496	780,695	826,284	894,212	998,645
109,923	135,044	137,966	144,018	193,385
316,279	314,483	316,522	512,982	512,343
30,458	0	0	69,431	145,498

1948	1949	1950	1951	1952
1,216,805	1,551,991	1,806,597	1,907,042	2,206,395
1,294,072	1,443,475	1,636,914	1,941,167	2,209,918
926,378	1,262,747	1,493,859	1,730,695	2,004,309
285,660	284,062	285,662	112,577	112,575
0	14,920	73,006	38,870	35,346
16,074	106,409	106,409	106,409	106,409

**This balance derived from a $1.5 million grant for building the D wing of the hospital in 1937. The figures in the endowment row show income derived from the endowment.

made to use most of the restricted endowment for the medical school rather than split the payout between medical school and hospital (Please refer to table 5-2), thereby enabling the former to climb out of its financial hole and place $69,431 in its reserve fund as of June 1951. The immediate crisis had passed.

Day-to-Day Effects of the Fiscal Crisis

The cracks in the system resulting from this brush with fiscal disaster took several forms. For example, on April 5, 1949, Dean

Goodpasture authorized reimbursement of a third-year student, Margaret Veller, for expenses associated with repairing the car used to transport female medical students to Thayer Veterans Administration Hospital on White Bridge Road. This car was a frequent recipient of repairs, mostly minor. On this occasion, Miss Veller had been able "through an uncle [sic] to replace the four old tires and tubes with new ones" at a cost of $19.78.[29]

On May 25, 1948, Dean Goodpasture was notified by Cobb Pilcher that several members of the surgical staff had contributed sufficient personal funds ($3,500) to air-condition operating rooms three and four. Contributors whom the school thanked were Doctors Barksdale, Daniel, Douglas, Larsen, McSwain, Regen, and Pilcher.[30]

On March 14, 1946, Dean Goodpasture thanked several Nashvillians for their contributions to a fund named by Dr. Hugh Morgan the "Desperation Fund" and entered on the university's ledgers as such. Expenditures "were restricted to the purchase of expensive drugs, such as penicillin, which the hospital is unable to furnish to charity patients." One thousand twenty dollars was given in 1946 by such well-known community leaders as Tony Sudekum, A. M. Burton, Jack Bass, John Cheek, J. C. Bradford, Brownlee Currey, and Hugh Morgan. By 1948, the name of the fund had been changed to the more dignified "Emergency Hospital Fund," to be used for "expensive life-saving remedies in desperate, emergency cases." Nashville's Big Brothers had in the meantime established a Penicillin and Streptomycin Fund to cover those important needs of indigent patients.[31]

These examples are compelling indicators of the day-by-day effects of institutional penury, but letters on file indicate that the basic science faculty were probably the most severely stressed. Their distress was caused by fighting to keep their research programs alive, fighting to maintain their standards in teaching, and trying to keep their loyal secretaries and technical support staff when there were no real prospects for improvement. For example, it must have been difficult for Dr. Paul Lamson, professor of pharmacology, to write to his colleague, friend, and dean to voice his dismay about the niggardly budget of his department, and for Dean Goodpasture to attempt to deal with his request. It would have been a particularly distressing situation for both, as they had come to Vanderbilt together in 1925 as professors and had shared the early good times. Nevertheless, Dr. Lamson pointed out on March 22, 1946,[32] that his departmental budget had been $21,170 yearly from 1930 to 1934, $19,476.40 from 1935 to 1938, and $18,892.11 from 1939 to 1946. Small sums from a research grant had been used to supplement the salaries of his secretary and two technicians for several years.

Three years later, in 1949, Dr. Lamson submitted a departmental budget of $21,892.11, justifying his request for increases because outside support by Mallinckrodt Chemical Works Fund had been reduced.[33] His letter contains these comments: "I restrain myself from asking for any salary increases although everyone here is due one. . . . If asking for an increase embarrasses you please do not feel any obligation to do so. Until the Board of Trust wakes up we are bound for Hell and it makes little difference to me how we get there." Perhaps Professor Conkin was right after all.[34] To have his colleagues give up hope would have made Dean Goodpasture heartsick.

Causes of the Financial Crisis

The financial crisis in the medical school and hospital was related to a combination of factors, some of which were not under local control. In Chancellor Branscomb's *Autobiography*[35] we are told: "The immediate cause for this was the inflationary effects of the previous five years of war. The more pressing and continuing cause, however, was the burgeoning program of medical services which had been maturing for two decades, programs which called for new medical departments, new facilities, supporting auxiliary personnel and greatly expanded research." For Conkin, the problem was that the "hospital had to depend on a fixed income even as prices soared."[36] Dr. Henry Clark later summarized the difficulties as follows:[37]

There was a large and growing hospital deficit, made worse by the serious inflation which followed World War II. This expanding deficit was eating into the capital endowment funds which supported both the School of Medicine and Hospital. Furthermore, there was long standing severe tension between the full-time members of the clinical faculty, based in the hospital, and the larger part-time clinical faculty, based in the community. Many of the part-time faculty steered their private patients to other community hospitals in Nashville. This left Vanderbilt Hospital with a bed occupancy rate of about 65 percent, far below the level needed for operating efficiency. Also about half the patients were indigent.

Salary levels for hospital personnel had been kept below those prevalent in other hospitals in the area because of the growing deficit. As a result, there had been serious losses of staff over many months. To make matters worse, the physical plant and equipment of the hospital had been allowed to deteriorate for several years to save money.

Because of all this, there had developed a general feeling of hopelessness among the once proud professional and lay staff of the hospital.

The crisis in the Vanderbilt Hospital had its counterpart in the School of Medicine. . . . More important, there seemed to be no prospects of new money, with the result that salaries of all faculty members were frozen and the Department of Preventive Medicine [actually, the master's program] was discontinued as an economy measure. Even more important, the scientific world was burgeoning in the wake of World War II and it was impossible to appoint new personnel and activate new programs to stay abreast of the times. Perhaps the unkindest cut of all was the growing realization in the clinical departments that Vanderbilt could no longer afford to pay for teaching patients from educational endowment funds. In the eyes of many faculty members the loss of selectivity of teaching patients would spell the doom of the Vanderbilt School of Medicine as a top quality institution.

Jacobson traced these problems to the central issue[38] that the hospital, as originally conceived by Canby Robinson, was an educational tool of the medical school and only secondarily a service institution to the community. Blatantly idealistic, this core concept of the Canby Robinson reorganization plan of 1925 was effected by dividing the income from the very generous endowment between the medical school and hospital. In the former, the income provided salaries of full-time faculty and some operational costs; in the latter, the income paid the health care costs of indigent patients admitted to facilitate the teaching of medical students and residents.

In the short term, this approach created an ideal environment for teachers, physicians, and investigators; in the long term, it isolated the hospital from the community and became overtly unrealistic when conservative investment policies and the practice of spending all of the endowment income caused the endowment to remain the same from 1940 to 1955,[39] when inflation escalated the costs of all goods, services, and personnel, and when specialization in medicine dramatically increased the needs for more sophisticated personnel and equipment. There were other local reasons for the timing of the crisis and the exacerbation of its effects. The bookkeeping system was antiquated and did not provide monthly summaries of expenses and income,[40] and there is suggestive evidence that Dean Leathers and Superintendent Connell were not able to provide the leadership and guidance necessary when the crisis began to unfold.[41]

Finding Solutions to the Financial Crisis

Deficits of great magnitude ripple through an institution causing despair at every level. Relief may come only through desperate measures, if at all. In this case, fiscal turnaround was achieved by raising patient charges so that the hospital became self-sufficient, by two key personnel changes, and by using most of the endowment income for the medical school. The latter transfer was authorized in 1950 to 1951, thereby increasing the payout to the medical school from endowment by $200,000.

On April 20, 1948, Chancellor Branscomb (Fig. 5-3) announced that Vanderbilt Hospital would require indigent patients to pay a flat rate of $8.50 per day for hospitalization.[42] This and subsequent rate hikes in 1949, coupled with increased room occupancy, dramatically raised hospital income. In announcing this change in policy, Chancellor Branscomb carefully explained to Nashville's Mayor

Cummings and news reporters that emergency cases would not be turned away and that this new policy had been necessitated by rising costs. He reminded the Nashville community that the university had absorbed indigent care costs of $6,189,916 over the preceding twenty-one years.[43]

The crucial personnel changes were the appointments of Dr. Goodpasture as dean of the medical school in 1945 and of Dr. Henry Clark as director of Vanderbilt Hospital in 1948. The latter had been trained in hospital management and had recently participated in a study of Vanderbilt Hospital[44] so he was aware of many of the problems and personality issues at Vanderbilt. Perhaps most importantly, he brought a high level of professionalism to the management of the hospital. By instituting a desperately needed system for tracking expenses and income, it became possible to institute and justify rational hospital charges. No less significantly, he was only thirty when appointed and rose to the various challenges with contagious enthusiasm and hard work. He, his wife, and two small children lived in a small apartment on the D wing, a fact that must have raised spirits hospital-wide (Fig. 5-4).

Fig. 5-3: Chancellor Branscomb, circa 1955. Dr. Branscomb was chancellor from 1946 to 1963.

Morale was also raised by such simple acts as cleansing grime and soot that had accumulated on walls in public areas over the previous twenty-three years from our bituminous coal-burning version of smog. A pay raise was negotiated for key personnel, a courageous act by the director and the chancellor. New nursing supervisors were appointed in medicine and

Fig. 5-4: Dr. Henry Clark and family. This picture was taken in North Carolina in the early 1950s. Dr. Clark reports that they have no pictures showing their family in the apartment on the D wing. Their third child was born after leaving Vanderbilt.

surgery, and even more miraculously several general duty nurses were hired.

In order to increase the use of hospital beds, admission policies were changed. By the winter of 1949, the responsibility for admission of all patients was transferred from the resident staff to the admissions office. This transfer had great symbolic and practical significance. Patients were no longer admitted to Vanderbilt Hospital principally for teaching purposes. Instead, the goal had changed to maximizing the patient census. Coupled with an increase in patient charges from $8.50 to $11.50 per day, the changed admission policy moved the hospital into the black.

The extent of Dr. Clark's energy and vision for involvement of Vanderbilt Hospital in community affairs is best exemplified by his actions in the summer of 1948. One month after his arrival in Nashville, a severe poliomyelitis epidemic struck the middle Tennessee area. Dr. Amos Christie, professor of pediatrics, suggested creation of a special ward for all of the regional cases. Such a ward was not available elsewhere in the state. There were natural concerns that the hospital had insufficient resources to assume additional responsibilities, particularly in terms of nursing staff. Nevertheless, the ward was opened and subsequently cared for forty-seven patients without a fatality. The local and National Polio Foundation provided support, while the Nashville papers fully described the success of this venture.

The story does not end there, as shown by this recollection from Dr. Clark:[45]

> In January 1949 the Junior Chamber of Commerce spear-headed the annual fund-raising campaign for the local chapter of the March of Dimes with the provision that most of the funds would be used to reactivate and up-date the Physical Therapy Department at the Vanderbilt Hospital, which was needed for polio patients but which had been closed for several years. Furthermore, as a part of that fund-raising the Jaycees organized an all-night, coast-to-coast radio auction sale, with major gifts provided by local merchants. This was staged in the old Ryman Theatre and featured entertainment by the full company of the Grand Ole Opry. Thus Roy Acuff and Minnie Pearl and all their associates joined the Vanderbilt team. And shortly thereafter the Jaycees agreed to organize and stage an annual Thanksgiving All-Star High School football game, to be played in the Vanderbilt stadium, with the proceeds to go toward the annual cost of operation of the expanding Physical-Occupational-Speech Therapy Department at Vanderbilt. This guaranteed that, henceforth, the sports pages of the Nashville newspapers would join the front pages and editorial pages in telling the Vanderbilt Hospital story.

This football game is still being played and the proceeds, which amounted to $4.5 million by 2000, are still used to support the physical therapy department at Vanderbilt.

Dr. Goodpasture's leadership was also indispensable. Behind the scenes, he was the only faculty member/administrative officer who had the academic stature and reputation for loyalty necessary to lead the faculty through the crisis. His willingness to take on the most difficult of administrative tasks, in addition to his professorial responsibilities, was palpable evidence of his faith in Vanderbilt Medical School and his commitment to its preservation. These same qualities also obtained for the medical school a degree of tolerance from the Board of Trust and chancellor that might not have been afforded a man with less local and national stature. Chancellor Branscomb[46] awards equal credit to Dr. Henry Clark and Dr. Goodpasture for weathering the storm. In retrospect, it is likely that neither would have succeeded alone.

Dr. Goodpasture's Controversial Proposals for Vanderbilt Medical School

Dr. Goodpasture's analysis of the problems in Vanderbilt Medical School and Hospital and his controversial proposals for their remedy are contained in three documents prepared between July 21, 1948, and January 22, 1949.[47] The first of these was an address to the medical faculty, and the last two were letters to Chancellor Branscomb dated January 7 and January 22. These three documents have been transcribed into the appendix in their entirety, because they are the most lucid available statements about our reasons for existence and survival as a medical school and because they describe quite clearly Dean Goodpasture's rationale for abandoning the undergraduate curriculum while stating his academic priorities. Segments of these documents are copied for emphasis in the pages that follow. Other relevant documents from this period include the yearly Dean's Reports to the chancellor and the report of the Christie Committee, which had been established November 26, 1948, and which responded December 30, 1948.[48]

The report to the faculty on July 21, 1948, echoes themes enunciated by Dean Goodpasture on May 3, 1946, in his first Dean's Report:[49]

- All medical schools were going through a trying period because of war time dislocations in personnel and programs, as well as postwar shortages in personnel and inflation.
- The budgets of the medical school had outpaced endowment return due to expansion of facilities and staffs, as well as to increased operating costs.
- The budgets of the hospital had outpaced its endowment and income because of the addition of new additional wings and increased operational costs.

- Most notably, it had become necessary to change the use of the hospital purely as a source of teaching patients by charging ward patients $8.50 per day and by converting the teaching ward on the eighth floor (8400) to a private ward.

Inevitably, the financial situation affected medical education at Vanderbilt in these two ways, as enunciated by Dean Goodpasture in his report to the faculty:

The preclinical departments and some clinical departments are laboring under the disadvantage of the same budgets but shrunken to 50 percent less in purchasing power than those during the twelve or fifteen year pre-war period, with the certainty of needing an unforeseeable resource of from 170 to 200 thousand dollars to operate during the year 1948–1949 at the same financial level as of today.

The Hospital notwithstanding endowment support cannot be sure of balancing its budget without increasing its charges to ward [indigent] patients.

These problems had created a dilemma, stated by Dean Goodpasture as follows:

Thus it would appear that our dilemma consists in operating a University Teaching Hospital as a quasi-private hospital supported by endowment income, while at the same time we are proceeding to dissipate our faculty and students by removing them from their primary base, in order to utilize the clinical facilities of other hospitals to carry out our teaching responsibilities. Would it be simpler and better under these circumstances to close the wards of Vanderbilt Hospital, release endowment income, and only operate that portion of the hospital whose private beds would pay for themselves and furnish accommodation for the patients of our Staff who assist in teaching?

To do this or to follow as a permanent arrangement the plan outlined for teaching next year would in my opinion destroy the one great source of strength that has made Vanderbilt Medical School an eminent institution namely an integrated and concentrated interest and effort under a single roof where intimate associations and mutual concerns of the entire faculty, preclinical and clinical, are devoted to the problems of Medical Education, research, and medical care. This is our *forte* and we must not lose it. With laboratories, library, common dining room, continuous consultations and common attack upon problems we can still maintain our prestige. With that situation at the heart of our School and Hospital we could then cooperate with other hospitals and institutions to advantage.

In his judgment, there was a solution that was ideal and practicable. Because Vanderbilt Medical School needed $250,000 in additional income and because the hospital needed patients for student teaching and to balance its budget, then the hospital should release endowment to the medical school and make up its deficit through increased bed occupancy while continuing to provide ward patients for teaching purposes. He then concluded: "To me this objective as briefly outlined makes sense and it can be achieved. Achievement will depend upon the earnest, loyal and diligent support of the faculty, upon wise and efficient management of the hospital, upon the united and concentrated effort of us all."[50]

This approach was consistent with all previous efforts to maintain the status quo and certainly represented the wishes of the senior faculty, as stated subsequently in their letters to Dean Goodpasture,[51] as well as by the Christie Committee. In line with this approach, a letter was sent to all medical alumni in August or September 1948, soliciting funds to help the medical center through the crisis.[52] On September 8, 1948,[53] a revised budget for the hospital indicated the possibility of a small surplus despite increased expenditures for nurses and new equipment. In view of these developments, it is somewhat surprising that Dean Goodpasture proposed a completely different solution in his letters to Chancellor Branscomb four months later. During this time, he had apparently become convinced that solving the problems of the hospital would so damage the teaching program that a more radical solution was necessary.

The formation of the Christie Committee (Fig. 5-5) is perhaps an indication that he had changed his mind about the solution proposed in his previous report to the faculty. This committee was formed after a special meeting of the executive faculty held on November 24, 1948, when the dean had learned that the occupancy rate of the hospital was about 66 percent, although the faculty had been urged in July to reach 80 percent. The committee was composed of Doctors John Burch, Henry Clark, Hugh Morgan, Cobb Pilcher, and Amos Christie, who were the most influential members of the clinical faculty, assuming Cobb Pilcher was more effective than the prickly Barney Brooks.

The committee's report[54] recommended a number of medium to long-range approaches, including a study of the financial affairs of the medical school similar to that carried out by MacLean in 1946 for the hospital. They further suggested that certain "town-gown" problems be addressed and that a constructive Community-University Hospital Plan be established in order to consider building a city hospital operated by the university. Their report concluded with the statement that the committee (with one dissenting vote) "believes that no thought of reduction of the Vanderbilt University School of Medicine to a two-year school should be considered at the present time." Dean Goodpasture was presumably disappointed in the failure of the committee to provide realistic short-term remedies in a crisis that was rapidly moving toward its denouement and in the failure of the clinical services to increase the hospital census after the call to arms on July 21. The committee, on the other hand, may have felt it was late in the game to have a meaningful study of such a complex

Fig. 5-5: Dr. Amos Christie, head and professor of pediatrics. Courtesy of Dr. Samuel Paplanus.

issue. In any case, it is unlikely that the dean waited for the formal Committee Report to be filed on December 30 before he began drafting his letter to Chancellor Branscomb with its controversial proposal on January 7, 1949, although he does state their report was "duly considered."[55]

This letter of January 7[56] was transmitted with a challenge to Chancellor Branscomb and the university: "The enclosed letter represents the stand on which I rest my case." Obviously, if the proposals were not accepted, Dr. Goodpasture would resign as dean. Eight days later, he sent members of the executive faculty a copy of this document, asking for strict confidentiality, and notifying them that the chancellor would attend an executive faculty meeting four days hence for "a full discussion of policy." Dean Goodpasture's letter on January 7 began as follows: "For the past three and one-half years I have been studying the problem of Vanderbilt Medical School endeavoring to interpret its position in relation to the changing local and national attitudes toward medical education and health services. In the meantime economic conditions have so altered our situation that our financial stability has become untenable." He then summarizes the changes he felt were necessary:

> The program I have in mind involves discontinuance at the earliest possible date, commensurate with our commitments, of the undergraduate curriculum of the medical school, and creating in its stead a School or Institute in which all our present facilities and resources, together with additional ones that should be added to them by means of a vigorous campaign over an indeterminate period, would be devoted to medical research and education at a graduate and postgraduate level.

There followed a brief summary of the extraordinary advances in medicine over the last fifty years, attributed to an integration of this new science into our American medical institutions. "The basic principle upon which this renaissance in American medical education was founded was the essential inseparability of research and education. . . . Research and training, it has been found, must go hand-in-hand—the one to advance knowledge, the other to apply it. Neither can stand alone nor should one disproportionately surpass the other in level of attainment."

Dr. Goodpasture portrayed Vanderbilt's current situation rather scathingly as:

At the present time Vanderbilt Medical School finds itself bankrupt financially and without a constructive program to fulfill its great mission. Locally it has been denied governmental support for its current teaching program, while it suffers the indignity of professional criticism on the disgusting level of economic competition and personal aggrandizement. Its faculty is being drained into the services of an antiquated City hospital and a temporary Federal hospital, while control of teaching resources is firmly held in the hands of politicians and practitioners with the dire implications of a settlement on the basis of unilaterally beneficial appeasement and degrading compromise. Its attenuated and dissipated staffs are being called upon by other local and regional hospitals to furnish the services of a rapidly depleting faculty and defensive agencies of government are restricting its liberty to choose freely and effectively its student body. In the meantime economic necessity has already removed from its use in large part its chief clinical asset—the Vanderbilt Hospital which through financial necessity is now converted into a private service institution of little teaching and research value. Lack of money and a constructive program leave the School understaffed, many of its teaching personnel ill-paid, departments temporarily organized and administered or carried on in skeleton form only. In spite of this disorganizing process no real headway is being made in the solution of an overall financial problem nor in an effective determination of its position in terms of fundamental principles. It is the element of tragedy in the latter circumstance that of course concerns me most; but there would be no regret in failure that refuses to compromise principle.

From the midst of this imbroglio we must extricate ourselves immediately in policy if not in material success. The purpose, policy and program of Vanderbilt Medical School for the past quarter century has been to foster research and medical education at the highest level. As we move into a new and changing period this philosophy must continue to prevail. The dubious path of appeasement and temporary expedient will neither fulfill our avowed ideals nor will it give us the needed inspiration to carry forward our mission of leadership which cannot succeed without freedom of imagination and courage to pursue our destiny along uncharted paths.

I have no apprehension or fears for the adequate accomplishment of undergraduate medical education in this country with the many excellent State and private schools and their organizations to preserve standards at the level attained during the past twenty-five years, in which accomplishment our School has so effectively participated. Existing undergraduate schools will be enlarged and others will be built. Public demand and governmental support will effectively see to this. My concern is with opportunities that might then remain, especially in the Southern Region, for a continuation at a higher level of the combination of research and education that inevitably must provide unusual talent for creative work and leadership if we are to go forward rather than sink to the low level of service distribution for which the demand is so compelling today. There is no middle road, we either go forward or backward.

There is consequently no justification in my mind for a Vanderbilt Medical School whose objective is only the graduation of its complement of physicians to serve the health requirements. There is and always will be need and a great need for advancement of knowledge and superior training. Our modern civilization, not its medical aspects alone, must be supported by the best minds of the Nation trained in the most advanced technical boundaries of science if we are to go forward intellectually.

Putting these proposals into effect meant converting Vanderbilt Hospital into an institution for postgraduate training in the advanced specialties of medicine and surgery, with "the primary emphasis even in the clinical fields upon research." Because of this conversion of the hospital's basic function, undergraduate medical education would be abandoned. The basic sciences would be continued; graduate and postgraduate students would be trained for master and doctor of philosophy degrees, and closer relationships would be established with the science departments of the college. The letter closed with these words:

This program so briefly outlined would immediately upon its accomplishment relieve the school of present difficulties on the economic level; it would enliven and uplift its waning enthusiasm and spirit and it would afford direction to a confused and foreboding complexity that lays such a heavy burden upon it. Controlling reins would be kept in University hands.

There was a follow-up letter to Chancellor Branscomb[57] on January 22 "in response to your request for a more detailed exposition of the general plan for the medical school." Admitting there was great reluctance to discontinuing the four-year undergraduate curriculum, Dr. Goodpasture proceeded to enunciate very clearly his credo:

> My own interest is in the preservation and improvement of medical research and advanced training at Vanderbilt. If this could be done and at the same time the four-year undergraduate course be continued, for example at Nashville General Hospital, I of course would not be opposed, although the latter would I am convinced be at a lower level. The hope of a better arrangement sometime in the future might seem sufficient justification for a temporary retreat. Nevertheless when it comes to a choice between maintaining undergraduate medical education at a lower level, and the elevation of research and advanced training at a higher level, I must always enlist on the side of the latter. It seems likely to me that we may now be confronted with that choice.
>
> In final analysis decisions under these circumstances are determined by one's own philosophy as to the basic functions of a University. To my mind a University should consist primarily of an environment congenial to scholars for the purpose of creative scholarship and teaching. In science that means opportunity for basic research irrespective of immediate application and in medicine it means the investigation of problems of health and disease.

We then come to three paragraphs that detail his concerns about the future of Vanderbilt Hospital as a teaching institution.

Basically, Dr. Goodpasture took the position that, in making the hospital solvent, its effectiveness for teaching undergraduates would inevitably erode. It was this judgment that ultimately led to the positions described in the letters of January 1949:

If we admit that the sole purpose of Vanderbilt Hospital is to facilitate medical education and research, and I take it that this is admissible for it is hardly conceivable that it could be operated as a hospital for financial gain as a resource of University income, let us examine what we are doing with it today in terms of the desired objectives. As you well know all means in use or under consideration are designed primarily to balance its budget and release income from endowment. It is obvious that the Hospital is not serving satisfactorily for teaching purposes because our students are going to Thayer and to the Nashville General Hospital for a large part of their training. It is not operated to the advantage of research, because with few exceptions clinical investigation is at a low ebb. The clinical faculty oscillates between Vanderbilt and Thayer [Veteran's Administration Hospital], between Thayer and Nashville General, between the last and their offices and so on back and forth again. Many of them in addition are up to the hilt in private practice.

What prospect is there, should we accomplish our objective of balancing the budget, that the Hospital would then meet the needs of undergraduate medical education? In my judgment there is none whatever. What we are doing is transforming the Hospital into a private service institution. In order to do this we are making its fine facilities more and more available for the patients of private practitioners and nothing else. Toward this end we have abolished the best teaching ward, namely 8400 [for black patients], and created in its stead a ward for private patients. We have made available for low cost private patients the two and four bed rooms on our previously subsidized wards, and we have of necessity raised the rates on the open wards so high as to price ourselves out of the market. So much in the name of economic necessity.

Suppose our plan of balancing the budget succeeds, what would be the result from the standpoint of teaching and research? The result would be that the School would have lost all the essential requirements that we have been able to procure in the past by purchase; namely,

professional control of patients as to variety, length of stay in the
Hospital, diagnosis, treatment and follow-up. Clinical teaching and
research would have gone by the board under our own roof.

Nine pages of this letter were then devoted to the specifics of
the operational plan proposed by Dean Goodpasture, including
prospects for clinical specialists, reorganization of the medical
school for purposes of graduate education and closer ties with
science departments of the university, creation of research laboratories, and proposed budgets. It was an idealistic yet practical
document, providing full details as to the administrative implemen-
tation of the various proposals.

The Vanderbilt faculty's written response to the proposal to
abolish the undergraduate curriculum was uniformly negative.
Each of the four correspondents with letters on file (Doctors Sam
Clark, Lamson, Luton, and Pilcher) felt the four-year curriculum
should be maintained for reasons varying from tradition to invigora-
tion of the faculty. The Christie Committee, composed of the most
influential clinical faculty, came to a similar conclusion. Most faculty
members believed that it might be possible to maintain high quality
teaching and research if the care of indigents admitted to
Vanderbilt Hospital were subsidized by the community and were
controlled by the university.

Dean Goodpasture's proposal was formally considered by the
Board of Trust at the midwinter session on Monday, February 7,
1949, although he was not invited to attend. Chancellor Branscomb,
as documented in the minutes,[58] carefully reviewed the reasons for
the crisis in the medical center and then discussed some of the
possible solutions, including affiliations with the city of Nashville. In
presenting Dean Goodpasture's proposals (made available in their
entirety to the board for consideration), the chancellor concluded
the issues could be condensed to the question: "Do we feel that the
contribution which we should endeavor to make should be that of a
broad social influence through the type of practicing physician
whom we graduate, or should it be through contributions to the
sum total of medical knowledge and the training of those who shall

in turn be the medical teachers and research workers in the future?" The chancellor recommended that the Goodpasture plan "not be accepted."[59]

The board formally took a middle ground in its resolution, indicating that the research program outlined by Dean Goodpasture should be "if possible . . . worked out in connection with a four-year medical school." The chancellor was then prepared to discuss the course of action to be taken in light of the above resolution. Alternate possibilities mentioned were a medical clinic, retaining in whole or in part for the School of Medicine the fees of the faculty for their services, and affiliation with local, state, or federal agencies. The chancellor recommended the latter course, in which assessment the board concurred.

By the judgment of history, Dean Goodpasture's proposals were flawed, at least in part. He was, of course, correct in defining the idealism appropriate for his time, and ours. He was correct in assuming that university medical schools had the major responsibility for educating students and faculty who were devoted to teaching and research, a situation which also holds true today. However, in Dean Goodpasture's proposal, Vanderbilt would abrogate this specific responsibility, in the expectation that universities such as Johns Hopkins and Harvard would continue to feed academicians into the system. His proposal therefore seems flawed in that Vanderbilt has its own role to play in this vital activity. This medical school has through the years, to the advantage of the profession of medicine and the honor of the university, placed its own imprimatur on medical graduates and faculty.

Dean Goodpasture was quite correct in predicting the future of the hospital as an institution suitable for teaching and research. Today, patient care in hospitals has generally evolved into a quasi-business, its success judged principally by financial returns, services provided, length of stays, and paucity of lawsuits. Such an evolution was in some ways inevitable, as the Canby Robinson plan to provide patients for student instruction and research was doomed by rising costs and sophistication of medical care. Vanderbilt and the city of Nashville have attempted to make mutually satisfactory arrangements for indigent care for decades, and an arrangement of this type may yet be made, meeting the needs of the community and region while providing patients for teaching and research.[60]

Inadequate Support Services in the Hospital

While attempting to deal with the financial crisis, Dean Goodpasture and Dr. Henry Clark also faced a second major problem—inadequate support services. Even in 1945, patient care in a university hospital was surprisingly complex. A veritable army was (and is) required:

- Administrative personnel for maintenance of records of all types, purchasing, and bookkeeping.
- Nurses and ward aides for administration of care and medications.
- Pharmacists for maintenance and dispensation of drug supplies.
- Laboratory personnel for performance of X rays and other tests.
- Dieticians for food preparation.
- Workers of various types for cleaning rooms and maintenance of utilities, or to provide laundry and transportation services.

Generalizations as to the efficiency of these personnel, their qualifications, and their morale in 1945 are not possible, but there is considerable evidence that the various components of this complex system at Vanderbilt were dysfunctional. It was not an issue of salary alone, although there had not been a pay raise for ten to fifteen years. There were also major inadequacies in leadership[61] and widespread pessimism about the future of the medical center.[62]

From an analysis of the records and correspondence of the period, the major problems of the hospital support systems included:

- Nurses and ward aides were in short supply, in part because of competition for trained nursing personnel with Thayer Veterans Administration Hospital, where pay and benefits were much better. In 1947[63] the beginning salary for graduate nurses was $175 per month, while the Thayer Hospital provided $225 per month, one meal a day and laundry service. There were inadequate numbers of nurses to staff the operating suites for maximal efficiency. Presumably because of working conditions, the turnover in ward aides in the year beginning April 1, 1946, was 160 percent, in ward clerks 92 percent, in orderlies 124 percent, and in maids 114 percent.[64]

- Laboratories were poorly equipped and inadequately staffed. There had been trivial expenditures for new equipment over the previous ten or more years, and old equipment had not been maintained. In particular there were repeated pleas from radiology to bring their machines up to standard. Centralization of laboratories with a twenty-four-hour operation was years away. In 1945, serologic and bacteriologic tests were the responsibility of pathology; hematology and clinical chemistry were the responsibility of medicine; and surgical pathology was the responsibility of surgery. At night and on weekends, routine procedures were performed by medical students and residents. During the day blood and urine examinations were the responsibility of medical students and residents.

- There were too few anesthesiologists to maintain efficient operating room schedules and provide the necessary expertise to undertake difficult operations. Long after Ben Robbins was made the first head of anesthesiology in 1946, "selected" third- and fourth-year students were providing some of the anesthesia services.

- The accounting services were reputedly inefficient and did not provide accurate monthly statements as to expenses. One of Dr. Henry Clark's first actions was to recommend to Mr. A. B. Benedict, university treasurer, that the chart of accounts and the general accounting practices of the American Hospital Association be adopted.[65] This system had been especially designed for hospital use and allowed comparison of the operating efficiency of departments at Vanderbilt with those in other leading hospitals. It is astounding that Dean Goodpasture had to approve *all* expenditures in the medical school, as well as transfers of funds. This letter from Dr. Hugh Morgan is illustrative of the mechanism for approval (Fig. 5-6) and provides some insight into inefficiencies of the system. Having seen Dean Goodpasture's in box in Figure 5-2, it is impressive that Dr. Morgan's letter had been processed by the second day. Miss Corbitt presumably stamped the signature on the bottom and sent a copy on to Mr. Miltenberger, the hospital's accountant. All expenditures were so approved by Dean Goodpasture, with the written "Approved," date, and initials. Incidentally, the expenses of Dr. Morgan's trip were paid by a private practice fund of the Department of Medicine, and in 1949 it was possible to have four days in Atlantic City for $144.04.

By 1945 the hospital had sadly deteriorated. Personnel throughout the institution were dispirited, in part because they were underpaid, and some components were significantly understaffed. Equipment had not been maintained or modernized. In other words, all components of the system were malfunctioning, with life expectancy *for the hospital* perhaps as short as one or two years when Dr. Goodpasture was put in charge on July 1, 1945. In many respects, the fact that the medical center emerged from the crisis five years later in reasonable condition borders on the miraculous.[66]

Loss of Master's Program from Department of Preventive Medicine

The story behind the loss of this program is symptomatic of the widespread institutional malaise and is also illustrative of the attempts made by Dean Goodpasture to enhance the academic potential of a particular department despite the financial crisis. On June 4, 1947, he went to New York to discuss with Dr. Clarence Scannan of the Commonwealth Fund the imminent loss of their support for the Department of Preventive Medicine. In a follow-up letter on June 10, Dean Goodpasture pleaded the case of the Medical School[67] by analyzing the financial status of this department over the years. This analysis indicates that the Department of Preventive Medicine (and several other departments) relied on external support for survival.

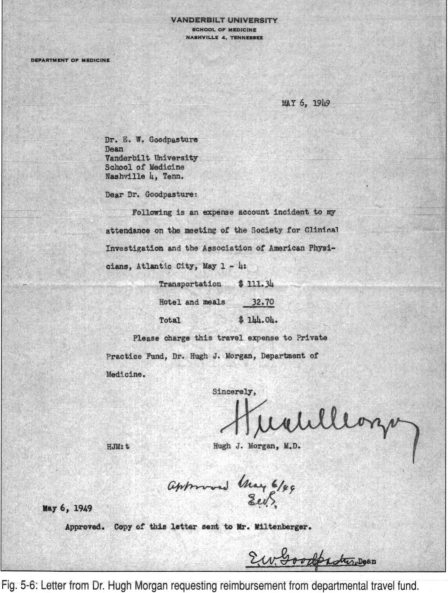

VANDERBILT UNIVERSITY
SCHOOL OF MEDICINE
NASHVILLE 4, TENNESSEE

DEPARTMENT OF MEDICINE

MAY 6, 1949

Dr. E. W. Goodpasture
Dean
Vanderbilt University
School of Medicine
Nashville 4, Tenn.

Dear Dr. Goodpasture:

Following is an expense account incident to my
attendance on the meeting of the Society for Clinical
Investigation and the Association of American Physicians, Atlantic City, May 1 - 4:

Transportation	$ 111.34
Hotel and meals	32.70
Total	$ 144.04

Please charge this travel expense to Private
Practice Fund, Dr. Hugh J. Morgan, Department of
Medicine.

Sincerely,

Hugh J. Morgan, M.D.

HJM:t

May 6, 1949

Approved. Copy of this letter sent to Mr. Miltenberger.

Fig. 5-6: Letter from Dr. Hugh Morgan requesting reimbursement from departmental travel fund.
Authorization for Mr. Miltenberger to repay was by Dean Goodpasture's initials.

As an example, the Department of Preventive Medicine from its
creation in 1930 had received $403,000 (by return from endow-
ment) from Vanderbilt, $128,150.03 from the Commonwealth

Fund, and more recently $67,500 from the United States Public Health Service. After 1941, the grant from the Commonwealth Fund was added to the budget of the department to create a degree-granting program (Master of Public Health), a program approved in 1946 by the Association of Schools of Public Health.

Dean Goodpasture then summarized the current perilous financial state of the medical school, showing how the 1947–48 budgets had been reduced in comparison to the previous year. The Department of Preventive Medicine had taken the largest cut of all departments due to an unexpected loss of $7,500 in United States Public Health funds. A new bill was to have been presented to Congress that would have restored money for support of schools such as Vanderbilt, but it had apparently died in committee. Dean Goodpasture estimated that $6,500 would provide sufficient support for the master's program to continue, but he was notified on June 23 that his request had been turned down. As a consequence, Dr. Frye resigned May 19 of the following year to take the professorship at Tulane, and the master's program was discontinued.

Dean Goodpasture did not give up. On May 14, 1948, he sent letters[68] to the most distinguished immunologists in the country, outlining his plans for the department:

> In reorganizing this department I am anxious to explore the possibility of securing as Professor and Head of the Department a scientist who is basically qualified and has achieved accomplishment in research in the field of immunity. We propose to emphasize preventive medicine rather than public health in the department, and I feel that an active program directed toward fundamental exploration of the immunity processes and the sensitization phenomena would greatly strengthen our research and teaching program.

Advice and recommendations were sought from the leaders in American science, including O. T. Avery at the Rockefeller Institute and Linus Pauling at the California Institute of Technology. Unfortunately, Dean Goodpasture's goals were ahead of the time

Table 5-3
Years in the Life of a Dean
Major Changes in Personnel and Programs

1945

June 7   Dr. William Frye appointed professor of preventive medicine, head of department
Sept. 20 Dean Goodpasture chairs his first executive faculty meeting
Sept. 20 Medical school resumes usual schedule of instruction, drops wartime accelerated program
Dec. 2   Dr. McGehee Harvey resigns from Department of Medicine

1946

Feb. 26 Death of Waller Leathers
Mar. 13 Department of Anesthesiology created; Dr. Ben Robbins made head
May 23 Motion to create unit of biophysics passed by executive faculty
June 27 Foreign language requirement dropped as criterion for admission to medical school
July 1   Dr. Glenn Millikan appointed professor of physiology, head of department
Nov. 12 Dr. John Youmans resigned from Department of Medicine
Dec. 19 Dr. John Burch appointed acting head, obstetrics and gynecology

1947

Feb. 4   Inauguration of Chancellor Branscomb
Mar. 20 Chancellor Branscomb was welcomed to his first executive faculty meeting
April 17 Blue Cross extended to all faculty
May 25 Tragic death of Dr. Glenn Millikan

Sept. 18 Dr. Howard Curtis appointed professor of physiology, head of department
Sept. 18 Department of Psychiatry authorized, Dr. William Orr made head

1948

May 19 Dr. William Frye resigned as head of preventive medicine
May 28 Dr. John Buddingh resigned as professor of bacteriology
May 31 Dr. Henry Clark arrives, becomes director of Vanderbilt Hospital
July 9   Contract with Veterans Administration to train residents
Dec. 16 Program of Dental Medicine approved by executive faculty

1949

Mar. 24 Dr. Goodpasture resigned as dean but continued to serve until replaced in March 1950
March   Clarence Connell, hospital superintendent, resigns
May 2   Dr. James Dawson resigns as professor of pathology
Oct. 1   Dr. William Darby made head of biochemistry
Oct. 27 Tragic death of Dr. Cobb Pilcher
Nov. 19 Dr. Youmans approved as dean by executive committee, Board of Trust

1950

Mar. 1   Dr. John Youmans assumes responsibilities as dean
Mar. 30 Executive faculty passes resolution thanking Dr. Goodpasture for serving as dean
May 1   Dr. Henry Clark resigns

and far ahead of the available resources. Ultimately, Dr. Alvin Keller was retained as acting head of preventive medicine, a move signifying maintenance of traditional departmental responsibilities and a very limited budget.

Major Changes in Personnel and Programs

After Waller Leathers's resignation as dean June 30, 1945, the new management team consisted of Dean Goodpasture, Associate Dean Sam Clark, and Assistant Dean Beverly Douglas.[69] Over the summer, two search committees were formed to replace retiring professors of physiology and obstetrics/gynecology. Dean Goodpasture served as chairman of both committees, and in addition he chaired a committee managing the affairs of the Department of Medicine, as Hugh Morgan was on loan to the surgeon general's office. The continuing shortage of anesthesiologists led to creation of the Department of Anesthesiology on December 29, 1945 (Table 5-3).

Dr. Ben Robbins moved his affiliation from pharmacology to this Department of Anesthesiology as its new head on March 13, 1946. Another important appointment was that of Dr. Glenn Millikan as head of the Department of Physiology, effective July 1, 1946 (Fig. 5-7). Changes in this year included the dropping of the foreign language requirement as a criterion for admission to the medical school, and the notable development of a program of cooperation in resident training and professional staffing at Thayer Hospital between Vanderbilt and the Veterans Administration. The executive faculty approved a resolution to create a "unit" of biophysics, probably an interdisciplinary cooperative group with the college, but financial pressures prevented its activation.

The looming financial crisis began to occupy more of Dean Goodpasture's energy by the fall of 1946, with letters to and from Kirkland Hall pronouncing the situation "extremely critical" and authorizing modest hospital rate increases. Initial efforts to find a replacement for Dr. Lucius Burch in obstetrics/gynecology were unsuccessful, leading to the appointment of his son, Dr. John Burch, as acting head in December.

The new year brought a new chancellor, Harvie Branscomb, dean of the Duke University Divinity School, a Rhodes Scholar, holding a Ph.D. from Columbia University in philosophy, and recognized for his writing on the New Testament. Inaugurated January 16, 1947, he attended his first executive faculty meeting in March, when he commented on the increasing

Fig. 5-7: Dr. Glenn Millikan, professor of physiology.

cost of medical education and the small class size of Vanderbilt Medical School. Chancellor Branscomb never understood why so much money was expended in the medical center and why so few students were graduated.[70] By March, he had read the recent study of Vanderbilt Hospital by MacLean, and he voiced support for one of its recommendations, a central purchasing office for the medical center.

It was Dean Goodpasture's sad duty to prepare the following resolution upon the tragic death of Dr. Glenn Millikan. In their eleven months in Nashville, Dr. and Mrs. Millikan had made many friends before he was killed in a rock-climbing accident in the Fall Creek Falls area.

It is with deep regret that the Executive Faculty records the death of Doctor Glenn Millikan who served as Professor of Physiology and Head of the Department from September 1946 until May 1947. Doctor Millikan came to Vanderbilt with a wealth of cultural and intellectual experience that made him an outstanding individual on the faculty. He had been reared in the atmosphere of scientific research created by his renowned father and his education had been directed to the development of his own talents and his keen interest in science. He graduated from Harvard with high honors. In the congenial environment of Cambridge University, where he pursued his graduate studies, his ability gained for him a fellowship in Trinity College, an honor rarely granted to Americans. Through his position in England and his paternal connections in the United States he had acquired a host of acquaintances who, under the influence of his vivid and attractive personality, became his friends. Nor were his associates limited to scientists. The variety of his activities and the energy with which he pursued them endeared him to all sorts of people. The Vanderbilt Faculty succumbed to the spirit of his enthusiasm, the stimulation of his discussions and his ardent desire to be accepted as a member of the group. His success in this last respect was complete, as is evidenced by the loss that is felt from his death after such a brief sojourn in the University. The Faculty takes this occasion to convey to Doctor Millikan's wife and to his parents their deep sympathy.

In the spring of 1947, the executive faculty approved the creation of a Department of Psychiatry if funds for its support became available. A search committee was constituted, consisting of Dean Goodpasture as chairman, Hugh Morgan, Cobb Pilcher, and Sam Clark as members. They recommended that Dr. William Orr be appointed head August 13, 1947, an action approved by all of the executive faculty save Dr. Paul Lamson. At this time there were no psychiatric beds, and it was necessary to renovate ward "1300" (now part of T corridor between A and B wings), using funds donated privately.

It is not clear whether Dr. Lamson objected to Dr. Orr's appointment on grounds that there were inadequate funds to support existing departments, much less create new ones. Dr. Frank Luton must have been surprised by this choice, as he had submitted a proposal in August,[71] certainly at the dean's request, for structuring a new Department of Psychiatry in which he would be the professor. In 1976, Dr. Luton attributed the appointment of Dr. Orr as head to his close friendship with Sam Clark.[72] At any rate, a grant of $35,000 per year from the National Mental Health Act made it possible to activate this new department.

In August, the dean also appointed a special committee to study the problem of nursing, or more specifically, the lack of nurses at Vanderbilt. This committee, consisting of Doctors Burch, Billings, Christie, Pilcher, and Director of Nursing Service Holtzhausen, was diligent in meeting its charge, enumerating the lack of simple amenities, lack of fringe benefits, and inadequate salaries as causes of the shortage of nursing personnel. The disabling turnover in ward personnel mentioned previously was also documented.

Personnel departing in 1948 included Dr. William Frye, who left to be professor of preventive medicine at Tulane, and Dr. John Buddingh, who became head and professor of microbiology at Louisiana State University School of Medicine in New Orleans. Dr. Buddingh was a particularly valued and competent colleague who was especially close to Dr. Goodpasture, as evidenced by his letter of resignation.[73]

> Above all else I leave here with my sincerest thanks to you. You are my teacher. I hope that, God willing, I may be able to continue as a teacher and research worker in such a way as to maintain the illustrious tradition which you have enhanced. If I succeed in a small measure it will be largely due to your guidance and constant interest in me and my work. Our association in all we have done and hoped for is one which is not ended by my going elsewhere. I shall always consider it a privilege to know that I can turn to you for counsel.

The loss of these key personnel was partially offset by the arrival of Dr. Henry Clark May 31, 1948, whose leadership was needed because the fiscal crisis had become all-consuming. Dr. Clark was recruited by Chancellor Branscomb,[74] probably because the medical center had not followed the recommendations of the MacLean Report of 1946. Chancellor Branscomb later wrote Dr. Goodpasture "Part of the credit for that [improvement in finances] goes to Henry Clark, but it was your judgment and decision that picked him."[75] In April 1948, the chancellor announced that the hospital would charge $8.50 per day for indigents as the university had spent $6,189,916 over the previous twenty-one years and could no longer bear the burden. Contributions to the "Desperation Fund" and the Hospital Emergency Fund were received, and the surgical staff paid for air-conditioning operating rooms three and four.

Vanderbilt's participation in the residency training program at Thayer was announced in October. Also in October, the chancellor convened a "Confidential Hospital Committee" (that did not include Dean Goodpasture or Dr. Henry Clark) to consider the problem of indigent care in Nashville.[76] As mentioned previously, the Christie Committee was formed in November 1948 to advise the dean about the conduct of the medical school and hospital. It might be expected that a program of Dental Medicine approved by the executive faculty in December was not activated probably due to lack of funds.

The year 1949 was very difficult for Dean Goodpasture. After his proposals for reorganization of the medical school were not accepted in February, he asked to be relieved of his duties on March 17. Dr. John Youmans was contacted and agreed to return, this time as dean, effective March 1, 1950. In May, Dr. Jim Dawson resigned to become head and professor of pathology at the University of Minnesota. Dr. Dawson had assumed major responsibilities for running the department at Vanderbilt over the previous three years, and his departure would have been a greater loss had not Dr. John Shapiro been available to take Dr. Dawson's place. Then, in October, the university was saddened by the untimely death of Dr. Cobb Pilcher, the senior faculty member in the Department of Surgery upon whom Dean Goodpasture relied.

There were a few pieces of good news. Dr. William Darby replaced Dr. Charles Robinson as head of biochemistry October 1, 1949, and thereby the university was able to develop very important and nationally recognized programs in nutrition. Further, Eileen Cunningham, professor of medical library science, was acknowledged for her contributions to the field with the Marcia Noyes Award.

Dr. Youmans relieved Dr. Goodpasture as dean, effective March 1, 1950. Dean Goodpasture signed his last *Executive*

Faculty Minutes on February 23, 1950. The last official act recorded in these minutes was the approval of a committee report recommending the appointment of a physician to direct the student health services. The abilities and energy of Dr. Henry Clark were recognized by the University of North Carolina with an invitation to become their vice-chancellor for Health Affairs. This was an offer that could not be refused, returning Dr. Clark and his family to one of their academic homes, and offering broader responsibilities than were available at Vanderbilt. Dr. Clark stayed on into the spring while training his replacement, Dr. Richard Cannon.

It was also time for Dr. Goodpasture, Dr. Sam Clark, and Dr. Beverly Douglas to move out of the dean's office. In the *Minutes of March 30, 1945,* the executive faculty recorded the following resolution:

> That the Executive Faculty expresses its deep and abiding apprecia-
> tion of the leadership and guidance provided this medical school
> through a difficult, critical period of its existence by the retiring Dean,
> Dr. Ernest W. Goodpasture, and its great satisfaction that he continues
> with us, Head of the Department of Pathology and member of this
> Executive Faculty.

These warm feelings were presumably mutual. The *Executive Faculty Minutes of November 17, 1949,* convey a more muted farewell from Chancellor Branscomb: "He [Vice-Chancellor Sarratt] also expressed on behalf of Chancellor Branscomb and the Administration their appreciation of the services rendered by Dr. Goodpasture as Dean of the School of Medicine during the past few years," while the *Board of Trust Minutes* are slightly more expansive:[77]

> NOW, THEREFORE, BE IT RESOLVED
> That the Board of Trust of Vanderbilt University, through its executive
> committee, express to Dr. Ernest W. Goodpasture its great appreciation of
> his services to the School during this difficult period as its chief adminis-
> trative officer, and assures him of the deep regard and appreciation which

it will always have for him personally and for his outstanding services to medical education in so many respects.

Such administrative succinctness probably reflects a lack of appreciation by the chancellor and Board of Trust that the medical center immediately after World War II was hanging by a thread. A few faculty stalwarts, by sacrificing their own peace of mind and careers, literally held the place together by force of will and loyalty to Vanderbilt. Foremost among these were Dr. Rudolph Kampmeier as the sole full-time faculty member of the Department of Medicine for two years, and Dr. Ernest Goodpasture, dean for five years. For their service in these periods alone, both deserve a permanent and prominent place in the pantheon of Vanderbilt University.

OVERVIEW OF DR. GOODPASTURE'S TENURE AS DEAN

Dr. Goodpasture left the deanship with friendships intact, honor and integrity preserved, and the school viable. By creating the Departments of Anesthesiology and Psychiatry, he recognized the necessity of specialization as medicine evolved after World War II. His appointment of Dr. William Darby as head of biochemistry was important in reinvigoration of the basic sciences at Vanderbilt. His support of Dr. James Dawson and Dr. John Shapiro strengthened the tradition of excellence in teaching in Vanderbilt Medical School.

Dr. Goodpasture's research career essentially ended owing to the combination of World War II (see Extramural Responsibilities, chapter 6) and his becoming dean. The decade of the 1930s was the most productive period for his laboratory, in large part due to the $250,000 "Fluid Research Fund" provided by the Rockefeller General Education Board. Dr. Goodpasture was successful in obtaining grant support subsequently, but he was unable to maintain high levels of productivity in the 1940–45 period due to war-induced personnel shortages and teaching responsibilities. However, the *coup de grace* for research came when he was appointed dean. This was a serious loss for the medical school and university, in addition to the personal toll on Dr. Goodpasture.

Fig. 5-8: Chancellor Carmichael, circa 1942. Dr. Carmichael was chancellor from 1937 to 1946.

Did Chancellor Carmichael (Fig. 5-8) have reasonable alternative options for the deanship? In 1945, there were only forty full-time senior faculty members in Vanderbilt Medical School; sixteen of these were professors. In the clinical departments, Dr. Christie had been on the faculty for only two years, Dr. Lucius Burch was ready to step down, Dr. Kampmeier was single-handedly managing the Department of Medicine, and Dr. Brooks was far more effective as a teacher and surgeon than he would have been as dean. In the preclinical departments, Dr. Sam Clark was the only alternative choice the chancellor might have considered. Professors of pathology have often been chosen as deans, in comparison to professors of anatomy, perhaps because the former have more clinical contacts and responsibilities. In addition, Dr. Goodpasture certainly had more stature than Dr. Clark nationally as a scientist. Recruitment of a dean from the outside was not likely, due to fiscal constraints and wartime disruptions of the usual pipelines of academic personnel.

Why was it necessary to appoint a new dean in 1945? There is considerable evidence that Dean Leathers was in failing health, a factor that might even have necessitated the appointment of Dr. Goodpasture as associate dean in 1943. In any case, Dr. Leathers died from a stroke shortly after his resignation in 1945.

In summary, at this interval in time, it appears the university had no reasonable alternatives to the appointment of Dr. Goodpasture as dean and that it was a responsibility he could not refuse.

Dr. Goodpasture made many interesting and useful speeches in his career, but one of the more remarkable was delivered on October 11, 1950, six months after his responsibilities as dean ended. He had been asked to represent the faculties at the convocation celebrating the seventy-fifth anniversary of the opening of Vanderbilt, a ceremony held in Neely Auditorium with Chancellor Branscomb presiding. A lesser man might have had more difficulty concealing the bruises from his recent administrative interactions with the chancellor and Board of Trust. Read this draft of his speech carefully (including the crossed-out words); it reflects wisdom, loyalty, and an honest appraisal of Vanderbilt's accomplishments and prospects:[78]

It is my valued privilege to bear to all of you the Greetings of the Faculty. Under almost any other circumstances it would be a rash undertaking to speak for a university faculty on the supposition that the speaker represented any sort of unanimity of opinion, but today in celebrating the 75th anniversary of Vanderbilt University, one of the few great independent institutions of higher learning in this country, there will be no dissent amongst us from the feelings of ~~high~~ profound respect for past performances and the best of good will for the journey forward that pervade our greetings at this milestone.

I have an especial pride in this honorable assignment. For almost two-thirds of the extraordinary period of educational enterprise which we celebrate today I have had a personal interest in and connection with Vanderbilt University, first as student, then as alumnus, and for the last third of its existence as a ~~grateful~~ member of its distinguished faculty.

These connections with an institution of such lofty purposes, high endeavors and congenial associations have been ~~most gratifying and~~ inspiring ones to me, and I value ~~beyond measure~~ the opportunity to take advantage of this occasion to make acknowledgements of my great indebtedness.

From the very beginning institutions of advanced education, founded and supported by private means, have set the standards in the ~~advance~~ progress of learning in our country. With increase in population and resources this forward movement made rapid strides during the past

75 years; and during that period responsibility for higher education was assumed more and more by individual States. . . .

In expressing their Greetings today I feel sure the Faculty joins me in the hope and expectation that as it proceeds upon its course from this anniversary dateline Vanderbilt University will be able to preserve the traditions of independent exploration into the fields of higher education. To do this it must maintain and cultivate the spirit of initiative and self-reliance directed by an abiding faith in and an understanding of excellence.

To withstand the immediate demand in favor of the long term need, balancing the practical with development of theory, preferring the basic inquiry to invention of the applicable product, will not be an easy accomplishment. To maintain the tradition of leadership, to hold the initiative with self-reliance, to preserve the climate of intellectual freedom will be a stern ~~task~~ ordeal for the independent university in the future; and the achievement of these ends by Vanderbilt will require the combined, determined and resourceful effort of Administration, Faculty, Alumni and Friends. The history of Vanderbilt for 75 years is reassuring.

The Faculty joins me in greeting the dawn of ~~a new day~~ another period of progress with confidence and good will.

At this particular moment in their respective lives, Dr. Goodpasture probably welcomed this public opportunity to extend his hand in collegiality and goodwill to the university. For his part, Chancellor Branscomb must have been pleased to witness that one of his most esteemed faculty was still aboard ship.

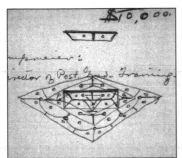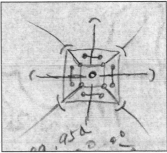

Fig. 5-9: Doodles by Dr. Goodpasture.[79]

Chapter Six

EXTRAMURAL RESPONSIBILITIES

In 1940, Dr. Goodpasture was fifty-four years of age, was the most distinguished scientist at Vanderbilt, and was recognized as one of the premier pathologists in the United States.[1] Nevertheless, the decade of the 1940s witnessed a dramatic decline in his research productivity, with his only significant studies those of viral infections on human placental membrane explants in 1942 and the discovery of the cause of granuloma inguinale in 1945.[2] After the work on granuloma inguinale, there was a thirteen-year hiatus during which no research papers were published. This dearth of research work is all the more noticeable because Dr. Goodpasture's laboratory in 1940 was at the forefront internationally in the study of viral and bacterial diseases, owing to imaginative and skillful exploitation of the chick embryo technique. Nor had he changed his lifelong commitment to conduct basic research into the mechanism of infectious diseases, as evidenced by his repeated declarations about the importance of research.

This seachange in research productivity is attributable in part to his assumption of responsibilities in the dean's office, as associate dean in 1943 and dean in 1945. The deanship was particularly trying, as there were many administrative crises for which he and the medical school were not prepared, the most demanding of which was the financial crisis following World War II that has been previously described in chapter 5.

World War II also dramatically changed the conditions for conducting basic research: applied research was the order of the day, and sources of basic research funding such as the Fluid Research Fund had evaporated; furthermore, trained manpower was diverted immediately into the war effort, and those on the home front faced year-round scheduling of medical school classes and coverage of civilian medical needs with skeleton staffs.[3] Dr. Goodpasture commented to his friend Watson Sellards in 1942:[4] "We are in such a state of confusion at the present time because of reorganization incident to accelerated teaching and the war in general that I don't know how we stand so far as investigative work is concerned but hope we will be able to continue."

Four years later, at the convocation honoring Chancellor Carmichael at his departure, Dr. Goodpasture summarized the effect of the war on the university as follows:[5]

> The major portion of your administration has been carried out under the impact of war, first abroad with Pearl Harbor, then engulfing our own country. The educational problems arising from the needs and demands of the armed forces were so varied, so urgent and so radical, the entire atmosphere of the campus changed suddenly from one of peaceful pursuit of learning to that of an intensified, directed and accelerated technological training camp. Much time will pass before the effects of this change cease to be felt, if ever.

Dr. Goodpasture also had personal problems that must have affected his ability to concentrate on research. His wife, Sarah Catlett Goodpasture, died July 17, 1940, from a chronic illness, followed by the death of his brother Ridley on October 8, 1942, his father A. V. Sr. on December 3, 1942, and his sister Mattie on December 28, 1944. Sarah died in Vanderbilt Hospital, and the latter two died in the Goodpasture home on Fairfax Avenue. These were sad times, when the sense of purpose might well have gone out of his life, but the decline in research productivity in all probability was due instead to the professional demands of the dean's office and the difficulties inherent to carrying on a basic research program during wartime.

This chapter examines another impediment to his research. During the 1940s a host of extramural responsibilities placed additional demands on his time and energies (Table 6-1). First, because of his professional stature and expertise in infectious diseases, he was asked during this time to assume major extramural responsibilities on committees attempting to reduce the spread of infections in U.S. troops. In 1941, he was appointed to a board for the investigation and control of epidemic diseases by the surgeon general's office and in 1942 to a subcommittee on epidemic and infectious diseases by the National Research Council (NRC).

His expertise in pathology shortly led to additional appointments to give advice and counsel about various special weapons, with NRC appointments to the Committee on Biological Warfare and the Atomic Bomb Casualty Committee, as well as appointments to a National Defense Research Committee on potential use of nitrogen mustard and to the Atomic Energy Commission Advisory Committee for Biology and Medicine. Finally, his stature as an academician led to challenging appointments as acting editor-in-chief of the *American Journal of Pathology,* as president of the American Association of Pathologists and Bacteriologists, and to key committees attempting to develop peacetime strategies for maintenance of research through federal funding.

The time and effort consumed by these various duties are difficult to estimate. There is no diary or log of his travels, and records of compensation are inconsistently available. Trips, particularly those to Washington or New York, were often multipurpose, mixing government and university business. Minutes of meetings listing attendees have not been uniformly saved, and some documents describing committee activities were coded SECRET and returned after his membership terminated. In terms of time involved in travel, most trips were via railway, and the most frequent commutes to Washington and New York required overnight journeys of twelve and twenty hours respectively.

Table 6-1
Boards, Committees, Foundations, Commissions, Showing Dates of Service**

1929–52
National Academy of Sciences, National Research Council: Committee on nasal sinuses, 1929
Subcommittee on epidemic/infectious diseases, 1942
Conference group, advisory to Surgeons General of Army and Navy, Chairman, 1942
Committee on biological warfare, 1942–45
Committee on atomic casualties 1950–53
Special mission to Hiroshima, Japan, 1950, to review Atomic Bomb Casualty Commission

1932–34
Leonard Wood Memorial for Eradication of Leprosy: Medical Advisory Board

1935–44
Board of Directors, American Society for Control of Cancer

1938–44
Rockefeller Foundation, International Health Division: Board of Scientific Directors, 1938–40 and 1942–44

1938–45
Cincinnati Children's Hospital Research Foundation: Scientific Advisory Council

1940–49
American Medical Association: Committee on Scientific Research

1941–46
Surgeon General's Office: Board for Investigation and Control of Influenza, Other Epidemic Diseases

1942–50
Tennessee Valley Authority: Consultant, Health Division

1943
Member, National Defense Research Committee (Burwell Committee)

1944–52
National Academy of Sciences: Council, 1944–47 and 1949–52

1944–47
Office of Scientific Research and Development: Medical Advisory Committee (Palmer Committee)

1945–49
Life Insurance Medical Research Fund: Advisory Board

1946–50
Special Consultant, U.S. Public Health Service: Member, Virus and Rickettsial Study Section

1946–52
Oak Ridge Institute: Board of Directors, Institute for Nuclear Studies

1947–52
U.S. Atomic Energy Commission: Advisory Committee for Biology and Medicine, 1947–52, Vice chairman

1951–55
Tennessee State Library Board

1949–54
Grayson Foundation: Board of Scientific Directors

1952–58
National Science Foundation: Divisional Committee for Medical Research, 1952–54
Committee to review support of research by Department of Health, Education and Welfare, 1955
U.S. Advisory Committee for the Living Cell Class, International Science Exhibition, 1957–58

** Dates for the various positions are based on correspondence or other archival material. In many cases the dates do not correspond precisely with those in the C.V. of Dr. Goodpasture prepared in 1958 when he was at the Armed Forces Institute of Pathology.

With these caveats, a conservative estimate of 25 percent of time and effort for extramural responsibilities seems justified, particularly during the 1941–47 period.

—

SECURITY CLEARANCE

Citizens interacting with the government in wartime faced issues of security clearance, loyalty declaration, and disclosure of heretofore private information that deserve brief comment. Dr. Goodpasture readily complied with these requirements, was given a SECRET security status, and often had special travel privileges. His correspondence files contain personnel security questionnaires and travel vouchers that provide information that is not available elsewhere in the records. For example, in 1950[6] a security clearance form records that his height was five feet, eight inches, weight was 145 pounds, eyes were blue, and hair gray.

The mechanics of interacting with the government did not come readily to citizen Goodpasture, and he frequently had problems complying with the letter of instructions in completing travel vouchers. On February 18, 1941, Major Paul Robinson, Medical Corps, an assistant in the Surgeon General's Office (SGO), returned a travel voucher because precise hours of departure and arrival at various stages of the journey had not been provided.[7] From the correctly filled out form, we are given a glimpse of travel from Nashville to Washington in 1941 and the time required to attend a single meeting, this of the SGO Board of Epidemic Diseases. Dr. Goodpasture left home at 7:00 A.M., on February 26, by taking a taxi to Union Station for a 7:25 departure for Washington via Cincinnati. Arriving in Washington at 7:45 A.M., February 27, he took a taxi to the Willard Hotel, from which he departed the next day at 4:00 P.M. for the 5:00 train to Nashville. Arrival at Union Station in Nashville was at 2:30 P.M., March 1, followed by a taxi to his home on Fairfax Avenue.[8]

There were other vexations, as indicated by the following problems in filling out a fingerprint card and handling SECRET documents. On October 2, 1941, another assistant in the Surgeon General's Office, Major R. J. Wilson, returned a fingerprint card because it was "not acceptable in its present form," in that it was not "completely filled out on both sides." There was this response on October 7 from Dr. Goodpasture:[9]

in re: S.G.O. 201 (Goodpasture, Ernest W.)

My dear Major Wilson:

In response to your letter of October 2, I am returning the finger print card. I wish to advise that I have filled out the card to the best of my knowledge. On one side of the sheet there is a blank space for a photograph the use of which is indicated as being optional. Below that is for additional information to be submitted only by applicants for firearm permits, and the remaining space is to be left blank. On the opposite side of the card there is a heading of classification, number and reference, as to the meaning and nature of which I have not the slightest idea.

Hoping that the finger print card is not [presumably now] satisfactory, I am,

Sincerely yours,

Rules about handling SECRET documents and meeting security regulations were elaborate and probably troublesome for civilians to understand or follow. In October 1951, Dr. Goodpasture was to view an atomic explosion as a member of the Advisory Committee for Biology and Medicine of the Atomic Energy Commission and was thereby responsible for returning the documents "Security Acknowledgement for Observers at Operations BUSTER-JANGLE" and "Instructions and Information for Observers at Operations BUSTER-JANGLE" to the central office for safekeeping.

Mr. Bryan F. LaPlante, chief of Washington Area Security Operations, wrote on October 12, 1951: "We wish to inform you that the above SECRET documents were received at this Headquarters in one envelope [instead of two] with no receipts." Dr. Goodpasture's attention was invited to the enclosed Security

Instruction GM-SEC-5 (formerly GM-37) entitled "Procedures for Processing Classified Matter," a fourteen-page document containing instructions about transmitting SECRET documents. His attention was particularly directed to paragraph 6c. (2) requiring the use of double envelopes and paragraph 7c. (3) requiring the use of Classified Material Receipts when change of custody was intended. Applying the law of mass action, Mr. LaPlante enclosed thirty copies of the receipt form for future use.

―――

WARTIME COMMITTEE ASSIGNMENTS

In order to understand the nature of Dr. Goodpasture's extramural responsibilities and his contributions to the deliberations of various committees and boards, we must take a brief foray into the realm of acronyms such as NIH, NRC, AEC, ABCC, NDRC, OSRD, and NSF. Some of these organizations sprang up during the war and then vanished; some affect our scientific policies now. Some were responsible for key scientific contributions to the war effort and generally are credited with producing the technological advances necessary to win the war—namely, radar, missiles, proximity fuses, mass production of penicillin, and the atomic bomb.[10] Through his membership on some of these committees, Dr. Goodpasture interacted with the most influential officials in Washington as well as the most distinguished scientists in the United States. He witnessed a test explosion of an atomic bomb, traveled to Hiroshima, had an audience with General MacArthur, and, most importantly, had an opportunity to influence the mechanism of research funding after the war.

Before World War II, philanthropic agencies of various types were the major contributors to basic research because there was minimal research support by the federal government.[11] At Vanderbilt Medical School, for example, the Fluid Research Fund, a $250,000 contribution by the Rockefeller Foundation, underlay most research in the 1930s. This fund was a block grant to the medical school, parceled out to individual investigators through applications reviewed by a committee of peers. Many investigators, including Dr. Goodpasture, felt this approach to research funding was ideal, promoting maximal freedom for the investigator and minimizing paperwork.

Scientists' concerns about governmental interference and the military establishment's attitude that wars should be left to the professionals resulted in minimal input by our scientific community into the conduct of wars preceding World War II. This lack of scientific interaction is all the more remarkable in view of the fact that the federal government had recognized the need for scientific and technical advice as early as 1863, when the bill establishing the National Academy of Sciences (NAS) was passed by Congress and signed into law by President Lincoln. NAS was intended to be the official scientific advisor to the government, but in its first fifty years, help from NAS was requested by the government in only fifty-three issues.[12]

Some of these issues were important: the Academy of Sciences had a major role in creating the Geological Service, the Forest Service, the Weather Bureau, and the National Bureau of Standards. However, NAS as constituted was not an effective partner with the government, the former being always concerned about its independence and the latter seeking more control of operations. In 1916, the academy concluded that an auxiliary organization was needed to function as its operating arm, and the National Research Council (NRC) was created.

Consultants with or without NAS membership could serve on the NRC, thereby greatly enlarging the pool of talent that the government and NAS could call upon without diluting the prestige of academy membership. A brochure in Dr. Goodpasture's correspondence files[13] emphasizes that the NRC was established in 1916 "primarily to coordinate the non-governmental scientific and technical resources of the country with the military and naval agencies of the Government, in the interests of national security and preparedness." Reorganized later by President Wilson as a "permanent organization for the promotion and maintenance of scientific research," the purpose of the NRC, as purported in 1916, was somewhat broader.[14] Its goals were to:

> bring into co-operation existing governmental, educational, industrial and other research organizations with the object of encouraging the investigation of natural phenomena, the increased use of scientific research in the development of American industries, the employment of scientific methods in strengthening the national defense, and other such applications of science as will promote the national security and welfare.

The NRC has had difficulties performing up to these expectations, despite or perhaps because of a staff of one thousand, with another six thousand outside scientists and engineers serving each year as volunteers on the NRC's committees, boards, and commissions. A recent review of NRC organization[15] concludes the NRC "takes too long to produce many of its reports, is not responsive enough to its sponsors, lacks clear lines of authority, and its staff is too often frustrated and stressed." These or similar problems have presumably always limited its usefulness, as evidenced by the creation of a far more effective agency in World War II, the Office of Scientific Research and Development (OSRD) and its operating arm, the National Defense Research Committee (NDRC).

The arm came into existence first, on June 12, 1940, when the recently appointed president of the Carnegie Foundation, Dr. Vannevar Bush, met President Franklin Roosevelt for the first time.[16] At this meeting, Bush solicited the support of the president for a new committee—the National Defense Research Committee—to harness the scientific and technological manpower of the United States in the event of war. This committee would be empowered to:[17]

> coordinate, supervise and conduct scientific research or the problems underlying the development, production and use of mechanisms and devices of warfare, except scientific research on the problems of flight [flight was already being addressed in the National Advisory Committee for Aeronautics].

After fifteen minutes, Bush had Roosevelt's endorsement.[18] The NDRC was comprised of twelve members appointed by the president, all serving without compensation; there were in addition two members each from the War and Navy Departments and from the National Academy of Sciences. The committee was authorized to contract for scientific studies with educational institutions, individuals, and industrial organizations. Vannevar Bush was appointed chairman of the NDRC, and its members included, among others, James Conant, president of Harvard; Karl Compton, president of the Massachusetts Institute of Technology; and Frank Jewett, chief of AT&T's Bell laboratories and president of the National Academy of Sciences.

The key instrument in NDRC's bureaucratic arsenal was the contract by which scientists were mobilized for defense efforts in their own laboratories. Conant[19] felt the system of contracts represented a watershed in the government's relationship with scientists. The contract method allowed researchers to remain in familiar surroundings, assemble their staffs there, and stay relatively free of federal bureaucracy. In effect, a national network of the best researchers was developed, over which Vannevar Bush and fellow committee members had enormous power and authority.

Fig. 6-1: Advisory Council of Office of Scientific Research and Development. Left to right: J. C. Hunaker, Harvey Bundy, James Conant, Vannevar Bush, Admiral Julius Furer, Newton Richards, Frank Jewett, and Bush aide Carroll Wilson. From Zachary's *Endless Frontier.* (Between pages 248–49.)

Their resources were greatly increased in May 1941 when Roosevelt approved the creation of the Office of Scientific Research and Development, or OSRD, to oversee NDRC. The NDRC had been funded from the president's emergency funds,[20] but OSRD received direct funding from Congress and thereby had access to large amounts of money. Bush became director of OSRD (Fig. 6-1), a post he retained until that organization was disbanded after the war.

OSRD undertook a systematic search for scientific personnel in government, universities, and industry, and then involved the most talented in specific research and development programs. From OSRD programs came:

- Victory in the Atlantic over German submarines by more effective detection and destruction of enemy submarines
- Greatly enhanced anti-aircraft measures through development of high frequency radar and proximity fuses
- Improved mechanisms for off-loading ships using amphibious trucks
- Development of weapons for specific combat needs, such as the flamethrower, napalm, and incendiary bombs
- Handheld rockets (bazooka) for use as an anti-tank weapon
- Medical advances such as anti-malarials, DDT, mass production of penicillin, and fluid replacement for injured troops
- Victory in Japan due to these advances and the atomic bomb

By December 1, 1944, the Committee on Medical Research in OSRD had authorized 496 research contracts with 120 different institutions at a cost of $15 million. Ninety-five percent of these contracts were with universities or teaching hospitals and involved the services of 553 physicians.[21] In retrospect, President Roosevelt, in June 1940, had prepared for the eventuality of war in establishing the best system devised by any of the warring powers to mobilize scientists.[22] In Vannevar Bush he had appointed an exemplary director for this system, a man who was recognized at his death in 1974 as "the engineer who marshaled America's technology for

World War II and ushered in the atomic age."[23] The word "engineer" hardly conveys the extent of his role in the war or his influence on the postwar interactions between government and academia.

The extent of civilian involvement in the research effort in the United States is indicated by the number of contracts between OSRD and major universities and industrial organizations (Table 6-2). Efforts on such a scale were possible because of the support of the president and Congress and required deferral of at least ten thousand eminently draftable scientists. Thus was created our first military-industrial-academic complex, signifying a revolution in the American way of life.[24] Dr. Goodpasture was part of this military-industrial-academic complex. His most significant roles

Table 6-2
OSRD Contracts with Major Universities and Industries

University/ Industry	Number of Contracts	Amount Expended*
MIT	75	116.9
California Institute of Technology	48	83.4
Harvard	79	30.9
Columbia	73	28.5
Western Electric	94	19.1
University of California	106	14.4
Johns Hopkins	49	10.6
Research Construction	2	13.9
General Electric	58	8.1
RCA	54	5.8
du Pont	59	5.7
Westinghouse Electric	54	5.1

* In millions

Fig. 6-2: Army Epidemiological Board, as of 1941. Left to right, the members are: Doctors A. J. Warren, Ernest Goodpasture, C. H. Perry Pepper, Francis Blake, Colonel James Simmons, O. T. Avery, Colonel Stanhope Bayne-Jones, K. F. Maxcy, and A. R. Dochez.

were as an infectious disease specialist involved in minimizing contagious diseases in military camps, as an expert pathologist sent to evaluate the effects of an atomic bomb at Hiroshima, and finally as a senior and trusted academician who held two key committee assignments seeking administrative strategies for converting wartime funding of research to a peacetime mechanism of support.

BOARD FOR INVESTIGATION OF INFECTIOUS DISEASES

In late January 1941, Dr. Goodpasture was informed[25] that he would be invited by the surgeon general of the Army to serve on a civilian Board for Investigation of Infectious Diseases.[26] This notification came from Dr. Francis Blake, in the Department of Internal Medicine, Yale University School of Medicine, the president-designate of the board. Dr. Blake noted in his letter to Dr. Goodpasture that "the main function will be to select personnel and organize civilian commissions to be sent to Army posts or camps for the study and control of any epidemic outbreaks of infectious diseases that may occur." The members of the board were remarkably distinguished (Fig. 6-2).

Orders were sent from the surgeon general's office to Dr. Goodpasture and presumably to all members, thus ensuring attendance at the organizational meeting of the board[27] in Washington, to begin at 9:00 A.M. on February 6, 1941, and to last approximately five days. Civilians of course served without compensation, save for a flat per diem of $5.00 in lieu of actual expenses. The board recommended that commissions be established to deal with the important infectious diseases, each commission to have a director and necessary consultant personnel. Commissions were expected to consult and advise with respect to control of epidemic diseases and to investigate improved methods of control by field studies or interim laboratory investigations.

At the first meeting the original board was enlarged to seven civilian members, and general agreement was reached on the makeup of the commissions. The board (now called Board for the Investigation and Control of Influenza and Other Epidemic Diseases) returned to Washington on February 27–28, 1941, to convene the various commissions and their directors, which were, respectively:[28] acute respiratory diseases, Dr. John H. Dingle; cross infections in hospitals, Dr. Oswald H. Robertson; epidemiological survey, Dr. S. Bayne-Jones; influenza, Dr. Thomas Francis; measles and mumps, Dr. Joseph Stokes Jr.; neurotropic virus diseases, Dr. John R. Paul; pneumonia, Dr. Colin MacLeod; meningococcal meningitis, Dr. John J. Phair; hemolytic streptococcal infection, Dr. M. Henry Dawson; and tropical diseases, Dr. Wilbur A. Sawyer.

Altogether there were 7 civilian members on the central board, including Dr. Goodpasture, and approximately 104 commission members. Biannual meetings, each lasting two days, were held

Fig. 6-3: Army Epidemiological Board, as of 1946. Colonels Simmons and Bayne-Jones have become brigadier generals.

throughout the war and seemed to be well-attended, perhaps because notices of meetings did come in the form of *orders* from the surgeon general's office. Remarkably, the original board did not change during the war, even in its military personnel (Fig. 6-3). The accomplishments of the board are best summarized in the citation accompanying the Lasker Award, given to the board as a group in 1946 by the American Public Health Association:[29]

> The Army Epidemiological Board, originally designated "The Board for the Investigation and Control of Influenza and other Epidemic Diseases in the Army," rendered exceptionally meritorious service to the country in the prevention of infectious diseases during the period from January 1941 to June 1946. . . . Fundamental investigations were carried on at some of the chief universities and scientific institutes in the United States, field studies were made at Army posts and camps in this country, and extensive investigations were conducted among American forces in all theatres of operation overseas. An effective virus vaccine against influenza was developed, tested

and applied. A vaccine for prevention of Japanese B encephalitis was developed and used. The nature, cause and mode of spread of the acute respiratory diseases were thoroughly investigated and measures for control were improved. The causative agent of infectious hepatitis was discovered and important information was gained concerning this disease. Meningitis was brought under control by prophylactic use of sulfadiazine. New and beneficial information was acquired from research on nearly all the infectious diseases of importance to the Army. The achievements of the Board and Commissions during the war constitute a notable gain in military preventive medicine, a permanent enrichment of medical science and a lasting contribution to the advancement of civilian public health.

Atomic Bomb Casualty Commission

This commission (ABCC) was funded by the NRC and conducted field operations for the Committee on Atomic Casualties appointed by the NRC's Division of Medical Sciences. As such, it had a joint advisory role to the Division of Biology and Medicine of the Atomic Energy Commission (AEC).[30] One hopes these interlocking committee arrangements were effective in practice, although they seem somewhat cumbersome and excessively entangled now. There undoubtedly was logic, if not practical value, in the arrangements. Many scientists, including Dr. Goodpasture, served simultaneously on all the committees and divisions mentioned in the paragraph above. For example, in 1947, Doctors Goodpasture, Bronk, Hastings, and Wearn were on the AEC Advisory Committee for Biology and Medicine (Fig. 6-4), and in 1951 these four and others were on the Committee on Atomic Casualties of the NRC.[31]

Dr. Goodpasture was sent to Japan in December 1950 to review operations of the ABCC. He left Nashville on December 14 with passport, military orders, Army identification card, Pan-Am Airlines tickets (for legs San Francisco to Tokyo via Honolulu and return), vaccination record, and, hopefully, towels and soap (not routinely available in Japan) all in hand. He arrived in Tokyo on December 18, and in Hiro

Fig. 6-4: Atomic Energy Commission Advisory Committee for Biology and Medicine. Left to right, members are: Doctors Joseph Wearn, E. C. Stakman, Alan Gregg, G. W. Beadle, A. Baird Hastings, Ernest Goodpasture, and Detlev Bronk.

on December 19, accompanied by Colonel Tessmer, director of ABCC, and Dr. Machle of the NRC. They were billeted in the BOQ (bachelor officer's quarters) at North Camp with the "privilege of the excellent mess [dining facilities] there." From Hiro, they commuted by stationwagon to the headquarters of ABCC in the Gaisenkan Building at Hiroshima for conferences and to carry out the daily program. The commute required three hours round-trip and was made each day of his visit, except for Sundays, December 24, and Christmas.

The available information about this trip to Hiroshima is contained in a lengthy report filed by Dr. Goodpasture shortly after his return to the United States. Leaving Hiro on December 28, he arrived in Tokyo via Kyoto on December 29 and departed from Tokyo on January 6 for Portland, Oregon. By January 9, his fifty-five-page report had been prepared for Dr. Shields Warren, director of the Division of Biology and Medicine of AEC, and was a subject of discussion by the Advisory

Committee for that division at its meeting in nearby Hanford, California, on January 12–13.

Before considering that report, recall that the peace treaty with Japan had not been signed at the time of Dr. Goodpasture's trip and that the United States was in the midst of the Korean War. When he visited Hiroshima, the ABCC had 1,061 employees, of whom 143 were Allied personnel and 918 Japanese. Among the former, there were seventeen M.D.s and Ph.D.s, four nurses, and ten technicians, while Japanese employees included thirty-nine physicians, forty-five nurses, and forty-two technicians.[32] ABCC's budget for fiscal year 1951 was $1.4 million, and the total expenditure for plant and equipment by that year was $1.37 million. The total number of Japanese exposed to the bombs who had survived until 1950 was estimated as eighty-five thousand in Hiroshima and seventy thousand in Nagasaki.

In this setting, Dr. Goodpasture's overall impression of the relationship between ABCC and the Japanese people is particularly interesting:[33]

> One can scarcely imagine so unique an enterprise so fraught with difficulties and uncertainties on every hand. To establish this undertaking de novo in a recent enemy land in the midst of a population lately suffering a new and awful catastrophe and now under occupation by a conquering nation, to do this and at the same time to cultivate the good will and cooperation of these people and to attract them to collaborate (although professionally they are ill prepared to participate in a modern clinic without . . . time consuming teaching and training) are accomplishments which one must indeed admire.

As one might expect, Dr. Goodpasture first defined the stated purposes of the ABCC:[34]

> The program as originally planned had two main objectives: (a) To determine the medical changes brought about in those exposed to the bomb explosion. The survivors are studied from the standpoint of the rate of recovery from the injury, development of late evidence of injury, alterations in their immunity to disease, changes in growth rate, if any, of

the exposed children, and any changes in fertility that may develop. (b) To determine the genetic changes, if any, of the ionizing radiations on the offspring of those exposed to the bomb explosion.

With these goals in mind, Dr. Goodpasture's report concentrated on the "broader aspects of the program, especially the scientific objectives," leaving administrative and budgetary issues to other NRC personnel on this site visit. There was time to deal only with the situation in Hiroshima, and planned trips to Nagasaki could not be wedged into the schedule. His report is more than a careful analysis of the complex scientific, political, and civic problems resulting from the atomic bomb. It also documents the difficulties of managing such a demanding field operation at a remove of eight thousand miles from "home base" (Washington). Some of the problems which should have been anticipated were:

- The AEC and NRC, as the two agencies responsible for the ABCC, had not clearly defined the goals, scientific program, and administration of the ABCC, and in some cases seemed to be in competition for resources (Goodpasture Report, page 4)
- There was ineffective liaison between the field operation in Japan and "home base," suggesting a lack of interest by the responsible NRC committee (Report, page 3)
- The Army Medical Corps officers providing leadership of the ABCC lacked innate scientific strength and wisdom (Report, page 2)
- Top Japanese leadership was not effective, except in understanding public relations (Report, page 3)
- Data collection was seriously hampered by lack of trained personnel and clearly defined projects (Report, page 16)

Some of the problems would have been difficult to anticipate: lack of housing and laboratory facilities in Hiroshima meant a daily three-hour commute for most American personnel (Report, page 3, discussion); Japanese physicians, nurses, and technicians were inadequately trained (Report, page 6, discussion); recruitment of American personnel was hampered by uncertainties of living arrangements for families (Report, page 2, discussion) and by instability in the region from the Korean War; and it was surprisingly difficult to document those Japanese actually exposed to radiation and their precise location in Hiroshima or Nagasaki. As Dr. Goodpasture commented (Report, page 10):

> It is curious to learn that the Japanese public locally have sublimated the A-bombing experience into a sort of honorable estate. Because of the activities of ABCC special advantages are considered to be available to those who were exposed and there seems to be some difficulty at times in discovering whether or not an individual was really present at the time.

From a scientific standpoint, there was very little to cheer about. The delay in establishing an effective field organization meant that the acute effects of irradiation could not be studied due to the death of the most heavily irradiated population. No scientific publications had been prepared, at least none for the public sector. The project which Dr. Goodpasture singled out as promising was the one showing an increase in the rate of leukemia, and even this study was of doubtful significance until laboratory methods for diagnosis were upgraded and statistical analyses improved.[35]

Dr. Goodpasture concluded the discussion section of his report in a surprising way. Rather than concentrating on the more immediate issues of bomb damage, he recognized that one of the most effective actions of ABCC might be the training of Japanese physicians in laboratory work, as a start in reinvigorating the medical profession (Report, page 7, discussion):

> From an educational standpoint it seems to me that full utilization of clinical laboratory resources of the Commission would be most beneficial. There is, I understand, no modern clinical laboratory in Japan, and no training at the present time that would make adequate use of such facilities [in] diagnosis and medical care. The training of well selected physicians in the use of the tools of the clinical laboratory, including surgical pathology and radiology, and the interpretation of values that can be derived from

them, with a subsequent seeding of these trained individuals into the medical schools and hospitals would be a most profitable contribution.

There was one more highlight of the trip to Japan—his appointment with General MacArthur. That appointment was on January 2, 1951, when Dr. Goodpasture presented a letter of introduction from Mr. Gordon Dean, chairman of the Atomic Energy Commission. Dr. Goodpasture "appreciated this courtesy very much and had an enjoyable and instructive visit with the General." At this meeting he was informed that a peace treaty would be consummated with Japan in 1951.

The AEC Advisory Committee for Biology and Medicine held its twenty-ninth meeting at the Las Vegas test site on October 28–29, 1951, and viewed operations BUSTER-JANGLE referred to previously. After the test, Dr. Goodpasture in his role as vice chairman of the committee wrote to Mr. Gordon Dean of AEC:[36] "For most of us this was the first opportunity to witness an atomic detonation and to observe first-hand the radiological safety operations in which the Committee has been vitally interested since its inception, and to which I hope we may have made some contribution." In this regard, Dr. Goodpasture closed his letter to Mr. Dean with the admonition that:

> Cancer is a specific industrial hazard of the atomic energy business. This significant fact justifies, in the opinion of the Committee, the continued exploitation of the Commission's [ABCC's] special facilities for radiation in cancer research, diagnosis and therapy. The Committee recommends the cancer program be vigorously pursued as a humanitarian duty to the nation.

COMMITTEES ANALYZING PEACETIME FUNDING OF RESEARCH

In 1944, when the end of the war in Europe was in sight, Vannevar Bush and Franklin Roosevelt attempted to organize an administrative framework for a peacetime coalition between government and science. The first public notice of this effort was a letter from Roosevelt to Bush dated November 17, 1944, which was barely two weeks after FDR had been elected to his fourth term. After briefly recounting the vital role of OSRD in the war effort, FDR asked Bush to address four questions:[37] (1) How can scientific knowledge developed in the war be released to the world quickly? (2) How can a program of medical research be organized to continue the attack on disease? (3) How can the government assist research in public and private institutions? (4) Can a program be suggested to develop the scientific talent of American youth to ensure high-quality research in the future? A copy of FDR's letter[38] was forwarded to Dr. Goodpasture on December 19 by Vannevar Bush, with the request that Dr. Goodpasture serve on a committee considering "the entire future of medical research in this country."[39]

Vannevar Bush obviously recognized the "extraordinary opportunity to lay before the President and the country well considered opinions and recommendations" about the interaction of scientists and government and recruited approximately fifty of the nation's most prominent scientists and educators to serve on four committees to address each of the questions stated above. Dr. Goodpasture promptly accepted the invitation to serve on the Medical Advisory Committee, with Chairman Dr. Walter Palmer, Bard Professor of Medicine, College of Physicians and Surgeons, Columbia University.[40] Dr. Palmer (and the other committee chairmen) moved quickly. On January 27, 1945, Dr. Palmer sent to his committee a seventeen-page document titled "Tentative Plans for Committee Action" in which he described their objectives and "plan of attack." Appendices were attached that summarized evidence presented on December 14–15 before the subcommittee of the Senate on Wartime Health and Education (the "Pepper Committee"), the interim report of the Pepper Committee, and issues Dr. Palmer suggested the committee should consider.[41]

The meeting schedule of the Palmer Committee has not been saved in Dr. Goodpasture's files, but the committee probably met only twice.[42] Dr. Palmer submitted the final report to Vannevar Bush on April 25, 1945, thirteen days after President Roosevelt's death. The report began with documentation of the success of OSRD's Committee on Medical Research in reducing the death rate of troops from 14.1/1000 in World War I to 0.6/1000 in World War II.

This reduction was attributed to mass production of penicillin and sulfa drugs, discovery of DDT, improvement in hygiene, and improvement in vaccines—thereby essentially eliminating the traditional wartime scourges of yellow fever, dysentery, typhus, tetanus, and pneumonia. Malaria had also been partially controlled, the disability from venereal diseases had been sharply reduced, and there had been dramatic progress in surgery on the wounded owing to improvement in transfusion therapies. In sharp contrast to this record of achievement, the effect of the war on basic research was completely negative:

- Hospitals and medical schools had seriously depleted staffs, while faculty had increased teaching and patient care responsibilities.
- The diversion of physicians into the armed forces and prohibition against graduate training had left the field of medical science "barren," so "it will be many years before medicine fully recovers."[43]

Because many of the achievements in medical care during the war were rooted in civilian research, the Palmer Committee felt justified in its goal: "Medicine must consider now how to attack the medical problems of peace." The committee further wished to emphasize that, "The entire history of science bears testimony to the supreme importance of affording the prepared mind complete freedom for the exercise of initiative" and that this process was traditionally the province of universities and their medical schools.

At this point, the Palmer Committee began to describe its version of an ideal relationship between government and science. Beginning with the observation that federal aid for medical research in the United States was mainly brought about by the war, the committee observed that government support of research had been widespread in Europe for many years. In particular, Great Britain had funded medical research through the Medical Research Council since 1920. This council could receive money both from Parliament and non-governmental sources and had considerable administrative autonomy.

In the arrangement suggested by the Palmer Committee, money would be made available to universities and their medical schools by block or unrestricted grants with a suggested grant lifetime of ten years, by fellowships, and by grants-in-aid for specific projects. It was important that the group dispensing the money be "free from political influence and protected against special pressures," for which purposes the Palmer Committee recommended an independent federal agency to be called the National Foundation for Medical Research.

This foundation would be administered by a Board of Trustees made up of five men "experienced in research," appointed by the president, and approved by the Senate. Expert advice and council would be provided by a technical board appointed by the Board of Trustees and containing twelve scientists representing special fields. The latter could appoint ad hoc committees to advise on particular medical problems. These recommendations naturally reflected the fierce independence of investigators of that period, coupled with suspicion of governmental control and their memories of the salad days when financial support like the Fluid Research Fund at Vanderbilt provided resources over a long period with minimal restrictions.

These recommendations also reflected an astonishing level of political naivete. Their report was sent to Vannevar Bush on April 25, 1945, with the endorsement of Dr. Palmer: "This report has the unanimous approval of my Committee and I submit it with the conviction that it has, almost without exception, the endorsement of the many individuals to whom the Committee is so deeply indebted for freely-given and valuable advice." In fact, on March 23, 1945,[44] Dr. Goodpasture retracted his support of an independent foundation that had apparently been agreed to at an executive meeting in Denver a few days before. Dr. Goodpasture stated in a letter to Dr. Palmer that: "It seems to me now that such a suggestion would be entirely impractical," a viewpoint apparently also supported by Dr. Doisy.

Dr. Goodpasture concluded his letter with the suggestion: "We should make every effort to explore the possibilities under government before abandoning hope . . . in that direction." This was late in the game to attempt substantive changes in the committee report, of which there is a draft document in the files that is essentially unchanged from the final report.[45] The draft is undated, and in it approval or comments were requested by Dr. Palmer. There are no notations on this document to indicate whether or not Dr. Goodpasture reviewed it.

The four committees appointed by Bush submitted their reports on time, allowing Bush two to three months for collation and word-crafting before the final report was submitted to President Truman on July 5, 1945. It was titled *Science: The Endless Frontier* (Fig. 6-5). Barfield, in *Science for the Twenty-First Century*, states: "By all contemporary accounts, the report became an instant success, enjoying widespread editorial support and commendation that transcended party, geography, and ideology."[46] The title came in for its share of commendation, creating the vision of scientist and engineer exploring the frontiers of knowledge.[47]

Science: The Endless Frontier is allegedly "the single most influential document

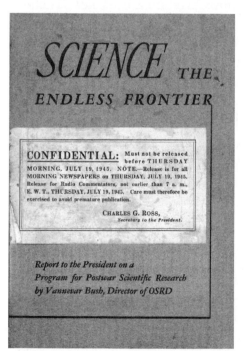

Fig. 6-5: The Bush Report that was sent to Dr. Goodpasture. Now filed in the Goodpasture papers in the Eskind Library, Special Collections.

shaping U.S. science and technology policy over the past half-century."[48] In this report, Bush proposed the creation of a National Research Foundation, which would have the following features:[49]

> The agency would sponsor studies in the physical sciences and medicine, set priorities for long-term military research and lend coherence to the diverse research efforts paid for by other federal departments. Sweeping in scope, the research foundation would elevate private experts to a governmental status heretofore accepted only in periods of national crisis. In order to limit the possibility of political interference, the foundation would allow expenditures to be dictated by researchers themselves. Even the foundation's director would be selected not by the president, but by an independent board of scientists appointed by the chief executive.

The proposed independence of this foundation was its undoing politically.

A bill following Bush's organizational plan passed Congress in 1947, but President Truman vetoed it on the grounds that he would not establish an executive agency with so little control by the chief executive.[50] Three years later, Congress passed a bill placing the foundation under the president's authority. This bill was signed by Truman in 1950, thereby creating the National Science Foundation (NSF).

A great opportunity for rational and sustained funding of basic research was lost in the five years between the filing of the Bush Report and the creation of the NSF—lost in part because the cold war had developed. Consequently, the Defense Department and AEC by 1950 had secured 90 percent of federal research and development spending.[51] Further, the National Institutes of Health had in the early 1950s garnered great support for a host of specific disease projects that were eminently appealing to various interest groups and congressmen. The consequence of not having the NSF as intended has been summarized:[52]

The failure of Congress and the White House to agree on such an agency [National Research Foundation] meant that postwar science policy has had a vacuum at its center, with little or no comprehensive review and assessment of the allocation of the federal basic research budget between military and civilian agencies and among different areas of research. . . . The current allocation of the federal basic research budget among different areas has little apparent logic. For all the undoubted benefits of biomedical research, is the nation well served by a situation in which the National Institutes of Health alone accounts for nearly 45 percent of total funding for basic research? What is the basis for such an allocation? Nowhere within the congressional or executive branch budgetary process are such broad allocation decisions being debated, let alone determined.

Bush, his committees, and the United States were in a position to establish an effective mechanism providing disciplined and informed review of the interaction between scientists and the government. Their collective failure is apparent now in allocations of resources seemingly based on special interests and competition between agencies. Admittedly, there was widespread academic animus against governmental control in 1945. However, President Roosevelt and Bush through OSRD had convincingly shown that government and scientists could work together. It is particularly poignant that such a wise and politically informed leader as Bush[53] did not foresee and take steps to avoid the veto by President Truman in 1947. President Roosevelt and Bush were an effective, seasoned team, with a level of trust and communication Bush did not have with President Truman.

We should hope that our government will ultimately decide that the current welter of competing interests for federal dollars and politically driven allocation of resources are so ineffective that the Bush Report deserves revisiting. There are several key sections, but the cornerstones of the report are found in the sections dealing with New Responsibilities for Government on page 25, and the Five Fundamentals on pages 26–27. Here are those sections, with "New Responsibilities . . ." first:

It is also clear that the effective discharge of these responsibilities [for promoting the creation of new scientific knowledge and the development of scientific talent in our youth] will require the full attention of some overall agency devoted to that purpose. There should be a focal point within the Government for a concerted program of assisting scientific research conducted outside of Government. Such an agency should furnish the funds needed to support basic research in the colleges and universities, should coordinate where possible research programs on matters of utmost importance to the national welfare, should formulate a national policy for the Government toward science, should sponsor the interchange of scientific information among scientists and laboratories both in this country and abroad, and should ensure that the incentives to research in industry and the universities are maintained. All of the committee advising on these matters agree on the necessity for such an agency. . . . Science is fundamentally a unitary thing. The number of independent agencies should be kept to a minimum. Much medical progress, for example, will come from fundamental advances in chemistry. Separation of the sciences in tight compartments, as would occur if more than one agency were involved, would retard and not advance scientific knowledge as a whole.

And here is the "Five Fundamentals" section (the basic principles that must underlie government support for scientific research and education):

(1) Whatever the extent of support may be, there must be stability of funds over a period of years so that long-range programs may be undertaken.

(2) The agency to administer such funds should be composed of citizens selected only on the basis of their interest in and capacity to promote the work of the agency. They should be persons of broad interest in and understanding of the peculiarities of scientific research and education.

(3) The agency should promote research through contracts or grants to organizations outside the Federal Government. It should not operate any laboratories of its own.

(4) Support of basic research in the public and private colleges, universities, and research institutes must leave the internal control of

policy, personnel, and the method and scope of the research to the institutions themselves. This is of the utmost importance.

(5) While assuring complete independence and freedom for the nature, scope, and methodology of research carried on in the institutions receiving public funds, and while retaining discretion in the allocation of funds among such institutions, the Foundation proposed herein must be responsible to the President and the Congress. . . .

Before considering Dr. Goodpasture's second (and last) major opportunity to influence the funding of medical research after the war, we must analyze briefly one of NSF's major competitors for the research dollar—the National Institutes of Health (NIH). The NIH had a rather modest beginning in 1930 when the Hygienic Laboratory underwent a name change to the National Institute (singular) of Health. Somewhat truncated initially because of the depression's economic constraints, bonds were loosened in 1944 by the addition of the National Cancer Institute as a component. Cancer had then and has now enormous appeal for support by Congress. More importantly, having an institute named for a disease was a political gold mine.[54] In 1948, language in the National Heart Act made the name of the umbrella organization the plural *Institutes*, and by 1998 the NIH had twenty-four institutes and centers, each undoubtedly with its own advocacy groups. Competition between NIH and academic medical centers was further exemplified by the construction in 1953 of a 540-bed research hospital on the Bethesda "campus."

NIH's administrative home was in the Department of Health, Education and Welfare (HEW), the first director of which was Oveta Culp Hobby. She requested on January 14, 1955, that NSF review the intramural and extramural programs in medical research at NIH as well as the other research programs conducted by the Public Health Service (PHS). Accordingly, Dr. Alan Waterman, NSF director, established a Special Committee on Medical Research, with Dr. C. N. H. Long, Yale University, as chairman. Dr. Goodpasture and other distinguished scientists, including three Nobel laureates, were members.[55] In her letter of January 14, 1955, Secretary Hobby noted that the intramural and extramural programs of HEW had grown rapidly since the war and would total approximately $66 million in the fiscal year. She further noted that this money constituted a major portion of federal support for medical research. Because NSF had as one of its responsibilities "the evaluation of scientific research programs undertaken by agencies of the Federal Government," Secretary Hobby authorized such a review.[56]

Director Waterman used five months to establish the review committee, perhaps delaying action in order to sound for dangerous implications in the request. He must have recognized that this review was politically comparable to putting a hen (the Waterman Committee) in a fox den. The Special Committee on Medical Research had its first meeting on July 22, 1955, with a deadline for its report of December 1955.[57] Because of the urgency, the committee had two-day meetings every two weeks during September, October, and November. The second, third, and fourth meetings were held at the NIH to review their intramural and extramural programs, while the sixth and seventh meetings were devoted to the formulation of the report. The first concrete action that is apparent in the local records is a ten-page letter from Dr. Goodpasture to Chairman Long dated November 10, 1955.[58] We do not know if this letter represented a voluntary act of a particularly conscientious committee member or was solicited.

In Dr. Goodpasture's view, basic conflicts of purpose had developed between NIH and universities. The rapid growth and aggrandizement of NIH programs had produced deleterious effects on universities, creating a serious imbalance in development of scientists. He had specific criticisms, which have been edited slightly here:[59]

> Criticism is directed primarily at (1) the rapid growth of NIH in size and in influence upon medical research and education without sufficient authority of over-all scientific advisory or administrative guidance, (2) too much responsibility is centered in the Director of NIH who is appointed by the Surgeon General possibly without benefit of duly constituted scientific and professional advisors. Rapid growth has been

accompanied by (a) lack of supervisory control over broad policies, selection and structure of leadership, balanced operations, inter-institutional relationships, especially with universities and medical schools . . . (b) an over-emphasis on the categorical approach to research and training (c) restrictions imposed by Civil Service [prevent] competition for the best talent in the nation (d) superposition of a vast extramural program of grants for research and training on an already overgrown and overbalanced intramural program of categorical research that attempts at once to be basic and programmatic.

[Thus, the NIH grants programs] had resulted in an unbalanced educational enterprise through neglect of the basic institution whose resources of training and research are being exploited. This imbalance is reflected in . . . lack of financial support for the basic needs of medical and graduate education by which teaching and research talents are attracted, screened, recruited, educated, trained and made available for teaching and for the nationwide needs of research.

Having made a "diagnosis," the cure proposed by Dr. Goodpasture was to remove the extramural grants program from the NIH and to place this program in a special division of NSF devoted exclusively to medical education and research. This arrangement would reestablish the relationship between the government and medical research intended in the organization of the National Research Foundation proposed by Vannevar Bush in *Science: The Endless Frontier*. In this plan, Dr. Goodpasture placed the ultimate responsibility for education squarely in the universities:[60]

Considerations of a proper balance of basic and categorical research must take into account that the home of scholarship is the university and the objective of scholarship is breadth of understanding rather than immediacy of application . . .

The Universities, our only source of experts in higher education, must be given the fullest opportunity to recognize and educate intellectual talent in all areas. Much could be done to aid them by means of block grants given unrestrictedly for the purpose of education at the graduate level as well as at the professional medical level. . . . Of all things, the most important is to provide a good atmosphere for scientists to work in freedom, in reasonable security and peace in order to make their maximum contribution to teaching and to understanding. For this there must be extended, through grants to educational institutions, opportunities for life careers, especially in the Universities . . . Basic research should not be divorced from teaching, nor, so far as possible, from Universities.

The report was still in draft form when presented to Secretary Folsom by Dr. Goodpasture, Dr. Waterman, and Dr. Pisani (executive secretary of NSF) on November 30, 1955, in Washington. Chairman Long was unable to attend because "of a prior commitment in New York City at the time selected (presumably by Secretary Folsom) for the appointment."[61] Dr. Goodpasture was designated spokesman for the committee. Nothing in his summary of the recommendations was likely to please the secretary, as they followed closely the criticisms and solutions in his letter cited above. Furthermore, Secretary Folsom may have been disgruntled because he had been on the job for only two months.

The committee recommended:

- The intramural program should not be increased and should be supervised by a newly appointed board of medical scientists in matters of general policy, upper level appointments, and promotions.
- The extramural program should be divested from the NIH, and there should be no increase in grants awarded.

Secretary Folsom commented that the committee's opinion (of a flat budget) put him in a difficult position, as "he had asked the PHS to submit a realistic budget which they felt they could justify, even if it called for a sizable increase, so as to avoid the embarrassment *created by the Congress raising the figures in response to citizen's committees, etc.*" [emphasis added]. Further, he was confident that the Congress "would not buy unrestricted grants to institutions."

Dr. Pisani's written remarks at this point become somewhat terse. Dr. Pisani declared that Dr. Goodpasture had made an excellent summary of the committee's position, and he wished to emphasize the committee had sought to give advice about an optimal long-range program rather than focusing on next year's budget. Secretary Folsom then closed the meeting by stating his preference that NSF stress the "long-range nature of their recommendations." He presumably wanted short-term freedom to maneuver, recognizing that long-term recommendations were more easily deflected. His written response, a single-page letter dated July 25, 1956, is masterful in rejecting all of the committee's recommendations, while blandly touting their value:[62] "I am happy, however, to report that many of your proposals are now being implemented or are being seriously considered for future adoption." The key word in that sentence is "or," as the NIH essentially rejected any shackles to its further growth.

The report of the Special Committee and the Bush Report represented the best efforts of academic scientists to control or at least influence the governmental presence in basic research. Unfortunately, by 1955 the genie was completely out of the bottle, and priorities were established in political arenas rather than in academic halls. Nevertheless, the core statement of principle in the *Long Special Committee Report* is worth recording:[63]

> Freedom to work and teach, in order to advance knowledge regardless of its immediate practical application, is the most treasured possession of an educational institution. It is also our best security for the future. Many see in the rapid growth of Government and private funds, restricted in use for special purposes, a present threat to the most vital attribute of our educational structure. The question may well be asked: had the capital expenditure, and the annual funds available for research in certain diseases been used for the support and expansion of existing educational institutions, might not progress in the relief of these disorders have come more rapidly than by the overemphasis and support of circumscribed areas.

A year later, Mr. Folsom commissioned a second study of NIH, after "spokesmen" from his office declared the NSF report "obsolete" owing to the rapid growth of the federal medical research budget.[64] Dr. Goodpasture's bemused and, for him, critical comment was:

It is difficult to understand the attributed "obsolescence" of the NSF report by virtue of a rapid increase of the very circumstances which its recommendations were designed to correct. I hope the new Committee will have no adverse fixations with respect to separation of intra[mural] and extramural functions, from fear of creating more problems than would be solved.

The new committee was chaired by Stanhope Bayne-Jones and bore the official title of "HEW Consultants on Medical Research and Education." Their task was "to bring the nation's total medical research effort into balance for the first time." Dr. Stanhope Bayne-Jones at age sixty-eight had come from retirement to chair this study. As a former dean of Yale School of Medicine, he was "primarily interested in bringing the nation's support for medical education into line with its support for medical research."[65] It has not been possible to obtain a copy of this report for comparison with the conclusions of the Long committee on which Dr. Goodpasture served.

Whatever Bayne-Jones reported did not alter the mushrooming of the National Institutes of Health. In 2001, the former director of the NIH (Dr. Harold Varmus) prepared for the Policy Forum section of *Science* an article titled "Proliferation of National Institutes of Health."[66] You will be interested to read in this article the concerns of Dr. Varmus about the proliferation of institutes and perhaps will not be surprised to learn that another study is being contemplated:

> We need to establish some general principles by which the NIH should be organized and attempt to use those principles to decide how it can, in practice, be reorganized, even if the reorganization occurs in slow stages.
>
> Happily, the Labor–Health and Human Services–Education Appropriations Bill for 2001 includes report language that directs the NIH to fund just the kind of study of its organization that is so badly needed. The report of this study, to be conducted by the National Academy of Sciences, is due one year after the appointment of a new director of the NIH. . . .

———

OFFICES IN PROFESSIONAL ORGANIZATIONS

Dr. Goodpasture apparently enjoyed professional meetings but held few major offices, and over the years he refused several opportunities to join professional societies. He was president of the American Society of Experimental Pathology in 1940 and president of the American Association of Pathologists and Bacteriologists in 1949. The latter position is of interest in that he certainly did not seek election and yet was elected, and the related correspondence reveals some details of his state of mind and body in 1948.

Dr. Goodpasture wrote Dr. Howard Karsner, secretary of the association,[67] on February 17, 1948, asking for the dates of the next council meeting and notifying Dr. Karsner he wished to resign from the council with these words:

> At the last meeting of the Association, which I was not able to attend, I was elected Vice-President. This honor I appreciated very much. I am not sufficiently familiar with the procedures and practices of the Association, I am sorry to say, to know whether or not election to vice-presidency has any implications with reference to possible succession to the presidency. If there should be such implication a statement at the present time of my attitude might be of help. To put it briefly, I do not wish to become a candidate for the presidency. Naturally, I have the greatest respect for this office and would feel deeply honored should the Association decide to consider me. However, I could not accept this distinguished position for several reasons, purely personal in character. In the first place, I have never taken an active part in the Association in the past and therefore would feel much embarrassment to receive such an honor at their hands. For the past two or three years my responsibilities at Vanderbilt Medical School and Hospital have been such that I have not been able to do any scientific work in the laboratory and am, therefore, rather out of contact. Finally, I find that the demands upon my times and energies, now none too abundant, resulting from administrative duties through a very critical period are such that I am

endeavoring to become released as soon as possible from many outside positions and responsibilities.

Dr. Karsner replied on February 19: "I hope you will reconsider your desire to resign from the Council. . . . The job of president carries little responsibility except that of presiding at the annual meeting." Dr. Karsner then set the date of the council meeting for March 11 (the site was Benjamin Franklin Hotel in Philadelphia). This letter from Dr. Goodpasture followed on February 26: "However, I have given considerable thought to the matter and believe that under my present circumstances it is best for me to do so [resign]." Dr. Goodpasture was unable to attend and consequently was notified on March 26 he had been elected president. He responded: "I am very sensible of the high honor which has been conferred on me and I want to express to you my sincere appreciation for your personal interest." Dr. Goodpasture was able to host a very successful president's dinner the following April in Boston. His guest list is of interest to us, as he invited Doctors Tom Fite Paine, John Enders, Sidney Burwell, and James Dawson.

~

ACTING EDITOR-IN-CHIEF, *AMERICAN JOURNAL OF PATHOLOGY*

Due to the "sudden and untimely" death of the editor, Dr. Carl V. Weller, on December 10, 1956, Dr. Goodpasture was asked by the secretary of the American Association of Pathologists and Bacteriologists to make an emergency visit to the editorial office in Ann Arbor on January 24–25, 1957, and to become acting editor-in-chief until a replacement might be found.[68] These are Dr. Gall's comments:

> The readiness of your acceptance of this onerous responsibility in the face of a major commitment of your time and energies to the Armed Forces Institute of Pathology is indicative of your understanding of the needs of this Association and of your great loyalty to it. We are all profoundly in your debt.

In six months a successor had been found. Dr. Goodpasture's letter to Dorothy Seiferlein, editorial assistant, about his brief editorship is not in the file, but her response is:

> Your letter of July 16 awaited me here upon my return from a short vacation. For your sake, I am happy that you have been relieved of all duties connected with the Journal, but I shall greatly miss you. Above and beyond the routine duties that you took over at Dr. Weller's death, which you carried out so beautifully, you gave me that extra intangible plus support that I cannot define but which was very real to me. It not only helped me to continue to publish the Journal, but brought back all of my satisfaction and pleasure in the work. . . . Words cannot express my appreciation of all that you have done to keep the Journal going during a very difficult period.

EPILOGUE

We should close this chapter by defining the words *alma mater*, and by recalling Dr. Goodpasture's speech given at Vanderbilt in 1943 about universities in wartime. *Alma* in Latin means nourishing or bounteous, and everyone knows the meaning of *mater*. The two words were first used together by Thomas Carlyle in 1866, in order to refer to the school, college, or university one attended.[69] In his speech Dr. Goodpasture crystallized his beliefs about the importance of universities in our society and tells us why he expended so much time and effort in extramural responsibilities when he was desperately fighting to hold his medical school together. The entire speech may be reread by returning to chapter 4; his conclusion is quoted below:

> In the search for common denominators, whose acceptance might bring the fundamental interests of the world closer together and inspire mankind to protect them with all their will and power, there is a challenge

to every man, and every group and nation of men. We believe these formulas should be expressions of an ideal of individual liberty, and as students of science and students of life we should realize that underneath and supporting all of our chartered modes of freedom lies a many-sided spirit; and the facet of that spirit, to my mind, that would be essential to the maintenance and growth of liberty is the spirit of rational inquiry. To question ourselves, to question our universe, to question our gods, our devils and our destiny, and to listen sensitively and intelligently to spontaneous and induced revelations of truth, is the last bulwark of our hope at least to know a better world. Seek and ye shall find.

Chapter Seven

SCIENTIFIC DIRECTOR, ARMED FORCES INSTITUTE OF PATHOLOGY

BACKGROUND

D r. Goodpasture became scientific director of the Armed Forces Institute of Pathology (AFIP) in 1955, at age sixty-nine. Many of his contemporaries retired at age sixty-five, in part because rules at most universities mandated that faculty routinely assume emeritus status at that age. His rationale for assuming this position of responsibility at the AFIP is not apparent from his correspondence. Nevertheless, by July 1, Katherine and Dr. Goodpasture had sold their home on Fairfax Avenue in Nashville, had left their academic home behind, and had begun a new life in Washington, D.C.

The AFIP is a military organization that traces its origins back to 1862 when it began as the Army Medical Museum. It has always been located in Washington, D.C., or its environs. From inception, the AFIP has assumed educational roles that are unusual for military organizations: civilians as well as members of the armed forces benefit from the teaching programs of the AFIP; pathologists, other medical specialists, dentists, and veterinarians are on its staff or attend AFIP-sponsored courses; its medical responsibilities are worldwide, ranging from diagnosis to prevention of disease; and the AFIP contains a medical museum that is very popular with the public, with more than 250,000 visitors yearly.

Through its long existence, the AFIP has developed unique features. It is invaluable as a repository of specimens and associated historic information, particularly relating to wounds inflicted in the Civil War, World War I, and World War II. In its responsibility as a museum, the AFIP has assembled the most complete collection of microscopes extant. It houses (and has studied) more than one million human tissue specimens of all types, including tissues injured in war as well as those affected by naturally occurring diseases. The AFIP has a veterinary science branch containing the country's largest staff of veterinary scientists. It is the central pathology laboratory for the Army, Navy, Air Force, Veterans Administration system of hospitals, and the United States Public Health Service, providing expert consultative services with review of diagnoses for service and civilian physicians.

The AFIP provides pathology support for the Atomic Energy Commission and is the repository for thousands of specimens from Japanese civilians and other victims of atomic bombs in Hiroshima and Nagasaki. It is an informal consultant to the Civil Aeronautics Board and Federal Aviation Agency and provides expert forensic pathology support for investigation of aircraft crashes. The AFIP houses the American Registry of Pathology, an arm of the National Research Council,[1] in which there are individual registries of diseases affecting specific organs.[2] Because of the wealth of material available for study, the AFIP provides study sets of all types for military and civilian use, each set containing microscopic sections and related syllabuses. The American Registry of Pathology has served an important educational role for civilians and military personnel by publishing a series of fascicles (books) written by leading authorities on tumors of various types.

As a military organization, the AFIP is also distinctive in that it is a hybrid professionally and in governance. While under the

administrative jurisdiction of the surgeon general of the Army, it is
under the command of a director chosen in rota from the Army,
Navy, and Air Force. The director is under the immediate supervision of a Board of Governors composed of the surgeons general of
the three armed services. The AFIP then is one of the very few
organizations that has tripartite governance by the branches of the
armed forces. It is also a hybrid in the extent of civilian participation
on the professional staff. Most registries are directed by well-known
civilian pathologists; furthermore, in 1955 the position of scientific
director of the Department of Pathology was created to provide
civilian oversight for this essential department, a position first held
by Dr. Goodpasture.

There are many reasons why such an important position might
have appealed to Dr. Goodpasture:

- The AFIP was highly respected in academic pathology circles
  and had a long history of contributions to the welfare of civilians
  and military personnel.
- The position of scientific director afforded an opportunity to
  foster the development of research at the AFIP and as a new
  position would be subject to his stamp.
- Close friends such as Howard Karsner and Shields Warren held
  influential positions on the Scientific Advisory Board.
- The break with Vanderbilt would be clean, giving his successor
  free rein.

Further, the AFIP was in an interesting city that offered many
cultural advantages. Financial considerations were probably not a
significant factor; salary and benefits would be slightly greater at
AFIP but any increase would be offset by higher housing and
living costs.

The history of the AFIP since its origins as the Army Medical
Museum may have also been impelling. In the latter part of the
nineteenth century, principal medical schools and larger hospitals
routinely assembled pathological and anatomical museums in order
to study normal and diseased organs.[3] The Army Medical Museum

adapted this approach to focus on the nature of wartime injury, ultimately publishing a vast assemblage of individual case records from the Civil War.[4] More primitive manifestations of aggression may be found in the AFIP collection of arrow injuries, surely the only one in existence.

The early curators of the Army Medical Museum also performed important investigations into the nature of certain infectious diseases that affected civilian and military personnel. An investigator of note was Dr. Walter Reed, who was responsible for identification of the mode of transmission of yellow fever. Staff members functioning as the Typhoid Fever Board discovered that flies and poor sanitation were responsible for the spread of typhoid in encampments. This board then instituted effective preventive measures including vaccination.[5] Another well-known curator at the Army Medical Museum was John Shaw Billings, who in 1883 at age forty-five became curator of the museum and librarian. By 1895, the library contained 115,000 bound volumes, and Billings had started the *Index Medicus* to list "every article, in every issue, of every journal, in every country."[6] In its current form the *Index Medicus* is the basis of a worldwide medical informatics system.

Distinguished scientists who have overseen the Army Medical Museum include Brigadier General George M. Sternberg (surgeon general of the Army from 1893 until 1902). General Sternberg[7] was an outstanding American bacteriologist who identified the pneumococcus as the bacterium responsible for many cases of pneumonia, who was the first to photograph the tubercle bacillus that had been discovered in 1882 by Robert Koch, and who published the first American text on bacteriology.[8] Surgeon General Sternberg focused the energies of the Army Medical Museum on bacteriology by founding the Army Medical School, in which courses of instruction were given "for four months, . . . annually at the Army Medical Museum, in Washington City." From the standpoint of historical perspective, it is noteworthy that pathologists at the Army Medical Museum were responsible for performing the autopsies of Presidents Lincoln and McKinley.[9]

—

OFFER AND ACCEPTANCE OF POSITION AS SCIENTIFIC DIRECTOR

In July 1954, Dr. Goodpasture received a confidential letter from Shields Warren[10] stating that he and General DeCoursey (then director of AFIP) wished to discuss in the near future "an extremely important job for the Armed Forces." Dr. Warren was a member of the AFIP Scientific Advisory Board. Face-to-face discussions were set up for Thursday, September 23, when Dr. Goodpasture was to be in Washington for a meeting of the Grayson Foundation.[11] Despite having to deal with an abscessed tooth during their discussion,[12] Dr. Goodpasture was very interested in their proposals and returned to Washington on October 21 for an all-day meeting with General DeCoursey "to look into the present operation of the Armed Forces Institute of Pathology and to become more familiar with the nature of the problems and its future outlook."[13]

General DeCoursey sent a handwritten note on October 22 confirming the level of appointment (GS 17) and salary ($13,000 per annum minus social security of $260.00). Recruitment proceeded rapidly, with acceptance by Dr. Goodpasture in early November and a formal invitation by General DeCoursey on December 3, 1954, confirming the appointment level and salary, as well as inviting Dr. Goodpasture to the dedication exercises for the new AFIP building on May 26–27, 1955.[14] As General DeCoursey phrased it for his civilian colleague, "It is anticipated that you will be able to be with us for this dedication," a direction duly followed by Dr. Goodpasture.

The dedicatory address was given by President Dwight D. Eisenhower. His address and those of other dignitaries are presented in full in the September 1955, issue of *Military Medicine*.[15] The themes of President Eisenhower's address[16] surely resonated with Dr. Goodpasture's ethos: that the new building reflected "concern for human life" . . . and efforts to improve the quality rather than length of life; that (quoting Lincoln) "the function of government is to do for people those things that they cannot at all or so well do for themselves, but in those things which people can do better, the government ought not to interfere." President Eisenhower's address concluded with: "And so I dedicate this building to the conquest of disease so that mankind, more safe and secure in body, may more surely advance to a widely shared prosperity and an enduring and just peace."

It is significant that the dedicatory ceremonies included scientific presentations, the most notable of which was that of Wendell M. Stanley, a Nobel laureate and distinguished biochemist at the University of California in Berkeley. Dr. Stanley is best known for crystallizing the tobacco mosaic virus, a tour de force in which a ton or so of tobacco leaves were processed to obtain a few milligrams of virus. Stanley's address presented a wide-ranging discussion of different life-forms, focusing on the relationship between chemistry and the structure of viruses, and on the significance of nucleic acids in viruses and other forms of life—all themes of great interest to Dr. Goodpasture.

The Newly Constructed AFIP

The new building contained 121,444 net square feet[17] and is probably one of the only structures in Washington designed and built to be blast resistant, hence its monolithic, largely windowless exterior, heavily reinforced concrete walls twelve to sixteen inches thick, and immediate inadequacies in storage space and ventilation. This, the sixth home of AFIP, like all of its predecessors, had inadequate space to house its museum and stored tissues.[18] In 1955 the completed structure had five floors above ground and three below. The sub-basement contained electrical and air-conditioning equipment, autopsy rooms, and areas for tissue preparation and storage.[19] The basement was for files or records and was also the location for the statistical branch and photography.

The ground floor was the site of the medical illustration service, exhibit preparation, medical museum laboratories, and the television studio. Offices of the director, other offices, the boardroom, lecture halls, conference rooms, and a few laboratories were located on the first floor, as was the snack bar. Various laboratories were sited on the second, third, and fourth floors, including the pathology laboratory

Fig. 7-1: Dr. Goodpasture at the Armed Forces Institute of Pathology (AFIP) in 1955.

for Walter Reed Hospital.[20] The Registry of Pathology was also located on the third floor. The fourth floor contained the library, editorial offices, and specialty laboratories such as the virus and tissue culture rooms. Animal rooms and the experimental surgery suite were located on the fifth floor.

Governance of AFIP, 1955–59

It is appropriate for military organizations to speak of missions, and those of the AFIP, as the central laboratory for the Department of Defense, are threefold: education (advanced graduate instruction in pathology and lay instruction via its museum), consultation (AFIP is the chief reviewing authority on pathologic diagnoses for the armed forces and many civilian hospitals), and research (classification of diseases, their causes and prevention). These missions were accomplished by four departments: the Department of Pathology, the American Registry of Pathology, the Medical Illustration Service, and the Medical Museum. The entire operation was under the control of the director, Captain William M. Silliphant, MC, USN, and two deputy directors from the Army and Air Force. These three officers were termed the directorate, itself undoubtedly directed or influenced by the surgeons general and by a Scientific Advisory Board containing twenty eminent specialists.[21]

Role of Scientific Director

Administration of the Department of Pathology was the duty of the scientific director, a post created in March 1955, to foster research at the AFIP and management of that department. As scientific director (Fig. 7-1), Dr. Goodpasture was responsible for supervising and coordinating the professional and administrative functions of the department and for advising the director on professional policies.[22] The Department of Pathology was far larger than the other departments at the AFIP, containing 45 to 50 pathologists, over 250 armed forces personnel, and over 200 civilians, consuming in personnel and supplies approximately 60 percent of the AFIP budget.[23] In contrast to his meager forces at Vanderbilt, Scientific Director Goodpasture had acquired a veritable army of trained personnel almost overnight.

Once he had adjusted to the size of the AFIP and to the newness of the building (Fig. 7-2), Dr. Goodpasture noticed that his current responsibilities bore a striking resemblance to those of a departmental chairman in an academic medical center.[24] After six months on duty, he commented on these similarities in his first speech to AFIP personnel, given on January 20, 1956. While observing it was a "very complex and ramifying scientific structure indeed," nevertheless its mission was simply "to preserve, transmit and to increase knowledge of disease." Before offering his analysis of the major problems at the AFIP—a diagnosis, if you will—and suggested treatment, he generalized by expressing his reaction to the Department of Pathology as a whole:

My experience in the past has been almost wholly an academic one. So it was from that habit of mind that I first looked upon this Institute, and I must confess that it seemed architecturally a bit formidable and forbidding from the exterior. But once on the inside and in the midst of its operations, I was pleased to recognize a sort of

Fig. 7-2: The first scientific director of the AFIP with the institute in the background.

congeniality with the structural and functional organization of a
Department of Pathology in a University School of Medicine. This
similarity is not due to the fact that the pursuit of pathology is necessarily of one pattern, for under different circumstances any of the
three major scientific functions [education, consultation, research]
might be developed to the virtual exclusion of the others; . . . Neither
the Department of Pathology of this Institute nor the Department of
Pathology of a school of medicine divorces these functions one from
another; but rather are they cultivated all together with variations of
emphasis in individual instances. If one should consider the hospital of
the medical school as comparable with the aggregate of hospitals and
other institutions which contribute pathological tissues to and receive
consultant services from the AFIP, and if for curricular classes in
pathology one would substitute our attention to residents, fellows and
special students, and if for the faculty of the academic department
which carries on the routine of handling autopsies and surgical specimens while bearing its load of teaching and investigation, one would
substitute our professional staff, the close similarity and congeniality
become obvious. The similarity is all the more striking when one real-
izes, as the Director has assured us, that we operate here professionally
under conditions of academic freedom.

The Department of Pathology at the AFIP may have been
similar to the department at Vanderbilt in function, but there
were differences administratively. At the AFIP, there was a
Division of Experimental Pathology[25] that contained the special
laboratories of biochemistry, biophysics, histochemistry, and
historadiobiology, as well as the basic laboratories of bacteri-
ology/immunology, tissue culture/virology, and electron
microscopy. Most investigative research at the AFIP was initiated
or facilitated by the personnel and equipment in these laboratories. The other major division—the Division of Pathology—was
responsible for the diagnostic and consultative services for the
armed forces and for community hospitals. In this division were
housed the histopathology laboratories along with the records and
clerical services.

The problems at the AFIP in activating an experimental research program were a heavy consultation load that left inadequate time for research and a long tradition of relying solely on histopathologic analysis for studies of archived material. Dr. Goodpasture was not fooled by the expanses of space and numbers of personnel in the new building, recognizing there were problems in institutional mind-set and organization inhibiting the research program:[26]

> For a newcomer during the first few months of his experience the scientific advantages and potential assets of the Armed Forces Institute of Pathology are so impressive that one finds it difficult to think of any difficulties that might be encountered in an endeavor to release its assets to the fullest extent. Problems as well as advantages must be recognized and realistically appraised, however, if solutions are to be sought.

He then described problems affecting all three areas of the scientific mission of the Department of Pathology. The first related to the major responsibilities of accessioning cases and providing consultative diagnoses. Although the accessioned cases were preserved for study and represented a unique asset of the institute, the sheer volume was already unwieldy and increases to millions of cases were anticipated. Problems of storage and availability were "assuming huge proportions and a proper analysis in terms of ~~actual~~ extent of usefulness had not been made."[27] Tentative guidelines were proposed for storage of tissue: incoming cases should be photographed if indicated and then selectively dissected to embed the choicest blocks of tissue, while discarding the remaining wet tissue; the maximal number of cases of a specific type should be established, so that old cases of that type would be discarded when fresh cases arrived; cases over ten years old should be discarded unless they were unique or rare examples; and certain tissues representing routine diagnoses (such as tonsils and appendices) should not be accepted at all. In other words, Dr. Goodpasture proposed establishing order and method in a system that had accumulated over the previous hundred years an unwieldy mass of specimens.

In Dr. Goodpasture's analysis, the high volume of incoming cases was creating "log-jams of varying dimensions" that were interfering with the prompt generation of reports by consultants, and were such a burden to the staff there was inadequate "time for performance of educational responsibilities, and for the pursuit of research." He then admonished his staff:[28] "If research does not constitute a significant part of professional activity, that fact should not be attributable to lack of time or opportunity, but rather to choice and aptitude for other significant enterprises."

The next area considered was the educational program. Dr. Goodpasture reminded his staff that "in its broad aspects, education is our most important function." He was not prepared at that time to make specific recommendations other than to note the need for reappraisal of the consultant and guest lecturer program "in order to assure a proper recognition of our total research interests and needs."[29]

The third problem area was that of experimental research—that is, research conducted on animals or on tissues *in vitro*. He then enunciated the credo that had guided his career:[30]

> Over the years, in the history of medicine, it has been a traditional and self-imposed obligation of the educated and cultured physician to leave the intellectual resources of his profession enriched by the addition of his own experience. To observe and record for mankind has been a worthy purpose and inspiration of the physician in the past and no less challenging should be the contemporary injunction to the medical scientist to experiment, observe, and record for humanity.

In the past, most of the research at the AFIP had consisted of observations made upon tissue sections prepared by conventional methods, but now the staff had a new institute provided with modern facilities. With these facilities, activation of the research program became in part a matter of time. The expected division of labor for the professional staff was one-third for service (consultation), one-third for teaching, and one-third for research. For his staff, as they were relatively inexperienced in research, Dr. Goodpasture offered warnings, encouragement, and support.[31] The warning came in these words:

> Analytical and experimental research is not easy; in fact it is a strict and hard task master. It requires time and physical facilities, of course, but it demands above all a desire and an ability to use controlled interference with nature as a means of learning. It requires doing; that is experience.

Words of encouragement were directed at the beginners: "To encourage and to provide the environment for scientific inquiry should be one of our proudest achievements." There were opportunities for collaboration with members of the senior staff at the AFIP and at the Walter Reed Medical Center. The junior staff were invited to make their interest in research known. At the end of this talk, Dr. Goodpasture distilled into his words of support the ethos by which he had conducted his career and especially the department at Vanderbilt:

> Finally, let us cultivate about us in this Institute an academic atmosphere in which, while recognizing our origin and dependence upon the Armed Forces and other governmental agencies, and discharging faithfully and proficiently our responsibilities for service to them, we shall maintain at the same time the sense and satisfaction of being a part of the great company of scholars whose knowledge and wisdom are dedicated through Medical Science to the health and dignity of man.
>
> In conclusion I want to tell you that I appreciate and enjoy your companionship in our respective professional endeavors, and I hope you will give me an opportunity to discuss your problems with you, for I shall always be concerned that you be content and productive in your work.

Dr. Goodpasture provided a more focused analysis of the personnel and support needs to activate a basic research program at the AFIP in a memorandum to Captain Silliphant.[32] In this memorandum, Dr. Goodpasture justifies a staffing and supply budget for four laboratories that had not been activated: Biochemistry; Microbiology/ Immunology, including tissue culture facilities; Biophysics; and Histochemistry. A total of $100,000 was needed for personnel and supplies. As was often the case with governmental agencies, equipment had been supplied but could not be made operational owing to lack of skilled personnel and supplies. The underlying problem was stated clearly by Dr. Goodpasture in a draft of a speech to the Naval Medical Research Institute staff at Bethesda on February 3, 1956,[33] and then softened in the final version:

> Full activation of our experimental laboratory resources has been retarded ~~because the Surgeon General of the Army was unable to provide us with the positions necessary~~ temporarily because of manpower shortage[34] for staffing these laboratories. In the opinion of the Scientific Director of Pathology, the activation of these resources is so important . . . that extraordinary effort is being made to find means for making these resources available at the earliest possible time.

Accomplishments at AFIP

Documents available for review indicate that Dr. Goodpasture focused his attention at AFIP on organizing the consultative load and activating the research program.[35] The consultative burden was so time-consuming that research had been assigned a low priority by most staff. Dr. Goodpasture's role in activating the research program was to provide encouragement, direction, supporting staff, and supplies. The guidelines for activation were enunciated in a talk "To Staff" by Captain Silliphant on January 3, 1956:[36] Research could not jeopardize the consultative and teaching programs; research must be in the field of pathology or allied topics; and priority was to be given to "subjects and programs of a medical-military nature." Captain Silliphant pointed out that approximately one hundred thousand dollars in research and development money was available and that funds from civilian organizations and foundations might be requested.

The new and expanded facilities, plus the leadership provided by Dr. Goodpasture and Captain Silliphant, apparently were successful in increasing research productivity. In 1955, the year of occupation of the new building, thirty-five articles were published. The numbers in succeeding years were forty-one, forty-three, seventy-seven, seventy-six, and eighty-two, with ninety-one articles published in 1961.[37] Virtually all of these articles are case studies or are descriptions of human diseases. However, in Dr. Goodpasture's tenure, the number of research reports increased from one in 1955 to ten in 1959, when the scientific director was able to practice his preaching by publishing an article about mutants of fowlpox.

This paper was submitted to the *American Journal of Pathology* on August 12, 1958,

Fig. 7-3: This illustration shows figures one through five from the 1958 paper in *American Journal of Pathology*. Figures one and two show the different gross lesion produced on the chick embryo chorioallantoic membrane, with figure one the lesion induced by a field strain. The membrane has been dissected out of the egg in figure two, and the membrane is floating in fluid. The two inclusions are shown in figure five.

and was from the Department of Pathology at Vanderbilt and from the AFIP. E. W. Goodpasture, M.D., was the sole author. Appropriately, this paper dealt with mutations in the fowlpox virus that produced unusual lesions when the virus was injected directly into the kidney. Not only was there massive overgrowth of renal tubular epithelium, but the epithelial cells contained "hitherto undescribed basophilic bodies reminiscent morphologically" of a vaccinial inclusion called Guarnieri body, as well as the typical fowlpox inclusion (Fig. 7-3). These experiments are described in greater detail in Chapter 3. It must have been a source of great satisfaction for him to see his name on a research paper again after a thirteen-year hiatus.

Fig. 7-4: The Goodpastures at a going-away party. His future activities are depicted on the sketch.

The 1958 Annual Report describes improvements in the laboratories of electron microscopy and biochemistry that greatly facilitated research by all personnel. More importantly for research, by 1958 research was stimulated by a Research Committee with Dr. Elson Helwig as acting chairman, and intramural scientific programs were being held.[38]

DEPARTURE FROM AFIP

Somewhat surprisingly, Dr. Goodpasture began discussions about retiring from the AFIP and returning to middle Tennessee in the fall of 1957. He attempted to resign as of December 1957, preparatory to moving "ultimately . . . [to] middle Tennessee— Basin Spring to be more exact."[39] Under pressure from the AFIP directorate, Dr. Goodpasture stayed until December 1958, when a replacement for scientific director was appointed (Fig. 7-4). Therefore, his decision to resign after two years at the AFIP was presumably a personal choice. He may have felt that there was too much administrative overlay or that a substantive change in the research climate at the AFIP was unlikely. In any case, an explanation for his abbreviated tour of duty as scientific director is not discussed in the archived correspondence.

Chancellor Branscomb had heard of his intended return by October 2, 1957, when he wrote Dean Youmans asking if some arrangements might be made at Vanderbilt to accommodate Dr. Goodpasture.[40] Dean Youmans was at best an unwilling participant in such an accommodation, replying on October 4: "I apologize for reminding you [Chancellor Branscomb], but the only thing in the nature of a policy in the Medical School on such a matter was a statement by you some years ago that you did not approve of making facilities available [to emeritus or retired faculty]. . . . Unfortunately, at the present moment the matter of space would be difficult. But if we should get the new floors on the Learned Hall, they would probably make it easy."

Chancellor Branscomb rejoined on October 14:

> You are quite right it is a general university policy upon retirement people shall give up offices and laboratories on the campus . . . , but exceptions have been made.
>
> I don't want to push this matter and I hold no particular grief or interest, except that his [Goodpasture's] contributions were so great that any courtesy we could extend him upon his return to Nashville would seem to me to be something we would all like to do. I don't think there is any chance of Learned Hall being built at the very best for two or three years, so it can't solve the problem [at] the outset. In other words, I think your answer would have to be either that there is simply no space without putting someone out, or that he might be allowed some area with the possibility of expanding it later if and as needed.
>
> I won't push this matter any further since you must deal with the particulars in the case.

With no claims to expertness in the nuances of meaning used by Chancellor Branscomb in communications with recalcitrant faculty, this letter reads as a directive; but it apparently was not enough, and an end run was necessary. On November 11, 1957, apparently not having heard from Dean Youmans, Chancellor Branscomb asked Dr. Sam Clark if there were space in the anatomy department. The affirmative response and a memorandum were then sent to Dean Youmans, who replied on November 18, 1957: "I think it possible that something might be arranged and I shall continue to study it. Should a suitable plan appear feasible, I shall present it to you for your consideration."

Warm invitations to use space in the Departments of Anatomy or Pathology were sent in November 1957 to Dr. Goodpasture by Doctors Clark and Shapiro, respectively, but the issue became moot when it was clear his retirement from the AFIP would be postponed. There is no written documentation that Dean Youmans ever capitulated on this issue before resigning in 1959. When Dr. Goodpasture was ready to return in 1959, Vice Chancellor for Medical Affairs Patterson notified Chancellor Branscomb that Dr. Clark was providing space in the Department of Anatomy, that the title emeritus professor of pathology was the most distinguished title available, and that some compensation would be available through "restricted federal funds to provide any payment which is arranged." He concluded: "We feel it will be an asset to have Dr. Goodpasture in residence and we are looking forward to his joining us in the Spring of 1960."

Dr. Goodpasture's correspondence files reveal that he considered several professional arrangements before receiving the invitation to return to Vanderbilt. One of these was prestigious, as a visiting professor at Duke, while others involved doing diagnostic pathology and managing hospital laboratories in Tennessee. Dr. Wiley Forbus, professor of pathology at Duke, extended an invitation on October 15, 1957, to spend at least two months beginning in January of 1958. This possibility was not pursued after it became clear that a replacement for Dr. Goodpasture would not be available before July 1958.

There also was correspondence with Dr. Billy Lyle of Clarksville, Tennessee, in February 1959, in which it is apparent there had been previous letters about openings in pathology there. Finally, there was an exchange of letters with Mr. James Arnhart, administrator of the Rutherford Hospital, and Dr. S. E. Abel at the Veterans Administration Hospital, both in Murfreesboro, about a joint coverage of those hospitals. This possibility was considered at a luncheon with members of these two hospital staffs when Dr. and Mrs. Goodpasture made a visit to Tennessee in October 1958. Dr. Goodpasture continued to express interest in a letter to Mr. Arnhart on November 5, 1958, but his situation at AFIP precluded further discussions. The appointment as visiting professor at the University of Mississippi began to take shape in March 1959 when a successor at the AFIP had been appointed. These arrangements are discussed in chapter 9.

Chapter Eight

HOME

In previous chapters, we have relied on documents, records, historical facts, and correspondence for guidance. However, in this chapter we must conjure up visions and memories of times in the past, of places and ways of life that seem nostalgic, even idyllic, of people known to us mainly by their names, oral histories,[1] and photographs. We should attempt to visualize the homes in which the Goodpasture family and their friends lived and died, laughed and cried, shared the good times and the bad. These homes we now collectively attempt to create, or recreate, were as real an entity as Hopkins, Harvard, or Vanderbilt in terms of their influence on Dr. Goodpasture and their importance to him, for in these homes was laid the foundation of the man Dr. Goodpasture became.

After spending many happy days of his boyhood on a farm, Ernest developed a belief that there was an interconnectedness and interdependence of the land with all living things. Even as a boy on the farm, Ernest apparently had nascent investigative talents, as described in this interesting story:[2]

> The farm was in a section where tobacco was a money crop [more likely, *the* money crop]. During his boyhood summers he became aware

of the ecological relationships between plants, animals, insects, and their environments. One summer his special project was the guinea fowl. Suddenly they began to die. Tobacco moths were active and a cobalt spray was being used in an effort to prevent development of crop-damaging tobacco worms. Studying this problem, young Goodpasture noted that cobalt killed the moths; they fell to the ground and were eaten by the guinea fowl which then died of cobalt poisoning.

The land, its occupants, its flora and fauna, were an integral part of the Goodpastures' thoughts and lives, while the pioneers and native peoples in Tennessee were so well-known historically by them as to create a presence as palpable as that of ancestors. There was a sense of purpose in the Goodpasture home, a belief that the occupants were part of a larger community to which all were expected to contribute through scholarship and citizenship, qualities exemplified by Dr. Goodpasture's father, A. V. Goodpasture. It was a home in which altruism ruled and like-minded people found an invigorating congeniality.

The Goodpasture homes were gathering and meeting places for family and friends, and were places where the special relationships usually reserved for kin were extended to close friends. There Ernest found, and fostered, a quiet, undemanding conviviality that left all around him yearning for more. There he found, and fostered, a sense of security and stability based on the primacy of the family unit, individual independence, self-reliance, and democratic principles.

Daily routines were established that were comfortable because of their predictability, thereby making holidays and birthdays more memorable. The pace of life was under some control. There may well have been a gentle hand at the controls, first in the form of his mother, Jennie Dawson Goodpasture, then of Sarah Catlett Goodpasture, and later of Katherine Anderson Goodpasture. Jennie was described as "cheery, gentle, and genteel,"[3] and her son's quiet and pleasant sociability was attributed to her. Sarah, who became Mrs. Goodpasture in 1915, was vivacious and vibrant, deeply loved and respected by family and friends. She was an enthusiastic participant in the academic career

Fig. 8-1: Octagonal home at Walnuthurst Farm. Pictured are Ernest on the horse, his siblings and mother nearby. On the left are his unmarried aunt and uncle who lived in the vicinity.

of her husband, as well as a spirited homemaker. Katherine, who became Mrs. Goodpasture in 1945, was equally at home in a laboratory or in the woods. She not only understood the full significance of Dr. Goodpasture's scientific and administrative contributions but was a wonderful companion in the out-of-doors.

If Dr. Goodpasture could be asked to recall his most carefree days, he would likely describe those on the Walnuthurst Farm in Montgomery County; this, the farm of his maternal grandfather, Dr. Stephen Dawson, was his birthplace and the place where he spent many days as a child and boy[4] (Fig. 8-1). This farm and land were in his blood, their memories calling to him throughout his life, especially during the period when Dr. Goodpasture, his wife, and daughter lived for one to two years each in Boston, Manila, Pittsburgh, and Vienna before settling in Nashville in 1925.

During this time his maternal and paternal grandparents lived in Clarksville and on their nearby farms in Montgomery County. The semblance of permanence in the arrangements of the Tennessee families was probably comforting to those who had left the nest. After 1925, visits by Dr. Goodpasture's young family to this home base became a regular, even ritualistic activity, with anticipated interweaving of the fixed living patterns of elderly people and the exuberance of youthful cousins. Such allegiance to land and place was then transferred to their Monteagle cottage and later to Basin Spring, in Williamson County, after the death of the parents.

The words *farm* and *firm* developed from the same Latin root *firmare*, "to strengthen, make fast, confirm, attest."[5] The common origin of these terms is particularly apt now, in the age of agribusiness. The year of Ernest Goodpasture's birth, 1886, was in the age of the small farmer. At this time, farming was a family activity, with youngsters progressively assuming their share of the chores after they became able to walk. In 1886 most children in the United States were born on farms, as was Ernest Goodpasture. His life differed from that of his peers in that his parents and grandparents were sufficiently well-to-do that Ernest could partake of the pleasures of farm life without undergoing the drudgery. His family was not so wealthy that they qualified as gentleman farmers, but their advanced education and general resourcefulness meant they were not completely dependent on that year's tobacco crop for comfort.

Goodpasture and Dawson Families

The more recent ancestors of Ernest Goodpasture emigrated from Virginia in 1800 to Overton County, in the mountain district of East Tennessee.[6] There they established a vigorous presence, contributing successive generations of responsible citizens to this upper Cumberland area. Ernest's paternal grandfather, Jefferson Dillard Goodpasture, was the first well-educated man in this family; he became a lawyer and state senator. By the time he moved to Nashville in 1879, he was probably the wealthiest citizen of Overton County, owning the first brick home built in that county and several thousand acres in the Hilham area now occupied by Standing Stone Park.[7] In Nashville, he subsequently traded extensively in real estate and made several trips to Europe to import cattle, horses, and jacks (a male donkey).[8]

Fig. 8-2: Woodland Street home of A. V. Sr. and Jennie Goodpasture.

Jefferson Dillard Goodpasture had five sons by his first wife, who died in 1868 at age thirty-three after sixteen years of marriage. Jefferson Dillard remarried in 1869.[9] He died November 2, 1896, and is buried in Mount Olivet Cemetery, Nashville. In the following year, two of his sons, Albert Virgil (Ernest's father) and William Henry, published a biography of Jefferson Dillard that contained an extensive Goodpasture genealogy. It is perhaps pertinent to the history of these sons to note that they were thirteen and nine respectively when their mother died in 1868 and that they were one year older when they acquired a stepmother.

Albert Virgil Goodpasture was born in Livingston, Tennessee,[10] the county seat of Overton County, on November 19, 1855. He attended local preparatory schools and then received advanced degrees from the University of Tennessee (B.A., 1875; M.A., 1882) and Vanderbilt University (LL.B., 1877). His status as a scholar and historian was certified when, as a twenty-two year old, he was asked to address the people of Overton County on the Fourth of July,

1876, about the history of the county. His speech was knowledge-able and lengthy, approaching ten thousand words, and was reprinted by B. C. Goodpasture in 1954.

A. V. began his law practice in Clarksville in 1877 with his older brother, Ridley,[11] and later formed a law firm with William Quarles and William Daniel. In 1880, Albert Virgil and Jennie Willson Dawson of Clarksville were married and established their home at Walnuthurst, a farm in Montgomery County. This farm belonged to her parents and was located about six miles from the nearest post office at St. Bethlehem.

Jennie's father, Stephen N. Dawson, was a native of Maryland who moved with his wife to Logan County, Kentucky, in 1816. All twelve of his children were born there. In 1842, Stephen Dawson obtained better access to the tobacco market at Clarksville by purchasing four tracts of prime farmland totaling 575 acres. The farm was named Walnuthurst for the mile or two of walnuts that were planted with the help of his son Stephen William, Dr. Goodpasture's maternal grand-father. In 1849 Stephen William Dawson graduated from Jefferson Medical College in Philadelphia, thus following Dawson family tradi-tion of becoming a physician.[12] His postgraduate training must have been exciting—he promptly became physician to a caravan of gold rushers bound for California. Four years later he returned east with ten thousand dollars in gold dust, married the daughter of family friends in Baltimore, and brought his bride (Martha Lucretia Willson, nicknamed Mat) to

Fig. 8-3: A. V. Sr. and family in 1896.

Fig. 8-4: Ernest in 1896.

Walnuthurst Farm. There he built an octagonal house, raised his family, and practiced medicine until his death in 1887.[13] Ernest Goodpasture attributed his early interest in medicine to the influence of his grandfather Stephen William Dawson.

At Walnuthurst Farm, five children were born to the Dawson's daughter Jennie Willson and her husband A. V. Goodpasture: Mattie, in 1882; twins William and Ridley in 1884 (William died after three days); Ernest, in 1886; and Sarah, in 1890. In 1888, A. V. was elected to the state house of representatives; and in 1890 he was elected to the state senate, serving on the Ways and Means Committees in both bodies. He resigned from the senate in 1891 to become clerk of the Supreme Court of Tennessee in Nashville, a post he held until 1897. Because of this appointment and the wish to have their children attend schools in Nashville, the A. V. Goodpasture family moved in 1891 to a home at number 226 Woodland Street in East Nashville, where their last child, Albert Virgil Jr., was born in 1893 (Figs. 8-2 and 8-3).

All five of the Goodpasture children attended Warner Elementary School, 622 Russell Street, within easy walking distance of their home (Fig. 8-4). Miss Hattie Cotton was the principal and presided over the study hall (Fig. 8-5). After graduating from Warner, Ernest attended Bowen Academic School at 1309 Broadway, a private high school with a superior record for education (Fig. 8-6).

Henry Goodpasture, a cousin of Ernest, wrote this account of a visit to the Goodpasture home on Woodland Street:[14]

About 1905 my Aunt Jennie, who married Uncle Albert, invited me to come in [from his family's farm near Nashville] and spend the day with them. Uncle Albert lived in a very comfortable house on Woodland Street which was probably a mile from the Public Square in Nashville. It was a modern house. Aunt Jennie was one of the loveliest women I ever knew. She had sunshine in her voice and a sweet smile and seemed to be always happy and thoughtful. At the back of their house they had a stable which was characteristic of houses of that neighborhood and behind the house was an alley. There were alleys all over town because the service entrances were in alleys and horses and buggies were all kept on alleys behind the houses. Aunt Jennie and Uncle Albert had a horse which they called "Chance" and a very comfortable buggy called a Brougham. I remember that I was upstairs . . . and went down a long hall where there was a bathroom. I had never seen an inside bathroom before. . . . Aunt Jennie and Uncle Albert had the most comfortable house that I had ever seen. They had warm open fires, burning coal. The lights were gas and

Fig. 8-5: Students and faculty of Warner School, circa 1897. Ernest is left, front row. Some of his classmates appear to need Miss Cotton's immediate attention.

Fig. 8-6: Bowen School graduating class in 1903. There were five students in his class, including John Crowe Ransom and Hillman Scales, the latter a neighbor. Both attended Vanderbilt with Ernest, as did Hillman's brother, E. P. Scales, who graduated with Ernest.

oil lamps. . . . Uncle Albert always smoked a pipe and sat under a good light and read. Aunt Jennie was busy about her reading or sewing.

In the house at that time was their daughter Mattie . . . who played the piano very well. The next child was Ridley Rose, a quiet gentle person. Next was . . . Ernest whom we always called "Doc" because from early childhood he said he would be a doctor. Doc played the violin and the mandolin—he was always picking at some musical instrument as we gathered around the piano. Next to Doc was Sarah, a very attractive girl. . . . The last child was Albert, Jr . . . It was a very happy and congenial family. I never remember hearing any sharp words spoken in the house.

The well-known Goodpasture Book Company[15] was opened for business and general erudition in 1897, stocked mainly from the libraries of the owners, A. V. and his brother William Henry.[16] This store was first located on Union Street; due to modest success and frequent gatherings of bibliophiles, it moved to larger quarters at 511 and then 608 Church Street. Henry Goodpasture, in his memoir, recollected that "Uncle Bill" Goodpasture worked in the store and lived in the family's Woodland Street home; he "was an old bachelor, a brilliant and handsome man who was rather eccentric . . . [but] seemed to be quite congenial with the family" (Figs. 8-7 and 8-8).

This is Sarah Junior's account of the bookstore, as given in her freshman theme for Dr. Edwin Mims at Vanderbilt in 1940:[17]

> It was then [1897] that he and his brother went into partnership and opened a bookstore, using their own private library as a foundation. I am convinced that my Grandfather's interest was primarily for his own personal satisfaction, for, always a great book lover and prodigious reader, he thrilled at the excuse to fondle so many precious volumes during the day. Each book, I am sure, he must have "censored" before allowing it to be purchased. For the small second hand bookstore flourished and grew: it moved several times to larger buildings and even took over its rival store. During this time my Grandfather, himself inspired by his surroundings, wrote, in collaboration with one of his professional colleagues [William R. Garrett], *The History of Tennessee* which was accepted throughout the state as the text on that subject.

The *Tennessee Encyclopedia of History and Culture* states that the Goodpasture Book Company "served more as a club for book lovers than a bookstore." There are previous comments in chapter 2 by John Crowe Ransom about the frequenting of this bookstore by historically inclined Nashvillians. A. V. Goodpasture edited the *American Historical Magazine*[18] and wrote *Early Times in Montgomery County* as well as numerous articles on

Fig. 8-7: Goodpasture Book Company on Church Street. A. V. Sr. is to the left with two unidentified companions.

Fig. 8-8: Interior of Goodpasture Book Company. "Uncle Bill" Goodpasture, A. V. Sr., and an unidentified employee are shown.

Tennessee history, "the best of which were a series in the *Tennessee Historical Magazine* entitled 'Indian Wars and Warriors of the Old Southwest.'"[19]

In 1914, A. V. Goodpasture, at age fifty-nine,[20] "wearied by the strain and demands which his business life required, . . . retired from an active life in the city and moved with his family to the summer home" on the Walnuthurst Farm[21] (Fig. 8-9). The bookstore was sold, but A. V. retained most of the stock to reestablish his own library.

Catlett Family

The maternal grandfather of Sarah Catlett Goodpasture was Asahel Huntington Patch, a successful inventor. Patch's Black Hawk Corn Sheller was displayed at the 1893 and 1903 world's fairs, and it was a necessary part of every farmer's equipment. Asahel Patch (born 1825, died 1909) of Wenham, Massachusetts, and his wife Sarah Marsh (born 1835, died 1917) of Claremont, New Hampshire, moved to Louisville, Kentucky, so that he might work for the Avery Plow Company (a manufacturer of farm implements). Then in 1891 the Patch family moved from Louisville to Clarksville and in 1892 purchased a house at 328 Home Avenue (Fig. 8-10). On the back of the property there he established a foundry to manufacture the corn sheller and set up an office for marketing and distribution. Asahel and Sarah's daughter Fannie married John Catlett, from a well-known Kentucky family, in 1887. In the early 1900s, upon the death of her husband at age fifty, Fannie Catlett with her five children (Sarah Marsh, Marion, Margaret, John, and Richard Catlett) moved from their farm nearby in Kentucky to the Patch home in Clarksville.

Sarah Marsh Catlett and Ernest William Goodpasture

Both Sarah Catlett and Ernest Goodpasture had roots in Clarksville but they did not meet until the summer of 1914.

Fig. 8-9: A. V. Goodpasture Sr. and family. This photograph was taken in July 1936, at the Walnuthurst Farm, probably on the occasion of a visit by Sarah Martzloff. The inscription on the back: "Very Merry Christmas and Happy New Year. Papa and the five of us July 1936," was probably written by Mattie, who was living on the farm. The house was the "summer home" at Walnuthurst, the octagonal home having burned. From left: Mattie, A. V. Sr., Sarah, Ernest, Ridley, and A. V. Jr. Jennie Goodpasture had died in 1932. The original of this photograph was loaned by Ann Wilson Goodpasture, daughter of A. V. Goodpasture Jr.

Fig. 8-10: Patch-Catlett House, Home Avenue, Clarksville. This house dates from 1869.

Clarksville was of such a size that an earlier meeting might have been anticipated, but such chances were diminished by Sarah's attending Science Hill, a girl's boarding school in Shelbyville, Kentucky, and Ernest's entering Vanderbilt University in 1903 and then leaving for Johns Hopkins Medical School in 1908.

Their meeting occurred in 1914 because that was the year A. V. Goodpasture moved his family from Nashville to the family farm in Montgomery County. During Ernest's visit that summer, he attended a house party at nearby Dunbar Cave, a popular meeting place for social events in that part of Tennessee[22] (Fig. 8-11). At the party, Sarah Catlett and Ernest were introduced by her good friend and his younger sister, Sarah (nicknamed by her family "Sook").[23] They married one year later on August 11, 1915, in the chapel of Christ Church Episcopal in Nashville.[24] An out-of-Clarksville site was chosen for the wedding because Grandmother Patch, who had helped raise Sarah, had recently suffered a heart attack and was in fragile health.

The *Clarksville Leaf Chronicle* of August 11, 1915, contains some of the details: The Reverend Raimondo de Ovies of Trinity Church, Clarksville, officiated. The service was at 3:00 P.M. "Only a few of the most intimate friends and relatives of the contracting parties were present." A small reception was held at the Leila Webb Howe (later, Campbell) home at the corner of Hillsboro Pike and Woodlawn Drive. None of their correspondence from 1914–15 has been saved, nor are pictures of the wedding available (Fig. 8-12). The August 11, 1915, edition of the *Leaf Chronicle* concluded the wedding article as follows: "The popular bride is greatly beloved in this city. She will be greatly missed upon her removal to her distant home, where she will carry the best wishes of lifelong friends." Both bride and groom might have objected to the choice of the words "her removal."

Sarah was not a tall person—her height is given variously as four-feet-eleven-inches or four-feet-nine-inches—but there is universal agreement that she had curly auburn hair, a vivacious personality, and an infectious laugh. Their honeymoon trip began with a ride via Tennessee Central Railway to Red Boiling Springs, in middle Tennessee, and then continued by rail to Boston. We do not know the

Fig. 8-11: Dunbar Cave entrance, showing dance floor, circa 1920.

Fig. 8-12: This picture shows Sarah and Ernest on the front porch of the Patch-Catlett home in Clarksville and probably was taken just before their wedding.

extent of their honeymoon, although there are pictures of Niagara Falls in their memorabilia from 1915 (Fig. 8-13).

Their only child, Sarah, was born in Cambridge, Massachusetts, on March 12, 1919 (Fig. 8-14). Sarah Junior joined the family shortly before the Goodpastures began the transient part of their lives. By her seventh birthday, Sarah and her parents had lived in Boston, Manila, Pittsburgh, Vienna, and Nashville, had cruised around the world, and had toured across Europe.

In Pittsburgh, the family initially lived in the city near the Singer Institute; but they moved shortly upwind from the industries to the neighboring town of Sewickley, from which there was rail service to Pittsburgh. Their comfortable home in Sewickley (Fig. 8-15) was of historical interest and still stands. After twenty-one months in Pittsburgh, Dr. Goodpasture received an invitation to return to Vanderbilt as professor of pathology with the bonus of a sabbatical year in Europe for additional training. Dr. Goodpasture chose the pathology institute in Vienna.

So, after a year in Vienna, they were at last ready to come home. The Goodpasture family returned from Europe on July 26, 1925, on the ocean liner RMSP *Ohio*. (See color section for place setting at dinner their last night before disembarkation.) We may well imagine their anticipation of coming home, to their home state, to his alma mater. There were the immediate challenges of organizing his department, setting up his laboratory, teaching the pathology course, and establishing themselves as a family in Nashville. Dr.

Goodpasture had used his time well in preparation for this greatly desired appointment, and the two Sarahs must have been ecstatic with the prospects for home and family.

This is Sarah Goodpasture Little's description of her mother's personality:[25]

> Mother was a very animated, garrulous person who immediately made friends easily. My father used to joke (though it was probably true) that she never went anywhere in the WORLD that she didn't meet someone from Clarksville! One lady (not from Clarksville) whom she met on a ship in Norway sent her a postcard addressed: "Dear Lady with the beautiful stars" (in her fragile knowledge of English she probably meant "eyes"). Dorothy Dix[26] inscribed a book to mother: "To dear Sarah who made angel food of life."

At Home in Nashville

While in Nashville, the Goodpasture family lived at 408 Fairfax Avenue (Fig. 8-16).[27] They purchased their first car, an Essex, and hired their first full-time household help, Gracie Edmondson. The Fairfax Avenue neighborhood was notable for the close friendships of the adults as well as those of the children. The William Wemyss family was at 409 Fairfax, the Donald Davidsons at 410, the Hugh Morgans next to the Davidsons for a while, and nearby were the Beverly Douglas and Walter Morgan families.[28]

Fig. 8-13: There are two copies of this photograph from Niagara Falls in their memorabilia, each with an inscription. The inscription in his writing reads: "This was not on our honeymoon," while the one in her hand reads: "This is what we saw all the others doing."

Peggy Wemyss (now Connor), who is four years younger than Sarah, remembers idolizing her and following her around the house and neighborhood. Billy Wemyss, Peggy's younger brother, was very attached to Dr. Goodpasture, to the extent of voluntarily giving him Christmas presents (such as a carefully chosen tube of toothpaste, for which Billy was thanked kindly). Billy undoubtedly was appreciative of the extension of the Goodpasture hospitality to all members of his family, including their terrier, who enjoyed napping in Dr. Goodpasture's chair. Billy, whose father was in shoe manufacturing, called Vanderbilt Hospital "Doc's factory," a designation that was more perceptive than he realized. The Wemyss children were often in the Goodpasture home, particularly after their mother died when Peggy was ten.

Susie Sims (now Irvin), daughter of Mr. and Mrs Cecil Sims, remembers Mrs. Goodpasture as "sweet and loveable, . . . with a beautiful, kind face." The Sims and Goodpasture families were good friends, had dinner in each other's homes, and occasionally attended cultural as well as sporting events together.[29] Mr. Sims was a prominent attorney and civic leader, who sat on the Board of Trust and Vanderbilt Hospital Board and shared membership in the Coffee House Club with Dr. Goodpasture. One of their favorite joint activities, in which the younger Sarah Goodpasture undoubtedly had a special interest (namely, Joe Little Jr.), was a trip to the Old Gym or the Hippodrome to watch Vanderbilt varsity basketball games.[30]

Gardening and painting were favorite hobbies during the years on Fairfax. There was an asparagus bed by the stone wall to the front of the yard; later roses were planted

Fig. 8-14: Sarahs Senior and Junior in Reading, near Boston, in 1919.

Fig. 8-15: Goodpastures at home in Sewickley, Pennsylvania, in 1922 or 1923.

there. Sarah remembers her father cutting yellow roses for his buttonhole and for their breakfast table.[31] There are glimpses of Dr. Goodpasture's familiarity with the natural world in photograph albums. Please see the color photograph inset for this naturalist observing a snapping turtle, obviously somewhere in Tennessee.

Several members of the Goodpasture family were amateur painters, and there is a portrait of Sarah ("Sook") by her sister Mattie that reflects her training and advanced technique. Dr. Goodpasture had been instructed at Hopkins by the master medical illustrator Max Broedel, and along with most classmates he had prepared detailed anatomical drawings as a course requirement for anatomy. Similarly, in pathology students drew images of various pathologic states seen by microscopy. His nonmedical efforts were mostly landscapes and still life, although he did a portrait of his first grandchild when she was two.[32] Both Dr. and Mrs. E. W. Goodpasture entered paintings in the amateur section of a

Fig. 8-16: Goodpasture home at 408 Fairfax Avenue in Nashville, circa 1930.

Tennessee Artists' Exhibition in the late 1930s. Her oil showed Miss Eloise's Cottage (at Monteagle), and his was of a view at Monteagle. He also painted "Wisteria," their Monteagle cottage.[33] (See color section for his painting of "Wisteria Cottage.")

During most of the year, the Goodpasture family alternated Sunday visits to the Clarksville families and attendance by Sarah with family friends or relatives at Christ Church Episcopal where she was confirmed on December 1, 1935. The following excerpts from Sarah's theme for Dr. Mims in 1936 describe a recent visit to Clarksville:

> Last Sunday I went down to the farm to be with Granddaddy [Goodpasture] on his eighty third birthday (Fig. 8-17). He lives in the same house that he moved to thirty years ago, and, in fact, I believe he has spent the ten hours a day that he has averaged reading in the same easy chair that

we found him rared back in when we were there last week. At his right hand he has a revolving book stand in which he keeps his ledgers, his accounts, and all of his favorite books which he likes to reread from time to time. Never has the installation of a telephone been allowed to disturb his peace, nor have even the conveniences of modern plumbing and heating been admitted to his house. He dislikes for anything around him to be changed, from his menu to his brand of tobacco, and he does not suffer interruptions of his routine. [Due to the death of his wife, Sarah's Grandmother, five years ago] there is a new stillness and lack of animation about the place. This setting may tend to increase the awe which always possesses me when I am in Granddaddy's presence, though he treats me in the simplest and gentlest manner possible. . . .

When we dropped in on him last Sunday he was tilted back in his easy chair, with his head reclined against its back, his eyes half closed, puffing on a pipe. He rose immediately to meet us and then, after all the greetings were exchanged, he settled back down in his old chair, resumed his pipe and began to draw us out. Of course he asked me about college and the courses I was studying, and I mentioned Mark Twain to him, knowing that Mark was an old favorite of his. Right then was I given the explanation for the beginning of Granddaddy's particular interest in him—and I am liable to get just such a story on most any subject I approach him with. . . .[34] I wish I had the opportunity to know my Grandfather better.

After a couple of hours on the farm, they then went to see "what was stirring on Home Avenue" at the Catlett household:[35]

Fig. 8-17: A. V. Goodpasture Sr., with a favorite rosebush, on Walnuthurst Farm.

For news and activity is just as much a characteristic of Home Avenue as the lack of it is of the farm. . . . As soon as I stepped in the house, I had to begin planning, to myself, my program: 1. Go admire the baby [a new grandson of Fannie Patch Catlett] for at least fifteen minutes; 2. Step over next door and see Aunt Polly and Uncle Joe; 3. Go down the street and ask about the Vaughn sister who has been so ill; 4. Mr. Sanders will have his feelings hurt if I don't run in and speak; and so on goes the canvass of the neighborhood, all of which must be completed in a couple of hours. Of course, I must allow for fifteen or twenty minutes of soundless lip-readable monologue with which I relay in detail to Grandma [who had been almost totally deaf for many years] all of my activities of the past month. The inhabitants of this little town live in the present and live on the animation within its own limits. Contact, sociability, and conversation interact to make the life of the community a busy one.

Sarah attended Peabody Demonstration School from 1925 until 1932. There she and Mary Jane Brooks (now Evans) began their lifelong friendship, frequently walking in the afternoon together from the school on Edgehill Avenue across 21st Avenue to Dr. Goodpasture's and Dr. Brooks's offices after school.[36] Grace Benedict (now Paine) and Miriam McGaw (now Cowden) became close friends of Sarah's during high school and college years. The McGaws lived on Dixie Place, a block or so from Vanderbilt Hospital, and then on Whitland Avenue. The Benedicts lived on Belcourt Avenue in the winter and Curtiswood Lane (then farmland) in the summer, while the Brooks had a home on Jackson Boulevard in the newly developed Belle Meade area.

Ward-Belmont was Sarah's high school, except for her junior year at Holton Arms in Washington, D.C., as "growing up time." Sarah, Grace, and Miriam were in the same high school sorority. As upperclassmen, they were allowed to attend dances in nearby towns such as Sewanee and Columbia. Sarah remembers that her mother had sewn two new evening dresses for one such occasion. The trip went smoothly until the girls were met by their dates in Cowan (the nearest railhead to Sewanee). In the general excitement, Sarah left

Fig. 8-18: Edith Brooks and Sarah Goodpasture undoubtedly conversing while admiring a rosebush in the front yard of the Fairfax home. Mary Jane and Sarah are on the porch. Barely visible is a brick walk laid by Dr. Goodpasture.

her suitcase containing the dresses behind in the train continuing on to Chattanooga. A telegram and a few anxious moments led to their retrieval the next day. Perhaps we should be reminded that sewing was an essential skill in most households until recent times:[37]

> Mother was popular with my friends—she taught several of them to knit. And one Christmas I remember she and my father made presents for six of my friends. They were luggage racks: my father painted the frames and mother cross-stitched the strips which held them together. She often made my evening dresses.

Mary Jane Evans, the daughter of Dr. and Mrs. Barney Brooks, has been a close friend of Sarah's for seventy-five years (Fig. 8-18)! She recalls the gentleness and wry wit of Dr. Goodpasture and the closeness of the Vanderbilt medical faculty.[38] The faculty wives were equally close. They were hostesses for their husbands' professional guests, and they also took on tasks that contributed to the comfort of the ward patients:[39]

> The 1930s were the Great Depression years and my mother [Mrs. Brooks] and Sarah's mother were prime movers in the Sewing Club. This was a group that met monthly and sewed for the hospital social service department. They made hospital garments and clothing for the ward patients and their families, particularly children, as requested from social services. Four or five of the wives had portable sewing machines and they had it organized on a sort of assembly line with people who cut out patterns, pinned, basted, machine-sewed. It was an all-day affair at somebody's house and they had lunch together and the younger wives got to meet and become friends with wives of the department heads.

Most southern towns and cities had garden clubs. Members were invariably of the fair sex and had varying levels of horticultural interest and expertise. Knowledge, cuttings and bulbs were shared at meetings in addition to discussion of topics of local interest. Meetings were usually held monthly at the homes of the hostesses, where light lunch or refreshments were provided and a paper was read. Sarah Goodpasture belonged to the Town and Country Garden Club, a group that still holds regular meetings. She accepted the invitation to membership on the condition that her husband would be responsible for her papers.[40] Two papers were prepared under these conditions: "Native Shrubs of Tennessee" and "Jonquils and Narcissus." In due course, Sarah Little and Katherine Goodpasture were members of this club as well.

Sarah recalled the pleasures of holiday times on Fairfax and Christmas caroling thusly:[41]

> One of my happiest memories is our caroling on Christmas Eve (being an only child, Christmas was often a lonely time). Christmas Eve, though, was special. Mother was on the Board, I believe, of the Fannie

Battle Day Home[42] and she encouraged me to invite my friends to sing carols as a group, in our neighborhood, for the benefit of the Home. One friend was a violinist and she played as we sang. The girls would gather for an early supper of (I still remember distinctly) turkey sandwiches with cranberry sauce and hot chocolate with marshmallows. When it began to get dark, we started out to visit our neighbors on Fairfax and Chesterfield [streets], collecting money which we turned in at Christ Church later. We did this for years.

The Goodpasture home on Fairfax and Wisteria Cottage at Monteagle were a beehive of friends and family.[43] In addition to the neighborhood children, there were numerous visitors with overnight stays by Sarah's friends. As for relatives, "Uncle John" Catlett was a frequent guest. Almost deaf, he relied on a hearing horn to participate in the conviviality; his grave is adjacent to the Goodpasture plot in Greenwood Cemetery in Clarksville. Sarah's aunt Marion Catlett Edmiston had so many children that her son Jimmy often spent the summers at Monteagle, to the mutual gratification of all. Another aunt, Margaret Catlett Lindamood, rented a cottage next to Wisteria Cottage on occasion; during her daughter's prolonged illness and treatment at Vanderbilt, they lived with the Goodpastures on Fairfax. Grace Benedict Paine recalls that friends were often dropping in and staying for several days at Wisteria Cottage and that meals were usually taken at Miss Ellie Sutherland's Boarding House. Boardinghouses at Monteagle were civilized precursors to motels, offering rooms as well as home-cooked meals, which were routinely enjoyed by guests in the cottages nearby.

Family and friends from more distant locations also shared the Goodpasture hospitality. The Martzloffs (Dr. Goodpasture's sister "Sook" and brother-in-law Karl Matrzloff) of Portland, Oregon, maintained a regular correspondence and apparently visited Tennessee biannually.[44] Their letters mention visits to Monteagle, to Nashville, and to the farm in Montgomery County. On one such visit in 1936, Karl was taken to dinner at the Idaho Springs Hotel near Dunbar Cave with Mr. and Mrs. Hyde, Mrs.

Catlett, Dr. and Mrs. Core, Aunt Sally, Aunt Lulu, "Sim" (A. V. Jr.), and his wife Sally. This hotel was known for the excellence of its kitchen, prompting enthusiastic appreciation by Dr. Martzloff.

West of the Mississippi, "Sook" was known as Sarah Jane, but Dr. Goodpasture was known to the Martzloff family only as "Uncle Doc." During a visit by the Martzloffs in 1936, Dr. Goodpasture received this urgent request from his nephew:[45]

On the farm
Clarksville, Tenn.
(8:00) June 21, 1936
Dear Uncle Doc,

   If you come to the farm next weekend please come on Friday if you can. It's my birthday and if you can come please write me. If you can come in the evening we'll save you some cake and you can see all my presents. We'll sure have a good time if you come. BE SURE TO BRING YOUR GUN! [GUN is written in letters approaching a half-inch in height] so we can shoot.

                                                      Much love, Tom

P.S. Be sure to write

No uncle could refuse such a charming request to go shooting, particularly with the inducements of cake, present-viewing, and assurances of a good time.

Karl Martzloff was very proud of his famous brother-in-law, and once accused Dr. Werner Henle, the professor of virology at the University of Pennsylvania, of a "most serious and inexcusable breach of fidelity" for failure to give Dr. Goodpasture proper credit for proving that mumps was a viral infection. The imbroglio developed after Dr. Martzloff, giving his affiliation as the Department of Surgery at the University of Oregon Medical School, reviewed in 1952 a multi-authored book on advances in medicine and surgery from the University of Pennsylvania.

Instead of being impressed with the extent of knowledge of this surgeon from west of the Mississippi about the mumps literature, Dr. Henle took refuge by stating that his chapter covered only the most recent advances. He probably did not know that family pride and not mumps was the issue, a secret also kept by Dr. Goodpasture in responding to Dr. Henle:[46]

> Thank you very much for your letter of December 4 with enclosures. I enjoyed reading your article on "Recent Advances in Control of Mumps" and see no reason why you should have referred to earlier work concerning etiology. There is certainly no need for apologies so far as I am concerned.

A favorite memory of Sarah's involved attending Camp Nagawicka in Delafield, Wisconsin. Sarah was a camp counselor for several summers, with particular responsibilities for teaching ballet. Joe Little Jr., who seems to have become a permanent part of this story, had been recommended by Mrs. Goodpasture as a waterfront counselor at the adjacent boys' camp (St. John's). Mrs. Albert Whitson was the Nashville representative for both camps as well as a regular member of Mrs. Goodpasture's bridge foursome. Her daughter Laura was a camp counselor. So there was a large Nashville contingent summering in Wisconsin, including the various counselors, campers Al Whitson and Susie Sims, and Mrs. Whitson. Sarah was often entrusted with the care of Susie on the rail trip to Chicago, overnight stay there, and a smaller rail line to the camps.

For Sarah, ballet was an absorbing interest, as described in her theme for Dr. Mims in 1936:

> Some way, back about fifteen years ago, it was noticed and remarked on that I had an infallible sense of rhythm. Since then, spasmodically, I have taken various kinds of dancing lessons from an assortment of teachers. Soon after moving to Nashville, however, I began studying with the most highly recommended teacher here.... For ten years I have been studying with her.... Gradually, with technical improvement, I have been able to, more and more, express myself through this medium. It gives me such a satisfaction as nothing else has been able to do, and I look forward eagerly to the four hours weekly which are to me all absorbing and peaceful....
>
> In addition, my dancing has been of use to me materially, particularly in the last two years. For both summers I have secured a position in a

Fig. 8-19: The Goodpastures welcoming visitors at Union Station, Nashville, circa 1938. Catherine (Mrs. Roy) Avery is behind Sarah, and John Buddingh is to the far right.

fine girl's camp as assistant dancing instructor. Not only has this given me further opportunities to pursue my interest, but it has enabled me to realize my potentiality in relation to my fellow creatures. The contacts that I have made in this environment have been some of the most interesting ones in my life. The routine which I followed there was the most perfect combination of my varied interests, and contributed satisfactorily to every part of my being.

Sarah entered Vanderbilt University in 1936, where she was a member of the Delta Delta Delta sorority.[47] In her freshman theme, this was Sarah's description of her parents:

My father, who could be the lowliest of human beings and yet be my idol, every day coming closer to that goal of "justifying his existence" which was placed before him upon graduation from medical school, has one of the foremost places in his particular field of medicine in the world. Yet, he too has been contemplating a "back to the farm" movement [as made by her Grandfather Goodpasture returning to the farm in Montgomery County at age fifty-five to lead a simpler life] for the last three or four years and will probably realize it when I have graduated from college.

My mother, red-headed and "highly energized," has entered top-speed into all of the activities here, large and small, that she has been called upon to attend (Fig. 8-19). She has made it possible for me to be associated, from my childhood, with the kind of people with whom I would be congenial, through the many friends that she has made during the eleven years that we have lived in Nashville.

Sarah Goodpasture and Joe Little received their bachelor of arts degrees on Wednesday, June 12, 1940, from Chancellor Carmichael. The commencement address was delivered by Dr. Dave Hennen Morris, distinguished lawyer and diplomat.[48] The yearbook *Commodore* notes that Sarah was president of the Tri Delta sorority and that Joe had been inducted into the honor society Omicron Delta Kappa.[49] This time must have been bittersweet because Mrs. Goodpasture was too ill to attend and was only able to observe the proceedings from their car (Fig. 8-20).

This is Sarah's account of her mother's illness:[50]

Mother became ill about the time of my 12th birthday. She had what was called malignant hypertension and had to be confined to bed for . . . several months. A nurse came each day to give her massages [specific treatment was not available]. Mother had a friend from Clarksville who worked in Nashville at Stokes and Stockell bookstore in the children's department. She came out to our house to "host" my 12th birthday party with games and contests appropriate for our age.

[In later years] no matter how sick she was with frequent "sick

Fig. 8-20: Sarah and her father at Vanderbilt commencement, 1940.

headaches," mother always bounced back and was ready for her weekly bridge foursome.[51] She was an especially good bridge player and loved the game.

These are a few of my memories of my mother who died in 1940— soon after I graduated from Vanderbilt. *Too soon.*

Mrs. Goodpasture's physicians were Dr. Hugh Morgan and Dr. David Strayhorn. She was admitted to Vanderbilt Hospital for five days early in 1939 for pneumococcal pneumonia. In the fall and winter of 1939–40, Sarah's health was "not at all good and a recent attack of flu and sinusitis has not helped"[52] Then in May of 1940 the pace of her illness accelerated. Dr. Goodpasture was scheduled to give the Shattuck Lecture in Boston on May 21, and he informed his friends there on May 13 that his visit would necessarily be truncated. In mid-May, Sarah had a few good days but was hospitalized with a hypertensive crisis in late May for almost two weeks.

The Goodpastures then sought comfort in the setting of their Monteagle cottage, with Dr. Morgan consulting from Nashville. In spite of considerable distress with abdominal and leg pains, Sarah was noted to "maintain her splendid courage and cheerfulness." Sarah Junior remembers that during this time Dr. Goodpasture was attempting to make some huckleberry jam by the "scientific method," while Sarah Senior called from her bedroom with remedial instructions. When the family was away for lunch at a nearby boardinghouse, she rose from her bed to finish the jam properly. Readmission to the hospital was necessary on July 16, and Sarah died from a hypertensive crisis on the following day. After services at the home on Fairfax with Dr. Prentice Pugh (an Episcopal clergyman) officiating, burial was in Greenwood Cemetery in Clarksville.[53]

The most helpful solace for Dr. Goodpasture must have come from daughter Sarah,[54] who was living at home on Fairfax; from Jim Dawson, who had returned to Vanderbilt in 1938; and from Joe Little, who was engaged to Sarah. Jim Dawson was "like a son" to Dr. Goodpasture as well as "like a big brother" to Sarah.[55] The Dawsons' eldest son was named for Dr. Goodpasture, and Jim's support after Sarah's death was acknowledged in a letter from Dr. Goodpasture in 1955.[56] Jim must have helped in several ways, including building a fishing boat in the garage on Fairfax. This boat had its maiden voyage in the fall of 1940 on the Red River near Clarksville.[57] In Joe's words: "When it became obvious that Sarah and I were serious about each other Dr. James Dawson decided he should make a fisherman out of me so that I would be more compatible with Dr. Goodpasture." An expedition to Clarksville was arranged, with Sarah visiting Grandmother Catlett, several Patch cousins, and other relatives while the gentlemen tried their luck on the Red River. They fished from noon until late afternoon without success, prompting this comment from their hostess: "Serves them right, fishing on Sunday!" There was the good news that the boat did not leak and that the tyro avoided hooking either of his companions.

It had become obvious that Sarah and Joe were serious about each other quite a while before this expedition. They had met during her freshman year at Vanderbilt. Joe apparently received considerable tactical support in his suit from Mrs. Goodpasture, who had recommended him as camp counselor and had also provided late afternoon meals and companionship while the two of them waited for Sarah to return from other dates. Joe had been raised in Bessemer, Alabama, where he was a standout student and athlete. His record and personality were so exemplary that he became the standard by which other boys in Bessemer were measured and universally found wanting.[58]

Sarah and Joe married in Christ Church on August 2, 1941, and received the wedding guests under a white tent at the Fairfax home[59] (Figs. 8-21 and 22). Tom Fite Paine and Joe Little flipped a coin to determine the order of their weddings, due to the tight schedules imposed by Reserve Officer's Training Corps and the opening of Vanderbilt Medical School on its accelerated wartime schedule.[60]

Joe was awarded the M.D. degree at Vanderbilt in 1943 and was inducted into the Army Air Force on December 30, 1943. Fortunately he had assignments in the United States until he was mustered out in

Fig. 8-21: Sarah Jr. and Joe Little's wedding.

July 1946. He then had residency training at Vanderbilt and at the Children's Hospital in Cincinnati. His academic career included faculty appointments at Children's Hospital in Cincinnati, University of Louisville, Vanderbilt University, and Louisiana State University School of Medicine in Shreveport. He was physician-in-chief at the Children's Hospital in Louisville from 1956 to 1962; and he was professor and head of the Department of Pediatrics at Shreveport from 1970 to 1983, at which institution he became professor emeritus in 1985.

The Littles have three children: Sarah Marsh, born in 1944; Susan McLaughlin, born in 1946, and Joseph Alexander III, born in 1950. Sarah and Susan Little were born in Vanderbilt University Hospital; Joe was in the Army Air Force from 1943 until 1946, but he was able to be in Nashville for both births. The Littles lived on Fairfax during his residency at Vanderbilt 1946–47. In 1949 the Littles moved to Louisville, where Joseph A. Little III was born. Joe Little was asked in May 2000 to describe having Dr. Goodpasture as a father-in-law. This is his response, in part:[61]

> Dr. Goodpasture was the ideal father-in-law to me. My own father died when I was 10 years old and, although I was in awe of Dr. Goodpasture, he was the most gentle and kind man whom I had ever known. I never heard him raise his voice to me, his daughter or his grandchildren. He helped me in so many ways that I cannot recall them all. In 1950 when I was operated for an eighth nerve tumor at Johns

Hopkins he supported me and his daughter despite having to go to Japan shortly after my operation for the Atomic Energy Commission. . . .

Marriage with Katherine Anderson

Katherine Anderson and Dr. Goodpasture married at Westminister Presbyterian Church in Nashville on May 23, 1945.[62] The home at 408 Fairfax was a busy household that next Christmas, for Joe, Sarah, and baby Sarah came home. Mother and daughter stayed until Susan was born in May 1946. Then the Little family returned en masse from the Air Force to live on Fairfax during Joe's 1946–47 residency in pediatrics at Vanderbilt. Fortunately, Bertha Davis became part of the household activities in 1945 and provided support and sustenance until the Goodpastures left for Washington in 1955.[63]Katherine and Bertha had other important responsibilities arising from Dr. Goodpasture's duties as dean and head of pathology. Many of the dinners and evening affairs attendant to

Fig. 8-22: The bride and groom.

professional activities in the medical school and university were held in homes during these times; in addition, there were departmental events, including the traditional New Year's eggnog party.[64]

Katherine was a gracious hostess, but she is better known for her interests in the outdoors. In her new role as Dr. Goodpasture's wife, she gave up her considerable competency as a bench-scientist and transferred her observational and investigative skills to the natural world. She became one of the leading ornithologists in Tennessee, if not the South, and a superb all-round amateur naturalist. Her love and respect for all life-forms were transmitted formally and informally to friends, family, and students.

As admirable as these achievements were, her most significant accomplishment was to become a beloved "grandmother" for the Little children.[65] Family reunions at holidays, as well as vacations at Rehobeth Beach and Mount LeConte, were greatly anticipated and became fondly remembered events. In particular, the farm at Basin Spring in Williamson County assumed such a treasured place in the lives of children and adults that it deserves special attention.

The Basin Spring Farm

This farm on Bedford Creek Road, in the First District of Williamson County, in the state of Tennessee, was purchased by the Goodpastures in August 1948. Bedford Creek flows into the South Harpeth River, which in turn is a tributary of the Big Harpeth or Harpeth River.[66] The central component of the Basin Spring Farm totaled 154 acres and was purchased for $3,750. It had the advantages, from the perspective of the Goodpastures, that it was readily accessible to Nashville by car, requiring forty-five minutes, and yet was sufficiently remote to have intrinsic privacy.

The lay of the land was appealing in that the spring, its drainage, and the homesite were nestled between gentle hills framing and protecting the view. The spring flowed year-round, providing water for wildlife and cattle as well as a marvelous wading stream for grandchildren and friends. (See color section for view of Basin Spring Creek.) Most of the valley land was cultivatable and bordered by wooded hills eight hundred feet or so above sea level.

The second-growth hardwood forest, interspersed ravines, brushy edges, and cleared land contributed to the ecological diversity of the property.

When purchased, most of the cleared land (about twenty-four acres) had been planted in corn; a tenant farmer lived in a small house within sight of the road, and a barn for livestock was located farther up the spring-fed creek. (See color section for view of farm house, Basin Spring.) Several generations of Tennesseans had lived at Basin Spring for the purpose of operating a post office that had opened on June 22, 1858.[67] A graveyard on a knoll above the creek contains graves of these postmasters and postmistresses and their families.

Ultimately, the Goodpasture holdings expanded to 210 acres. The Basin Spring Farm instantly filled a need both Goodpastures felt for being outdoors, working with the land, and observing nature.[68] There were demands imposed by the property on their time—gentle, yet insistent, ones associated with the change of seasons: searching for treasured flowers in their restricted locales; identification of birds at expected times and in expected places; tramping and exploring the woods as the flora responded to the seasons and weather. There were more insistent demands associated with gardening, keeping bees, and raising cattle: working the ground, putting in fenceposts, stringing barbwire, and cutting firewood, all physically demanding tasks (Fig. 8-23).

These demands established a regularity in their presence at the farm that was invigorating

Fig. 8-23: Dr. Goodpasture in working attire at the Basin Spring Farm.

Fig. 8-24: Sketch by Dr. Goodpasture for a cabin at Basin Spring.

and satisfying. In 1949, one or both of the Goodpastures were at the farm on ninety-seven occasions; approximately one-half of these were on the weekend. Other than the expected trips on weekends, the only hint of a ritual about their visits may be found in the logbooks described below, when Katherine mentioned on several occasions the need to "start the new year right" with a trip to the farm on January 1. There is no evidence they ever spent the night there, although the cabin would have afforded rough accommodations and a fire. They considered building a cabin at Basin Spring, as several sketches by Dr. Goodpasture were made, including this exterior view (Fig. 8-24).

Dr. Goodpasture started a notebook on August 28, 1948, recording the purchase of the farm, and entered notations of expenses until November 30 (such as two ounces of purple top turnip seeds for ten cents, a foot adze for $1.75, seven spools of barbed wire for $52.50, panes of glass, and green paint) (Fig. 8-25). Fortunately, Katherine kept a detailed record of their trips to Basin Spring. From her logbooks we may appreciate this special part of their lives from the descriptions of the weather, activities, visitors, flora, and fauna for each trip.[69]

The 1949 log documents in their first year on the farm a formidable amount of physical work, even hard labor, by the Goodpastures, then aged sixty-three and forty years. They shunned hired help and cheerfully tackled the following: they disked and weeded the bottomland fields and established permanent pastures; a "complete" vegetable garden was planted and the produce used immediately or stored; over one hundred fruit and nut trees were planted and cared for; seventy-five loblolly pines were also planted; an impressive amount of fencing was put up;[70] and a rail fence with rails they split was built across the front by the road.

Their greatest pleasure came from identification and study of the various life-forms on their own land, as stated by Katherine in a summary at the end of the 1949 log:

> Untold observations on plant and animal life on Basin Spring farm have increased not only our knowledge of natural history as a whole but the pleasure, relaxation and refreshment derived from each trip there. We always want to go back because each time we discover something "new" to our own experience.
>
> During the year we have identified 92 species of birds on the farm. That includes migrants. A complete list of migrating warblers would push this list upward considerably! A summer nesting population will be an interesting one. Sixteen nests were observed and 3 additional species were observed feeding. . . .

A constant source of interest has been to find and learn an increasing number of species of trees and shrubs. Among the shrubs are several species of huckleberries one of which tends to be arboreal. . . . Beautiful coral red honeysuckle which is our native species and eglatine are indeed spring beauties. . . . The bright red flowering buckeye was a real find as was the indescribably lovely flowering native crab. . . .

Observation and study of the wildflowers has been constantly stimulating. A definitive list of those studied, identified specifically and sketched would be cumbersomely long.[71] Suffice it

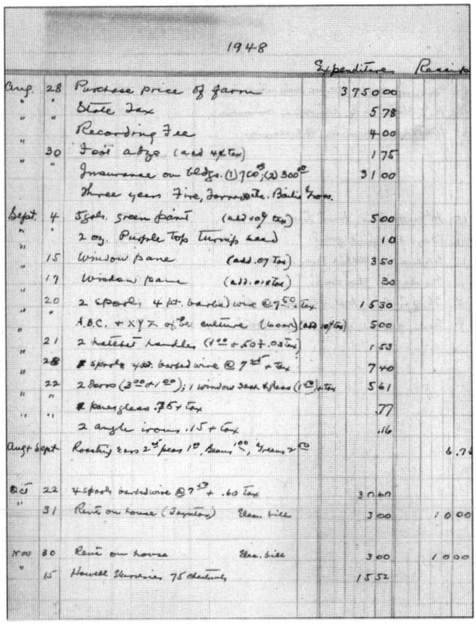

Fig. 8-25: Notations by Dr. Goodpasture about initial purchase of Basin Spring Farm and supplies in 1948.

to mention a few "finds" that have been especially pleasant and notable. To find patches of pepper and salt, trout lily, wild poppy, phacelia, pachysandra, Indian pink and spider lily are real botanical experiences, not to mention 5 *species* of native wild orchids. *One day* during mid-fall we identified 40 species of wild flowers in bloom—this included the lovely blue lobelia.

Then we find a remarkable sentence: "The geological history of Basin Spring Farm will lead us into an almost new world figuratively speaking. We have collected and specifically labeled some twenty fossil forms of marine animals which inhabited the area some 500,000,000 years ago." Their intellectual curiosity about life on earth was truly all-encompassing! The 1949 log closes with these New Year prospects: "So many challenges to one's ignorance of the world about here and so many stimuli to one's five senses will surely make the Next and New Year one of great fun and expectations!"

Basin Spring was certainly a paradise for children. No trip to Nashville was complete for the Little children until they had ridden in "Gran's" Jeep to the farm, checked out the cows, drunk from the spring, splashed in the creek, and hunted berries, fossils, and arrowheads.[72] Lunch was anticipated because it always included deviled eggs, a specialty of "Kafun's." There was also a hidden curriculum, the courses including respect for the land and the life it supported; the simple pleasure of exploring a creek in middle Tennessee; the unending wonder of the natural world. Fifty years later, the graduates of this school still treasure their memories of Basin Spring.

Modernists are probably incapable of forming such deep attachments to land as the Goodpastures felt for Basin Spring. There the pace of life was established by the seasons, and the seemingly infinite variety of life was gradually revealed to the patient observer. It was an oasis of life, sheltered from the mobilization of society and the threat to treasured places from roadways, sprawl, and pollution. It must have been very difficult for them to leave for Washington in 1955.[73] Here are Katherine's words about leaving Basin Spring:

1955—Basin Spring Log—1955

January 2. Sunday. We begin our New Year at Basin Spring on the second day of January again in deference to the Dept. [of] Pathology and an eggnog party on the first. Twas a good party seemingly enjoyed by everyone but this is a farm log—so let us onto an account of the first day there [in] 1955. Weather: Warm, sunshiny; official temp. 61 degrees. The day was bright, warm and pleasant as only a warm January day can be. Up leisurely, packed lunch with gumdrops & nuts & current cake along with ham sandwiches left from the party. Off at 10:00 A.M.—took a somewhat casual bird count along the way.

Fed 3 head of cattle: cottonseed meal, chopped corn, hay. Pastures are green but cropped to the crowns. Speck & Cleo & Sylvia [all cows, presumably] seem in good state of repair. . . . and so on home after an especially fine day out-of-doors.

A somewhat more than casual bird count gave a check of 32 species, including: myrtle, winter wren, waxwings, redheaded [woodpecker] at 4th bridge. Especially notable were flocks of goldfinches, about 30 waxwings, 5 shrikes, 10 chickadees (most since blizzard [of 1951]), 3 white-brown nuthatches.

We are faced with the prospect of development of a federal highway, right by the front gate during the next year and a half and I can hardly fail to add that all my observations are overshadowed by the prospect of our not being able to watch another cycle of seasons through to the end because we may be away from 408 [Fairfax] and Basin Spring for an interval before the year is out. I shall not write of this except as our activities are directed toward preparation for such an event but I shall have my previous records of the seasons at Basin Spring with me and shall be able to follow in my imagination the turn of the seasons there.

This was the last entry in 1955, dated March 24:

K. out all day. Dug bulbs at 408 for an hour and half to transplant to Basin Spring. [Planting locations were then given in detail for bulbs, especially daffodils, and crabapple seedlings.] A good planting. I very much hope these fine bulbs live! Have others to take out. Whether I'll ever know where they are or have opportunity to see them I cannot tell.

. . . Walked to big oak. No black and white or sycamore [warblers]. Trout lilies in beautiful bloom. Two-leafed Deuteria fresh and pretty . . . one mayapple [opening]. Purple finch.

The next journal entry was in 1962 in a separate notebook and is included below. There is no journal for 1960, although one would have expected records of their visits in the spring of that year after their return to Nashville, even though they would have been busy moving into a new home and setting up their laboratory. Following Dr. Goodpasture's death in September 1960 (a subject for chapter 10), Katherine's routine in terms of visits to Basin Springs was presumably not reestablished until 1962.

1962—Basin Spring Log

The Journal is picked up again after lapse of a good many years. Fundamental changes in the whole structure of my relations to these acres have taken place. Natural beauty is the same but my spirit is less light, my security in these hills is lessened, my responsibilities greater. Time takes its toll, but Man is part of a changing environment. I feel part and parcel of this ecological niche and shall be happy here as long as I can . . .
Jan 1, 1962

In years past, I have liked to "begin the New Year right" so made special effort to stick to an old custom. Drove out alone about noon to Basin Spring. There was light snow on the ground. . . . Had a wonderful tramp to the back pasture thru the snow. Tramped up second hollow, over the hill to the "saw-whet" cedars looking for owls—down into Shale Hollow.

[A number of birds are listed.] Good first day of the year 1962.

The last entry in 1962 was on July 29. Similarly, the log books of 1973 and 1975 end prematurely, with entries in May and April, respectively. By this time, Katherine was an expert ornithologist and all-round naturalist. Her good friend Ann Tarbell traced this expertise to experiences in Washington:[74]

Although she had studied biology, her education in the natural history of the out-of-doors was sparked and fanned by the years she and her husband Dr. Goodpasture spent in the Washington, D.C. area. There she became acquainted with well-known and enthusiastic ornithologists in the government Office of Migratory Bird Studies. On field trips with them on the East Coast, she learned her skills of bird identification and habits and the art and purpose of bird-banding. At that time she witnessed the setting up of new and wide-spread research projects on the patterns of bird migration. In turn she was recognized as a coming co-worker in the field. By her self education through reading and study and her own banding projects to document Tennessee birds through the seasons, she fulfilled this in Nashville. . . .

Katherine worked responsibly at birding. She kept records and counts, valuable in migratory and nesting studies; she documented TV tower kills of birds in fall migration; for twenty years she directed Tennessee's part in significant national Breeding Bird Surveys; she served in official capacity in the Tennessee Ornithological Society in Nashville and the state and received from them the Distinguished Service Award in 1990 at the 75th Anniversary Meeting of the Society. Of great importance, she published her results with meticulous accuracy in national journals and our state journal, *The Migrant*.[75]

Katherine Goodpasture died on February 12, 1995, after a period of progressive enfeeblement that required nursing care for more than twenty-four months. Her activity was initially restricted by a broken hip and remedial surgery. It was finally necessary for her to leave the home she and Dr. Goodpasture bought in 1960 and move to Richland Place Health Center in Nashville, where she lived for two years. Friends and family made frequent and determined efforts to bring reminders of the outside world to Katherine, but her spirit was at Basin Spring.[76] A memorial service at Benton Chapel on the Vanderbilt campus concluded with remarks by her "grandson" Joseph Little III, M.D., in which her impact on the lives of others was summarized:[77]

> For those times when we forget how all things on this earth are connected and interdependent, for those times when we forget the wonders that the study of the natural world can provide, for those times

when we forget what a difference one, quiet person can make—I give you the memory of Katherine Goodpasture and Basin Spring.

Special Friends

There is some presumption and potential embarrassment involved in making a list of friends of Dr. Goodpasture, and especially a list of close friends, but the latter appear to have included: Sam Clark, Barney Brooks, Jim Dawson, Watson Sellards, Sidney Burwell, Cecil Sims, William Wemyss, Andrew Benedict, and Tom Fite Paine.

Dr. Goodpasture's personal correspondence is not available for review, with the exception of the extensive correspondence he conducted with Jim Dawson and Watson Sellards in which they routinely mixed business and pleasure. The list above is principally based on recollections of neighbors on Fairfax and of Sarah Goodpasture Little's close friends as well as Dr. Goodpasture's correspondence file in the Eskind Library archives.

The friendships with the Benedict and Paine families were special because of their multiple relationships to the Goodpastures. Grace Benedict Paine at this point is well known to us, so we should begin with her parents, Anne Hillman Scales and Andrew Benedict. The Scales and Benedict families lived across the street from one another in North Edgefield and near their mutual close friends the A. V. Goodpastures on Woodland Street. Many prominent Nashvillians lived in East Nashville in the late 1800s and early 1900s, before Belle Meade was developed and Nashville began to grow to the west and south. Hillman Scales graduated from Bowen School and was at Vanderbilt with Ernest Goodpasture, as was his brother E. P. Scales. Anne Scales graduated from Vanderbilt in 1905,[78] Ernest Goodpasture in 1907, Andrew Benedict in 1908,[79] and Tom Fite Paine Sr. in 1908.[80]

Andrew Benedict Sr., after becoming treasurer of Vanderbilt University in 1941, had extensive interactions with Dean Goodpasture during the financial crisis of the medical school (from 1945 to 1950). Following the marriage of Grace Benedict and Tom Fite Paine Jr. in 1941, Dr. Goodpasture was instrumental in finding positions for Tom and Grace in Rochester, New York; meanwhile (1941–42) Sarah became secretary to Miss Annie Allison, headmistress at Ward-Belmont, probably with Mr. Benedict's support. Both Tom Fite Paine and Joe Little had academic careers, and their families have maintained close personal ties to the present.

The shared interest of the Sims and Goodpasture families in basketball has been mentioned previously. Cecil Sims was a very influential and effective member of the legal community and made repeated efforts to resolve issues between Vanderbilt Medical School and Nashville General Hospital relating to health care of the indigent. Friendship with the Goodpastures was partially based on professional interactions, as Mr. Sims was on the Vanderbilt Board of Trust and the Hospital Committee. They also shared membership in the Coffee House Club.[81]

Dr. Sam Clark may have been Dr. Goodpasture's closest faculty friend, but the Barney Brooks family was also very close. The interactions between Dr. Brooks, professor and head of surgery, and Dr. Goodpasture must have been interesting and sometimes contentious, as both held opinions strongly. However, both had farming backgrounds, had expressed interest in becoming physicians as boys, had attended Johns Hopkins Medical School, had come to Vanderbilt as professors at the same time, and were committed to the Vanderbilt ideal. Their friendship undoubtedly flourished with the guidance of Edith Brooks and Sarah Goodpasture, who must have been kindred spirits because their daughters Mary Jane and Sarah were also close friends.[82]

The Goodpasture persona had the quiet, dignified side presented to medical students and the congenial side known fully by family, personal friends, colleagues, classmates, and neighbors. The gulf that students and casual acquaintances had to cross to experience the warmth of his friendship was wide, a gulf created in part by his native reserve and in part by their natural respect for his stature and accomplishments. He may not have been aware of the gulf, in part owing to humility, and certainly did not deliberately foster its development.

When medical graduates taught by Dr. Goodpasture (from 1929 to 1959) were solicited for information about him, those responding universally described their respect and even awe of this professor.[83] There were no descriptions of jokes or casual interactions. A few graduates described diagnostic coups when Dr. Goodpasture reviewed particularly difficult cases, or his professional demeanor when interacting with families of patients. There were no nicknames. There are no pictures of teacher with students. And yet here is Jim Dawson's description of Dr. Goodpasture in the memoir prepared for the *American Journal of Pathology* in 1961:[84]

> Away from the laboratory he was a charming person with many diverse interests, including history, painting, gardening, hunting, fishing, and just plain talking. A wonderful sense of humor and a fine ability to recount stories appropriate to the occasion made him a most perfect companion either in the living room or on a bass stream.

Esmond Long in his biographical memoir summarizes Dr. Goodpasture's personality thusly: "Goodpasture's range of association with colleagues and friends was very wide. Personally he was unostentatious, reserved, good-humored, and quietly friendly."

Thomas Francis Jr. in his biographical memoir for the American Philosophical Society has these comments about Dr. Goodpasture's personality:

> Throughout his career Goodpasture stressed the value of research in vitalizing the teaching of students and staff. Frequently stern and laconic, a fine sense of humor coupled with an understanding patience made him at once a valuable critic and preceptor readily available for discussion with students and colleagues.

There is a common theme to these three descriptions, but they also become progressively more analytical and less personal. The heartfelt description, that of Jim Dawson, rings true owing to the advantage Jim had in interacting with Dr. Goodpasture repeatedly, inside the medical center as well as outside. We should also recognize that more may be learned about the character of a faculty member in a few minutes in the field, on a stream, or even on a golf course, than is apparent by detailed scrutiny of a curriculum vitae or letters of reference.[85]

The faculty members in those good, early days managed to entertain each other at parties with some regularity. Dr. Kampmeier described a costume party in 1934 at the Cunninghams' (professor of anatomy and librarian, respectively) attended by the full-time faculty, apparently in nonacademic regalia. Dr. Kampmeier "lacked the temerity, although strongly tempted" to include photographs of the assembled professors in his book *Recollections*.[86] Mrs. Albert Evans (Mary Jane Brooks) describes the medical school faculty as a "close knit, fun loving group":[87]

> I remember one garden party at the home of the Sidney Burwells [later dean of the Harvard Medical School]. After the picnic supper, the entertainment of the evening was an original play, the side porch over-looking the back yard serving as stage. It was a murder mystery, at the conclusion of which the actors froze in their stage positions. And then they did the whole thing backwards, reciting their lines, repeating the action, all in reverse. The murder victim leaped to his feet and then the gun fired. Some of the backward lines were excruciatingly hilarious . . .

This kind of activity was apparently still going on in 1946, when Clare and Glenn Millikan (Glenn was the recently appointed head of physiology) entertained the senior faculty at their home on Stonewall Drive on August 21.[88] The party featured some type of competition involving falls from ski and horse. Dean Youmans admitted to nine falls from ski; former Dean Goodpasture to six? from ski, with the question mark not further explained; Dr. Darby (professor of biochemistry) had seven from ski and seven from horse, while Nancy Ward (her husband Jim was associate professor of anatomy) won (or lost) with fifteen from ski.

Dr. Goodpasture could hardly be described as a partygoer, but there are hints in his correspondence that he was an active partici-pant in all types of convivial activities. There are many letters from

Watson Sellards in which socializing with each other and a few friends was anticipated or recalled with pleasure. In 1953, Dr. Goodpasture was asked to send a letter to Dr. E. C. Stakman, head of plant pathology at the University of Minnesota, on the occasion of his retirement:[89]

> I can't quite get adjusted to the thought of your retirement so soon (so young, so vigorous, so recently). But if that's the way things go nowadays I certainly want to be amongst those present to make an ado about it.
>
> Association with you on the [Atomic Bomb Casualty Commission] was an experience that gave me much pleasure and satisfaction. As we met here and there for serious discourse and decision your wisdom was enlightening and elevated by your spirit of kindliness; and while traveling over the road together with congenial friends your presence always bespoke good humor, good company, and conviviality. (I wish I had a copy of your Swedish song that wouldn't bear translation.). . . .
>
> Good luck, Stak, and thanks for your good company along the way.

Dr. Goodpasture's closest friend may well have been Dr. Sam Clark, professor and head of the Department of Anatomy from 1937 until his death on July 1, 1960 (Fig. 8-26). They were both of local origin, almost the same age, and identical in their loyalty to Vanderbilt and belief in the primacy of universities in civilized society. Both espoused a close physical and intellectual association of medical schools with universities, and both were committed to the melding of research and teaching.

In 1945, a time of crisis for the medical school, Dr. Goodpasture turned to Dr. Clark for help in the dean's office. They

Fig. 8-26: Dr. Sam Clark at his desk, circa 1955. Courtesy of Dr. Samuel Paplanus.

were similarly highly principled, with wide-ranging interests; both were excellent albeit amateur historians. At a more personal level, their personalities were similar, and each had lost his wife to disease. At the memorial service for Dr. Clark in July 1960, Dr. Goodpasture praised his colleague with words that were equally appropriate for both of these men:[90] "No better justification of the 'Athens of the South' has ever emerged from his native city than this exemplary physician, teacher, scientist, gentleman and scholar."

Fig. 8-27: William Gunter, longtime factotum in the Departments of Pathology and Anatomy.

Their loyalty to Vanderbilt was mirrored in the loyalty of their departmental personnel. Dr. Goodpasture's secretary, Miss McGovern, worked throughout his tenure. Another long-term employee, William Gunter, had joint responsibilities in pathology and anatomy. On August 23, 1943, faculty and alumni honored William Gunter (Fig. 8-27) for fifty years of service to the medical school by participating in a ceremony in the amphitheater (now C2209, Medical Center North). Bill Gunter had held several positions over that period, the most important of which were to serve as photographer and factotum for Dr. Goodpasture and to prepare cadavers for the anatomy class. Both Dr. Goodpasture and Dr. Clark had a role in organizing this thoughtful and appropriate recognition of Bill Gunter's role in the medical school. Dr. Goodpasture's comments on the occasion exemplify his innate courtesy, sense of humor, and respect for his fellow man:[91]

He has helped educate hundreds of doctors and has made their student life happier and more profitable by his labors; he has raised a fine family of sons some of whom are now efficiently carrying on his work; he has helped in indirect ways to restore the sick to health, and he has witnessed the rising of the dead.[92]

Watson Sellards was one of Dr. Goodpasture's two close friends in Boston. They maintained a lifelong correspondence, the analysis of which is complicated by the lack of dates on the letters from Sellards; also, replies were not copied, nor were they saved at Harvard. Mrs. Goodpasture also corresponded with Watson Sellards, who uniformly asked in his letters to Dr. Goodpasture to be remembered to the "two Sarahs" and later to Sarah Little.

Watson Sellards was a Kansan by birth. He entered Johns Hopkins Medical School in 1905, graduating in 1909. His training overlapped with that of Dr. Goodpasture in medical school, their residencies at Hopkins (Sellards in medicine), faculty appointments at Harvard, and for the year 1921–22 in the Philippines when they collaborated extensively in research. Dr. Sellards came to New Orleans in 1929 at Dr. Goodpasture's invitation to present results of his research on yellow fever to the Southern Medical Association. Their friendship was based on a common interest in research on infectious diseases and their shared training experiences. Contact was maintained through intermittent meetings in Boston or New York. Watson Sellards had traveled extensively throughout the world; and, judging by his letters, he must have been a good conversationalist. His most important research contributions were to find additional evidence that yellow fever was a viral infection and to develop methods for transporting infectious material from the field to laboratories where sophisticated studies could be carried out.[93]

Dr. Sellards was described as heavily built, with a large, balding head.[94] Hypertension was presumably responsible for an episode of transient cerebral ischemia in October 1940. That winter he was on sick leave, but he still joined Sarah and Dr. Goodpasture for a week on their Christmas trip to New York in December 1940.[95] Other strokes and attempted treatment led to marked deterioration of health and ultimately his death on December 1, 1942. His last letter to Dr. Goodpasture was dated October 23 and read in part:[96]

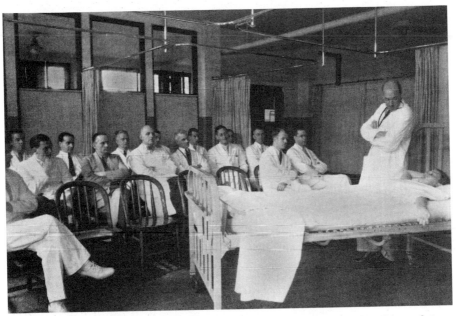

Fig. 8-28: Sidney Burwell conducting ward rounds at Vanderbilt Hospital, circa 1934. Doctors Cate, Morgan, and Weinstein are identified.

"Nothing would please me more than a visit at Nashville but this convalescent period is a joke and drags on through the months. . . . Many thanks and Best of wishes, Watson."

Sidney Burwell, Dr. Goodpasture's other close friend in Boston, sent notification of Watson Sellards's death by telegram. The foundation for the Burwell and Goodpasture friendship was laid in Nashville while Dr. Burwell was professor of medicine from 1928 until 1935 (Fig. 8-28), when he became dean of the School of Medicine at Harvard. They maintained close contact thereafter for twenty years. One of Dr. Burwell's first semiofficial acts at Harvard was to host a dinner party featuring Tennessee country ham, grits, and eggnog on ice cream. Anticipating questions about the ham-curing process, he naturally turned to Dr. Goodpasture for the specifics:[97]

Pack fresh ham in dry salt for six weeks. Hang in smokehouse. Smoke slowly about two months. Sack and hang in smoke house a year or two.

Old well seasoned smoke house indispensable for best flavor.
Hickory wood smoke choice. Age important factor. It's a ham what am.

Happy days, Ernest

The cordial relationships between Vanderbilt and the Burwells
are illustrated by the ceremony at the presentation of Canby
Robinson's portrait to the university in May 1938 at the Belle
Meade Club in Nashville. Dr. Burwell was asked to officiate,
although Dean Leathers or Hugh Morgan as professor of medicine
might have felt it was his responsibility.[98]

Shortly after arriving in Boston, the Burwells purchased a
summer cottage at Ipswich, on the North Shore of Massachusetts
approximately twenty-eight miles from Boston. Ipswich claims to be
the birthplace of American independence; it certainly was one of
the earliest sites of smallpox inoculation for prevention of that
disease. Somehow, Dr. Goodpasture knew that a Dr. Manning of
Ipswich was the pioneer involved in the smallpox inoculations and
wrote Dr. Burwell as follows on October 31, 1938:[99]

> Recently I read a life of Nathaniel Hawthorne in which it was stated that
> his Mother was a Miss Manning of Concord, I believe. Hawthorne himself
> was born about the time or a little after Dr. Manning of Ipswich was making
> his experimental inoculations, and it occurred to me that she was possibly
> related to him, perhaps a sister, which if true would add some interest.
>
> In regards to the Ipswich records it must be borne in mind that
> Manning made his vaccine inoculations no doubt some weeks or perhaps a
> few months before authority was granted him to reinoculate with smallpox
> virus. I hope you will be able to find out something about the gentleman.

Dr. Goodpasture dined at the Burwell home in May 1939, when
he appeared before the New England Pathological Society, and he
stayed in their home in 1941 before presenting the Cutter Lecture.
Sarah and Joe Little were warmly received at Ipswich in July 1943.

The Kober Medal presentation in 1944 must have meant a great
deal to these two old friends. Dr. Burwell forwarded a copy of his
remarks, to which Dr. Goodpasture responded:[100]

I can't tell you how much I appreciated your presentation remarks in transmitting to me the Kober Medal. I am so glad you sent me a copy of them, because as I stood alone and forlorn on the rostrum I am afraid I was not in the state of mind to appreciate fully, or even reasonably well, the fine quality and rare spirit of your words. I did realize, however, that they gave a lift and gracefulness to the whole proceedings as everyone realized and commented upon it. My best thanks. . . .

We can hardly contain ourselves until little Sarah presents us with a little Sarah Little or something. She expects to do so on June 6 or thereabouts, and as misfortune will have it, I must be in Washington on the 7 and New York on the 9 and instead of the Army slogan, "Hurry Up and Wait" I hope she will hurry up or wait until I get back.

Dr. Burwell returned to Nashville in 1948 to present the Alpha Omega Alpha lecture, an arrangement Dr. Goodpasture must have facilitated. Dr. Burwell died on September 3, 1967.

Social Clubs

Dr. Goodpasture was a member of a scientifically oriented social club, the Medical Exchange Club in Boston, and of a group with mixed professional interests, the Coffee House Club of Nashville. The Medical Exchange Club had its first meeting on May 13, 1920, with the stated purposes of having dinner and exchanging thoughts about different fields of medicine.[101] It was a very exclusive club; in 1956 there were only twelve active members who had been admitted at irregular intervals after 1920. Six members had died; four, including Dr. Goodpasture, were emeritus, and there was *one* honorary member, Dr. Richards of Philadelphia.[102] Membership was probably limited to twelve so that the monthly dinner meetings would be manageable and maximally conducive to exchange of information. It goes without saying that strong ties to Boston were a requirement for admission, and many of Boston's most distinguished physicians were members, including Doctors John Enders, Chester Keefer, Howard Means, Francis Moore, and George Minot. Dr. Goodpasture as an expert on viruses and as a member of the Harvard faculty was asked to join in 1920 or 1921, an invitation that probably originated with his friend Watson Sellards, who had joined the previous year.

Invitations to meetings were faithfully sent through the years to their one representative in the South and respectfully declined except when the Medical Exchange Club meetings were coordinated with Dr. Goodpasture's lectures at Harvard in 1939–41. Detailed minutes were kept of each meeting, including subjects, attendees, and personal notes about the members' health and accomplishments. These notes were collated and published periodically; they provide a behind-the-scenes account of medical life in Boston, at least as viewed from one of the establishments.[103]

Criteria for admission to the Coffee House Club initially included the enlightened state of bachelorhood.[104] Due to the preference by members for matrimony, the survival of the club was threatened, and this requirement was dropped. In Dr. Goodpasture's time, admission presumably was by invitation from this men's group composed of leaders in all professions in the Nashville community.[105] Doctors Carmichael and Branscomb, while chancellors of Vanderbilt University, were members, as was Dean Madison Sarratt. Prominent businessmen such as Alec Stevenson, John Sloan, and Mason Houghland were listed as members, as was the publisher of the *Nashville Banner*, James Stahlman.

Other medical school faculty with membership included Hugh Morgan, Sam Clark, and Beverly Douglas. Dr. Goodpasture would have particularly enjoyed regular meetings with Cecil Sims (prominent lawyer), Donald Davidson (professor of English, Fugitive), John Crowe Ransom (professor of English), and Stanley Horn (historian). There are two manuscripts in the Goodpasture memorabilia cited as being presented before the Coffee House Club: "Science and Federal Policy," presented January 19, 1950, and "Medicine Prescribes Freedom for Prometheus," given on February 17, 1955. A third manuscript that qualifies for presentation in terms of style, syntax, and length dealt with smallpox vaccination, but it does not have a cover page. The "Science and Federal Policy" paper discussed the Vannevar Bush Report and the creation of the National Science Foundation; please see chapter 6, Extramural Responsibilities, for details. In "Medicine Prescribes Freedom for Prometheus," Dr. Goodpasture stated his views on the role of medicine in the current scientific era.

EPILOGUE

There are eleven definitions of the word "home" in the *American Heritage Dictionary of the English Language*, Third Edition. The first eight are: 1. A place where one lives; a residence. 2. The physical structure within which one lives, such as an house or apartment. 3. A dwelling place together with the family or social unit that occupies it; a household. 4.a. An environment offering security and happiness. b. A valued place regarded as a refuge or place of origin. 5. The place, such as a county or town, where one was born or has lived for a long period. 6. The native habitat, as of a plant or animal. 7. The place where something is discovered, founded, developed, or promoted; a source. 8. A headquarters; a home base.

Tennessee, Nashville, and Vanderbilt University were Dr. Goodpasture's home. From his home came his values, his sense of tradition, his sense of duty, and his respect for all forms of life. He had an unusually broad and effective perspective because he was intimately familiar with the history of his land, his people, and his profession. He was proud of his home and strove continually to make it a better place.[106]

Chapter Nine

HONORS AND AWARDS

BACKGROUND

Professional stature in academic circles is measured by a variety of standards that include the reputation of the university in which the academician holds an appointment, level and type of professorial title (assistant, associate, or full professor—any of which may be tenured or nontenured), grant support, quality and quantity of published articles and/or books,[1] membership in prestigious professional societies, and invited lectures or visiting professorships. Additional indications of accomplishment are the number and success of trainees, recruitment by other institutions, and leadership positions in universities, academic departments, or professional societies.[2] Finally, there are medals, honorary degrees, and other honors that may be awarded to particularly meritorious faculty members.

Professional stature is therefore an amalgam of many factors, most of which are quantifiable and allow comparison of peers.[3] For each of the standards cited above, there are one or more mechanisms for review that are intended to provide unbiased evaluations of the academician vis-à-vis the position, appointment, or honor under consideration. Two of the most important review mechanisms are those involved in publication of articles and grant applications. Each journal has a peer-review process to determine suitability for publication of proffered articles. The procedures for review of a research grant to determine whether it should be funded are basically similar to those for reviewing manuscripts to determine whether they should be published, although in the former, scores are established by committee action. In both cases the review is carried out by investigators from other medical centers who are experts in the field and whose identity is not known to the academician whose work is being reviewed. The conditions for awarding medals or honorary degrees vary widely among institutions and foundations, but in most cases the intention is to honor research accomplishments.

The description of these standards for evaluating professional stature indicate the complexity of the process, its multiple interlocking and interdependent features, its potential to reward accomplishments as well as its susceptibility to bias and manipulation. A review of the process also shows that its cornerstone is publication of research articles or books. Publishing and grant application are guided by the twin maxims of academia: "Publish or perish"[4] and Juvenal's "Who will guard the guards?"[5] Investigative, scholarly activities gain credence by publication, as the peer-review process serves to ensure reliability of the work. Publications are displayed in the curriculum vitae of academicians, along with a summary of one's education, professional history, and grant support. In Latin, *curriculum vitae* means "the race of life;" these words and their abbreviation *c.v.* reassume their original meaning when investigators attempt to publish studies that may ensure promotion or attempt to obtain additional grant support. As for the reviewers, the words of Juvenal are frequently invoked, while academicians work within the peer-review system and ponder whether the review process for publication and grants is fair and informed.

The professional standards as described are public and are subject to review and analysis. It would be naïve, even foolhardy, to assume that a parallel private and confidential process does not exist. Trusted friends exchange information about the accomplishments and potential of colleagues or junior faculty that may be obfuscated when presented for public consumption. Behind the curriculum vitae, and more difficult to quantify, are the most valuable of attributes, those of honesty, loyalty, trustworthiness, motivation, and collegiality.

By all standards, Dr. Goodpasture was eminently successful. His curriculum vitae is appended for a detailed review.[6] Articles are arranged by year of publication. Invited lectureships, fifty-five in total, are shown by date, title if known, and location. The named lectureships from this larger group are described next, as they are more prestigious and yet are representative of the group as a whole. Finally, his exceptional achievements were recognized by other kudos as detailed in sections that follow.

Named Lectureships

Dates, occasions, titles, and sites of presentation are included in his curriculum vitae (appendix A). Dr. Goodpasture gave seventeen lectures of this type from 1929 to 1957; we concentrate on four of these lectures because their printed texts offer insights into Dr. Goodpasture's research career as it was flowering in 1929, show his view of the development of medicine as a scientific discipline, explain his rationale for tying research to the practice of medicine, and demonstrate his conviction that universities and their medical schools were inextricably and wholesomely linked for the betterment of humankind. These subjects reflect the central themes in his career and are thereby particularly appropriate for detailed consideration. The other named lectures are no less important, but in general they are based on research already described in chapter 3.

The Harvey Lectures

The Harvey Lectures were initiated in 1905 as the major function of the Harvey Society of New York City. They honor William

Harvey, discoverer in 1628 of the circulation of the blood. Harvey had established an annual oration to be given to the Royal College of Physicians in London, in which "fellows and members of the college were to be exhorted to search out and study the secrets of nature by way of experiment and to continue in mutual love and affection among themselves."[7] Invitations to lecture before the Harvey Society had over the years been extended to distinguished investigators in the United States and abroad and certainly indicated recognition by the "Eastern establishment."

Dr. G. Canby Robinson, as president of the society and shortly after his move to Cornell, mailed the invitation on July 12, 1929, for Dr. Goodpasture to give a Harvey Lecture.[8] His lecture "Etiological Problems in the Study of Filterable Virus Diseases" was delivered on December 19, 1929,[9] and was the second ever given on viral diseases to the Harvey Society. The first had been given the previous year by Dr. F. d'Herelle on bacteriophages.[10]

Virology was *terra incognito* in 1929, as shown by the ongoing controversy as to whether viruses were living agents or not. Virologists were in the same position bacteriologists had held in the previous century before methods were discovered for the culture and morphologic identification of microorganisms. This was Dr. Goodpasture's summary of the state of knowledge in virology in 1929:[11]

> The nature of any filterable virus is . . . entirely unknown, and the group of virus diseases, now very large, is loosely hung together mainly by the thread of filterability of the active agents which cause them. . . . It seems almost hopelessly confusing to one newly introduced to the subject of filterable viruses to find such a formidable array of apparently unrelated or at most seemingly superficially related morbid entities grouped together nominally only on the basis of the fact that their active agents can . . . be forced through the small pores of so-called antibacterial filters of various kinds. What possible congenial relationship might the virus of small-pox, for example, bear with that of the wilt of caterpillars or the transmissible lysis of bacteria?

Dr. Goodpasture then attempted to bring some order to chaos by establishing stringent criteria for that group of viral infections in which there was a propensity to affect specific tissues, a phenomenon called cytotropism. The chief significance of this attempt was his effort to correlate the morphologic changes produced by viruses with their ability to grow at the site where lesions were produced. The long process of classification of viral diseases was thus begun. His Harvey Lecture ended with a detailed analysis of his recent investigations of the fowlpox inclusion, with the significant disclosure that he and Dr. Woodruff had shown that the inclusions contained discrete, infectious, and filterable particles known as Borrel bodies. Their demonstration was the first proving that viral inclusions contained active virus units.

Canby Robinson wrote Sarah Goodpasture immediately after the lecture:[12]

> No doubt you want to know how Ernest's Harvey Lecture was received, and no doubt you cannot get a very satisfactory estimate from him. I think that under the circumstances you may be glad to hear from me that his lecture was *immense*. All the best people, scientifically speaking, were tremendously impressed, and I was very proud, not only of Ernest, but also of the Vanderbilt Medical School, which he represented. I can honestly say that I never heard a better Harvey Lecture. But that is not all. It was a great pleasure to Marion and me to see Ernest and to get direct news of you and little Sarah, and of our other good friends in Nashville.
>
> I hope next time you will be with him. I want so much to get down to Nashville, but it is hard to find enough free time to make the trip worth while. We have not lessened our interest and affection for the place and for all you good people in it.
>
> With best wishes for a very Merry Christmas and Happy New Year, in which Marion joins me.

It must have been a very happy Christmas for the Goodpasture family and the Vanderbilt community, knowing full well that the scientific credentials of the new medical school and of its professor of pathology had been firmly established on a national if not international stage.

The Gorgas Medical Society

The Gorgas Medical Society of the University of Alabama honors a native son who was instrumental in eliminating the scourge of yellow fever. The secretary of this society notified Dr. Goodpasture that he had been elected an honorary fellow February 24, 1933, leading to his addressing the society and guests on April 28, 1933, in Tuscaloosa, Alabama. His choice of title and subject for this talk is surprising in view of the short amount of time available for preparation. After paying due respect to Dr. Gorgas, "A Medical Pageant" reviews the full sweep of medicine from Hippocrates to the present. It is impressive that the subject matter was so familiar to him that a written text of this scope and detail was prepared in two months, particularly in view of the vigorous research program underway in his laboratory. He did not use this historical material as a unit again, at least not in a presentation to a scientific group. The title was a subject of his own choosing, as most presentations to the Gorgas Society were on clinical topics.

This talk was potentially of great value to medical students and faculty who were interested in the evolution of ideas and knowledge, as Dr. Goodpasture encapsulated the interrelated advances improving the health of humankind over the centuries. Apropos of Dr. Gorgas, recent breakthroughs had conquered yellow fever, the ravages of which had been sufficiently cataclysmic to alter the course of history, particularly in the South. This is his tribute to Dr. Gorgas:[13]

> Is it not a sufficient cause for wonder and admiration that of a sudden such cares [ravages of yellow fever] should be lifted from us, our fears allayed, and our civilization extended to regions theretofore uninhabitable? You members of the [Gorgas] Society have a just pride in sharing largely by universal acknowledgement of the contribution to humanity of that great benefactor, Doctor Gorgas. You partake in part of his honor in thus recognizing him as your inspiration. Born of Alabama, he died in a

foreign land, decorated by a king: and as he lay in state in St. Paul's Cathedral at London, Sir Patrick Manson [famed English specialist in tropical diseases], soon to follow him, acknowledged the indebtedness of the medical world by laying upon his bier a solitary wreath.

Dr. Goodpasture's understanding of history gave perspective to the evolution of knowledge in the conquest of this particular disease:

> General Gorgas, the disciple of Walter Reed, was the practical exponent of the knowledge discovered by the Yellow Fever Commission at Havana of which Carrol, the lamented Lazear, and Agramonte were members. Reed was directed more immediately by Carter's demonstration of an extrinsic incubation period of yellow fever and by the hypothesis, long maintained by Carlos Finlay of Havana, that the virus is transmitted by the Stegomyia [*Aedes aegypti*] mosquito. Perhaps more remotely, but no less significantly, was Reed influenced, trained, and directed by Professor Welch, who so effectively disseminated from Johns Hopkins the newer knowledge of pathology and bacteriology brought to this country from the workshops of Koch, Cohnheim, and Virchow in Germany, and from those of Pasteur and Claude Bernard in France, augmented by the contributions from his own productive laboratory.

Passano Award

In its May 27, 1946, edition, *Time* magazine announced that Dr. Goodpasture had received the Passano Award [on May 15] in Osler Hall, Baltimore. Under a paragraph header titled "Wanted: Freedom," the article summarized Dr. Goodpasture's acceptance speech as "philosophic, rambling and often brilliant," a speech in which he deplored the lack of freedom of "researchers . . . to follow their own keen noses." The talk referred to in the *Time* article was titled "Research and Medical Practice" and was published in *Science* in 1946.

In its published form, the talk is not rambling, nor would Dr. Goodpasture have been comfortable with its characterization as "brilliant." His comments were to the point and heartfelt: basic research was not receiving the support it needed from the government,

philanthropies, or universities. Here is Dr. Goodpasture's summary
of the problem:

> I believe the crux of the situation lies in the fact that exploratory
> research—teaching research, if you will—research that seeks basic prin-
> ciples, inapplicable until thoroughly understood, entails relatively great
> financial waste. The university does not have the financial resources to
> absorb the waste or rejections in its budgets, and donors of grants-in-aid,
> often not scientists themselves, try to select "projects," preferably of a
> developmental type, with as little risk of waste and failure as possible.
> *But the true interests of science require investigations that involve great
> risk, and if ultimate progress is to be expected in the application of scien-
> tific knowledge to human needs, the cost of the waste of original research
> must be met.*

Here is his solution:

> Let each social order therefore give the scientist a free hand and
> provide him with the environment and the tools he needs; make him
> accessible to students, for he is essentially a teacher; make the university
> his home; and otherwise, for humanity's sake, leave him alone.

Ivy Day Celebration

Tulane University School of Medicine honors its graduating
seniors on Ivy Day, the day before commencement, in a ceremony
dating back to 1908. Dr. Goodpasture, having been awarded an
honorary Doctor of Laws by the administrators of the Tulane
Educational Fund in 1957, was invited to speak on June 7 as a part
of the Ivy Day festivities. It was an opportunity for him to describe
the beneficial interactions between medical schools and universities, an interaction that began in the United States around the turn
of the twentieth century. He deemed this relationship fitting and
proper, since "the university is the home of the medical school and
the entire great edifice of learning will continue to profit by association with its [the medical school's] science, its art [the practice of
medicine] and its humanity."

He then spoke of a recurring concern that the universities and their medical schools were not being properly supported:[14]

> All the magic of wishful thinking and all the money in the world can't add one iota of scientific knowledge without the cultivation of intelligence. Neglect of our universities and their schools, improvidence in encouraging and training our best mental talent will bring us eventually and certainly to a point of diminishing returns. In fact I might add, insofar as medical education is concerned, unless the millions going now into the directed study of selected diseases are matched by other millions designed to support the fundamental programs of our universities and their schools, the failure of a continuous and maximal supply of superior talent, developed under the best educational environments, will prevent the union of science and the arts from protecting us against the physical ailments and social diseases which will always threaten. We just can't afford to kill the academic goose that lays the golden egg-head of science, notwithstanding the antipathy in some quarters to this worthy, though often unrewarded, product.

Despite these concerns, the prospects for the future were strengthened by a grand historical perspective:

> The observational methods of the Greeks were later supplemented by the fresh and bold techniques of the Renaissance which eventually established the potentialities of the controlled experiment. Since then, and especially for the last two centuries, scientific methods have made possible for better or worse, the revolution which enabled medicine to combat and conquer heretofore unyielding diseases and to set up a rational program of progressive research from which we may confidently expect greater conquests. But science is not for the exploitation of the moment nor for ourselves alone. Once acquired, it becomes a part of human culture and its evolution must be sustained and so far as Western civilization is concerned the scientific method is here to stay. It is to be hoped that it is here not only to serve humane purposes, but by its elegance, beauty and magnitude, to uplift the spirit, and in time to take its place in humanistic literature.

> Over the now quiet centuries come with tranquil assurance the unhurried words of Aristotle seeming to invite our patience: "The search for truth . . . is in one way hard and in another easy. For it is evident that no one can master it fully nor miss it wholly. But each adds a little to our knowledge of nature, and from all the facts assembled there arises a certain grandeur."

He closed his Ivy Day address with these statements, which are his last public pronouncements about the intrinsic role of universities in society:[15]

> To the achievement of these ends, the university as conservator, educator, creative builder of knowledge, evaluator and disperser of the arts and science should, above all civic institutions, be respected, protected, supported and promoted in the interest of human culture.

Honorary Degrees

Academic degrees can be awarded *in absentia* or *honoris causa*, in addition to the usual mechanism. The honorary degree, as defined by the *Oxford English Dictionary*, is "a recognition of distinction, or a tribute of honor." In the United States, the honorary degree recognizes outstanding service or achievement which in England is rewarded by orders of knighthood.[16]

Honorary degrees were awarded Dr. Goodpasture by Yale University in 1939 (master of science), University of Chicago in 1941 (doctor of science), Washington University in 1950 (doctor of science), and Tulane University in 1957 (doctor of laws).

Yale University

This first honorary degree may have been the most gratifying. Yale University is one of the great American universities and was the alma mater of his mentor, Dr. Welch. In 1939 the research laboratory of Dr. Goodpasture was at the peak of its productivity and was recognized worldwide for its innovative studies of infectious diseases. The Vanderbilt experiment in academic medicine, the complete integration of a medical school with its university, was a great success, and Vanderbilt's fabled collegiality was fully savored by the faculty. The problems attendant to war, inflation, and Dr. Goodpasture's assumption of the deanship were in the future and not yet imagined. He must have been gratified and quietly pleased to know he was in such a distinguished company of recipients.[17] Finally, he was able to take this celebratory trip to Yale with his family and daughter Sarah's close friend Grace Benedict.

They had "a most pleasant motor trip to New Haven, West Point [the young women had been invited to a dance], the World's Fair in New York, the Tide Water section of Virginia, and mountainous North Carolina."[18] The citation for the Yale degree reads in part:[19]

> He is a tireless hunter: he hunts for the parents of diseases, the so-called viruses. These minute particles seem to be the causes of many diseases in plant and animal life. In human beings they include Measles, Influenza, Smallpox, Infantile Paralysis. Using the membranes of the developing chick egg, he has made discoveries of the first importance in the understanding of virus diseases.
>
> This excellent southern gentleman is thus a research scholar who has made definite contributions to science, to education, and to human well-being.

University of Chicago

The awarding of the doctorate by the University of Chicago in 1941 was a part of ceremonies recognizing the fiftieth anniversary of that university. This was a three-day-and-night affair, with a grand dinner at the Palmer House on Friday night, September 26, alumni assembly on Saturday, a service of thanksgiving and commemoration on Sunday, and convocation for awarding of degrees on Monday.

The citation for his degree reads: "a teacher and investigator in the field of experimental pathology who has made distinguished additions to our knowledge of the virus diseases."[20] Representatives of many universities and colleges were in attendance,[21] as were delegates of well-known societies, mostly from the United States but including a generous representation from abroad. Dinner on Friday was notable for the number of tables in the grand ballroom of the Palmer House (ninety-two) and for the distinctions of the guests. This dinner and the three-day ceremony were a gathering of the academic elite.[22] Heretofore, the University of Chicago had awarded eighty-six honorary degrees, but on this occasion recognized thirty-five of the world's most distinguished scientists.[23]

On Friday, September 26, Dr. Goodpasture read the paper "Virus Infections of the Mammalian Foetus" as a part of the academic celebration. This lecture was subsequently published in *Science* in 1942 and drew extensively on the investigations by Katherine Anderson and Goodpasture using placental grafts on chorioallantoic membranes. (See chapter 3.) A complete review of the subject concluded with these observations:

> Owing to the obvious importance of the placental union in determining whether or not infection of the fetus takes place, it is rather surprising to find so little knowledge concerning placental infection, and the relative specific resistance of placental and fetal membranes.
>
> Our experimental observations concerning the inoculation of human fetal membranes grafted on the chorioallantois of chick embryos indicate that the human chorionic epithelium is naturally a resistant membrane to a number of viruses, and the relative rarity of fetal infection by the active agents of the great contagions leads one to conclude that it is resistant to others which it was not practicable for us to test.

Washington University

The ceremonies on Tuesday, February 21, 1950, commemorated the fiftieth anniversary of Washington University. Festivities began with a dinner on Monday evening at the home of Dr. and Mrs. Robert Moore, chairman of the Department of Pathology, and continued the next day with a convocation at which honorary degrees were conferred (Fig. 9-1), laying of the cornerstone of the Cancer Research Building, and a scientific program in the auditorium of the medical school.[24]

Dr. Goodpasture's citation was prepared by Dr. Robert Moore:

> It is fair to say that the studies of Dr. Goodpasture have been major contributions in this rapidly developing field [that of viral infections] of

Fig. 9-1: Recipients of honorary degrees, Washington University, 1950. Shown are Ernest Goodpasture, Abraham Flexner, Edwards Park, and Charles Huggins.

the last three decades: the first demonstration of the virus causing mumps, identification of inclusion bodies as actually virus, a concept of the transmission of virus along nerves, and the use of the chorio-allantoic membrane of the chick embryo for the growth and study of virus. From these facts, concepts, and techniques stem much of our present knowledge and control of viral diseases. . . . But, above all, he has seen beyond the horizon of the laboratory and lecture room into the world. To quote his own words, "We are committed to research for we know well its power; but with this added strength come broader fields of influence and usefulness. Medicine in the days to come will make no greater extra-professional contribution to human well-being than by the application, as never before, of its great spirit and moral prestige to the cause of justice and righteousness among men and nations."[25] Mr. Chancellor, I present Dr. Ernest William Goodpasture, investigator, teacher, administrator, and citizen of the world, for the honorary degree of doctor of science.

Tulane University

Dr. Goodpasture was one of five selected by Tulane University to receive honorary degrees (doctor of laws) in 1957. His speech on Ivy Day has been described previously in this chapter. The citation reads:

> Dr. Goodpasture has made notable contributions to medical educa-
> tion, to public health, and to science, over a period of thirty years. He
> has served as advisor and director of important government agencies and
> private philanthropic foundations. His skillful inquiries have greatly
> increased our knowledge of the pathogenesis of infectious diseases.
> From his laboratory first came the demonstration that chick embryonic
> tissues would support the growth of viruses and microbes harmful to
> man, a finding which served microbiologists throughout the world as a
> starting point for many fundamental studies and practical applications
> leading to control of important human and animal diseases.

Honors and Awards

Dr. Goodpasture received twelve medals or awards, as shown in Table 9-1; this table also shows, by year, honorary degrees and elected membership to prestigious professional groups. The breadth of recognition of Dr. Goodpasture's contributions is noteworthy. The Gold Headed Cane, awarded in 1958, is probably the most prestigious award given to American pathologists by a major professional organization of that discipline. He was elected to the Association of American Physicians in 1938; the "Old Turks" have long represented senior leadership in academic medicine, particularly in internal medicine. As noted in Table 9-1, Dr. Goodpasture was later awarded the Kober Medal by that group. He also received a high award (the John Phillips Memorial Award) from the American College of Physicians, comparable in stature to the Association of American Physicians mentioned above. Illustrious prizes were received, both for basic research and for prevention of disease. He was elected to the most distinguished scientific group in the United States—the National Academy of Sciences, and to the even more exclusive American Philosophical Society, a group "unusual among learned

Table 9-1
Medals, Awards, Honorary Degrees, and Elected Memberships

1937
Southern Medical Association's
  Research Medal
National Academy of Sciences

1938
Association of American Physicians

1939
Honorary M. S. Yale University

1941
Alvarenza Prize of the College of
  Physicians, Philadelphia
Honorary D.Sc. University of Chicago

1943
The Kober Medal by the Association
  of American Physicians
American Philosophical Society

1944
The Sedgwick Memorial Medal by
  the American Public Health
  Association

1945
The John Scott Medal, awarded by
  the city of Philadelphia

1946
Kappa Sigma "Man of the Year"
  Award

The Passano Award by the Passano
  Foundation

1947
New York Academy of Medicine,
  Honorary Fellow

1948
The John Phillips Memorial Award
  from the American College of
  Physicians

1950
Honorary D.Sc. Washington
  University

1955
Howard Taylor Ricketts Award from
  the University of Chicago

1956
Elected to Vanderbilt University
  Board of Trust

1957
Honorary LL.D. Tulane University

1958
Jesse Stevenson Kovalenko Medal
  from National Academy of
  Sciences
The Gold Headed Cane by
  American Association of
  Pathologists and Bacteriologists

societies because its membership is comprised of top scholars from a wide variety of academic disciplines."[26]

Among the medals and awards, five have been selected for our concentrated attention because they probably had special significance for Dr. Goodpasture. The Southern Medical Association's Research Medal was the first prize he received. The Kober Medal represented recognition by distinguished senior academic physicians, and the medal was conferred by his good friend and colleague Sidney Burwell. The Passano Award recognized accomplishments principally in basic research, as did the Jesse Stevenson Kovalenko Medal from the National Academy of Sciences. Finally, he relished receiving the Gold Headed Cane, as it had been held by the founders of pathology in America.

Southern Medical Association Research Medal

With the exception of the Southern Medical Association, Dr. Goodpasture did not participate actively or regularly in the affairs of professional societies. This association was managed and controlled by Mr. C. P. Loranz, longtime secretary, who officially became secretary-manager by 1937. There is extensive correspondence in Dr. Goodpasture's files with Mr. Loranz and other members from 1928 to 1938, in part a reflection of Dr. Goodpasture's election in 1928 to secretary of the pathology section of the association. He was elected secretary at the 1928 meeting in Asheville, although he was not yet a member, prompting this letter to Mr. Loranz:[27]

> I was unable to attend this last section meeting and the information [his election as secretary] came as somewhat of a surprise in as much as I have not yet formally joined the Association. This has not been through lack of interest in the activities of the Southern Medical Association, but through ignorance as to the necessary qualifications for membership. In 1912 I passed the State Board examination in Maryland but have never taken out a license to practice.
>
> Judging from the fact of my election as Secretary, I assume that I am eligible and will gladly remit to you my dues. . . . Please send me

> . . . the constitution, bylaws, rules and regulations of the Southern
> Medical Association as I wish to be informed more exactly concerning
> the organization.

Communications with the association over the decade indicate a certain lack of organization somewhere in the system. Dr. Goodpasture learned on November 5, 1937, that he was to be given the Research Medal at the upcoming meeting scheduled for December 1, a meeting he had not planned to attend. The medal had been awarded only five times since 1912,[28] and techniques for informing the recipients had apparently not been codified.

Dr. Goodpasture received the medal at the thirty-first annual meeting of the Southern Medical Association, at the general session held in the grand ballroom of the Roosevelt Hotel in New Orleans. The citation read "for his outstanding achievements through his research on the cultivation and the nature of viruses." His response was notable for the generous acknowledgment of the role colleagues had played in his research laboratory; in particular, he mentioned Oscar Teague, although it had been fifteen years since Dr. Teague's death:[29]

> Among other favorable circumstances it has been my good fortune
> to have collaborated, amidst congenial environments, with associates
> whose disinterested and generous labors have seemed to me to mani-
> fest the true spirit of research; and it is that spirit, I believe, which you
> wish to recognize and encourage by this award. . . . Some fifteen years
> ago, shortly before his untimely death, Dr. Teague, fresh from Vienna
> where he had familiarized himself with the recent developments, intro-
> duced me to the field of virus diseases, and stimulated me by his help
> and example to cultivate an interest in this subject, for which he envi-
> sioned the rapid expansion that we have witnessed in the last few years.

Then he made a plea for the support of research:

> Permit me to say just a word about research. It would be superfluous
> for me to tell you that we must look to research for all progress in the

control, treatment, and prevention of disease. Yet, up to the present time medical research, though making great strides, has led a rather haphazard and precarious existence. Whose responsibility is research, anyway? I would say in final analysis, that the responsibility for fostering and conducting research ultimately falls upon our universities. . . .

This medal could not have been sweeter praise than the congratulatory telegram he received from his daughter.[30]

The Association of American Physicians' Kober Medal

The Association of American Physicians' Kober Medal is awarded annually to a member of the Association of American Physicians "who has contributed to the progress and achievement of the medical sciences or preventive medicine."[31] The full text of Dr. Sidney Burwell's presentation speech and Dr. Goodpasture's acceptance are in chapter 1. These two speeches in 1943 epitomize the time in terms of collegiality in medicine and perhaps should be reread now. In his acceptance, Dr. Goodpasture again refers to his work with Oscar Teague, now dead twenty-one years, and to collaboration with his good friend Watson Sellards, who had died two years previously, as well as to his collaborators at Vanderbilt:

> I realize that you have it in mind, by means of awarding this symbol of your concern for the promotion of medical research, to recognize and to honor all of those earnest investigators who have devoted themselves to the advancement of knowledge for human needs; nevertheless I feel it would be no infringement upon the special privilege you have allowed me today if I should mention a few of my own past and present associates who have made possible my preferred status on this occasion. Only a deep sense of indebtedness to their friendship and their comradeship in research could prompt me to call the names of Watson Sellards and Oscar Teague, and to add likewise with affection those of Alice and Eugene Woodruff, James R. Dawson, John Buddingh, Katherine Anderson and Claud Johnson, for I know all of them would have preferred at this time to maintain a generous anonymity.

Fig. 9-2: Dr. Goodpasture receiving the Passano Award in 1946 from Mr. Passano.

The Passano Foundation Award

The Passano Foundation Award had been instituted in 1945 and remains to this day a prestigious award. From 1945 to 1961, twenty persons[32] had shared the award as joint prizes were given on three occasions. Five of these twenty subsequently received the Nobel Prize. The following excerpt outlines the criteria for the Passano Award, as stated in their brochure:[33]

Beginning in 1945, the [Passano] Foundation has each year presented an award of $5000 to an American citizen who recently has made an outstanding contribution to the advancement of medical science. The Directors give prime consideration to work that has immediate clinical value, or that gives promise of practical application in the near future. To help them make a truly representative and irreproachable Award, the Directors annually seek the opinion of a nation-wide group of men and women engaged in medical research or practice. This group includes many teachers and researchers in the medical schools of the country, since they are especially likely to be well informed on such matters.

Dr. Goodpasture was selected for the 1946 award (Fig. 9-2) for the studies that "have led to a better understanding of the host-parasite relationship, and opened up a new and important chapter in the history of the conquest of disease."[34] His acceptance speech was discussed earlier in this chapter. Dr. Goodpasture received notice of this award from the president of the Passano Foundation, Mr. Robert Gill, in a letter dated March 2, 1946:[35]

> In my official capacity as president of the Passano Foundation, there falls to me the honor, and I may add the very great personal pleasure, of announcing to you that the Passano Award of five thousand dollars[36] has been made to you by unanimous action of the Board of Directors on March 1, 1946. The Award is made for distinguished service to clinical medicine with particular reference to your work on virus diseases.

The Jesse Stevenson Kovalenko Medal

The Jesse Stevenson Kovalenko Medal, first bestowed in 1952, is "awarded approximately every three years for important contributions to the medical sciences."[37] Dr. Goodpasture was selected in 1958 for "outstanding contributions to medical science and for long and continued devotion to the study of his chosen field of Pathology."[38] The award was given to Dr. Goodpasture by Dr. John R. Paul at the annual meeting of the National Academy of Sciences, in Washington on April 28, 1958, with these accompanying remarks:[39]

> Dr. Goodpasture has become the acknowledged Dean of American pathologists. He has won this position by virtue of long experience and *continued*, effective activity in this field. His contributions, which are many, indicate that he has interpreted his subject—*"Pathology"*—in the truest and broadest sense of the word, namely the "Study of Disease" . . .

Here he has been concerned with the natural history of host-parasite relationships, particularly in virus diseases. He has furnished proof that the *elementary bodies* of fowlpox were really infectious units. He has demonstrated the etiological agent of mumps . . . and developed the use of the chick embryo for the propagation of viruses in the laboratory. From this last discovery came many practical applications in the field of preventive medicine. Notable among them has been the development of certain vaccines, in which the antigen was propagated in hen's eggs. This was a forerunner of tissue culture methods for the growth of viruses, which today have so revolutionized the science of virology. The gate which he found and opened has lead into truly green pastures for a host of medical and biological scientists. . . .

Added to these achievements in the laboratory stands Dr. Goodpasture's record as a teacher. Two generations of students have sat at his feet. He has also served as the Dean of Vanderbilt University School of Medicine.

During the past two decades, year after year has found him serving on important government boards here in Washington. He has been one of the Nation's wise and devoted servants in the general field of medicine.

Today, at a time when many of his colleagues have relinquished their professional duties, we find him not only active but occupying a most responsible position as [Scientific] Director of the Armed Forces Institute of Pathology in Washington. In this capacity he is still being called upon to use that particular asset with which he is so well endowed, namely the ability to teach and guide others through the convincing example of a life *patiently dedicated* to the development of his own special gifts and skills.

The Gold Headed Cane

The Gold Headed Cane has been awarded to Americans who "represent the highest ideals in pathology and medicine."[40] First awarded in 1919 by the Association of American Pathologists and Bacteriologists, the cane given Dr. Goodpasture in 1958 was the eighth one awarded. The progenitor of this cane is "the original and world-famous British Cane that rests on display in the Royal College of Physicians in London."[41] The recipients of the American version have had two common elements: each was a teacher, and each was devoted to research. Most recipients have also been pathologists.

There have been relatively few recipients since 1919, as it has been the custom for the cane to be held until death. Dr. Howard Karsner received the cane in 1952 and made two substantive changes in the traditions of its transmittal: the cane was to be exhibited permanently at the Armed Forces Institute of Pathology, and it was released for award before his death.[42] The first change is easily understood, owing to Dr. Karsner's long interest in the AFIP.

Fig. 9-3: Dr. Goodpasture with Gold Headed Cane, awarded in 1958.

Because of the second, it was possible for Dr. Goodpasture to have this highly cherished recognition for the two years remaining in his life.[43] For his part, Dr. Goodpasture was deeply touched by this award (Fig. 9-3). In his acceptance speech he mentioned that the previous recipients were all known to him, that some had been his mentors, and that all were illustrious physicians and scientists. Their careers spanned the golden age of pathology. Recipients (and year of award) were: Doctors Harold Ernst (1919), William Henry Welch (1923), Theobald Smith (1930), Frank B. Mallory (1935), James Ewing (1942), Ludvig Hektoen (1944), and Howard Karsner (1952).

Member of Association of American Physicians, National Academy of Sciences, and American Philosophical Society

The Association of American Physicians

The Association of American Physicians is unique as a clinically oriented society in electing basic scientists to membership.[44] This policy notwithstanding, it is distinctly unusual for pathologists to be

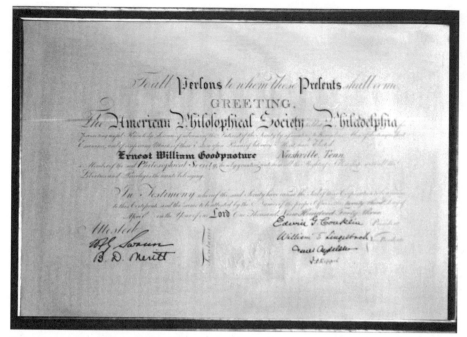

Fig. 9-4: Notice of election of Dr. Goodpasture to American Philosophical Society. This framed notice is in the Eskind Library, Special Collections.

elected to membership and rare for them to receive the ultimate recognition from the association in the form of the Kober Medal. The first pathologist to receive the medal was William Welch in 1927, followed by Frank B. Mallory in 1935, George Whipple in 1939, and Ernest Goodpasture in 1943.[45]

The National Academy of Sciences

The National Academy of Sciences is the most prestigious association to which scientists may be elected, a statement supported by the scarcity of Vanderbilt physicians in that group. Dr. Goodpasture was the first to be elected, in 1937. He was followed by Dr. Earl Sutherland in 1966, by Doctors William Darby and Sidney Colowick in 1972, by Dr. Charles R. Park in 1980, and by Dr. Grant Liddle in 1982. Details about Dr. Goodpasture's long and effective interaction with the National Academy of Sciences may be found in chapter 6.

American Philosophical Society

American Philosophical Society records show that only one other member of the Vanderbilt faculty has been invited to join this group, Professor James Barr (elected in 1993). Dr. Goodpasture (Fig. 9-4) was the only Tennessean in the society until 1948 when Professor Samuel Colville Lind of Oak Ridge was elected. There were precious few other southern members in the 1940s and 1950s.[46] In 2001, the only Tennessean listed is Professor Alvin Weinberg of Oak Ridge Associated Universities, who was elected in 1977 in the mathematical and physical sciences category.[47]

Member of the Vanderbilt Board of Trust

The *American Heritage Dictionary* (Third Edition) has thirteen definitions of the word *board*; the eighth is "an organized body of administrators or investigators." The word *trust* and its synonyms *faith, confidence, reliance,* and *dependence* convey more precisely the vital importance of this group to Vanderbilt University. The Board of Trust is legally responsible to the state of Tennessee for the university. More importantly, the Board of Trust establishes policy and maintains fiscal integrity, as evident in the current mission statement of Vanderbilt University's Board of Trust that was approved by the board in November 1997.[48]

The code of bylaws states that "the general government of The Vanderbilt University is vested in its Board of Trust," and that, "The Board shall elect the Chancellor of the university, who shall serve at the pleasure of the Board."[49] The board had similar powers in 1957, although the conditions for selecting board members have changed considerably. In 1957, alumni trustees might be elected by alumni ballot for a term of eight years. There were forty-three trustees total, meeting in general session twice a year. Dr. Goodpasture was notified by Chancellor Branscomb on May 9, 1956,[50] that he had been elected to an eight-year term as an alumnus:[51]

You don't know how delighted I was when the returns from the alumni ballot came in, and I found, as I had expected, that you were one of the two elected. I think you will be able to make a great contribution to the university, particularly in connection with the problems of the Medical School. While, of course, there is no panacea for a big problem of this sort, yet there are ofttimes alternatives on which knowledge and judgment are needed, and I shall feel that we have a great resource in the Board with your presence. Nor do I think of your contributions as limited to the Medical School by any means. We may face problems in the next several years as to whether we can justify expenditures for scientific equipment of certain sorts, as, for example, a nuclear reactor, and many problems in this area. You will help us on them all. . . . Congratulations. I will enjoy working under you for a change.

Other trustees with terms expiring in 1964 were Henry Alexander, Parkes Armistead, Lipscomb Davis, Robert Henry, O. H. Ingram, N. Baxter Jackson, Cecil Sims, and William Waller. Many of the trustees were known to him, including a classmate from his Bowen School days, James Souby. In Robert Henry's future was a commission to write an account of the first hundred years of the Armed Forces Institute of Pathology, a book he finished in 1964.

On April 28, 1960, Dr. Goodpasture submitted his resignation as a trustee on the grounds that he had recently been placed on the payroll of the university and was being paid through a training grant to the Department of Pathology.[52] He made these additional comments about his membership on the board:

With this spring meeting I shall have completed four years of membership on the Board. A termination at that time would therefore make my tenure harmonize with recent recommendations of the Milton Underwood Committee dealing with questions of Board membership, and would be in keeping with my own view that four years is long enough for a person of my age.

To serve as a member of the Board of Trust of Vanderbilt University has been a signal honor. It is an experience which has given me the opportunity to witness and to realize the devoted service which Members of the Board render to the University. For the privilege of association with the present Board I feel a deep sense of appreciation.

Additional comments about his status were given in a cover letter to Chancellor Branscomb:

> Since my return from a very pleasant and profitable sojourn at the University of Mississippi Medical Center last winter, Katherine and I have been staying at her Mother's old home, otherwise unoccupied, at Williamsport, while we undertake the problems of settling in the vicinity of Nashville. I am looking forward with much pleasure to operating a laboratory and assisting with research in the Department of Pathology at the Medical School.

This was the chancellor's reply:[53]

> Needless to say, I can present your resignation only with the deepest sense of appreciation for your services on the Board, and your contributions to the University in this additional capacity. You added not only a voice of wisdom on several important issues, but a touch of distinction in which we all shared to some extent. I am deeply grateful to you for this service.

Dr. Goodpasture had one more contribution to make as a board member, and that was a challenge to his alma mater. In informal comments at his last meeting of the board, the May 1960, meeting, Dr. Goodpasture left this legacy for his university: "If there is a typical Vanderbilt image, let it reflect the presence of an independent and unregimented mind, unfettered in its continuing search for the truth."

Portrait Presentation to Vanderbilt University

Portraits, busts, and statues have been used for centuries to memorialize famous men and, less frequently, women. Among the original Vanderbilt Medical School faculty, portraits were locally commissioned for G. Canby Robinson, Hugh Morgan, Sam Clark, Barney Brooks, Lucius Burch, Horton Casparis, and Ernest Goodpasture.

The university's intention to commission a portrait of Dr. Goodpasture was announced at a testimonial dinner held at Belle

Fig. 9-5: Participants in the party at Belle Meade at which the portrait commissioning was announced. From the left, they are Hugh Morgan, John Youmans, Ernest Goodpasture, Katherine Anderson Goodpasture, Amos Christie, and John Shapiro.

Meade Country Club in Nashville on Friday, November 18, 1955 (Fig. 9-5). Guests numbered between 215 (*Nashville Banner*) or more than 300 (*Nashville Tennessean*). Both of these Nashville papers covered the event in some detail in their November 19 editions. Tributes were paid by Chancellor Branscomb, Dean Youmans, Dr. Hugh Morgan, and Dr. John Buddingh, while the toastmaster for the occasion was Dr. C. S. Robinson, professor emeritus of biochemistry. The significance of the dinner and tribute was highlighted by the presence of Mr. Harold Vanderbilt, president of the Board of Trust.

Dr. Branscomb noted, "A university consists of the great names associated with it. It is a privilege of everyone of us here to be associated with one of the greatest of them all—Ernest Goodpasture. It was wonderful to have been on the same team with him." Dr. Youmans was quoted as saying about the portrait: "We want a perpetual remembrance of Ernest Goodpasture," an interesting comment in view of the difficulties the actual Dr. Goodpasture had returning to Vanderbilt in 1959.[54]

There was a prolonged standing ovation when Dr. Goodpasture rose to speak: "You have made Katherine and me very happy with this occasion, and I know we will be happy with the days of tomorrow when we will look back on this. You have made this an enlightened experience for us."

Arrangements for the portrait were made with Martin Kellogg, whose portraits of Dr. Goodpasture and several other original faculty now hang in Light Hall. (See color section for the portrait of Dr. Goodpasture. It may be viewed also in Light Hall, Room 208, Vanderbilt University Medical Center.) Mr. Kellogg wrote Dr. Goodpasture on May 29, 1956, at the behest of Dr. Shapiro and the other members of the portrait committee. Twenty hours of sittings were required, two hours at a time, with breaks every twenty minutes or so. Mr. Kellogg was very good at his profession, as evidenced by the quality of his portraits and this confident declaration: "I should mention that if the painting is undertaken, it has to be satisfactory to you and those concerned or there is no transaction of any sort, or obligation to anyone."[55]

Visiting Professor, University of Mississippi

By the spring of 1959, the Goodpastures were attempting to sell their home in Washington and were considering very tentative options for him to practice pathology in the community hospitals of Clarksville or Murfreesboro. The opportunity to serve as a visiting professor at the medical school in Jackson instead was offered by Dr. Joel Brunson, a protégé of Jim Dawson, and the recently appointed chairman of pathology at the University of Mississippi. Dr. Brunson, in a letter dated March 2, 1959, expressed his "hearty agreement" with the suggestion from Dr. Batson and others at Mississippi that Dr. Goodpasture come to Jackson on a full-time or part-time basis. Dr. Goodpasture responded on March 13:[56]

I have an abiding interest in medical education in the south and my many friends with the school at Jackson afford especial ties to that youthful and growing institution.

Fig. 9-6: Dr. Goodpasture (lower right) with second-year class, University of Mississippi, 1959–60. The inscription reads: "Best wishes, and thanks for a stimulating visit. Ole Miss Med School Class of 1962."

Your suggestion that there might be an opportunity for me to participate in the activities at the medical school of the University of Mississippi intrigues me, and I should like to give further consideration to that possibility.

I do not know what might be expected of me and must await further clarification from you as to that and the feasibility and conditions of a position for which I might be suited.

The initial suggestion to offer a position to Dr. Goodpasture was at the instigation of Dr. Blair Batson, professor of pediatrics and chairman, as shown in a letter dated March 17, in which he further urged favorable consideration:

Our faculty is young and often impatient and impetuous. We have no senior statesman and scientist to whom we may turn for intellectual stimulation or advice concerning problems of research, education, administration or to help us hone down our own philosophies concerning these areas.

Your vast experience in the field of Pathology and your long identification with medical education and research would be of inestimable value, not only to the Department of Pathology, but to the house staff in all departments, the senior staff whose clinical and research interests impinge or hinge on pathology and to all staff members interested in building a better school.

These expressions of goodwill and collegiality were echoed by Doctors Peter Blake, Fred Allison, and Charles Randall, all former students of Dr. Goodpasture. He replied to Dr. Batson on March 22:

I am understandably proud to think that you and your group feel that I might be of some assistance in the advancement of your school and whatever the event I do thank you cordially for the expression of your thoughtfulness and interest in my behalf.

A site visit was arranged for early September, to the complete satisfaction of all concerned. This from Dr. Goodpasture to Dr. Brunson on September 7 from Williamsport, Tennessee:

Your generous proposal, endorsed by friendly expressions from friends and former colleagues on your faculty, that I join your group as a member of your staff, has been constantly on my mind and I have felt greatly honored to receive this consideration, especially from you who have known me less well than the others. That you were willing to receive me on a part-time basis was especially appreciated.

I have given this proposal very serious consideration I assure you and it has been difficult for me to accommodate my lingering doubts as to my qualifications for such an important position of influence as that in which you propose to place me.

But for better or worse I am willing to try another adventure and will endeavor to do my best to forward the interest of your great enterprise in medical education and research, if on reflection your offer stands.

So it was arranged. An office, laboratory (generously equipped by Charles Randall), salary (one thousand dollars per month), and title (associate in pathology) were provided effective December 1, 1959, until March 7, 1960. Lectures to the second-year students were scheduled for December 3 and 5, and Dr. Goodpasture was to participate in a student research and journal review club on December 2. The visiting professorship was a stimulating experience for the class of 1962, as evidenced by their inscription on a class photograph taken with Dr. Goodpasture (Fig. 9-6). The reunion of the Goodpastures with Charles Randall and other former students and colleagues was a welcome back to the South that was mutually treasured and remembered.

EPILOGUE

Honor is a good word, with unambiguous meanings and clear intent. When a person is honored, as Dr. Goodpasture was, he has been shown great respect and has been distinguished by the recognition of his peers. When a person is honored, it is natural and usually appropriate for his institution (in this case Vanderbilt University), his region, and for some colleagues to share in the glory, although it is reflected. The rank order of universities (in quality or reputation) is often defined by the number of Nobel Prizes won by their faculties, or the number of faculty members elected to membership in the National Academy of Sciences.

This sharing of honor by university and faculty creates opportunities as well as obligations for the university. It is to be hoped that universities uniformly view distinguished faculty members as models for the development of subsequent generations of scholars. The greatest honor for Dr. Goodpasture would be for his alma mater to foster the scientific idealism and intellectual curiosity he personified.

Chapter Ten

PROPHET

S eptember 20, 1960, was a Tuesday. Dr. Goodpasture was in his
laboratory on that workday, just as he had been on the nineteen
previous days in September. The laboratory notes from that
period are written in his hand in a somewhat decrepit loose-leaf notebook identified only with title Book #3 and a date (8-27-60) (Fig.
10-1). During September he was attempting to establish a new field
strain of fowlpox, and he recorded his experiments in this book.[1]

These experiments with fowlpox were an extension of the
studies Doctors Goodpasture and Katherine Anderson began in
Jackson, Mississippi, early in the winter of 1960 when they trapped
a junco[2] with pocks on its feet. The causative virus (a juncopox) had
been established in serial passage on chorioallantoic membranes of
chick embryos. Microscopic sections showed that the original pocks
on the junco and the membranal lesions were unusual in that inclusions were produced not only in the cytoplasm of affected cells as
expected but also in the nuclei.

After returning to Nashville in March 1960, Doctors Goodpasture
and Anderson were attempting to define the relationship of the newly

isolated juncopox to other members of the pox group, including fowlpox. On September 20, Dr. Goodpasture harvested the lesions from five eggs for cultures and smears to detect bacterial contaminants, as well as for microscopic sections. Pieces of membrane were set aside for special stains and for electron microscopy. His last note (Fig. 10-2) is quoted in full:[3]

> 9/20 All eggs alive. All show good lesions.
>
>   # 7-10-12-13-15 [the numbers for 5 of 16 eggs inoculated on September 14] opened, cultured on chocolate agar, smears for bacterial stain, sections in Zenker's fixative, and two pieces of each in separate Petri dishes. Small piece for lyophilization if no infection. Remainder for deep freeze or other stock. Smaller piece from center of lesion where culture was taken and is less exposed to accidental contamination.
>
>   All membranes show a gross trabecular pattern, whitish bands and lines enclosing pink or transparent areas of membrane. The whitish bands scrape off easily and seem evidently a tracery of hyperplastic infected ectodermal epithelium. Therefore several pieces of scrapings about 1 mm in diameter were fixed in Osmic acid [for electron microscopy], together with small, but a little larger pieces of whole membrane. Both from #13 which had best epithelial bands. Pieces of membrane from #15 also. A piece of membrane #13 (shorter) and one from #15 (longer) fixed for Feulgen stain [for nucleic acids]. Mr. Hamilton in Anatomy assisted with Osmic preparations. Other eggs continued in incubator for further observation. #16 has a fungus growing from shell inside, but kept for observation.
>
>   Bacterial stains show: #7 = frequent groups of staphylococci

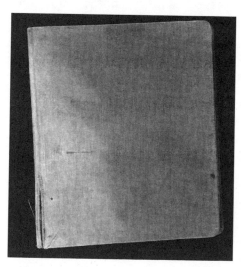

Fig. 10-1: Last laboratory notebook used by Dr. Goodpasture.

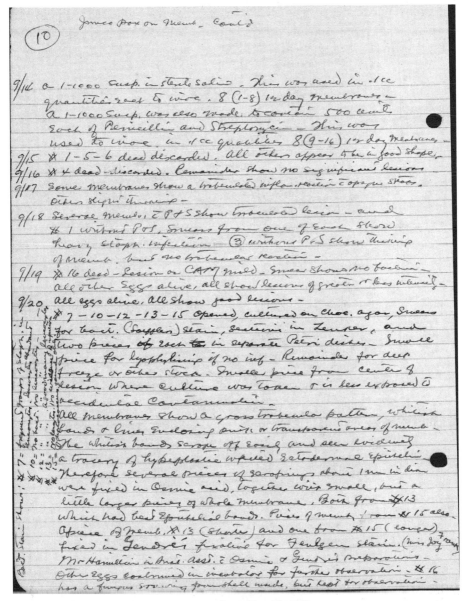

Fig. 10-2: Notes made by Dr. Goodpasture on September 20, 1960.

in leukocytes. Leukocytes abundant. #10 = No bacteria. No leukocytes #12 = No bacteria. No leukocytes #13 = No bacteria. A good many leukocytes #15 = No leukocytes. No evidence of infection. One staphylococcus found only.

Six days previously, he had written his daughter Sarah a long letter that is a comprehensive account of the status of the Goodpastures and is quoted extensively below:[4]

Sept. 14–60

Dearest Sarah:

It would be better to scatter our letters, but neither of us has written recently, so despite the fact I'm mailing Katherine's today, I'll just send this along too. . . .

We have finished (almost) moving things from Williamsport but are not yet fully established "at home" [on Hopkins Lane]. This is migration time so Katherine and the birds are taking to Basin Spring for a few days. After that episode we'll probably get the 17 boxes now stored on Uncle Sim's farm and call it a day.

I am working every day in the laboratory carrying on experiments, consulting, etc. Now that school has started there will probably be seminars, conferences (I don't know the difference but with symposiums they seem to constitute the great trinity these days) and a lecture now and then. I will try to stick it out for a while. . . .

Earlier in the summer I spent a good deal of time writing memoirs— one for Dr. Leo Loeb for the National Academy of Sciences, and afterward the Dean appointed me with Jim Ward and Billy Orr to write one for Sam Clark. They assigned me the task—which I considered a privilege, for I appreciated the opportunity to express my admiration for such a good friend and colleague. That has been completed and given to Jim Ward. What will be done with it I don't know. Now I'm trying to work up some of my research into a couple of papers, if the results on balance seem worthy. So I'm taking photos, looking up references when I'm not cleaning cages and feeding baby chicks or looking at slides.

Things must be humming at your house now that school has started. I hope all goes well and every body likes teachers, subjects and books. I'm getting mighty anxious to see my pardners [partners] and learn first hand how things are going. I hope it won't be long now. . . . Love to DeDe [Sarah's husband, Joe Jr.], Pardner [granddaughter Sarah], Suzie Pie [granddaughter Susan], my old friend Jo Jo [Joe III].

Affectionately, Gran

On the afternoon of the 20th, while it was still light, he was planting grass in the backyard of their recently purchased home on Hopkins Lane.[5] He apparently collapsed around 6:00 P.M., was found to be lifeless, and was pronounced dead approximately one hour later. His death was presumably due to an arrhythmia from a coronary occlusion.[6] Funeral services were held at Benton Chapel on the Vanderbilt campus at 2:30 P.M. on September 22, and burial was in Greenwood Cemetery in Clarksville beside the grave of Sarah Catlett Goodpasture (Fig. 10-3). (See the color section for a view of the Goodpasture headstone at Greenwood Cemetery.) A. L. Currie, minister of Westminister Presbyterian Church, officiated at the services; honorary pallbearers were Chancellor Branscomb and Vice Chancellor for Medical Affairs John Patterson, as well as the heads of departments and faculty in the medical school.

The contributions of Dr. Goodpasture to medicine and to Vanderbilt were detailed[7] in a front-page obituary and editorial in the *Nashville Tennessean*, obituaries in the *Nashville Banner*, *New York Times*, and *Washington Post*, and biographic memoirs by Doctors John Youmans, Thomas Francis, and Esmond Long. Dr. James Dawson prepared obituaries for the *Archives of Pathology* and the *American Journal of Pathology*. An editorial was prepared for the *Southern Medical Journal* by its editor, Dr. Rudolph Kampmeier. Sir Macfarlane Burnet wrote a tribute for *Perspectives in Biology and Medicine* titled: "The influence of a great pathologist: A tribute to Ernest Goodpasture." There were appropriate resolutions by the executive faculty of Vanderbilt School of

Fig. 10-3: Gravestones of Sarah Catlett and Ernest William Goodpasture, Greenwood Cemetery, Clarksville. (For a picture of the Goodpasture headstone, please see color section.)

Medicine and the Board of Trust extolling his contributions. Perhaps the most succinct and yet encompassing description of his importance to Vanderbilt was the Board of Trust resolution adopted on October 7:

ERNEST WILLIAM GOODPASTURE
A.B., M.D., M.S., D.Sc., LL.D.
October 17, 1886—September 20, 1960

Dr. Ernest W. Goodpasture loved Vanderbilt University. From the day that he enrolled as a freshman in 1903 until his death September 20, 1960, he never wavered in his loyalty and his support. He was related to the University in as many ways as is given to one man—as an undergraduate, as a teacher and head of a department, as a Dean, as a member of the Board of Trust and finally, as Emeritus Professor whose sage counsel was heeded by all.

As a scientist and teacher, Dr. Goodpasture earned international renown. His discoveries in the field of virus diseases extended medical knowledge immeasurably, saved thousands of lives and placed him in the position of being a medical immortal while still in his prime. His unique contribution to Vanderbilt never will be duplicated. The least that can be said of him is that in his life he summed up everything that Vanderbilt University stands for and believes in.

It is impossible to measure accurately the total contribution of a man to an institution but it is of men that an institution is made. If it can continue to deserve loyal and devoted service such as was given freely by Dr. Goodpasture, the future of Vanderbilt University is assured.

It is with sorrow and a feeling of great personal loss that the Board records the death of Dr. Ernest W. Goodpasture.

Dr. Dawson and Dr. Shapiro also recognized the legacy of Dr. Goodpasture at Vanderbilt in their tributes. First, Dr. Dawson's:

With a life full of service and accomplishment behind him and undiminished physical and mental vigor, Dr. Goodpasture returned [from the Armed Forces Institute of Pathology and University of Mississippi] to his beloved Middle Tennessee to be near his family and his friends and to engage in those activities which he enjoyed so much. He returned to Vanderbilt Medical School whose fine reputation had resulted so largely from his creative thinking and contributions. In this familiar and congenial environment, in the early evening of September 20, 1960, Ernest William Goodpasture went out to work in his garden. Shortly thereafter this truly great man collapsed and died.

This was the concluding statement in the executive faculty resolution prepared by Dr. Shapiro, with the advice of Dr. Hugh Morgan:

A lifelong academician, Dr. Goodpasture pictured the ideal university as a place conducive to individual, independent development and expression and providing an environment immune to tyranny of convention, custom, pressure and prejudice. When asked by Chairman Harold Vanderbilt on the occasion of his resignation from the Board of Trust for parting words of advice for the administrative officers and trustees of the University [he responded] "If there be a typical Vanderbilt image, let it reflect the presence of an independent and unregimented mind, unfettered in its continuing search for truth." Thus he spoke for the last time to the university that he had chosen above all others as the one for his life's work. In this extemporaneous talk he revealed the core of his concept of a university and its mission. This statement may well be included as part of the unique legacy left to Vanderbilt University by E. W. Goodpasture.

Thus the university had in the space of three months lost two of its most loyal and effective scholars from the medical school faculty. On July 1, 1960, Dr. Sam Lillard Clark Sr. had died after a six-month illness due to cancer. Dr. Goodpasture, as one of his closest friends, was chosen to be a pallbearer and was responsible for preparing the resolution accepted by the executive faculty in honoring Dr. Clark. They were kindred spirits, and it was most appropriate that the respective services for both were held in Benton Chapel on their campus under the officiation of Chancellor Branscomb.[8]

Fig. 10-4: Dr. Goodpasture, circa 1958.

Prophet

The word *prophet* suggests that a person is a teacher with wisdom, dignity, and the ability to see into the future. Since ancient times, societies have turned to prophets and to elders for guidance and enlightenment. Prophets may have honor in their own country,[9] but it is rare indeed for a faculty member to have the stature to guide a university or to speak for a university. It is also rare for a faculty member to have the stature to guide a profession or to speak for a profession. Has Ernest William Goodpasture (Fig. 10-4) not earned those prerogatives? If so, what can he say that is of value now to universities, particularly Vanderbilt University? What can he say that is of value now to the profession of medicine?

> 1943
>
> Even at the risk of chauvinism I would say that no other group of human beings in our midst by personal aptitude, by selection, by opportunities, training, traditional humanitarian objectives, ethical standards and preference in the hearts of mankind, has so great an opportunity and with it so profound a responsibility for leadership along paths of sane and healthful living in the broadest sense, in this sick world of ours, as does the medical profession, of which this Association [Association of American Physicians] is so distinguished a representative. All people will look to them for help and understanding, and they will not fail.[10]

> 1949
>
> There is consequently no justification in my mind for a Vanderbilt Medical School whose only objective is the graduation of its complement

of physicians to serve the health requirements. There is and always will be need and a great need for advancement of knowledge and superior training. Our modern civilization, not its medical aspects alone, must be supported by the best minds of the Nation trained in the most advanced technical boundaries of science if we are to go forward intellectually.[11]

1957

But the university is the home of the medical school and the entire great edifice of learning will continue to profit by association with its science, its art and its humanity. . . . Medicine is the most universally acceptable example of what education and science can do in the interest of well being. . . . The university as conservator, educator, creative builder of knowledge, evaluator and disperser of the arts and science should, above all civil institutions, be respected, protected, supported and promoted in the interest of human culture.[12]

1943

. . . as students of science and students of life we should realize that underneath and supporting all of our chartered modes of freedom lies a many-sided spirit; and the facet of that spirit, to my mind, that would be essential to the maintenance and growth of liberty is the spirit of rational inquiry. To question ourselves, to question our universe, to question our gods, our devils and our destiny, and to listen sensitively and intelligently to spontaneous and induced revelations of truth, is the last bulwark of our hope at least to know a better world. Seek and ye shall find.[13]

1957 or 1958

Perhaps the greatest tragedy a human being can experience is the failure to find himself. The tragedy is not merely an individual one when it involves a person of great creative stature, for then the failure to realize full potentiality may constitute not only a national or international calamity but a deprivation of humanity itself. It should be the untiring effort of society ever to provide constructive ways and means for youth to discover itself— ways designed to afford the highest probability of success in achieving this basic personal revelation. Know thyself, admonished Socrates; the Kingdom of God is within you, taught Jesus.[14]

What can we say to Ernest Goodpasture in 2002 about the profession of medicine and the status of university medical schools?

As a basic scientist, and as someone with analytical tendencies, you would be surprised and concerned to learn that medical students in 2002 spend two years in the basic sciences just as you did in 1908–09, although we live in a time when each issue of major journals contains important new information about how the body works, or how it defends itself in a hostile environment.[15] Yet the understanding by students of these basic processes has not kept pace with the flow of information. Worse, the *interest* of students in basic processes has waned. The forced memorization of minutiae is so stultifying that most students pass through their initial exposure to medical school with the fervent intention of never revisiting the classroom or research laboratory.

The pace of life in medical schools is frenzied not only for students but for residents and faculty as well. Faculty find that the quantity of essential information, the instant worldwide availability of information, the number of journals, the number of national meetings, and the number of deadlines create demands on time and energy that are very difficult to sustain. In particular, the academically inclined are enormously frustrated because no one can stay abreast of the information load in a broad sense. The pace has also quickened in regards to patient care. Pressures to reduce the length of hospital stay and increased patient load in the clinics inhibit or prevent deliberative interactions between patients and physicians.[16] It is not yet apparent how students and residents will learn clinical judgment in this frenetic environment.

You might well believe that these problems were not intrinsic to the system, and that minor adjustments would result in their correction. Therefore, I suspect you would be most concerned about the gradual and seemingly inevitable involvement by university medical centers in the creation of businesses. Business enterprises have been initiated by full- or part-time faculty members, fostered by universities, and promoted on the basis of profits for the faculty and university. Discoveries in medicine are routinely patented. Conflicts of interest have thereby developed that would have been inconceivable in your time and have not been resolved in ours.

The Measure of the Man

Shall we now pass judgment on Ernest William Goodpasture? Albeit intrinsically presumptuous, it is our custom and perhaps our responsibility to judge, so that we may review our own values and usefulness.

He was, first of all, a consummate investigator, searching for an understanding of the factors underlying the relationships between living things. Beginning with a thorough knowledge of the literature and mastery of histopathologic features, he and his colleagues successfully addressed central issues in viral and bacterial diseases. His research style was determined, even dogged, but not plodding.

He was a gentleman and a gracious colleague, while being fiercely independent and uncompromising in values.

He believed universities among social institutions were best constituted to acquire as well as transmit knowledge and values.

He believed in education in the broadest sense and that through education lay the path to good government and social justice.

He believed the profession with the greatest opportunity and responsibility to improve the lot of humankind was that of medicine.

He was justly proud of his heritage, fortunate in his upbringing, comfortable with life in his native state, and devoted to his family.

He liked the word *congenial* and was guided in his life by the sense of balance implicit in that word.

He had lifelong friends who relished his company.

He delighted in knowledge of all types, be it biological, historical, or mechanical.

He was a practical idealist, fortunate to live in a time when a man's word might be taken at face value.

He was a scientist, gentleman, and scholar.

CURRICULUM VITAE

ERNEST WILLIAM GOODPASTURE
M.D., A.B., M.S., D.Sc., LL.D.
CURRICULUM VITAE
August 20, 1958
Washington, D.C.

I

Ernest William Goodpasture, A.B., M.D., M.S., D.Sc., LL.D

1. Born October 17, 1886 on Walnuthurst Farm, in the 6th District of Montgomery County, Tennessee, located near the Russellville Pike (now State Highway No. 13) about 7 miles east of Clarksville, Tenn. and 5 miles west of Guthrie, Ky. The nearest post office at that time was St. Bethlehem, Tenn., 3 miles to the west.

2. Parents: <u>Father</u>, Albert Virgil Goodpasture Sr. (1855–42), Lawyer, farmer, historian and author; a native of Tennessee, born at Livingston in Overton County. He was a graduate of the University of Tennessee, B. A. 1875, Hon. M. A. 1882, and of Vanderbilt University, LLB, 1877. He practiced law in Clarksville, Tennessee, and was elected to the State General Assembly, House, 1888, and Senate 1890; served as Clerk of the Supreme Court of Tennessee (1891–97); founded the Goodpasture Book Co. (1897–14) and served as Secretary of the Tennessee Historical Society and Editor of the American Historical Magazine.
    <u>Mother</u>, Jennie Willson (Dawson) Goodpasture, a native of Tennessee, born in Montgomery Co., (1857–32).

3. Siblings: Mattie Madge, unmarried (1882–44). Ridley Rose, unmarried (1884–42). Sarah Jane (Martzloff) m. Dr. Karl H. Martzloff, 2 children, Thomas H. and Albert D., Residence, Portland, Oregon. Albert Virgil Jr. m. Sally Hammil (d. 1958), 4 children, Ann Willson, Albert V. III, Martha, Sally—Residence, Nashville, Tennessee.

4. Married (1) Sarah Catlett (Clarksville, Tenn.) Aug. 15, 1915. d. 1940.
1 child, Sarah, b. 1919, m. 1941, Dr. Joseph A. Little; 3 children, Sarah Marsh, Susan McG., Joseph A. III. Residence Anchorage, KY.
Married (2) Francis Katherine (Anderson) May 23, 1945.

5. Education:
a. Public Schools, Nashville, Tenn., 1893–99.
b. Bowen's Preparatory [Academic] School 1899–1903.
c. Vanderbilt University, B.A., June 19, 1907.
d. Teacher, Allegheny Collegiate Institute, Alderson, W. Va., 1907–8.
e. Johns Hopkins University, School of Medicine, 1908–12. M.D., June 11, 1912.

6. Licensed in Medicine. Certificate of permanent license, State Board of Medical Examiners, Tennessee, December 19, 1936.

II

Professional Positions

1. 1912–13, Rockefeller Fellow in Pathology, Department of Pathology, Johns Hopkins University Medical School under Prof. W. H. Welch and Prof. G. H. Whipple.

2. 1913–15, Instructor in Pathology, Johns Hopkins Medical School, and (1915) Acting Resident Pathologist Johns Hopkins Hospital and Visiting Pathologist to the Union Protestant Infirmary.

3. 1915–18, Resident Pathologist to the Peter Bent Brigham Hospital and Instructor in Pathology, Harvard University Medical School, under Prof. Wm. T. Councilman.

4. 1918–22, Assistant Professor of Pathology, Harvard Medical School and
a. 1918-19, on leave Chelsea Naval Hospital, as Lieut. (j.g.) USNRF, MC (Pathologist) Hon. discharge May 9, 1922; end of enrollment Sept. 30, 1921. Total service in NRF 3 1/4 years.
b. 1921–22 on leave, Manila, P.I. as Asst. Prof., then Prof. of Pathology, School of Medicine and Surgery, University of the Philippines, and Pathologist-in-Chief, Philippine General Hospital.

5. 1922–24, Director, Wm. H. Singer Memorial Research Laboratory (Associated with Allegheny General Hospital), Pittsburgh, Pa.

6. 1924–55, Professor of Pathology and Head of the department, Vanderbilt University School of Medicine, and Pathologist to Vanderbilt University Hospital, Nashville, Tenn., and
a. 1924–25, Rockefeller Scholar, General Education Board, Institute for General and Experimental Pathology of the University of Vienna, Acting Director: Prof. Dr. T. C. Rothberger.
b. 1942–45, Associate Dean (with Dean W. S. Leathers), Vanderbilt University, School of Medicine. 1945–50, Dean, School of Medicine. 1955—Professor Emeritus, Vanderbilt University, Dept. of Pathology.

7. 1955—Scientific Director of Pathology, Department of Pathology, Armed Forces Institute of Pathology, Washington, D.C.

III

Membership in Professional Societies
1. American Association of Pathologists and Bacteriologists, 1915—.
2. American Society for Experimental Pathology, 1925—.
3. American Association for the Advancement of Science, April 4, 1924.
4. American Medical Association, 1925—.
5. Southern Medical Association, 1928—.
6. Nashville Academy of Medicine, 1937—.
7. National Academy of Sciences, Member, April 28, 1937.
8. Association of American Physicians, 1938—.
9. New York Academy of Science, May 22, 1940.
10. American Philosophical Society, Member, April 23, 1943.
11. Sigma Xi (Charter member of Vanderbilt Chapter), April 15, 1944.
12. New York Academy of Medicine, Honorary Fellow, April 24, 1947.
13. Washington (D.C.) Academy of Medicine, December 1956.
14. Tennessee Academy of Science, 1960 (Posthumous election).

IV

Offices in Professional Societies
1. 1940—American Association for the Advancement of Science, Vice President for the Medical Section.
2. 1939–1940—American Society for Experimental Pathology, President 1940, Meeting at New Orleans, La.
3. 1948–49—American Association of Pathologists and Bacteriologists, Council 1945–49; President, 1949, Meeting at Boston, Mass.

V

Membership in Social and Honorary Fraternities and Clubs
Social
1. Kappa Sigma Fraternity (Vanderbilt University).
2. Nu Sigma Nu Medical Fraternity (Johns Hopkins Medical School).
3. Omicron Delta Kappa (ODK), Vanderbilt University, June 10, 1940.
4. Coffee House Club, Nashville, Tennessee.
5. Commodore Club, Vanderbilt University, 1906.

Honorary
1. Alpha Omega Alpha, Vanderbilt Medical School, 1929.
2. Sigma Xi, Vanderbilt University, April 15, 1944.
3. Phi Beta Kappa, Vanderbilt University, November 5, 1936.
4. Gorgas Medical Society, University of Alabama College of Medicine, Birmingham, Alabama (1933).

VI

Special Appointments
1. 1930–32—Member Scientific Advisors, Leonard Wood Memorial for the Eradication of Leprosy.
2. 1935–41—Member Scientific Advisory Board, Children's Research Foundation, Cincinnati, Ohio.
3. 1938–40—Member Board of Scientific Directors, International Health 1942–44 Division, Rockefeller Foundation.

4. 1941–46—Member, Board for the Investigation and Control of Influenza and Other Epidemic Diseases in the Army, Preventive Medicine Division, S.G.O., U.S. Army, Washington, D.C.
5. 1942—Chairman, Conference Group on Pathology, Medical Division, NRC, 1942.
6. 1942–45—Member, Committee on Biological Warfare, NAS-NRC.
7. 1942–50—Consultant, Health Division, Tennessee Valley Authority.
8. 1945–51—Member Advisory Board, Life Insurance Medical Research Fund, New York City.
9. 1945–48—Member Council, National Academy of Sciences, Washington, D.C. 1949–52.
10. 1946–50—Member, Study Section on Viruses and Rickettsia, National Institutes of Health, U.S. Public Health Service, Washington, D.C.
11. 1946–52—Member Board of Directors, Institute for Nuclear Studies, Oak Ridge, Tenn.
12. 1947–52—Member and Vice chairman, Advisory Committee to Division of Biology and Medicine, Atomic Energy Commission, Wash., D.C.
    (a) 1950—Special Mission to Japan to Report on the Atomic Bomb Casualty Commission Activity, Hiroshima, Japan.
13. 1951–57—Member Editorial Board 1951—; Acting Editor, 1957 (Jan.–July), *American Journal of Pathology*.
14. 1952–55—Member Commission on Tennessee State Library and Archives, Nashville, Tenn.
15. 1954–55—Member Divisional Committee for Biological and Medical Sciences, National Science Foundation, Washington, D.C.
16. 1955—Member Committee appointed by National Science Foundation (Chr. Dr. C.N.S. Long) to review support of Medical Research by the Department of Health, Education and Welfare (Secy. Folsom).
17. 1956—Member Board of Trust (Alumni Member) Vanderbilt University, Nashville, Tenn.

VII
**Asterisks indicate that the text for the lecture is unavailable.

Special Lectureships
1929
The DeLamar Lecture, February 26
"Herpetic Infection, with Especial Reference to Involvement of the Nervous System."
Johns Hopkins University, School of Hygiene and Public Health, Baltimore, Maryland
The Harvey Lecture, December 19
"Etiological Problems in the Study of Filterable Virus Diseases."
New York Academy of Medicine, New York City

1930
Chairman's Address, November 13
"Cytotropism, and Virus Infection of the Nervous System."**
Section on Pathology, Southern Medical Association, Louisville, Kentucky

1932
Lecture, April 22
"Cytotropic Viruses, with Reference to Filterable Forms of Bacteria and Cancer."
Duke University, School of Medicine, Durham, North Carolina
Lecture, Title: UNKNOWN,** November 4
New York State Association of Public Health Laboratories, Albany, New York

1933
Gorgas Medical Society Lecture, April 28
"A Medical Pageant."
University of Alabama School of Medicine, Tuscaloosa, Alabama

1935
Lecture, January 18
"A Review of Human Virus Diseases."**
Kansas City Academy of Medicine, Kansas City, Missouri
Speaker, date unknown
"Intracellular Parasitism and the Cytotropism of Viruses."
Virus Symposium, Southern Medical Pathological Section, St. Louis, Missouri

1936
Lecture, October 20
"Immunity to Virus Diseases."
Epidemiology Section, American Public Health Association, 65th Annual Meeting, New
    Orleans, Louisiana

1937
Ludwig Hektoen Lecture (XIII) of the Frank Billings Foundation of the Institute of
    Medicine of Chicago, January 22
"Vaccinia."
Palmer House, Chicago, Illinois

1938
The Leo Loeb Lecture, March 24
"Some Uses of the Chick Embryo for the Study of Infection and Immunity."
Washington University School of Medicine, St. Louis, Missouri
Lecture, April 2
"Pathogenesis of Infectious Disease."**
Centennial Celebration, University of Louisville School of Medicine and Alpha Omega
    Alpha Society, Louisville, Kentucky
Lecture, April 5
"Experimental Virus and Bacterial Infection of the Chick Embryo."
Bacteriological Society, University of Kentucky, Lexington, Kentucky
Thayer Lectures, November 8 & 9
"Virus Infections, with Especial Reference to the Use of Skin Grafts on the Chorio-
    allantois";
"Experimental Bacterial Infections of the Chick Embryo."
Johns Hopkins Univ. School of Medicine, Baltimore, Maryland

1939
Lecture, March 28
"Virus Infections of the Chick Embryo."
American College of Physicians, New Orleans, Louisiana
Rachford Lectures, April 13–15
"Experimental Virus Infections of Chick Embryos."**
"Experimental Bacterial Infections of Chick Embryos."**
Children's Hospital Research Foundation, Cincinnati, Ohio

Lecture, May 18
"Viral and Bacterial Infections of Chick Embryos."
New England Pathological Society, Boston, Massachusetts
Lectures, October 23, 24, 25
"1. Investigations of Viral Infections and Immunity by Means of the Chick Embryo Technique.
2. Experimental Bacterial Infections of the Chick Embryo.
3. A Consideration of Pathogenesis of Virus and Bacterial Infection, with a Review of Some Human Virus Diseases."
Portland Academy of Medicine, Portland, Oregon
Eastman Lecture, December 12
"A Consideration of Pathogenesis in Viral and Bacterial Infections."
The University of Rochester School of Medicine and Dentistry, Rochester, New York

1940
The Shattuck Lecture, May 21
"Immunity to Virus Diseases."
Massachusetts Medical Society, Boston, Massachusetts
Symposium on Virus Diseases, November
"The Pathology of Virus Disease."
American Academy of Pediatrics, Memphis, Tennessee

1941
The Alvarenga Prize Lecture I (Award XXXV), March 5
"The Cell-Parasite Relationship in Bacterial and Virus Infection."
The College of Physicians of Philadelphia, Philadelphia, Pennsylvania
Cutter Lectures on Preventive Medicine, March 7
"Intracellular Infection and Some of Its Possible Implications."**
Harvard Medical School, Boston, Massachusetts
Lecture IV, April 14
"The Pathology and Pathogenesis of Poliomyelitis."
Vanderbilt Lectures on Infantile Paralysis, Vanderbilt University School of Medicine, Nashville, Tennessee
Lecture, September 26
"Virus Infection of the Mammalian Fetus."
Fiftieth Anniversary of the University of Chicago Symposia (Sect. B-17), University of Chicago, Chicago, Illinois
Chairman's Address, December 30
"Intracellular Parasitism in Human Infectious Diseases."
Section N, American Association for the Advancement of Science, Dallas, Texas

1943
Commencement Address, December 16
"The Spirit of Inquiry."
Vanderbilt University, Nashville, Tennessee

1944
Sigma XI Lecture, May
"Education and Aid for Research."
Vanderbilt University, Nashville, Tennessee

Speaker, July 28
"The Doctor Looks at the Humanities."
Humanities Conference, Vanderbilt University, Nashville, Tennessee

1945
Sigma XI Lecture, March 16
"Can Scientific Research Develop Wisdom"**
Vanderbilt University, Nashville, Tennessee

1946
Convocation, February 6
Address honoring Chancellor Carmichael, on his departure
Vanderbilt University, Nashville, Tennessee
The Passano Foundation Award Lecture, May 15
"Research and Medical Practice."
Baltimore, Maryland

1947
Speaker, March 2
"Agents of Infectious Disease."
New York Philharmonic Symphony Program, New York, New York

1948
The John Phillips Memorial Lecture, April 21
"The Intracellular Environment for Infectious Agents."
American College of Physicians, San Francisco, California

1950
Lecture, February 21
"Some Aspects of Twentieth Century Research on Infectious Diseases."
Fiftieth Anniversary Program, Washington University School of Medicine, St. Louis,
    Missouri
Lecture, April 8
"The Influence of William Henry Welch upon the Development of Pathology."
Welch Centennial Program, Johns Hopkins School of Medicine, Baltimore, Maryland
Speaker, October 21
"From the Faculties"
Convocation Celebrating the 75th Anniversary of the Opening of Vanderbilt, Nashville,
    Tennessee

1952
Lecture, January 11
"The Significance of the Experimental Approach to the Cancer Problem."
Inauguration of Radiation Therapy Unit, University of California School of Medicine, San
    Francisco, California
Lecture, October 29
"The Role of Research in the General Hospital Laboratory."
Singer Research Laboratory Celebration, Pittsburgh, Pennsylvania
Lecture, November 14
"The Pathology of Pneumonia Following Influenza Infection."

Symposium on Acute Respiratory Disease, Auspices of Knoxville Academy of Medicine
and Tennessee Academy of General Practice, Knoxville, Tennessee

1953
Lecture, April 23
"State Library System of Tennessee in Transition."
Tennessee Library Association, Jackson, Tennessee

1954
Max Brodel Memorial Lecture, October 6
"Max Brodel and the Role of the Medical Illustrator in Modern Medical Education."
Ninth Annual Convention of the Association of Medical Illustrators, Nashville,
Tennessee
Alpha Omega Alpha Lecture, May
"Reaction of Host-cells to Viral Mutants."**
Vanderbilt University School of Medicine, Nashville, Tennessee

1955
The Howard Taylor Ricketts Lecture, May 9
"Host-Cell Response to Viral Mutants."
University of Chicago School of Medicine, Chicago, Illinois

1956
Lecture, February 3
"Research in the Armed Forces Institute of Pathology."
Naval Medical Research Institute, Bethesda, Maryland
Lecture, May 4
"Host Cell Responses to Mutants of Fowl-Pox Virus."
Department of Microbiology, Yale University School of Medicine, New Haven,
Connecticut
The Stoneburner Lectures, May 21–22
"Advances in Knowledge of the Pox Group of Viral Diseases:
1.   Herpes Simplex, Varicella and Zoster
2.   Vaccinia and Fowl-Pox in Mutations and Host-Cell Responses."
Medical College of Virginia, Richmond, Virginia
Speaker, October 13
"Research in the Armed Forces Institute of Pathology."
Armed Forces Institute of Pathology Luncheon, Chicago, Illinois
Lecture
Subject: AFIP
Washington Branch, American Society of Microbiology, Washington, D.C.

1957
Lecture, March 7–9
"The Pathology of Virus Neoplasia."
Eleventh Annual Symposium on Fundamental Cancer Research, M.D., Anderson
Hospital and Tumor Institute, Houston, Texas
Ivy Day Celebration Lecture, June 7
"Medicine and the Ivied Walls."
Tulane University, School of Medicine, New Orleans, Louisiana

1958
Lecture, April 19
"Influences of Medical Technology on the Development of Pathology."
Eleventh Annual Seminar, District of Columbia Society of Medical Technologists, Washington, D.C.
Lecture, December 3
"Influences of Pathology on the Changing Patterns of Medicine."
Washington Society of Pathologists, Washington, D.C.
Lecture, Occasion, Site, and Date unknown
"Alma Mater for Pathology's Spirit of Inquiry."
Lecture, Occasion, Site, and Date unknown
"Research at AFIP: Facilities, Projects, Programs."

1960
Lecture, January 24
"The Influence of Leo Loeb upon Pathology in America."
Washington University School of Medicine, St. Louis, Missouri

VIII

Honorary Degrees
1939
1.　M.S. Yale University, at Commencement, New Haven, Connecticut, June 11, 1939.

1941
2.　D.Sc. University of Chicago. Presented at the Fiftieth Anniversary of the University of Chicago, September 29, 1941, Chicago, Illinois.

1950
3.　D.Sc. Washington University. Presented at the Fiftieth Anniversary Program, Washington University, February 21, 1950, St. Louis, Missouri.

1957
4.　LL.D. Tulane University. Presented at Commencement, June 8, 1957, Tulane University, New Orleans, Louisiana.

IX

Medals
1937
1.　SMA Achievement in Medical Research, December 1, 1937.
　　Southern Medical Association, Annual Meeting, New Orleans, Louisiana

1943
2.　The Kober Medal, Presented May 9, 1943.
　　Fifty-eighth Session, Association of American Physicians, Atlantic City, New Jersey.

1944
3.　The Sedgwick Memorial Medal, October 3, 1944.
　　American Public Health Association.

1945
4.　The John Scott Medal. Awarded by the City of Philadelphia, November 16, 1945.

1948
5.   The John Phillips Memorial Award, presented February 21, 1948.
     Annual Meeting of the American College of Physicians, San Francisco, California.

1955
6.   Howard Taylor Ricketts Award, presented May 9, 1955.
     University of Chicago, School of Medicine, Chicago, Illinois.

1958
7.   Jesse Stevenson Kovalenko Medal, presented April 28, 1958.
     National Academy of Sciences, Washington, D.C.

Awards
1.   Kappa Sigma "Man-of-the-Year" Award, presented 1946, Nashville, Tennessee.
2.   The Passano Foundation Award, presented May 15, 1946, Baltimore, Maryland.
3.   The Gold Headed Cane, presented by the Council at the Fifty-fifth Annual Meeting of the American Association of Pathologists and Bacteriologists, Annual Dinner, Cleveland, Ohio, April 24, 1958.

BIBLIOGRAPHY

1913
With G. H. Whipple. Acute haemorrhagic pancreatitis. *Surg Gynecol and Obstet,* 17:541–47.

1914
Fibrinogen. II. The association of liver and intestine in rapid regeneration of fibrinogen. *Am J Physiol,* 33:70–85.
Fibrinolysis in chronic hepatic insufficiency. *Bull Johns Hopkins Hosp.,* 25:1–17.

1916
With G. B. Wislocki. Old age in relation to cell-overgrowth and cancer. *J Med Res,* 33:455–73.
Double primary abdominal pregnancy. *J Med Res,* 34:259–61.

1917
Crystalline hyalin. *J Med Res,* 35:259–64.
A contribution to the study of pancreas intoxication. *J Exp Med,* 25:277–83.
An acid polychrome-methylene blue solution for routine and special staining. *JAMA,* 69:998.

1918
An anatomical study of senescence in dogs, with especial reference to the relation of cellular changes of age to tumors. *J Med Res,* 38:127–90.
Observations on mitochondria of tumors. *J Med Res,* 38:213–24.
With Victor C. Jacobsen. Occlusion of the entire inferior vena cava by hypernephroma, with thrombosis of the hepatic vein and its branches. *Arch Intern Med,* 22:86–95.

1919
With F. L. Burnett. The pathology of pneumonia accompanying influenza. *U.S. Naval Med Bull,* 13:177–97.
Bronchopneumonia due to hemolytic streptococci following influenza. *J Am Med Assoc,* 72:724–25.

A peroxidase reaction with sodium nitroprusside and benzidine in blood smears and tissues. *J Lab Clin Med*, 4:442–444.

The significance of certain pulmonary lesions in relation to the etiology of influenza. *Am J of Med Sci*, 158:863–871.

1921

With Fritz B. Talbot. Concerning the nature of "protozoan-like" cells in certain lesions of infancy. *Am J Dis Child*, 21:415–25.

Myocardial necrosis in hyperthyroidism. *JAMA*, 76:1545–51.

The influence of thyroid products on the production of myocardial necrosis. *J Exp Med*, 34:407–23.

1923

With Andrew Watson Sellards and Walfrido de Leon. Investigations concerning yaws. *Philipp J Sci*, 22:219–89.

Histopathology of the intestine in cholera. *Philipp J Sci*, 22:413–21.

Complement fixation in treated and untreated leprosy. *Philipp J Sci*, 22:425–37.

A poisonous constituent in cholera stools. *Philipp J Sci*, 22:439–45.

With Oscar Teague. The occurrence of intranuclear inclusion bodies in certain tissues of the rabbit inoculated directly with the virus of herpes labialis. *Proc. Soc. Exp. Biol. Med.*, 20:400.

With Oscar Teague. The transmission of the virus of herpes febrilis along sensory nerves with resulting unilateral lesions in the central nervous system in the rabbit. *Proc. Soc. Exp. Biol. Med.*, 20:545–47.

With Oscar Teague. Experimental herpes zoster. *JAMA*, 81:377–78.

With Oscar Teague. Experimental production of herpetic lesions in organs and tissues of the rabbit. *J Med Res*, 44:121–28.

With Oscar Teague. Transmission of the virus of herpes febrilis along nerves in experimentally infected rabbits. *J Med Res*, 44:139–84.

With Oscar Teague. Experimental herpes zoster. *J Med Res*, 44:185–200.

With Robert H. McClellan. A method of demonstrating experimental gross lesions of the central nervous system. *J Med Res*, 44:201–6.

1924

Spontaneous encephalitis in rabbits. *Journal Infect Dis*, 34:428–32.

With Dorsey Brannan. The pathology of pneumonia caused by Bacillus influenza during an inter-epidemic period. *Arch Intern Med*, 34:739–56.

1925

Intranuclear inclusions in experimental herpetic lesions of rabbits. *Am J Pathol*, 1:1–9.

The axis-cylinders of peripheral nerves as portals of entry to the central nervous system for the virus of herpes simplex in experimentally infected rabbits. *Am J Pathol*, 1:11–28.

The pathways of infection of the central nervous system in herpetic encephalitis of rabbits contracted by contact; with a comparative comment on medullary lesions in a case of human poliomyelitis. *Am J Pathol*, 1:29–46.

1925

Certain factors determining the incidence and severity of herpetic encephalitis in rabbits. *Am J Pathol*, 1:47–55.

A study of rabies, with reference to a neural transmission of the virus in rabbits, and the structure and significance of Negri bodies. *Am J Pathol*, 1:547–82.

1927

With Howard King. A cytologic study of molluscum contagiosum. *Am J Pathol*, 3:385–94.

Nuclear changes of ganglion cells in experimental herpetic encephalitis. *Am J Pathol*, 3:395–99.

With J. D. Wilson. Yellow atrophy of the liver; acute, subacute and healed. *Arch Intern Med*, 40:377–85.

1928

Virus diseases of fowls as exemplified by contagious epithelioma (fowlpox) of chickens and pigeons. In: *Filterable Viruses*, ed. by T. M. Rivers, pp. 235–70. Baltimore, The Williams and Wilkins Company.

The pathology of certain virus diseases. *South Med J*, 21:535–39.

The pathology of certain virus diseases. *Science*, 67:591–93.

With S. John House. The pathologic anatomy of tularemia in man. *Am J Pathol*, 4:213–26.

With S. John House. Spontaneous arteriovenous aneurysm in the thorax. *Am Heart J* 3:682–693.

1929

Vanderbilt University School of Medicine Department of Pathology. In: *Methods and Problems of Medical Education*, Thirteenth Series, pp. 51–58. New York, The Rockefeller Foundation.

Cellular inclusions and the etiology of virus diseases. *Arch Pathol*, 7:114–32.

Herpetic infection, with especial reference to involvement of the nervous system. *Medicine*, 8:223–43.

With Alice M. Woodruff and C. Eugene Woodruff. Fowl-pox. II. The nature of the virus as indicated by further morphological data, and by experiments with certain chemicals. *Am J Physiol*, 90:560–61.

Etiological problems in the study of filterable virus diseases. Harvey Lectures, 25:77–102, 1929–1930.

With C. Eugene Woodruff. The infectivity of isolated inclusion bodies of fowlpox. *Am J Pathol*, 5:1–9.

1930

Cytotropismus und das Vordringen der Virusarten im Nervensystem. Zeitschrift fur die gesamte: *Neurol Psychiat*, 129:600–16.

With Alice M. Woodruff. The nature of fowlpox virus as indicated by its reaction to treatment with potassium hydroxide and other chemicals. *Am J Pathol*, 6:699–711.

With C. E. Woodruff. The relation of the virus of fowlpox to the specific cellular inclusions of the disease. *Am J Pathol*, 6:713–20.

1931

With C. E. Woodruff. A comparison of the inclusion bodies of fowlpox and molluscum contagiosum. *Am J Pathol*, 7:1–7.

With William A. DeMonbreun. Etiological studies of granuloma inguinale. *South Med J*, 24:588–97.

With W. A. DeMonbreun. Infection of monkeys with Donovan organisms by injections of tissue from human lesions of granuloma inguinale. *Am J Trop Med*, 11:311–22.

With Alice M. Woodruff. The susceptibility of the chorio-allantoic membrane of chick embryos to infection with the fowlpox virus. *Am J Pathol*, 7:209–222.

With Alice M. Woodruff and G. J. Buddingh. The cultivation of vaccinia and other viruses in the chorio-allantoic membrane of chick embryos. *Science*, 74:371–72.

1932

With W. A. DeMonbreun. Infectious oral papillomatosis of dogs. *Am J Pathol*, 8:43–55.

Yellow fever encephalitis of the monkey (Macacus Rhesus). *Am J Pathol*, 8:137–50.

With Alice M. Woodruff and G. J. Buddingh. Vaccinal infection of the chorio-allantoic membrane of the chick embryo. *Am J Pathol*, 8:271–81.

The use of experimental procedures in teaching pathology. *South Med J*, 25:991–95.

1933

Cytotropic viruses, with references to filterable forms of bacteria and cancer. *Am J Hyg*, 17:154–67.

Borreliotoses: Fowl-pox, molluscum contagiosum, variola-vaccinia. *Science*, 77:119–21.

Use of embryo chick in investigation of certain pathological problems. *South Med J*, 26:418–20.

With W. A. DeMonbreun. Further studies on the etiology of granuloma inguinale. *Am J Trop Med*, 13:447–68.

A medical pageant. *The Diplomate*, 5:251–63.

With G. J. Buddingh. Human immunization with a dermal vaccine cultivated on the membranes of chick embryos. *Science*, 78:484–85.

1934

With Claud D. Johnson. An investigation of the etiology of mumps. *J Exp Med*, 59:1–19.

The pathogenesis of neurocytotropic virus diseases. In: *The Problem of Mental Disorder*, pp. 241–54. New York, McGraw-Hill Book Co., Inc.

With W. A. DeMonbreun. An experimental investigation concerning the nature of contagious lymphosarcoma of dogs. *Am J Cancer*, 21:295–321.

Cancer and viruses. *Bull Amer Soc Control of Cancer*, 16:4–5.

With G. J. Buddingh. Immunisation de l'homme par un vaccin dermique, cultive' sur les membranes de l'embryon de poulet. *Bulletin de l'Office international d'hygiene publique*, 26:1226–32.

1935

A review of human virus diseases. *Trans Kansas City Acad of Med*, 1933–35, pp. 119–35.

With Claud D. Johnson. The etiology of mumps. *Am J Hyg*, 21:46–57.

With G. John Buddingh. The preparation of antismallpox vaccine by culture of the virus in the chorio-allantoic membrane of chick embryos and its use in human immunization. *Am J Hyg*, 21:319–60.

1936

Intracellular parasitism and the cytotropism of viruses. *Southern Med J*, 29:297–303.

With Claud D. Johnson. Experimental immunity to the virus of mumps in monkeys. *Am J Hyg*, 23:329–39.

With C. D. Johnson. The histopathology of experimental mumps in the monkey, Macacus rhesus. *Am J Pathol*, 12:495–510.

With G. J. Buddingh. The protective action of rabbit serum for vaccinia virus at high temperatures. *Science*, 84:66–67.

Immunity to virus diseases. *Am J Public Health*, 26:1163–67.
With Leland M. Johnston. Acute encephalitis in a child with cerebellar lesions like those of louping ill in monkeys. *Am J Dis Child*, 52:1415–23.

1937

Vaccinia. *Proc Inst Med Chi*, No. 11, Volume 11, pp. 206–20. Thirteenth Ludvig Hektoen Lecture of the Frank Billings Foundation.
With Katherine Anderson. The problem of infection as presented by bacterial invasion of chorio-allantoic membrane of chick embryos. *Am J Pathol*, 13:149–74.
Concerning the pathogenesis of typhoid fever. *Am J Pathol*, 13:175–85.
Comments on virus diseases and their control. *South Med J*, 30:731–35.
With Mae Gallavan. Infection of chick embryos with H. pertussis reproducing pulmonary lesions of whooping cough. *Am J Pathol*, 13:927–38.

1938

With Alice Polk and G. J. Buddingh. An experimental study of complement and hemolytic amboceptor introduced into chick embryos. *Am J Pathol*, 14:71–86.
Some uses of the chick embryo for the study of infection and immunity. *Am J Hyg*, 28:111–29.
With Beverly Douglas and Katherine Anderson. A study of human skin grafted upon the chorioallantois of chick embryos. *J Exp Med*, 68:891–904.

1939

With S. H. Auerbach, H. S. Swanson, and E. F. Cotter. Virus pneumonia of infants secondary to epidemic infections. *Am J Dis Child*, 57:997–1011.
Virus infection of the chick embryo. *Ann Inter Med*, 13:1–11.
Virus and bacterial infection of the chick embryo (abstract and discussion). *Arch Pathol*, 28:606–9.

1940

Immunity to virus diseases; some theoretical and practical considerations. *NEJM*, 222:901–10.
With Katherine Anderson. Immunity to fowlpox studied by means of skin grafts on chorioallantois of chick embryo. *Arch Pathol*, 30:212–25.
The developing egg as a culture medium. *J Lab Clin Med*, 26:242–49.

1941

The cell-parasite relationship in bacterial and virus infection. *Trans Stud Coll Physicians Phila*, 9:11–24.
The pathology and pathogenesis of poliomyelitis. Symposium on Infantile Paralysis, pp. 85–125. Vanderbilt University.
The pathology of poliomyelitis. *JAMA*, 117:273–75.
With M. M. Cullom: Boeck's sarcoid; a case of bilateral tumor of the lacrimal gland. *Arch Ophthal*, 26:57–60. (Old series, Vol. 83.)
The pathology of virus disease. *J Pediatr*, 18:440–46.

1942

Virus infection of the mammalian fetus. *Science*, 95:391–96.
With Katherine Anderson. Infection of newborn Syrian hamsters with the virus of mare abortion (Dimock and Edwards). *Am J Pathol*, 18:555–61.
With Katherine Anderson. Virus infection of human fetal membranes grafted on the chorioallantois of chick embryos. *Am J Pathol*, 18:563–75.

1943
Herpes zoster. In: *Cecil's Textbook of Medicine*, 6th ed., pp. 37–40. Philadelphia, W. B. Saunders Company.

1944
The spirit of inquiry. Vanderbilt Alumnus, 29:5–8.
With Katherine Anderson. Infection of human skin, grafted on the chorioallantois of chick embryos, with the virus of herpes zoster. *Am J Pathol*, 20:447–55.

1945
With Katherine Anderson and W. A. DeMonbreun. An etiologic consideration of Donovania granulomatis cultivated from granuloma inguinale (three cases) in embryonic yolk. *J Exp Med*, 81:25–40.
With Katherine Anderson and W. A. DeMonbreun. Immunologic relationships of Donovania granulomatis to granuloma inguinale. *J Exp Med*, 81:41–50.
With Katherine Anderson and W. A. DeMonbreun. An experimental investigation of the etiology and immunology of granuloma inguinale. *Am J Syphilis*, 29:165–73.

1946
Research and medical practice. *Science*, 104:473–76.

1948
The internal environment for infectious agents. *Ann Intern Med*, 29:991–1002.
With G. John Buddingh. Chick-embryo technics. In *Viral and Rickettsial Infections of Man*, edited by Thomas M. Rivers. J. B. Lippincott Co., Philadelphia, 97–113

1949
In memoriam, Cobb Pilcher (October 7, 1904–September 22, 1949). Nashville, Tennessee, Vanderbilt University.

1950
Some aspects of twentieth century research on infectious diseases. *Wash Univ Med Alumni Quart*, 13:96–106.
The influence of William Henry Welch upon the development of pathology. *Bull Johns Hopkins Hosp*, 87:3–11.

1952
With Stewart H. Auerbach and Oscar Mims. Pulmonary fibrosis secondary to pneumonia. *Am J Pathol*, 28:69–87.
Francis Gilman Blake (1887–1952). *Year Book of the American Philosophical Society*, 302–7.

1955
Max Brodel and the role of the medical illustrator in modern medical education. *J Assoc Med Illustrators,* 7:39–43.

1957
The pathology of viral neoplasia. *Tex Rep Biol Med*, 15:451–61.

1959
Cytoplasmic inclusions resembling Guarnieri bodies, and other phenomena induced by mutants of the virus of fowlpox. *Am J Pathol*, 35:213–31.

1960
The influence of Leo Loeb upon pathology in America. Read at the Leo Loeb Memorial Service, Washington University, St. Louis, Missouri, January 24.
Leo Loeb, 1869–1959. *Trans Assoc Am Physicians*, 73:19–23.

1961
Leo Loeb. September 21, 1869–December 28, 1959. *National Academy of Sciences, Biographical Memoirs*, 35:205–51.

1962
With Katherine Anderson. Isolation of a wild avian pox virus inducing both cytoplasmic and nuclear inclusions. *Am J Pathol*, 40:437–53.

FACULTY MEETING NOTES

JULY 21, 1948

This meeting was called to acquaint you with the present condition of the Medical School. Medical Schools in this country are going through a trying period, with maintenance of the high standards of medical education achieved during the past twenty-five years hanging in the balance; Vanderbilt Medical School is no exception.

Following a war period of several years in which an accelerated program of teaching, together with a depleted and disorganized faculty, disrupted continuity of development, we are experiencing now a post-war period of readjustment. The prevailing scarcity of professional and other personnel and inflationary conditions not only make more acute the movement of teachers and investigators among universities, but accentuate greatly the economic disadvantage an educational institution must bear in competition with governmental and industrial organizations, as well as the lures of a private professional career.

The shortage of professional personnel which results in greater competition between the Medical Schools cannot be remedied until a sufficient number of qualified persons are trained for teaching and research. On the other hand the competition for present and future professional and technical personnel between faculties of Medical Schools, government institutions, industry and private practice has an economic basis, and can only be remedied by increased financial resources of the schools.

In addition to these problems, which are difficult enough, Medical Schools must provide patients for clinical teaching. There are a number of ways in which this is done but the most expensive way, and perhaps the best way at least for a private school, is by ownership of its teaching hospital. Economically this is a hazardous enterprise. Vanderbilt University Medical School is one of the few private schools that own and operate a hospital for teaching purposes. It is my judgment that the distinguished place Vanderbilt Medical School has attained is due to the ownership of its teaching hospital which permitted concentration and unification of its educational program under one roof thus creating an integrity of objective and resources.

In order to accomplish this integration of its energies and thereby to achieve an intimate collaboration of its faculty and facilities it has been necessary to spend relatively great sums under the plan by which we have operated, for the purchase, so to speak, of clinical teaching material by means of subsidy of ward patients. In the years 1946–1947, and 1947–1948, this amounted according to my estimates to about $350,000.00 annually, more than two-thirds of which came from endowment and reserves.

It is evident that this situation could not continue under present conditions.

With this general background I should like to acquaint you somewhat more in detail with the financial situation as it has developed and now exists.

The Medical School and its Hospital have at present an endowment of approximately $14,000,000.00. This endowment has been yielding recently something less than 4 percent. In 1947–1948 endowment income amounted to approximately $512,000.00 which was divided almost equally between the budgets of the Medical School ($268,847.42) and the Hospital ($243,583.33).

As things go this is a sizeable endowment which places Vanderbilt Medical School in a more favorable financial situation than most schools of its size. However it is equally evident that it is not enough under present conditions to meet the needs of the school and of its hospital as operated in the past.

For the sake of simplification perhaps, I would like to discuss first and briefly the financial situation of the Medical School, then in a cursory and overall fashion the finances of its hospital.

Medical School

Vanderbilt Medical School did not reach its present physical stature until 1938 when the new wing which houses the Departments of Pediatrics, Obstetrics and Gynecology, Preventive Medicine and Public Health as well as private wards was opened.

This expansion of the facilities and consequent increase of the faculty of the Medical School are clearly indicated in the curve of annual budgets.

The period of greatest intellectual activity as manifested by accomplishments in research and in training I believe occurred in the decennium 1930–1940 during which a special grant of $250,000.00, to be spent by the Faculty over a ten-year period, was made available by the Rockefeller Foundation. This gave us funds over and above budgetary allowances, purely for research purposes.

Since the addition of the new wing in 1938 the annual budget of the Medical School has been rising—steadily at first, lately at alarming speed. For the year 1926–1927 it stood at $284,420.00. In 1936 it was $368,754.60. Last year (1947–1948) it was $576,205.00, a rise of over 100 percent.

How has this great expenditure, unaccompanied by equivalent increase in endowment, come about? And how has it affected departmental budgets?

Analysis of Budgetary Graphs

It is thus seen that the great increase in expenditure from budgets of the Medical School has come about in the following ways:

1. Expansion of facilities and staffs for the departments of Pediatrics, Obstetrics and Gynecology, and Preventive Medicine and Public Health.
2. The assumption by the Medical School of the budgets of the Department of Radiology, and the Clinical Laboratories of Chemistry and of Bacteriology and Serology.
3. The creation of departments of Anaesthesiology and Psychiatry.

4. Greatly increased operational expense, 1926–1927—$61,750, 1947–1948—$101, 812.79.

This leaves the budgets of most departments less than or approximately equal to those obtaining during the twelve year period 1927 through 1939 just preceding the war. Since 1939 however inflation has reduced the value of the budgetary dollar to almost half. It is hardly to be expected that the volume of high quality work carried on by these departments can continue with a budgetary cut of virtually 50 percent. Let us turn to the hospital.

Hospital

Receiving approximately half the total income from endowment, how has Vanderbilt Hospital fared? In 1928–1929 the Hospital budget totaled $403,072.00. In 1947–1948 the budget was $1,085,049.55.

This enormous increase in hospital expense has been due to:

1. Opening of the additional wing in 1938.
2. Increasing operational cost as a result of inflation—(Nurses and food).
3. Increased census.

Practically all of the increase in hospital expense has occurred since 1938 during which period there has been no significant increase in endowments.

It is to be recalled that the Medical School and its Hospital share approximately equally in the endowment income. During good years before the war there accumulated a considerable reserve fund.

In recent years, in order to meet inflationary conditions, it has been necessary for both the Medical School and the Hospital to supplement their income by inroads on these accumulated reserves.

Last year (1947–1948) fortunately the Hospital came out of the red and balanced its budget with a little left over, I hope. The Medical School however withdrew from the common reserve store the sum of $141,862.92.

The Medical School budget that has been adopted for 1948–1949 provides a withdrawal from reserves of $170,667.90 despite an increase of tuition from $500.00 to $600.00 per year.

This large withdrawal from reserves will not, I regret to say, improve materially the budgets of the departments, although it will completely exhaust the reserve funds.

Consequently as of June 30, 1949, the Medical School will face the problem of devising a budget under inflationary conditions, I hope no worse than they are today, without recourse to reserve funds, which during the current year provide $170,000.00 of a $600,000.00 budget. The financial problem of the Medical School after June 30, 1949 can be stated very concretely, namely the need of a minimum of $170,000.00 to provide a budget equal to that under which it is operating today. If costs should increase, if endowment income should diminish, or if we should be able to improve the departmental budgets, a total sum of $250,000.00 or more would be required.

At the present time no source for such funds is in evidence, but efforts are being made to provide them.

Medical School and Hospital

Inevitably this financial situation of the Medical School and Hospital is having its effect upon medical education at Vanderbilt and especially in the following ways:

1. The preclinical departments and some clinical departments are laboring under the disadvantage of the same budgets but shrunken to 50 percent less in purchasing

power than those during the twelve or fifteen year pre-war period, with the certainty of needing an unforeseeable resource of from $170,000 to $200,000 to operate during the year 1948–1949 at the same financial level as of today.

2. The Hospital notwithstanding endowment support cannot be sure of balancing its budget without increasing its charges to ward patients.

These situations necessitated careful review, and a revision of the relationship of Vanderbilt Hospital as a teaching resource of Vanderbilt Medical School which I hope may be of a temporary nature.

During the year 1946–1947 and the year just concluded, according to my estimate, Vanderbilt Hospital spent a sum of approximately $350,000.00 annually for the purpose of subsidizing patients for teaching purposes. That is to say: the actual cost of caring for patients was $350,000.00 more than they paid. Of this amount approximately $250,000.00 was provided by endowment. The purpose of this huge expenditure was, in bald terms, the purchase of patients for teaching purposes. From the standpoint of income from endowment approximately the same amount of money was spent to procure patients for clinical teaching as was expended for the entire budget of the Medical School.

Notwithstanding this huge expenditure it was evident that the hospital could not be sure of balancing its budget if it continued to utilize all its available resources for subsidizing ward patients.

Furthermore it became evident that the Medical School must exert every effort to provide additional funds for its budget, heretofore supplemented by reserves which will be exhausted as of June 30, 1949.

No increase of endowment or annual gifts that would yield the necessary two hundred to two hundred and fifty thousand dollars are yet in sight. No arrangements have materialized thus far whereby the cost of medically indigent patients could be provided by governmental or other sources. Consequently the only potential resource existing appeared to be the release of endowment income, previously and presently allocated to operation of the hospital, for use by the entire Medical School.

This might be accomplished it was thought at least in part, if the ceiling of medical indigency were raised so that income from ward patients would increase. Although the results were unpredictable, it appeared to be reasonable, and in fact imperative to increase the charges for ward patients. On May 1 of this year the policy was adopted and put in to effect of charging every ward patient the flat rate of $8.50 per day. It was further determined that Ward 8400 should be converted to a private ward in order to increase its earning power.

It was only on the basis of these changes that an acceptable budget for the hospital for the current year was prepared.

With a little thought it is obvious that this emergency situation and the means used to meet it temporarily place the Medical School in an as yet unresolved dilemma.

In the first place there is no complete assurance that, even with the imposition of increased charges for ward patients plus the usual allocation of endowment income, the hospital will on June 30, 1949 be able to turn back to the Medical School a sufficient surplus to support its budgets adequately in the absence of available reserves next year. I will say more about this a little later.

The uncertainty that sufficient patients for our teaching purposes would be able to pay the established charges has caused the Medical School to prepare to meet such a contingency by a revision of its curriculum in such a manner as to be able to utilize the facilities in Medicine and Surgery at Thayer Veterans Hospital for clinical teaching and, in addition to the facilities at Vanderbilt Hospital, to utilize certain available opportunities at

Nashville General Hospital particularly for the departments of Pediatrics and Obstetrics and Gynecology.

Thus it would appear that our dilemma consists in operating a University Teaching Hospital as a quasi-private hospital supported by endowment income, while at the same time we are proceeding to dissipate our faculty and students by removing them from their primary base, in order to utilize the clinical facilities of other hospitals to carry out our teaching responsibilities. Would it be simpler and better under these circumstances to close the ward of Vanderbilt Hospital, release endowment income, and only operate that portion of the hospital whose private beds would pay for themselves and furnish accommodation for the patients of our Staff who assist in teaching?

To do this or to follow as a permanent arrangement the plan outlined for teaching next year would in my opinion destroy the one great source of strength that has made Vanderbilt Medical School an eminent institution namely an integrated and concentrated interest and effort under a single roof where intimate associations and mutual concerns of the entire faculty, preclinical and clinical, are devoted to the problems of medical education research, and medical care. This is our *forte* and we must not lose it. With laboratories, library, common dining room, continuous consultations and common attack upon problems we can still maintain our prestige. With that situation at the heart of our school and hospital we could then cooperate with other hospitals and institutions to advantage.

Is it possible to solve our problems and the critical uncertainties they produce by our own means and effort in such a way as to reintegrate our Hospital and Medical School so that the needed funds would be provided for the budgets of the latter and an adequate supply of patients would be available for our clinical teaching in our own hospital? I believe this difficult achievement can be realized but it would require the unremitting effort of the entire faculty, especially the clinical staffs, and it might require the subsidy of medically indigent patients from sources other than those now available to us.

How might this be brought about? My primary object in calling this meeting was to acquaint you with the present condition of the Medical School and its Hospital, but I feel it would be a neglect of my responsibility if I did not at the same time give you my judgment as to a possible solution—ideal perhaps but reasonably practicable.

Vanderbilt Medical School needs at the present time an addition to its budget of approximately $250,000.00 to supply funds now and formerly afforded by reserves. Our teaching hospital needs patients for the instruction of our students and a balanced budget.

In view of this situation I have obtained a statement from the hospital administration as to the possibility of Vanderbilt Hospital operating in such a way as to release to the Medical School the endowment income the hospital now receives, and to provide in its wards the patients needed for teaching, and last but not least to balance its budget. Here are the figures: (see attached sheets).

Potential Income of Vanderbilt Hospital

There is the possibility of accomplishing what we drastically need to place our Medical School in a sound position to teach our students, to take advantage of grants-in-aid of research, and to extend our influence for good in this community and in this region. Can it be done? It can be done if our occupancy rate is kept high and if ward patients can pay the now established charge or secure support from other sources. Those "ifs" are large but not insurmountable if we work hard together and receive the reasonable support that we need.

When private and low-cost private beds are lying idle in Vanderbilt Hospital we cannot subscribe to the need of additional such beds in Nashville. We should take every justifiable measure to fill them. When there are medically indigent patients in this community who need but do not have hospital care we can see no sense in beds on the wards of Vanderbilt Hospital lying idle because of lack of community support.

To me this objective as briefly outlined makes sense and it can be achieved. Achievement will depend upon the earnest, loyal and diligent support of the faculty, upon wise and efficient management of the hospital, upon the united and concentrated effort of us all.

This plan which I believe is attainable is not the only solution. Reorientation of our hospital operating plan in the direction of a unified clinic is a possibility for example. Perhaps a better solution might be found through provision of local or national governmental aid. Before these more extreme and perhaps unlikely eventualities are forced upon us, we would, I am sure, do well to work diligently in the direction I have indicated, that is, to build up our hospital census until receipts will release endowment income. In this undertaking we would welcome outside aid from local government or other sources.

Appendix C

CORRESPONDENCE WITH
CHANCELLOR BRANSCOMB

January 7, 1949

Chancellor Harvie Branscomb
Vanderbilt University
Nashville 4, Tennessee

Dear Chancellor Branscomb:

For the past three and one-half years I have been studying the problem of Vanderbilt Medical School endeavoring to interpret its position in relation to the changing local and national attitudes toward medical education and health services. In the meantime economic conditions have so altered our situation that our financial stability has become untenable. An earlier decision on my part has not been possible because of the difficulty I have had in analyzing and evaluating a problem so inherently complex. Nevertheless I have constantly been aware of the necessity to arrive at a conclusion as to policy and program for the future at the earliest possible moment, for it is evident that nothing constructive can result from a course of fragmentary and impromptu, even though seemingly expedient, adjustments along a blind alley.

An overall view of the situation has finally led me to a judgment of a course of action which I believe to be sound, constructive, practicable and in keeping with the ideals which have made Vanderbilt Medical School preeminent in its field of academic endeavor. The conclusion I have reached represents my considered and best judgment. To its accomplishment I would be happy to make any contribution in my power. I realize, however, that a temporizing policy in the midst of the present welter of conflicting views and change might seem to the University Administration to be wiser and more expedient.

The plan I wish to present involves a radical departure from the paths of the past in practice only. In principle it adheres firmly to those ideals that have guided us so successfully since the reorganization of the medical school in 1925. Because it would bring us to a parting of the ways with a long tradition it is the more important that my reasons for

424

recommending such a change be presented as clearly as possible, though briefly at this time.

The program I have in mind involves discontinuance at the earliest possible date, commensurate with our commitments, of the undergraduate curriculum of the Medical School, and creating in its stead a school or institute in which all our present facilities and resources, together with additional ones that should be added to them by means of a vigorous campaign over an indeterminate period, would be devoted to medical research and education at a graduate and postgraduate level.

The present reorganized Vanderbilt Medical School came into existence toward the end of a pioneering period in medical education. Rapid development of scientific knowledge applicable to medicine in the first quarter of the present century was founded upon an immediately preceding quarter century of scientific discovery resulting from a comprehension and an acceptance of the principles of the scientific experimental method and their application to biological problems as brilliantly exemplified by the work of such leaders as Louis Pasteur, Robert Koch, and Claude Bernard. The phenomenally rapid accumulation of useful medical knowledge that followed in the succeeding half century captivated the imagination of leaders in medical education and directed the philanthropy of American wealth toward an integration of this new science into our American educational institutions. The basic principles upon which this renaissance in American medical education was founded was the essential inseparability of research and education. No teacher of medicine could henceforth divorce himself from research and remain in the advancing forefront of medical progress. In order to train and to seed the necessary teacher-investigators into our then inchoate system of medical education it was necessary to create new Medical Schools and to renovate old ones that they might be implemented with sufficient money and facilities to accommodate the new science and prepare its leaders. This was done first at Johns Hopkins, then at other universities and among the last at Vanderbilt. The wisdom of this revolutionary undertaking has been abundantly vindicated by experience of the past twenty-five years in the rapid advance of medical knowledge through research and the application of that knowledge to the prevention and cure of disease. Research and training, it has been found, must go hand in hand—the one to advance knowledge, the other to apply it. Neither can stand alone nor should one disproportionately surpass the other in level of attainment.

It is in the nature of science that its techniques become more complicated, varied and abstruse as it progresses. It is an obvious corollary that training in application must likewise become more intricate and specialized in order to supply the professional competence to administer new knowledge.

General education always lags behind the forefront of knowledge and to maintain the advancing frontier especial facilities and abilities must be provided. Consequently twenty-five years ago it was necessary to concentrate great wealth and effort upon undergraduate medical education to supply competence for medical practice at a higher level and to discover talent for training in advanced methods of research. In the meantime the general public was becoming conscious of the effect this system as having on its life and fortunes, and this public has at last determined that it will have in full measure the fruit of discoveries and the services of the profession trained to administer them. There is, however, the inevitable lag between the forefront of research and training, upon which all such hopes finally rest, and the accomplishment of desire for service at the current level, which lay and inexpert knowledge cannot perceive or evaluate. We, therefore, witness at the present time a great avalanche of funds for research along particular lines that have a public appeal, coupled with an inordinate and unprecedented demand for services, with what seems to be a complete absence of comprehension, even on the part of potent influences, of the underlying essential element of adequate support for the structure from which both research and application must depend; namely, our institutions of higher learning. This foundation which was laid less than a half century ago and upon which all hope of sustaining our position in health and welfare must now and always rest is rapidly crumbling under our eyes and if not reinforced very soon will be unable to support longer the super-structure which ill-advisedly is being heaped upon its weakening pillars.

In the rapid reorientation of emphasis upon service at current levels, educational and research potentials are becoming dissipated and weakened except perhaps in a few temporarily fortunate institutions. Because the public wants medical service it will have it, and we can see the handwriting distinctly on the wall. The American Medical Association is decorating and idealizing the general practitioner as a service arm; the United States Public Health and Armed Services are shouting for more physicians, and not necessarily better trained physicians; the social-minded are crying for rural ministra-tions; bills before Congress give precedence, in plans for Federal aid, to numbers of graduates rather than quality, and so it goes while our universities and their schools of medicine sweat in poverty in the midst of plenty and stand as targets of public disapproval because of their failure to deliver.

In the midst of this demand for service even at a low level of competency in this country at the present time Vanderbilt Medical School finds itself bankrupt financially and without a constructive program to fulfill its great mission. Locally it has been denied governmental support for its current teaching program, while it suffers the indignity of professional criti-cism on the disgusting level of economic competition and personal aggrandizement. Its faculty is being drained into the services of an antiquated City hospital and a temporary Federal hospital, while control of teaching resources is firmly held in the hands of politi-cians and practitioners with the dire implications of a settlement on the basis of unilaterally beneficial appeasement and degrading compromise. Its attenuated and dissipated staffs are being called upon by other local and regional hospitals to furnish the services of a rapidly depleting faculty and defensive agencies of government are restricting its liberty to choose freely and effectively its student body. In the meantime economic necessity has already removed from its use in large part its chief clinical asset—the Vanderbilt Hospital which through financial necessity is now converted into a private service institution of little teaching and research value. Lack of money and a constructive program leave the school understaffed, many of its teaching personnel ill-paid, departments temporarily organized and administered or carried on in skeleton form only. In spite of this disorganizing process no real headway is being made in the solution of an overall financial problem nor in an effective determination of its position in terms of fundamental principles. It is the element of tragedy in the latter circumstance that of course concerns me most; but there would be no regret in failure that refuses to compromise principle.

From the midst of this imbroglio we must extricate ourselves immediately in policy if not in material success. The purpose, policy and program of Vanderbilt Medical School for the past quarter century has been to foster research and medical education at the highest level. As we move into a new and changing period this philosophy must continue to prevail. The dubious path of appeasement and temporary expedient will neither fulfill our avowed ideals nor will it give us the needed inspiration to carry forward our mission of leadership which cannot succeed without freedom of imagination and courage to pursue our destiny along uncharted paths.

I have no apprehension or fears for the adequate accomplishment of undergraduate medical education in this country with the many excellent State and private schools and their organizations to preserve standards at the level attained during the past twenty-five years, in which accomplishment our School has so effectively participated. Existing undergraduate schools will be enlarged and others will be built. Public demand and governmental support will effectively see to this. My concern is with opportunities that might then remain, especially in the Southern Region, for a continuation at a higher level of the combination of research and education that inevitably must provide unusual talent for creative work and leadership if we are to go forward rather than sink to the low level of service distribution for which the demand is so compelling today. There is no middle road, we either go forward or backward.

There is consequently no justification in my mind for a Vanderbilt Medical School whose objective is only the graduation of its complement of physicians to serve the health requirements. There is and always will be need and a great need for advancement of knowledge and superior training. Our modern civilization, not its medical aspects alone, must be supported by the best minds of the Nation trained in the most advanced technical boundaries of science if we are to go forward intellectually.

Therefore, the program which I envisage would lead the school out of the current morass onto the higher ground of creative research and the most advanced technical medical training. Such a move could not fail of inspirational values but its success must depend upon the assessment of practical considerations. I believe there would be no dissent from the philosophy inherent in the program, and I am personally convinced that the university possesses the resources to accomplish its aims and could acquire abundant additional means because of the inspirational appeal the program would have to the highest type of academic persons and to philanthropy, as well as the practical advantages inherent in any program of medical service of a superior order.

An abandonment of undergraduate medical education would be required to effect this program with the application of all resources to the maintenance of research and specialized medical training. Scientific departments would be continued with modifications as seemed most useful to the attainment of our objectives. To these departments graduate and postgraduate students would be invited. Master and Doctor of Philosophy degrees would be conferred, and a closer relationship with the science departments of the College would be developed. Vanderbilt Hospital would be converted into an institution for postgraduate training in the several advanced specialties of medicine and surgery. The primary emphasis even in the clinical fields would be upon research and the particular specialties admitted would depend upon the availability of competent staffs. Under the circumstances I have no doubt that available beds could be filled with patients supported personally or through agencies. An immediate attempt would be made however to acquire a large endowment or current funds to help finance patients unable to pay for such special and expensive service. In general, the members of the professional staffs would collect fees for service and thus finance themselves under conditions of such a superior environment. A specialty hospital of this sort would fulfill a great need in the local medical community and would attract patients from far and wide, referred and direct. It would thus serve as an ultimate resort for those cases requiring highly specialized techniques and competency.

It is by no means out of the picture that the facilities of other local hospitals could be effectively used for the purposes of postgraduate courses for general practitioners who desire to keep abreast with developments. The wards of Nashville General Hospital and its staff could serve admirably in such a scheme and the school could continue its relationship with Thayer Veterans Hospital where already we cooperate in its program of postgraduate training.

On the research side both the scientific and clinical departments would be in the most advantageous position to make use of the number of resources that now exist for grants-in-aid. Government aid could as now be accepted for this purpose without the dread and apprehension that overshadow government subsidy of education. Problems of current interest and financial support could be recognized and exploited, such as heart disease, cancer, nutrition, tuberculosis and the like.

This program so briefly outlined would immediately upon its accomplishment relieve the school of present difficulties on the economic level; it would enliven and uplift its waning enthusiasm and spirit and it would afford direction to a confused and foreboding complexity that lays such a heavy burden upon it. Controlling reins would be kept in university hands.

So far as I personally am concerned I give this program my blessing and respectfully present it to you for your consideration.

Sincerely,
[signed] Dean Ernest W. Goodpasture

EWG: LC

January 22, 1949

Chancellor Harvie Branscomb
Vanderbilt University
Nashville 4, Tennessee

Dear Chancellor Branscomb:

In response to your request for a more detailed exposition of the general plan for the Medical School which I proposed to you recently, I wish to submit the following statements.

As you well understand it would be a very considerable undertaking to change from one type of Medical School to another with all the inertia that necessarily weighs upon a traditional routine of performance, and I do not wish to underestimate the difficulties. There would be great reluctance I am sure to a discontinuance of the four-year under-graduate curriculum and a sincere difference of judgment as to the need and wisdom of such a move. My own interest is in the preservation and improvement of medical research and advanced training at Vanderbilt. If this could be done and at the same time the four-year undergraduate course be continued, for example at Nashville General Hospital, I of course would not be opposed, although the latter would I am convinced be at a lower level. The hope of a better arrangement sometime in the future might seem sufficient justification for a temporary retreat. Nevertheless when it comes to a choice between maintaining undergraduate medical education at a lower level, and the elevation of research and advanced training at a higher level, I must always enlist on the side of the latter. It seems likely to me that we may now be confronted with that choice.

In final analysis decisions under these circumstances are determined by one's own philosophy as to the basic functions of a University. To my mind a University should consist primarily of an environment congenial to scholars for the purpose of creative scholarship and teaching. In science that means opportunity for basic research irrespective of immediate application and in medicine it means the investigation of problems of health and disease.

Scholars must have disciples, for these constitute the life of the environment. But there must be scholarly disciples, not merely trainees for a vocation or profession. Selected graduate and postgraduate students therefore would seem to me to be excellent and adequate human resources for teaching and training.

In keeping with this philosophy not only would the medical sciences be maintained and fostered but provision was made, in the plan I proposed, for the continuance of Vanderbilt Hospital, but at a high level of performance.

The question you raise, which of necessity is in the minds also of the clinical group, is twofold. From your standpoint there is the practical problem of operating the hospital as compared with present conditions, and from theirs is the question of how the plan would affect each member individually. Details regarding the latter, you will understand, involve personal relationships which can hardly be surveyed completely until it is decided to give serious consideration to the practicability of the plan. I have therefore not undertaken to explore this involved area extensively as yet.

As to the broader aspects of the proposal you and members of the Executive Faculty were justified in your assumption that I had given thought to means of operating the Hospital to better advantage than is now being done.

In the first place under my plan Vanderbilt Hospital would again become an integral part of the school with its assets and facilities integrated into a program of research and specialized training. To contrast this type of operation with that required for undergraduate education it will be necessary to refer to our past experience and to point out again how a fruitful period came to an enforced termination under present financial conditions.

When the Medical School was reorganized a compromise, perhaps an unwise one, was effected in order to integrate the school more closely with the university. The purpose was unquestionably sound, because Medicine had already become dependent upon scientific research. But to teach medicine it was necessary to have patients and in order to provide patients for a medical school such as was designed, it seemed advisable for the University to buy them, in realistic terms. Undoubtedly the designers of the School foresaw the weakness in this arrangement and anticipated future difficulties such as we are now experiencing. But there were obstacles in the way and as a result a direct solution on a financial basis was decided upon. This involved the appropriation of sufficient endowment to provide income for the purchase of patients at the then prevailing price. However, in anticipation of future difficulties a deliberate attempt was made to induce the community to build a hospital adjacent to the Medical School in which tax-supported indigent patients would become available for teaching purposes. As an inducement, I am informed, it was proposed that the University undertake to secure as much as a million dollars and to provide the land for the proposed hospital building. Furthermore the Medical School would agree to furnish the professional service needed for the best care of the community's medically indigent citizens. Unfortunately this plan failed for the same reasons I believe that the Branscomb Plan failed. These reasons were chiefly two—the one political, the other professional. Politically it was preferable to have Vanderbilt University foot the bill for indigent patients so long and to such an extent as it would consent to do so. Professionally it was desirable to utilize a tax-supported hospital for private patients and to keep a determining hand upon medical affairs by controlling essential teaching material.

In order to obtain sufficient patients in variety and quantity for teaching undergraduate students it has now become necessary to abandon Vanderbilt Hospital as a basic source and to send both faculty and students to other hospitals. It became advisable to abandon Vanderbilt Hospital in anticipation of its possible collapse financially because the school can no longer afford the expense of purchased patients.

It is important at this point to explain what is needed of a hospital as an asset to the training of undergraduate medical students. In the first place these students need variety and quantity—variety to exemplify current diseases and practices and quantity to secure and to accommodate the needs of the number of students which we undertake to teach. Not only are quantity and variety needed but the patients used for teaching purposes must be under direction of the Faculty of the School in order that the Faculty can determine not only the professional program of diagnosis and treatment, but likewise the availability of these patients for teaching purposes, such as for example their length of sojourn in the hospital, their home environment and their future schedule of reexaminations to observe progress and results. There must therefore be available to students both an outpatient general clinic as well as accommodations for inpatients.

Naturally one might ask why a hospital full of private patients, who are paying their own way, would not serve the purposes of the undergraduate teaching. The answer hinges upon the following considerations; namely, professional control by the Faculty and adequate variety. The only way by which a hospital for private patients could satisfy the first of these requirements would be by means of a "clinic" type of operation. Otherwise the patients would be the responsibility of individual physicians and consequently of limited availability for teaching purposes, for there would be no control by the faculty of diagnosis, treatment, length of stay in the hospital or follow-up observations. Furthermore it would be necessary to operate two types of clinic, the one for outpatients, the other for inpatients. In the case of patients who are being subsidized the outpatient clinic operates as a "feeder" for the inpatient clinic. This is not necessarily the case with private patients. From the standpoint of variety, which is an especially important problem for a small teaching hospital such as ours, it would not be possible in a hospital for private patients to exercise judgment in selecting cases suitable for teaching purposes as can be done so effectively if the patients are paid for by the University. Even though the Faculty operated a clinic free selection would not be practicable.

Whenever insurance coverage becomes sufficiently broad to include the clientele of a small teaching hospital, variety will become limited because of lack of selection; length of hospitalization will become out of control and teaching value will in consequence become reduced.

These limiting factors are of especial concern to Vanderbilt Medical School because it is almost unique as a private school in the ownership of its hospital without the availability of an immediately adjacent cooperating hospital under public auspices.

It is difficult for those who are particularly interested in undergraduate medical education to understand insistence upon the maintenance of Vanderbilt Hospital as the basic teaching unit of our school. Why, they inquire, cannot the students go to the patients in other hospitals such as the Nashville General Hospital and the Veterans Hospital? If one were concerned only with supplying the public with fifty additional graduates per year there would indeed be no good reason. If however it is deemed important to bring these students into an atmosphere of scientific approach to their clinical problems, and to maintain a full-time faculty of teachers who are likewise investigators capable of and engaged in the advancement of knowledge in their respective fields, it would hardly be sensible to separate either from their laboratories, from their library and from association with the preclinical and other university science departments which are engaged in creative investigations. So far as the preclinical staffs are concerned it would do them great harm likewise to part company with clinical problems and contacts. The environment for research by the clinical faculty would be lost under these circumstances as it largely is now, and when we come to seek Heads for our departments, as we must do in the not too distant future, there would be little appeal to the investigative, scholarly type of person, which as a university we cannot do without.

If we admit that the sole purpose of Vanderbilt Hospital is to facilitate medical education and research, and I take it that this is admissible for it is hardly conceivable that it could be operated as a hospital for financial gain as a resource of University income, let us examine what we are doing with it today in terms of the desired objectives. As you well know all means in use or under consideration are designed primarily to balance its budget and release income from endowment. It is obvious that the Hospital is not serving satisfactorily for teaching purposes because our students are going to Thayer and to the Nashville General Hospital for a large part of their training. It is not operated to the advantage of research, because with few exceptions clinical investigation is at a low ebb. The clinical faculty oscillates between Vanderbilt and Thayer, between Thayer and Nashville General, between the last and their offices and so on back and forth again. Many of them in addition are up to the hilt in private practice.

What prospect is there, should we accomplish our objective of balancing the budget, that the hospital would then meet the needs of undergraduate medical education? In my judgment there is none whatever. What we are doing is transforming the Hospital into a private service institution. In order to do this we are making its fine facilities more and more available for the patients of private practitioners and nothing else. Toward this end we have abolished the best teaching ward, namely, 8400 for negroes, and created in its stead a ward for private patients. We have made available for low cost private patients the two and four bed rooms on our previously subsidized wards, and we have of necessity raised the rates on the open wards so high as to price ourselves out of the market. So much in the name of economic necessity.

Suppose our plan of balancing the budget succeeds, what would be the result from the standpoint of teaching and research? The result would be that the School would have lost all the essential requirements that we have been able to procure in the past by purchase; namely, professional control of patients as to variety, length of stay in the hospital, diagnosis, treatment and follow-up. Clinical teaching and research would have gone by the board under our own roof.

What would be necessary to restore the Hospital to its previous status? The answer to this is simple under existing conditions. It would require the annual expenditure of about $350,000.00 more than we now have, or the income of approximately $10,000,000.00 additional endowment, for the Medical School departmental and operational budgets now need all available present income. The best approximation to a restoration of its previous status would be to fill its wards, including 8400 and the two and four bed rooms adjoining open wards, with patients supported by local government. Under this circumstance we would probably only lose a certain freedom of selection, and some freedom of operation. The next best approximation would be the filling of these beds with patients who are able to pay only their hospital bills. We would lose thereby freedom of selection, control of hospital stay and to a certain extent follow-up observations.

None of the above three methods of renewing the status of Vanderbilt Hospital, or approximating it, for undergraduate teaching and for research, seems to me at all likely under present conditions.

I think this general background is important to a more detailed consideration of the proposal I made to you in brief outline previously. It will be necessary to contrast with it the objectives I had in mind with reference to a reorientation of the Medical School and Hospital toward graduate and postgraduate education and toward research.

Postgraduate students in the first place would not require the variety of patients so important for undergraduates. On the contrary they would in the various specialties be concerned primarily with patients in restricted categories. These could be either private or subsidized for they would not be indiscriminate run-of-the-mill group of patients we have required and dealt with in the past. They would be special patients, highly selected because of the particular competence and facilities of the service to which they were admitted. The Head of each of these services would be a specialist in his restricted field and patients would come to him directly or be referred because of that fact. Each specialty therefore could be expanded or contracted according to needs and available facilities. The staff of each specialty would be concerned only with the problems involved within a well-defined area, both in teaching and research. A great deal of liability therefore would be possible in the operation of the Hospital from an economic standpoint. To be more specific it would be stipulated that the Hospital must operate at cost. We cannot make this demand now and preserve or rather reconstitute adequate teaching conditions for undergraduate students.

You are concerned practically with the operational plan I have in mind whereby the Hospital could become self-sustaining and at the same time serve the academic purposes desired and outlined, and I shall try to be as specific as possible.

It would be my effort to disturb the present clinical faculty as little as possible, because an evolutionary process would better serve our ends, I think, than a revolutionary one. Besides we have the professional ability now available to inaugurate the reorientation I propose. I will confine myself therefore first to a consideration of hospital operation and then discuss the academic aspects.

Let us take as an example the Department of Psychiatry, our latest addition for which we are receiving support from the Federal Government. Only a few beds are now available to this Department, but owing to a lack of facilities for mental disease in this area I am sure the number could be doubled, or perhaps tripled and filled with patients able to pay at least their hospital costs. Psychiatry has a public appeal, and although we have received relatively small support for the undertaking up to the present, very little effort has been directed to raising funds. Authorities of the State of Tennessee have for some time been considering the advisability of building a small psychiatric hospital possibly in association with Vanderbilt Medical School. Perhaps some arrangement could be worked out whereby the hospital could lease say fifty beds to the state for patients who would be under the professional supervision of the department. At least an enlargement of our own facilities and staff would be an inducement to the building of such a hospital in our vicinity. The Veterans Administration furthermore can under contract send their service connected cases to a nongovernmental hospital.

Another case in point would be that of a specialty we have long needed but could not develop largely because by providing beds for it we would reduce our resources for undergraduate teaching or deprive our staff of teachers of needed beds. I refer to ophthalmology. So important a specialty is this that large endowments from philanthropic sources have been devoted to it, such as for example that founding the Wilmer Opthalmological Institute at Johns Hopkins. It would surprise me greatly if a ward of perhaps twenty-five or thirty beds could not be filled with paying patients from this specialty alone under suitable direction. Doctor Carroll Smith was anxious to undertake this not long ago and perhaps would do so now. He would be competent to head a successful department.

Among our own surgical group we have a number of outstanding specialists whose potentialities might justify expansion of their available hospital facilities, notably, neurosurgery under Doctor Cobb Pilcher, chest surgery under Doctor Rollin Daniel, and there are others. In the Department of Medicine there are likewise competent individuals who could develop their specialties with a little encouragement. I think of Doctor William Darby and Doctor Edgar Jones in nutrition. Already they have available funds to support patients in hospital beds, and I believe they could get more support from certain industrial companies like Merck and Company and Massengill which are now greatly interested in their work. A beginning is being made in the specialty Endocrinology under the direction of Doctor Morgan. Doctor Albert Weinstein could possibly expand this field to use more hospital beds, especially for metabolic studies and Doctor Beverly Towery is already organizing a special laboratory for investigations in this area.

It has long been my view that a scientific and continuous attack on the problem of tuberculosis in this state should be undertaken by Vanderbilt Medical School. We have the nucleus for such a project in the persons of the medical specialist Doctor Hollis Johnson, the surgical specialist Doctor Rollin Daniel and the bacteriological specialists Doctors Roy Avery and Edgar Woody. The last two investigators have recently announced their experimental work which indicates the beneficial effects in treatment of a combination of streptomycin and potassium iodide. In the Department of Pharmacology is a distinguished chemist, Doctor Bush, who is working on certain antibiotics that repress the tubercle bacillus.

In view of the interest of these investigators and specialists it would be highly desirable to provide a group of beds in the hospital for the study and management of pulmonary tuberculosis. The State of Tennessee is currently planning to erect in this area a hospital for tuberculous patients at great expense. Possibly Vanderbilt Hospital could lease a ward for this purpose. If not the possibility could be explored of making a contract with the Veterans Administration. The Hoover Committee has already advised greater use by Veterans Administration of existing nongovernmental hospitals.

The Department of Medicine might explore likewise the establishment of a ward for the study and treatment of cardiovascular disease, a specialty so prominent in the public eye today and to which vast sums will be contributed. Perhaps one phase of this field, as for example hypertension, could be explored to advantage.

We should put our Department of Obstetrics on a better footing and make gynecology a specialty under its own leadership. These two specialties could, I believe, easily be expanded with encouragement and more substantial and permanent professional direction.

The Department of Pediatrics is already reaching out and receiving aid for its program and for hospitalization of certain patients. Prematurity, rehabilitation, and physiotherapy for poliomyelitis are all possible sources for a larger use of bed capacity.

This cursory review of potential expansion in the use of bed-capacity through the development of specialties is not of course complete. There are other areas we have not begun to develop. Dermatology, for example, is one of the most neglected specialties for the standpoint of research and teaching in this country. It could well use some hospital beds. Radiobiology and active isotope therapy is as yet scarcely touched. Orthopedics, urology, otolaryngology, plastic surgery are others to be mentioned. However, I believe I have stated enough to indicate the direction of my thought, so far as the relation of specialties to hospital facilities are concerned. We can disregard, at least for the present, the Outpatient Department, because this could be abandoned, I believe, under the plan I am considering. I should like now to proceed with a discussion of a reorganization of the Medical School to adjust it to the proposed program of teaching and research.

Recruitment of house officers under the plan I would have to explore with the clinical group and the director of the hospital.

Reorganization of the Medical School

At the present time the only major change in existing preclinical departments would be abandonment of the Department of Preventive Medicine and Public Health, and the transfer of biostatistics to another department. At later dates other departments might be added or discontinued depending upon persons rather than upon fixed curricular divisions. There could be a wholesome flexibility in the respect which undergraduate education has not thus far readily permitted. Certain important readjustments could be made in respect to bacteriology and immunology which I shall mention later. Each medical science department could receive graduate and postgraduate students. The latter would be largely medical graduates who desired special experience of a particular subject matter. I cannot predict how many students a department might recruit, but I know that wherever good research is going on there are always inquiring minds seeking such an environment. Now when so many fellowships are available, most of them carrying stipends for laboratory aid, and others on a larger scale being proposed, it seems reasonable that a department so disposed could admit sufficient students to satisfy its wishes and requirements. All of these students majoring in a department would engage in research, and would be in contact with all investigations in other departments. Tuition could be charged.

A real effort under these circumstances could be made to effect a closer relationship with the scientific and other departments of the university in order that the impact of the Medical School might be brought to bear upon them and vice versa. On the other hand closer ties and dependencies could be established with staff and students of the clinical departments. I shall point out how this might be done.

Creation of Division Laboratories

We have experienced great need in the past for research laboratories offering facilities and direction for clinical investigations. Little isolated laboratories to meet especial needs are now widely scattered throughout the school. As examples are the Asheim-Zondek laboratory in Obstetrics and Gynecology, the Rh laboratory in Pediatrics, the E.K.G. laboratory in Medicine, the E.E.G. laboratory in Anatomy. These are small but they indicate available special services.

We need very badly for research, teaching and clinical practice several large laboratories well equipped with men and material for the conduct of significant research. The best example I have in mind would be such a laboratory for Nutrition. Owing to the unique and productive development of this field under Doctor Darby a Division of Nutrition, intermediate between departments and extending labilely and usefully through many channels transcending departmental barriers, was established. To serve similar functions in special areas we should have well supported division laboratories with chiefs and staffs for

1. Nutrition under the direction of Doctor Darby.
2. Parasitism and Immunity.
3. Endocrinology and Metabolism.
4. Cellular Growth and Cancer.
5. Cardiovascular physiology.
6. Radiobiology.

I could elaborate <u>in extenso</u> on the need and value of each of these areas of clinical research, and would be glad to do so at an appropriate time. At present I will only state that their establishment would do more to recruit able young men to vitalize research and teaching in this school than anything I can imagine. Their influence under proper direction would extend throughout the medical community and the university as a whole. Furthermore each represents an area of interest that should be able to acquire considerable financial aid from already existing sources, and appropriate clinical specialties would be available to cooperate with them.

Clinical Departments

Clinical departments as they now exist should under the plan be broken up into individual specialties headed by a chief of each service. At least this should be done whenever there is a competent leader available. Thus neurosurgery, thoracic surgery, gynecology, orthopedics, and so forth, would become separate units. Each specialty service would be required to fill an allotted though variable number of beds. That would be one of the conditions of continuation. Office space would be rented to staff members as available and they would be allowed to collect fees perhaps with a percentage return for departmental use. All patients would be available for teaching.

According to these arrangements one would expect that the hospital would become self-sustaining and that teaching and research would be carried on in each specialty as conditions permitted.

Medical School Budgets

It is assumed that all income from endowment of the school ($14,000,000.00) would be expendable upon teaching, research and overhead operation. Income from endowment is now approximately $560,000.00 per annum.

Preclinical departments

The average budget of these departments is at present $27,000.00. This should be raised to $30,000.00, totaling $150,000.00.

Divisional Laboratories as proposed (6)

To establish these research laboratories at total of about $100,000.00.

Clinical departments

It would be my plan to make each specialty service as nearly independent as a unit and as self-supporting as possible. The staff would be allocated enough beds to support all their patients; they would collect fees for services, and would pay office rent. Laboratory space and research facilities would be provided by the school. I believe $100,000.00 would be sufficient to accomplish this. The Department of Pediatrics would need the greatest subsidy and should receive about $35,000.00 for the present, leaving $65,000.00 or more to be divided as needed among the specialties. Certain present commitments to faculty members would have to be honored of course. If possible some fellowships might be created.

Receipts from endowment and expenditures could be roughly estimated as follows:

Receipts	$560,000.00
Expenses: Preclinical departments	150,000.00
Divisional Laboratories	100,000.00
Clinical Specialties	100,000.00
Overhead	170,000.00
Unallocated (possibly in part for Fellowships)	40,000.00
Total	$560,000.00

This does not take into account any overhead charges payable from grants-in-aid which could amount I believe to $10,000 to $15,000. Nor does it reckon income from tuition nor laboratory stipends from fellowships.

The budget outlined above does not take into account certain items now listed in the Medical School accounts that properly belong to hospital expense; namely, those for radiology, anesthesiology, and the clinical laboratories for bacteriology, serology and chemistry.

These laboratories and services would contribute only to hospital patients and they are self-supporting in that respect.

While these figures are tentative and represent rather rough estimates, they indicate to me the practicability of operating a school for Advanced Medical Training and Research at a high level of performance within the financial resources that might be at our disposal.

Undergraduate Medical Curriculum

At the present rate of tuition medical students pay annually $120,000 in addition to income from endowment. This might be increased as some schools now charge $800. There might be a 25 percent increase by teaching four quarters annually.

If the first two years were taught in the preclinical departments as is now done and the last two years at Nashville General Hospital as has been proposed and at the same time the pattern for research and advanced training at Vanderbilt Hospital were undisturbed perhaps we could continue to operate the undergraduate courses in the hope that better times would come. It would be a serious mistake to do this however if research and advanced training were hampered thereby. A separate clinical faculty might be organized to carry the responsibility for teaching students of the third and fourth years, making use as they desired and were able the assistance of Vanderbilt Hospital staff. Some students would no doubt elect to work at times in the research laboratories.

The plan for Vanderbilt Hospital could I believe be worked out along these lines in such a way as to become self-sustaining. If so the undergraduate curriculum might be possible.

Sincerely,
[Dean Ernest W. Goodpasture]

EWG:LC

Appendix D

PATHOLOGY COURSE DESCRIPTION

Of interest and value to the students is the assignment to groups of two, of each autopsy performed during their course of instruction. The students abstract the clinical history, make a gross description of the autopsy, fix and imbed tissue, and make their own histological preparations from which they write a microscopic description. The case is reviewed by a member of the staff and finally presented before the entire class, including a demonstration of gross specimens, and the projection on the screen of microscopic slides.

At each laboratory period the class is met by an instructor and the work for the day is briefly reviewed. In the laboratory the instructors are present to assist the students and to acquaint themselves with the work each is doing. The laboratory work follows with a study of gross specimens and the corresponding microscopic sections. Frequent laboratory periods are devoted exclusively to the study of gross specimens. The students may handle and dissect, if necessary, these preparations and there is such a rotation that each student has an opportunity to study a great number of specimens. Frequent tests, both written and practical, are given during the course. Sufficient lectures are added to orient the students and to connect their work more systematically. The public health aspects of the diseases under consideration are emphasized as much as possible.

Bacteriology is taught concurrently with pathology during the first trimester of the academic year. In this way an intimate connection is established between the bacteriology and pathology of infectious diseases.

Autopsies take precedence over all other work and when they are held during the teaching hours are attended by the class. In order that students may witness and assist at autopsies performed out of hours, certain groups are kept on call and are notified of each examination.

The laboratory classroom is a long [one hundred feet], well-lighted hall facing the north and provided with desks and cabinets for fifty students. Each student provides his own microscope.

The lecture-room is separate and is equipped with projection apparatus both for lantern slides and microscopic sections.

NOTES

Preface

1. *American Heritage Dictionary*, Third Edition, 1992.
2. Mark Twain's *Autobiography*, Vol. 1, 1924.
3. For the status of notebooks and other archived materials, see the correspondence between Esmond Long and Katherine Goodpasture in 1962. Dr. Long was writing Dr. Goodpasture's memoir for the National Academy of Sciences, and had written Katherine on August 9, 1962, as a member of a committee to assemble records of noteworthy research at the Registry of the Armed Forces Institute of Pathology. Specifically, Dr. Long requested: "In Ernest's case, we thought we would like to have whatever is available in the way of original hand-written manuscripts, notebooks, photographs, gross specimens, microscopic slides, small apparatus and equipment, and comparable material from Ernest's investigations in the early years at Vanderbilt on the method of growth of the herpes and other viruses. Can you tell us if a significant amount of this material is still in existence, and if the projected Registry could have it?" Katherine responded on November 27: "I would say there is a minimum of items you mention though I am sure a representative number could be assembled. I know many old blocks of tissue and old slides have [been] junked. There are no gross specimens. I think there are only a few handwritten manuscripts and notebooks and I am still using a number of the original small apparatuses." See Collins papers, VUMC Archives, Box 1, Katherine Goodpasture file.

Chapter One

1. Collins papers, VUMC Archives, Box 1, Goodpasture speeches—The Spirit of Inquiry and Vanderbilt Commencement, 1943.
2. See Appendix A for EWG, *Science*, 104:473–476, 1946.
3. *Transactions of the Association of American Physicians*, 48:45–48, 1944 and see Kober acceptance speech by EWG, Collins papers, VUMC Archives, Box 1, Awards file.
4. Collins papers, VUMC Archives, Box 1, Esmond Long's *Memoirs*.
5. Collins papers, VUMC Archives, letters from alumni; Also see Craighead, *Pathology and pathogenesis of human viral disease*. Academic Press, 2000, frontispiece.
6. van Helvoort, *ASM News*, 62:142–145, 1996.
7. *Virology*, edited by Fields, 1996, 4.
8. Important business might be transmitted when personal relationships were strengthened by rustic ambiance. For example, Lake Ahmic in Ontario was a favorite summering spot for fishing enthusiasts Abraham Flexner of Rockefeller's General Education Board and Chancellor Kirkland of Vanderbilt University.
9. EWG papers, VUMC Archives, Box 11, General correspondence.
10. Leathers papers, VUMC Archives, Department of Pathology Reports, 1940.
11. Youmans papers, VUMC Archives, Department of Pathology Reports, 1955.
12. Galbraith, *The Great Crash 1929*, 168.
13. Ibid.
14. Klingaman, *1929 The Year of the Great Crash*, 338.
15. Ibid., 337.
16. A privately funded research laboratory affiliated with Allegheny General Hospital in Pittsburgh. For more details see chapter 4 and Collins papers, VUMC Archives, Box 1, Singer Research Institute.
17. Richard T. Johnson, "The pathogenesis of herpes virus encephalitis," *J Exp Med*, 119:353–354, 1964.
18. Peter Wildy, "Herpes virus," in: *Portraits of Viruses*, edited by Fenner and Gibbs, Karger Publishers, 1988. See 239 for Wildy citation.
19. Johnson, *J Exp Med*, 119:353–354, 1964.
20. EWG papers, Eskind Library, Special Collections: Louise Davis, "America's Pasteur," *Nashville Tennessean Magazine* Oct. 16, 1955, Collins papers, VUMC Archives, Box 1, EWG acceptance speech of Research Medal, Southern Medical Society, 1937 in chapter 9.
21. Personal communication to author, 1955.
22. Rivers, *Filterable Viruses*, 1928. See EWG "Virus Diseases of Fowls . . ." 237.
23. Levine, "Origins of Virology," Fields *Virology*, *Long History of American Pathology*, 315; Dalldorf, *Introduction to Virology*, 7.
24. See Appendix A for EWG and Buddingh, *Am J Hygiene*, 21:319–360, 1935.
25. Plotkin, "Short History of Vaccination," in *Vaccines* Saunders, 3rd ed., 1999 and *History of Immunization*, Parish E&S Livingstone, 1965.
26. Parish, *History of Immunization*, 1965.
27. Theiler & Smith, *J Exp Med* 65:787, 1937.
28. See Appendix A for EWG, "A study of rabies," in *Am J Pathol*, 1:547–582, 1925 for detailed description of rabies inclusions and EWG, "Cellular inclusions and etiology of virus disease," *Arch Path*, 7:114–132, 1929 for descriptions of inclusions.
29. See Appendix A for Woodruff and EWG, *Am J Pathol*, 5:1, 1929.
30. See Appendix A for EWG and Woodruff, *Am J Pathol*, 6:699–711, 1930.

31. See Appendix A for EWG, *Am Jour Hygiene*, 17:154–167, 1933.

32. Ibid.

33. van Helvoort, *ASM News*, 62:140–145, see 145 for Lwoff citation.

34. K. Anderson, *Science*, 90:497, 1939.

35. See Appendix A for EWG, *Am J Pathol*, 35:213, 1959.

36. A. S. Evans, *Yale Journal Biology and Medicine*, 49:175–195, 1976.

37. R. J. Huebner, *Ann NY Acad Sci*, 67:430–445, 1957.

38. T. Rivers, *Jour of Bact*, 33:1–12, 1937 and R. J. Huebner, *Ann NY Acad Sci*, 67:430–445, 1957.

39. A single passage involved emulsifying affected salivary glands and inoculation of this emulsion into another monkey.

40. EWG file, Eskind Library, Special Collections "America's Pasteur," by Louise Davis, *Tennessean*.

41. Collins papers, VUMC Archives, Box 1, Student Questionnaire.

42. Collins papers, VUMC Archives, Box 1, Hopkins recruitment.

43. VUMC Archives, Leathers papers, Dept of Pathology Annual Report, 1943.

44. EWG papers, VUMC Archives, Box 11, Blalock correspondence, 1941.

45. Collins papers, VUMC Archives, Box 1, Harvard recruitment.

46. The festivities included a dinner at the club of Watson Sellards at Dover on the upper Charles River. Dr. Thomas Weller described a "formal dinner for his friend, Dr. Ernest Goodpasture who was lecturing at Harvard, the guest list consisted of Dean Burwell, five professorial heads of departments, and three medical students. See Harvey, *Bull J Hopkins Hospital* 144:45–55, 1979.

47. EWG file, Eskind Library, Special Collections. See: *Time Magazine* May 27, 1946; Louise Davis, *Tennessean*, 1973; Tinsley Harrison letter to Kampmeier, May 6, 1976; Dawson to Goodpasture, August 26, 1951. Louise Davis in the 1973 article quotes Sir MacFarlane Burnet without specific attribution as saying Dr. Goodpasture should have had the Nobel Prize he received in 1960 instead of him. However, there are no confirmations of that opinion in the Nashville papers describing Burnet's prize in 1960, or in Burnet's autobiography *Changing Patterns*. It is also suggested by Greer Williams in *Virus Hunters*, pages 268–269 that Enders felt his prize should have gone to Dr. Goodpasture.

48. EWG papers, VUMC Archives, Box 11, Warren correspondence, Dec. 26, EWG, Dec. 31.

49. Greer Williams, *The Plague Killers*, Scribner's, 1969.

50. Feldman in *The Nobel Prize*, 246, states "Max Theiler . . . contributed little new in that he used methods by then decades old."

51. Feldman, *The Nobel Prize*, 241, 246.

52. *Science*, 291:567–568, 2001.

53. *Science*, 290:1284–1286, 2000. The other junior collaborator was Rita Levi-Montalcini. In support of the position taken by the Nobel Committee, Cohen and Levi-Montalcini were also selected for Lasker awards.

54. Collins papers, VUMC Archives, Box 1, chapter 1 file: Correspondence about awards, July 11, 2000.

55. EWG papers, VUMC Archives, Box 11, Warren correspondence to EWG, Dec. 1952.

56. Collins papers, VUMC Archives, Box 1, Memoirs.

57. M. Burnet, *Perspectives in Biology and Medicine*, 16:333–347, 1973.

58. *Trans of the Assoc of Am Physicians*, 48:45–48, 1944 and Collins papers, VUMC Archives, Box 1, Awards file.

59. Craighead, *Pathology and pathogenesis of human viral disease*, 2000, frontispiece.

Chapter Two

1. Collins papers, VUMC Archives, Box 1, Memoirs, "Resolution to Executive Faculty" by John Shapiro, 1960.

2. Watson Sellards was a close friend who had trained at Hopkins, collaborated with Dr. Goodpasture in the Philippines, and was a frequent correspondent. Sellards is not shown as a faculty member in a brochure from the University of the Philippines brought home by EWG. See Collins papers, VUMC Archives, Box 1, Philippines file. EWG is listed as associate professor of pathology. There is a description of the university and the curriculum for medical studies, showing extensive responsibilities for Dr. Goodpasture.

3. Vanderbilt held its first classes in 1875.

4. BOT minutes, 1907.

5. A literary movement founded at Vanderbilt.

6. Registrar's office, Vanderbilt University. Grade book 1902–1908, 21.

7. Collins papers, VUMC Archives, Box 1, VU undergraduate.

8. *Hustler*, Oct. 18, 1906. The student involved, R. S. Henry, became a distinguished historian, and was commissioned to write a history of the Armed Forces Institute of Pathology. He was an expert on railroads, about which he wrote several books. He was also on the Vanderbilt Board of Trust.

9. *Vanderbilt Alumnus*, January–February 1945.

10. Conkin, *Gone with the Ivy*, 180–182.

11. Kirkland papers, Heard Library Archives, Box 100, File 21.

12. Batts, *Private Preparatory Schools*, 10, 37, 1957.

13. Ibid.

14. EWG papers, VUMC Archives, Box 11, Branscomb correspondence, May 12, 1955.

15. Collins papers, VUMC Archives, Box 1, Memoirs, etc. Katherine Anderson Goodpasture to John Youmans in Feb. 1961.

16. Dixon, *Rise and Fall of Alderson*, 1967.

17. Esmond Long, "Ernest William Goodpasture 1886–1960: A Biographical Memoir" in *Biographical Memoirs*, 38:11–144, 1965.

18. Dixon's *Rise and Fall of Alderson*, 1967. Allegheny Collegiate Institute's principal in 1905 was Professor H. A. Scomp, former vice-chancellor of the American Temperance University in Harriman, Tennessee, and a Greek scholar "of wide repute," perhaps known by the literary cronies in Goodpasture's bookstore.

2

However, his reputation was not of sufficient width to merit a place in John Trotwood Moore's *Biography of Distinguished Tennesseans.*

19. Collins papers, VUMC Archives, Box 1, Hopkins file.

20. Corner, *Biography of Whipple,* 23.

21. Collins papers, VUMC Archives, Box 1, Hopkins file.

22. Ibid.

23. EWG papers, VUMC Archives, Box 11, EWG correspondence with Chesney, October 9, 1956.

24. Chesney, *Johns Hopkins Hospital and Medical School,* Volume III. Photographs and list of faculty between pages 72–73.

25. Osler returned to the states a total of five times; this was the only visit while Ernest was a student and occurred when the latter was at Lake Saranac for suspected tuberculosis—see below. Osler also returned in April 1913 when Dr. Goodpasture was a pathology house officer.

26. Broedel's famous "Welch Rabbit" sketch was the featured place setting—Dr. Goodpasture's papers included two copies. One bears Broedel's signature and inscription and was sent at Blalock's request in 1941; the other hung in Dr. Goodpasture's office.

27. Bliss, *Biography of Osler,* 386.

28. Chesney, Vol. III, 83–84.

29. EWG papers and photos, Eskind Library, Special Collections. Dr. Goodpasture in 1949 wrote his Hopkins classmate Lewis Weed: "Your being at Saranac Lake recalls my own experience there now many years ago and I still remember with much gratitude your many kindnesses to me while I was in Johns Hopkins Hospital and after my return to Baltimore. It was a pretty drastic experience at the time. . . . The worst part of it was the two or three weeks I spent in the Village before being admitted to Trudeau under Lawrason Brown."

30. Chesney, Vol. III, 171–172.

31. Collins papers, VUMC Archives, Box 1, Hopkins file, copied from Chesney, Vol. III.

32. Ibid.

33. Collins papers, VUMC Archives, Box 1, Hopkins file.

34. Collins papers, VUMC Archives, Box 1, EWG speeches. In 1954, in a talk about the pioneering illustrator at Hopkins, Max Broedel, Dr. Goodpasture reminisced: "In the medical school session of 1908–09 Max held a class in medical drawing in the anatomy building. I don't remember its title, but it was a wonderfully inspiring experience to be a member of that class. . . . I learned the texture of stipple board and how to shade a cerebral convolution with a rolled chamois and to scratch in a highlight with an etching tool. But, more important, I learned from Max Broedel the value of careful, detailed and meticulous observation."

35. Corner, 52 and ff.

36. Ibid., 52.

37. *Who Was Who,* Marquis Company.

38. Corner, 54.

39. Corner, 66–67. In 1921, Dr Whipple accepted the deanship of Rochester Medical Center and the professorship of pathology, and remained at Rochester for the rest of his career.

40. Bashford in particular had recognized that senescence was associated with cancer in humans and other animals. Imperial Cancer Research Fund, 1904 and 1905.

41. See Appendix A for for: EWG and Wislocki, 1916.

42. Collins papers, VUMC Archives, Box 1, Hopkins file. The date of this letter indicates family often spent their summers on the farm. A V Sr did not officially change residence to Montgomery County until 1914.

43. There is a brief description of Dr. Councilman's training and interests in Esmond Long's *History of American Pathology,* pages 153 and 154.

44. Winternitz published a far more extensive and elaborate book (Winternitz 1920) on influenza in which there are a number of color illustrations; this book was based on 1100 cases admitted to Yale Medical Center, 280 of which were fatal. Eighty-two autopsies were performed. Winternitz does not cite the study of Dr. Goodpasture, nor did he clearly recognize the probability of an underlying viral infection, or produce useful hypotheses.

45. EWG papers, Eskind Library, personal correspondence, unaccessioned. Copy of letter in Collins papers, VUMC Archives, chapter 2 file.

46. We do not know the total number autopsied at Chelsea during this period. Thirty cases are described in detail in the *U.S. Naval Bulletin* 13:177–197, 1919 article by Dr. Goodpasture, but all of these had bacterial superinfections. The total number with influenza he autopsied was probably seventy-five to one hundred.

47. See Appendix A for EWG, *Am J Med Sci,* 1919.

48. Stanton and Tange, *Aust Ann Med,* 7:132, 1958.

49. Burnet, *Perspectives in Biology and Medicine,* 16:333–347, 1973.

50. Personal communication to the author in 1960.

51. Robert Colvin, Professor of Pathology, Massachusetts General Hospital, personal communication to the author in 2000.

52. A contemporary discussion of a case of Goodpasture's syndrome in a *New England Journal of Medicine* case discussion contained more disturbing misinformation. One of the discussants claimed Dr. Goodpasture was "moonlighting" from Harvard when he did the autopsies at Chelsea. A letter to the editor from Robert Collins with pictures of Dr. Goodpasture in his naval uniform, his c.v., and Dr. Goodpasture's disclaiming priority in describing pulmonary-renal syndromes was rejected for publication by the journal. For case discussion in question, see *NEJM* 329:2019–2026, 1993.

53. See Appendix A for EWG, *Philippine Jour Science,* 22:413–421.

54. See Appendix A for EWG, *Philippine Jour Science,* 22:439–445.

55. Harvey, *Bull J H Hosp,* 144:45–56, 1979. Also contains reference to Sellard's postulate about toxin in cholera.

56. Collins papers, VUMC Archives, Box 1, chapter 2 file.

57. See Collins papers, VUMC Archives, Philippine file for letters of appointment, passport details. On

April 5, Dr. Goodpasture was given permission to shorten his appointment from July 26 to June 30. EWG had U.S. passport 47989, issued June 6, 1921, on which the two Sarahs were shown.

58. Collins papers, VUMC Archives, Box 1, Philippine file.

59. This picture may be seen in chapter 3.

Chapter Three

1. EWG Virus diseases of fowls . . . in Rivers's *Filterable Viruses*, 1928.

2. Fields, *Origins of Virology*, 1999.

3. Sanders, "Cultivation of virus," *Archives of Pathology*, 28:541–586, 1939.

4. Burnet, *Med Res Council*, 220, 1936.

5. van Rooyen and Rhodes, *Virus Disease*, 1948.

6. Burnet, *Perspectives in Biology and Medicine*, 16:333–347, 1973.

7. Literature searches of publications by software PubMed.

8. Thomas Francis Jr., Ernest William Goodpasture (1886–1960), see Collins papers, VUMC Archives, Box 1, Memoirs.

9. See Appendix A for EWG, *Southern Medical Journal*, 26:1–7, 1933.

10. His subsequent publication: "Some uses of the chick embryo for the study of infection and immunity" is in *Am J of Hyg*, 28:111–129, 1938.

11. This was another landmark study, for which Rous later received a Nobel Prize; it was actually much later, as his prize was not awarded until 1966.

12. See *Am J of Hyg*, 28:111–129, 1938.

13. EWG papers, VUMC Archives, Box 11, Correspondence with Blalock, 1955.

14. See J. D. Ratcliff's *Lifesaver*. *This week* magazine reproduced in *Vanderbilt Alumnus*, March 1945.

15. Dr. Stevenson wrote in 1937 to congratulate him on developing the embryonated egg technique. Dr. Goodpasture responded: "I recall very distinctly the interest which I had in your early experiments with the chick embryo in Baltimore. We have had a lot of fun with the method and have succeeded in making it useful in the solution of several problems, and I believe that it has wide application in the study of infection and immunity." See Collins papers, VUMC Archives, Box 1, chapter 3 citations. Dr. Goodpasture cited Dr. Stevenson's work in his 1938 *Am J of Hyg*, volume 28 publication on use of the chick embryo.

16. For Woodruff correspondence with EWG, see Collins papers, VUMC Archives, Box 1, chapter 3 file—Chick embryo.

17. See Appendix A for EWG, *Annals Internal Medicine*, 13:1–11, 1939.

18. J. B. Murphy, *Jour Experimental Medicine*, 19:181, 1914.

19. See Appendix A for EWG & Anderson, *Amer J Path*, 18.563, 1942.

20. See Appendix A for EWG, *Science*, 95:391, 1942.

21. See Appendix A for EWG, Douglas and Anderson, *Jour Experimental Medicine*, 68:891–904, 1938.

22. See Appendix A for EWG and Anderson, *Amer J Path*, 18:563–575, 1942.

23. See Appendix A for EWG and Woodruff, *Amer J Path*, 7:209, 1931.

24. See Appendix A for EWG et al., *Science*, 74:371, 1931.

25. See Appendix A for EWG et al., *Amer J Path*, 8:271, 1932.

26. Elementary bodies in vaccinia Guarnieri bodies had been described first by Paschen but the relationship between vaccinia inclusions and elementary bodies was first established by the chick embryo studies.

27. See Appendix A for EWG and Anderson, *Amer J Path*, 20:447, 1944.

28. See Appendix A for EWG and Buddingh, *Am J of Hyg*, 21:319–360, 1935.

29. Glycerin was used at this time as a storage medium for viruses. Now cultures containing virus are frozen for storage and maintenance of stock cultures.

30. See Appendix A for EWG and Buddingh, *Am J of Hyg*, 21:319–360, 1935.

31. See EWG papers, VUMC Archives, Box 3, File 3 for 1937 correspondence with Dr. John Lentz about vaccination of children in Davidson County.

32. See EWG and Buddingh, *Am J of Hyg*, 21:319–360, 1935.

33. See EWG papers, VUMC Archives, Box 2, File 10 for correspondence with the Eli Lilly Company. On September 17, 1935, the president, Mr. Eli Lilly, wrote: "It would be inexcusable if we did not send you our sincere thanks and appreciation for the cooperation which you and your people have given us in connection with the commercial development of your smallpox vaccine produced in the chorio-allantoic membrane of the chick embryo. It has been on the market now for about sixty days and many reports of its successful use are coming in." Dr. W. A. Jamieson, director of Lilly's Biological Division, stated on May 18, 1939, that English workers had "had very good success" with the method.

34. See Appendix A for EWG and Gallavan, *Amer J Path*, 13:927, 1937.

35. Now called Bordetella pertussis after the first researcher to isolate and grow the bacillus in 1906, Jules Bordet.

36. See Appendix A for EWG "Cell-parasite relationship" in *Transactions and Studies of College of Physicians of Philadelphia*, 9:11–24, 1941.

37. See Appendix A for Anderson, DeMonbreun and Goodpasture, 1945.

38. Kharsony et al., *Clinical Infectious Disease*, 22:391, 1996.

39. See Appendix A for Anderson et al., *J Exp Med*, 81:41–50, 1945.

40. In the Ricketts Lecture, May 9, 1955, at the University of Chicago, in the Stoneburner Lectures March 21–22, 1956, at the Medical College of Virginia, and at a Seminar in the Department of Microbiology, May 4, 1956, at Yale University School of Medicine.

41. See Appendix A for EWG, *Amer J Path*, 35:213–231, 1959.

42. See Buddingh, *J Exp Med,* 67:921–932, 1938.

43. See Appendix A for EWG, *Amer J Path,* 35:213–231, 1959.

44. EWG-Stoneburner Lecture II. For the text of these lectures, see Collins papers, VUMC Archives, Box 1, Speeches.

45. See *Genetics,* 28:491–511, 1943. Delbruck and Luria subsequently shared a Nobel Prize for their extensive investigations that basically inaugurated the field of molecular biology by showing how genetic information determined the structure and function of an organism.

46. EWG Stoneburner Lectures. For text see Collins papers, VUMC Archives, Box 1, Speeches.

47. Burnet, *Virus as Organism,* Harvard University Press, Cambridge, 14, 1946

48. Avery et al., *J Exp Med,* 79:137–158, 1944.

49. See Appendix A for EWG, *NEJM,* 222:903–910, 1940.

50. See Appendix A for Polk, Buddingh, and EWG, *Am J Pathol,* 14:71–85, 1938.

51. See Appendix A for EWG and Anderson, *Arch Path,* 30:212, 1940.

52. See Appendix A for EWG, *Am J Pathol,* 1:547, 1925.

53. See EWG, "Virus disease of fowls" in Rivers *Filterable Viruses,* 1928, 235–270.

54. For Dr. Goodpasture's Harvey Lecture, see Collins papers, VUMC Archives, Box 1, Speeches file.

55. See Appendix A for EWG and Woodruff, *Am J Pathol,* 5:1–9, 1929.

56. This observation, probably fortuitous, enabled subsequent studies of the bodies contained in fowlpox inclusions. The force of surface tension presumably ruptured the drying inclusions.

57. Borrel was a French bacteriologist (1867–1936) who described elementary bodies in fowlpox in 1904 by microscopic examination of smears from squashed inclusions. Buddingh and Goodpasture estimated that individual inclusions contained 5–20,000 Borrel bodies.

58. See Appendix A for Teague & EWG, *JAMA,* 81:377, 1923. In the Annual Report of Singer Research Institute dated July 11, 1923, Dr. Goodpasture stated that they had been working since "last fall" on herpes.

59. Louise Davis, *Tennessean Magazine,* October 16, 1955.

60. See Appendix A for EWG, *Am J Med Science,* 158:863, 1919.

61. See Appendix A for EWG and Talbot, *JAMA,* 21:415, 1921.

62. The author reviewed Index Medicus and Teague reprints, University of Alabama Medical School Archives. Although Teague had not published on viral diseases, he had spent the summer of 1922 studying viruses in various laboratories in Europe, as noted by Dr. Goodpasture in his speech at Singer Laboratory Celebration in 1952.

63. See Appendix A for EWG and Teague, *JAMA,* 81:377–378, 1923.

64. See Appendix A for EWG and Teague, *J Med Research,* 44:139–184, 1923.

65. See Fenner et al., *A History of Virology,* Karger Publisher, 1988.

66. See Appendix A for Johnson and EWG, *Am J Hyg,* 21:46, 1935.

67. See Appendix A for Johnson and EWG, *J Exp Med,* 59:1, 1934. Peyton Rous, editor of the *Journal of Experimental Medicine* wrote upon receiving the manuscript: "What splendid work! You must be very happy. To say that we are glad to publish this is to say very little." See Collins papers, VUMC Archives, Box 1, chapter 3 file.

68. See Appendix A for Johnson and EWG, *Am J Hyg,* 21:46, 1935.

69. Louise Davis, *Tennessean Magazine,* October 16, 1955.

70. In 1933, Dr. Burt Wolbach of Boston wrote Dr. Goodpasture to affirm that he was sending slides from testicular biopsies in two cases of mumps. See Collins papers, VUMC Archives, Box 1, chapter 3 file, Wolbach to EWG, June 6, 1933.

71. See Appendix A for Johnson and EWG, *J Exp Med,* 59:1–19, 1934.

72. See Baum and Litman, *Mumps Virus,* 1496 in Douglas Mandell, and Bennett's *Principles and Practice of Infectious Diseases,* Fourth Edition. Churchill Livingstone, 1995.

73. See Appendix A for Johnson and EWG, *Am J Hyg,* 21:46, 1935.

74. See Appendix A for Johnson and EWG, *J Exp Med,* 59:1, 1934.

75. See Appendix A for Johnson and EWG, *Am J Pathol,* 12:495, 1936.

76. Ibid.

77. These experiments are reviewed in Craighead, *Pathology and Pathogenesis of Human Viral Disease,* 381. The observation is correctly made that such experiments could not be done today.

78. See Appendix A for Johnson and EWG, *Am J Hyg,* 23:329, 1936.

79. See Appendix A for Johnson and EWG, *Am J Hyg,* 23:329, 1936 and letter from Dr. Levant of Pasteur Institute dated November 29, 1935, in Collins papers, VUMC Archives, Box 1, chapter 3 file. It is a comment (and criticism) to note that in one of the confirmations (Habel, *Pub Health Rep* 60:201, 1945) Stensen's duct of monkeys was inoculated with infected saliva as described by Johnson and Goodpasture, but their paper was not cited. To add insult to injury, this same author then reported growing the mumps virus in embryonated eggs, again without acknowledging Dr Goodpasture's work in developing that technique.

80. See Appendix A for EWG, *Ann Int Med,* 13:1, 1939.

81. See Habel, *Pub Health Rep,* 60:201, 1945.

Chapter Four

1. In 1945 the official title for the academic director of a department was *Head.* In about 1965, the title was changed to *Chairman.*

2. Collins papers, VUMC Archives, Box 1, Singer file, Haythorn history, 1917.

3. Ibid.

4. Dr. Felton subsequently had a distinguished career: a 1916 graduate of Johns Hopkins Medical School, he was at the Rockefeller Institute from 1920 to

3

1922, at Harvard from 1922 to 1935, and in the United States Public Health Service from 1938 to 1949.

5. Long's "History of Harvard" in *Am Soc Exp Path*, 1972, 79.

6. Collins papers, VUMC Archives, Box 1, Singer file, Board minutes, Feb. 14, 1921.

7. Collins papers, VUMC Archives, Box 1, Singer file.

8. Collins papers, VUMC Archives, Box 1, Singer file. Dr. Goodpasture visited the Singer Laboratory early in 1921 before leaving for Manila around July 1, 1921. See Dr. Goodpasture's speech at the Singer Celebration in 1952.

9. Collins papers, VUMC Archives, Box 1, Singer file, Board minutes, November 6, 1922.

10. See Board minutes for each date in this paragraph in Collins papers, VUMC Archives, Box 1, Singer file, Board minutes.

11. Collins papers, VUMC Archives, Box 1, Speeches (1952).

12. Esmond Long's *Biographical Memoir* notes on page 116 that Oscar Teague "had left a position in bacteriology at the College of Physicians and Surgeons of Columbia University for a summer of study in Europe in 1922, and had returned to the United States full of ideas on promising research. Teague, who had had abundant experience in tropical medicine, and who, while at Columbia, had begun studies of herpes and other virus diseases, joined the Singer staff shortly after his return from Europe. . . . Goodpasture and Teague promptly confirmed the reports of the Vienna pathologist Benjamin Lipschutz on intranuclear inclusion bodies in the epithelial cells of rabbits in experimental herpetic keratitis (inflammation of the cornea). . . .

13. Vanderbilt's campus was initially divided into a south site near Nashville General Hospital and the main campus on the western side of Nashville.

14. Chancellor Kirkland was an avid fisherman and had a summer cottage at Lake Ahmic, in Ontario; he made it possible for Flexner to purchase a cottage from Vanderbilt's Professor of Old Testament Literature, Dr. J. H. Stevenson. The Flexners used their camp for forty years, and Chancellor Kirkland chose to spend the last days of his life there, attended by Dr. Hugh Morgan.

15. Kirkland papers, Heard Library Archives, letter to Leathers dated March 15, 1937.

16. Eskind Library, Special Collections, VUMC catalogs.

17. See Canby Robinson's *Adventures in Medical Education*, 1957, page 153; the original source in Kirkland–Flexner papers in Heard Library Archives gives an expanded version.

18. Conkin, 272.

19. Canby Robinson's *Methods and Problems of Medical Education*, 13th series, Rockefeller Foundation, N.Y., 1929. This volume is in Special Collections, Eskind Library, and contains a detailed discussion of the reorganized Vanderbilt Medical School.

20. Conkin, 270–272.

21. See Robinson papers, VUMC Archives and Collins papers, VUMC Archives, Box 1, chapter 4 file.

22. Conkin, 272.

23. Ibid., 273.

24. Mims, 357.

25. Robinson, *Adventures in Medical Education*, 157.

26. Ibid.

27. Conkin, 272.

28. Robinson, *Adventures in Medical Education*, 158.

29. Conkin, 278.

30. Robinson, *Adventures in Medical Education*, 187.

31. Ibid.

32. VUMC Archives, Executive Faculty Minutes, November 8, 1928.

33. Ibid.

34. Robinson papers, VUMC Archives, 1928 correspondence.

35. J. B. Youmans, *J Tenn Med Assn*, 59:39–51, 1966.

36. Spirit of Inquiry, *Vanderbilt Alumnus*, 1944; Ivy Day address, Tulane, 1957, in Collins papers, VUMC Archives, Box 1, Speeches.

37. Robinson papers, VUMC Archives, correspondence with Leathers, 1930.

38. EWG papers, VUMC Archives, Box 11, Robinson correspondence.

39. EWG papers, VUMC Archives, Box 11, letter from Burwell, 1938.

40. Kirkland papers, Heard Archives, address on June 7, 1938.

41. EWG papers, VUMC Archives, Box 11, letter from Robinson, April 8, 1938.

42. Robinson, *Adventures in Medical Education*, 185.

43. Mims, 382.

44. Conkin, 273.

45. Kampmeier, *Making of a Clinical Teacher*, Private Printing, 1985, 43. See Eskind Library, Special Collections for this book.

46. Conkin, 275, 277.

47. *U.S. News and World Report*, April 14, 2000.

48. J. B. Youmans, *J Tenn Med Assn*, 59:39–51, 1966.

49. Robinson papers, VUMC Archives, 1924 correspondence.

50. VUMC Archives, Robinson-Kirkland correspondence.

51. He left Vanderbilt in 1918 to become professor of pathology at Columbia; when approached in 1920 he apparently declined to move back and remained at Columbia until 1945.

52. VUMC Archives, Robinson-Kirkland correspondence.

53. At Rockefeller, Brown was extremely productive, publishing twenty-five articles between 1920 and 1922; most of these dealt with experimental induction of syphilis. He remained there until his death in 1942.

54. VUMC Archives, Robinson-Kirkland correspondence.

55. Heard Library, Archives, Kirkland-Robinson correspondence.

56. Heard Library, Archives, Kirkland-Goodpasture correspondence, 1924.

57. A prominent physician in Nashville and dean from 1914 to 1920. He became acting dean in 1920 after

4

Canby Robinson was appointed, a position he held until 1925. He subsequently became head of the Department of Obstetrics and Gynecology.

58. Dr. Goodpasture's signature may be found in the old register of autopsies of Pathologische Anatomisches Institute in Vienna. See Christie Collection, VUMC Archives, Box 27, Photograph 151. Long in his *Biographical Memoir* states that Dr. Goodpasture worked under Carl Rothberger, an investigator of the pathology of the circulatory system, and at the time acting director of the Institute for General and Experimental Pathology at the University of Vienna.

59. Eskind Library, Special Collections, Robinson file.

60. Ibid.

61. Ibid., 3-4.

62. Collins papers, VUMC Archives, Box 1, Speeches, *Vanderbilt Alumnus*, 1944.

63. Collins papers, VUMC Archives, Box 1, Speeches, Ivy Day speech, 1957.

64. Dr. Goodpasture wrote Dr. Wiley Forbus at Duke in 1929 about the responsibilities of the Department of Pathology at Vanderbilt, in response to a query from Dr. Forbus: "The best arrangement [about tissue or surgical pathology] . . . is to turn it over to some member of your staff. One of the disadvantages which I do not like and shall try to eliminate is the request for frozen section diagnosis. One must be ready to drop at any time what he is doing, rush over and make a diagnosis, usually on a specimen which any intelligent surgeon should make from the gross." See EWG papers, VUMC Archives, Box D, File 4.

65. EWG papers, VUMC Archives, Box 11, Robinson correspondence of April 17, 1925.

66. Robinson papers, VUMC Archives, Department of Pathology Annual Reports, 1926 and 1927.

67. EWG in *Problems in Medical Education*, Rockefeller Education Series, 1929.

68. Additional details about the organization of the pathology course may be found in the appendix.

69. Collins papers, VUMC Archives, Box 1, Grisham notes. Also see EWG papers, VUMC Archives, Box 11, (Leathers correspondence—January 16, 1942) for a description of Dr. Dawson's role in the department's educational program.

70. Dr. Philpot, M.D., 1944, has described Dr. Goodpasture's lectures in some detail: "We knew in advance the first time Dr. Goodpasture was to lecture to us. All my classmates were present—none came late. The entire pathology department staff filed in and took seats in the lecture hall. During the seating the diener even came in to clean the blackboard spic-and-span. We were in a state of high anticipation. Then quite punctually, in a most unceremonious entrance, comes a white-coated, plain-looking gentleman, in his late middle years; and there's such a silence that the soft sounds of his steps are audible. Speaking not a word, he reaches his station behind a podium . . .; he sets and opens a stack of notes atop the podium, also sets an elbow on the podium, then . . . proceeds to deliver one of the dullest lectures I have ever heard." See Collins papers, VUMC Archives, Box 1, chapter 4 file.

71. Collins papers, VUMC Archives, Box 1, Grisham notes.

72. EWG papers, VUMC Archives, Box D, File 25. Later in this questionnaire, when asked to describe the characteristics of a good teacher, participation in fundamental research and practical application of subject matter were endorsed strongly by Dr. Goodpasture. Additional necessary features listed by him were "interest, curiosity, youth."

73. VUMC Archives, papers of Deans Robinson, Leathers, and Goodpasture.

74. Ibid.

75. Twenty-five hundred dollars contributed by Mr. Pouch of New York to the Pathology Department and used in 1930–31 to study the viral causation of cancer.

76. A total of $250,000 from the Rockefeller Education Board, was supplied on request to the office of Dean Leathers and expended by 1940; see Jacobson, 214–217 for a description of the method of allocation and amounts given.

77. Leathers papers, VUMC Archives, departmental yearly reports. See 1940.

78. Youmans papers, VUMC Archives, Pathology departmental report, 1955.

79. EWG papers, VUMC Archives, Box 11, Youmans letter dated June 27, 1955.

80. For the correspondence with Branscomb in this section, see EWG papers, VUMC Archives, Box 11, Branscomb correspondence.

81. Youmans papers, VUMC Archives, Branscomb correspondence in 1950. Also see Minutes, Executive Faculty Minutes, March 24, 1950.

82. Dean Youmans did not handle the extension of Dr. Goodpasture's appointment appropriately either, if the record is a guide. An extension was requested on November 7, 1951, by Dr. Goodpasture. In his response on November 12, Dr. Youmans stated "I shall arrange to talk about our plans within the next few days." There is no further correspondence on this topic until January 29, 1952, when Chancellor Branscomb solicited a letter from Dr. Goodpasture. The latter replied on January 30, 1952: "It is gratifying to know that you are willing to proceed with a nomination for my reelection. I would be happy to continue as an active member of the Vanderbilt faculty for the three year period."

83. Youmans papers, VUMC Archives, March 24, 1955, Minutes of Pathology Search committee. Chancellor Branscomb raised the possibility of retaining Dr. Goodpasture as chairman owing to inadequate funds to recruit his replacement.

84. A portrait of Dr. Goodpasture was subsequently commissioned and presented with appropriate dignity and ceremony, as described in chapter 9.

85. Heard Library, Special Collections, Record Group 300, Box 197, File 14.

86. Heard Library, Special Collections, Record Group 300, Box 197, File 14.

87. Bacteriology was placed in 1932 under Pathology's administrative wing.

4

88. Collins papers, VUMC Archives, Box 1, Miscellaneous Pathology faculty. For all Woodruff correspondence quoted in this section.

89. EWG papers, VUMC Archives, Box 11, DeMonbreun correspondence.

90. EWG papers, VUMC Archives, Box 11, correspondence with Youmans, 1950. Also see Collins papers, VUMC Archives, Box 1, DeMonbreun file, EWG to DeMonbreun, 26 February 1957.

91. EWG files, VUMC Archives, Box 11, Dawson correspondence, 1935.

92. EWG files, VUMC Archives, Box 10, EWG letter to Graves 1937, and Collins papers, VUMC Archives, Box 1, Dawson file.

93. EWG papers, VUMC Archives, Box 11, Dawson correspondence to EWG, Aug. 5, 1937.

94. EWG papers, VUMC Archives, Box 11, Dawson correspondence, March 1938.

95. EWG papers, VUMC Archives, Box 11, letter to EWC, March 11, 1938.

96. VUMC Archives, Executive Faculty Minutes, 1949.

97. *Minnesota Medicine*, April 1967

98. EWG papers, VUMC Archives, Box 11, Dawson correspondence, letter from EWG, May 17, 1955.

99. Youmans papers, VUMC Archives, Box 24A, Pathology Search Committee file.

100. Ibid.

101. EWG papers, VUMC Archives, Box 11, Dawson correspondence, 1935.

102. Collins papers, VUMC Archives, Box 1, Dawson file, article by Poser, 1983.

103. Collins papers, VUMC Archives, Box 1, Shapiro file, tribute by Randolph, 1972.

104. Collins papers, VUMC Archives, Box 1, Shapiro file, tribute by Branscomb.

105. See Collins papers, VUMC Archives, Box 1, Shapiro file for this letter from Dr. Mauricio, who in 1972 became chief of cytology owing to the illness of Dr. Shapiro. Her letter closes with this comment: "Dr. Shapiro became my closest ally, he was very dependable, loyal, unselfish, and deeply committed to the discipline, and we worked very well together. So . . . I found myself teaching my teacher, who became . . . then my partner and my friend. I knew I had arrived when each Christmas Eve, Dr. Shapiro brought to my doorstep at home a huge bag of bird seed!"

106. The M.D./Ph.D. program was recommended for the basic science departments by the Curriculum Committee under Bill Darby in 1964 (Vanderbilt Planning Study—School of Medicine, 1964, 44–46).

107. Collins papers, VUMC Archives, Box 1, Shapiro file, tribute by Branscomb, 1983.

108. Collins papers, VUMC Archives, Box 1, Buddingh file.

109. Collins papers, VUMC Archives, Box 1, Randall file.

110. Most viruses produce nuclear *or* cytoplasmic inclusions, not both. The cytoplasmic inclusions in juncopox were quite similar to those in fowlpox, as might be expected. Because of the rarity of nuclear

inclusions in the pox group, Dr. Goodpasture raised the possibility of a coinfection with two viruses in this junco.

111. These notebooks are now housed in Eskind Library, Special Collections, EWG papers.

112. Collins papers, VUMC Archives, Box 1, McGovern file, correspondence in 1925.

113. Nashville City Directory, 1925.

114. Obituaries, *Nashville Tennessean*, January 16, 1986.

Chapter Five

1. Branscomb, *Purely Academic*, 177, 1978.

2. Long, *Biographical Memoirs*, 1965.

3. Conkin, 494. As for "ablest faculty leaving for better paying jobs," Doctors Dawson and Buddingh left for purposes of academic advancement, moves fully supported by Dr. Goodpasture. Dr. Frye did leave because funds for the Preventive Medicine Department were no longer available.

4. EWG papers, VUMC Archives, Box 12B.

5. Conkin, 421–422.

6. EWG papers, VUMC Archives, Box 11, Burwell correspondence, July 18, 1945. Dr. Burwell had written to offer congratulations and advice: "I very often doubt whether anyone should be congratulated on being Dean except I am sure it is important to do the work of a Dean and to do it well. It is my belief that the correct principle is for a Dean of a Medical School himself to be active in research and teaching and I know you can't help being that kind of a Dean. Anyhow, my blessings on you and I hope we see you soon."

7. EWG papers, VUMC Archives, Box 11, Clark correspondence, March 3, 1950.

8. Advertisement for position of dean, 2000, Vice Chancellor's Office, Vanderbilt University Medical Center.

9. Executive Faculty Minutes, March 9, 1962. This committee consisted of Doctors Bass, Orr, and Scott, in addition to Dr. Shapiro.

10. Executive Faculty Minutes, May 22, 1961.

11. Conkin, 498.

12. Register, Vanderbilt Medical School, Eskind Historical Collection, 1926 and ff. The dean's duties had previously only been described as: "The Dean is ex officio a member of all standing committees of the faculty."

13. The Executive Faculty Minutes for March 9, 1962, state on 1666 A-4: For tenure appointments . . . there shall be appointed by the Chancellor a Committee on Tenure Appointments and Promotions. . . .

14. Louise Corbitt was the dean's secretary and Howard Miltenberger was the registrar-treasurer.

15. EWG papers, VUMC Archives, Box 14C.

16. EWG papers, VUMC Archives, Box 14C, Branscomb to EWG dated Feb. 8, 1949, and BOT minutes, Vol 32, 99.

17. MacLean Report, 34, 1946, Eskind Library Special Collections; Ziegler to EWG correspondence, VUMC Archives, Box 10, and Collins papers, VUMC Archives, Box 1, Dean file.

5

18. EWG papers, VUMC Archives, Box 14A, letters to Vice Chancellor Sarratt, April and June 1946.

19. EWG papers, VUMC Archives, Box 14 C.

20. BOT, Vol. 31, 237.

21. Clark to Branscomb, EWG papers, VUMC Archives, Box 14C.

22. File Group 300, Heard Archives, Box 178, Clark to Branscomb, Sept, 3, 1948.

23. Record Group 300, Box 197, File 15, Branscomb to EWG, Dec. 7, 1949.

24. Record Group 300, Box 178, File 20, Branscomb to Clark, Jan. 26, 1948.

25. File Group 300, Heard Archives, Box 178.

26. BOT, 1666A, 1962.

27. BOT, 1614A-2.

28. Heard Archives, Treasurer's Report, 1945.

29. EWG, VUMC Archives, Box 13A, Miltenberger file.

30. EWG papers, VUMC Archives, Box 12A, Surgery file and 14C, EWG to Pilcher, May 21, 1948.

31. EWG papers, VUMC Archives, Box 12A, Desperation-Emergency Hosp Fund.

32. EWG papers, VUMC Archives, Box 11B, Pharmacology.

33. Ibid.

34. Conkin, 494.

35. Branscomb, 176.

36. Conkin, 493.

37. Clark papers, VUMC Archives, material sent to Dr. Roscoe Robinson in 1991 and Clark Oral History, Collins papers, VUMC Archives, Box 1, Clark file.

38. Jacobson, 257.

39. The endowment for the medical school and hospital was $14,214,317.04 in 1940, $14,026,440.59 in 1955 per Treasurer's Reports. The failure of the endowment to grow was at the root of many problems. Medical School faculty suspected money was being diverted for other purposes on the campus, but the truth seems to be that each year all of the return from a very conservative investment policy was spent, and none of the return was added to principal.

40. Record Group 300, Heard Archives, File 178, letter from Clark to Benedict, July 23, 1948.

41. Record Group 300, File 178, letter from Clark to Branscomb, September 3, 1948.

42. EWG papers, VUMC Archives, Box 14C.

43. Ibid.

44. MacLean Report, 1946, Eskind Library, Special Collections.

45. Clark papers, VUMC Archives, chapter III, Heard to Robinson letter.

46. File Group 300, Box 178, File 19, Branscomb to Clark, Sept. 8, 1950.

47. EWG papers, VUMC Archives, Box 14C.

48. The Christie Committee report was titled: "Report of the Committee on the Financial Crisis of the Vanderbilt University School of Medicine and Hospital"; several letters from senior faculty to Dean Goodpasture in January and February 1949, and the Board of Trust Minutes of February 1949.

49. EWG papers, VUMC Archives, Box 18A, letter to Sarratt, May 3, 1946.

50. The closing page or pages of this document may have been misplaced. The sentences above are on page ten, and the text extends to the bottom of the page. An adjacent four pages in the file are numbered eleven through fourteen, but were typed on a different typewriter, and are mismatched contextually.

51. EWG papers, Box 14C, letters from Lamson, Pilcher, Clark, and Luton.

52. EWG papers, VUMC Archives, Box 14C, letter to alumni.

53. EWG papers, VUMC Archives, Box 14C.

54. Ibid.

55. EWG papers, VUMC Archives, Box 14 C, letter to Exec Fac, Jan. 15, 1949.

56. EWG papers, VUMC Archives, Box 14C, EWG to Branscomb, Jan. 7, 1949.

57. EWG papers, VUMC Archives, Box 14C, EWG to Branscomb, Jan. 22, 1949.

58. BOT, Vol. 32, 79 and ff.

59. Jacobson, 266 and Branscomb, *Autobiography*, 178.

60. In 1985, Dr. Joseph M. Merrill, then at the Baylor College of Medicine in Houston, summarized Dr. Goodpasture's position during this crisis (*JAMA* 254:912–913, 1985). His letter to the editor concludes with: "Since that time the growth and evolution of academic health science centers has been achieved largely by federal expenditures for health care and biomedical research. These have flowed to academic health science centers with the talent and leadership that Goodpasture clearly identified. Proposals to abandon public and university hospitals to commercial enterprises and to reduce funds for research and patient care have created a provocative agenda for university policy makers. Will those with Goodpasture's ideals and the spirit to carry them out please come forward?"

61. EWG papers, VUMC Archives, Box 14C, Clark to Branscomb, Sept. 3, 1948.

62. Record Group 300, Heard Archives, Box 178, File 20, Clark to Branscomb; EWG papers, VUMC Archives, Box 11B, Lamson to EWG, 1949; Letter to editor by Joseph Merrill, *JAMA*, 254:911, Aug. 16, 1985.

63. EWG papers, VUMC Archives, Box 14C, Report of nursing committee.

64. EWG, VUMC Archives, Box 14C, Nursing report.

65. Record Group 300, Heard Library Archives, Box 178, File 20, Clark to Benedict, July 23.

66. A folder titled Henry Clark papers in VUMC Archives contains letters written by Dr. Henry Clark to the medical faculty during the 1948–50 period. These letters, plus sections in the accompanying *Oral History* of Dr. Clark, detail the steps taken to produce major improvements in Vanderbilt Hospital operations and finances during those years.

67. EWG papers, VUMC Archives, Box 11C, Preventive Medicine folder.

68. EWG papers, VUMC Archives, Box 11C, May 14, 1948.

69. The various changes described in this section are documented in Executive Faculty Minutes, School of Medicine, 1945–50.

70. Branscomb, *Autobiography,* 177.

71. EWG papers, VUMC Archives, Box 12A.

72. Kampmeier files, VUMC Archives, Box 52, interview with Luton.

73. EWG Papers, VUMC Archives, Box 14A, Buddingh to EWG, May 28, 1948.

74. Henry Clark papers, VUMC Archives, *Oral History,* 47.

75. Citation; Branscomb to EWG, Record Group 300, Box 197, File 14.

76. EWG papers, VUMC Archives, Box 14C, Branscomb to EWG, Oct 5, 1948.

77. BOT Minutes, Vol. 33, 63.

78. Collins papers, VUMC Archives, Box 1, Speeches. Before the chancellor spoke about the future of Vanderbilt, there were addresses by Chester Barnard, president, Rockefeller Foundation and General Education Board, and by Goodrich C. White, president of Emory University.

79. The papers of Dr. Goodpasture bear very few doodles. Most were on administrative papers of various types, and they usually had a box shape with radiating lines as shown in these examples. These are from his time as dean.

Chapter Six

1. He had been elected to the prestigious National Academy of Sciences in 1937, at which time he was the only southerner; and invitations to assume professorships at Harvard and Hopkins would be tendered in 1941 and 1942, respectively.

2. Katherine Anderson was probably responsible for most of the technical work on these papers, with assistance from William DeMonbreun on the etiology of granuloma inguinale.

3. In this context, it is appropriate to note that the productivity of all investigators at Vanderbilt declined over this period. Judging by the size of Index Medicus, productivity of all universities and medical schools declined.

4. EWG papers, VUMC Archives, Box 11, Sellards correspondence in a letter dated February 25, 1942.

5. EWG papers, VUMC Archives, Box 11, Carmichael correspondence, 1946.

6. EWG papers, VUMC Archives, Box D, File 2.

7. EWG papers, VUMC Archives, Box A, File 31.

8. The taxi rides in Nashville cost seventy-five cents each, while those in Washington were twenty cents. Transportation in Washington to and from the surgeon general's office was provided by "The Transportation Service." There was a flat per diem of $5.00 in lieu of actual expenses, excepting the round trip rail cost of $32.80 and $10.60 for Pullman accommodations.

9. EWG Papers, VUMC Archives, Box A, File 30.

10. Zachary, *Endless Frontier,* 1–2.

11. Barfield, *Science for the 21st Century,* 7.

12. Greenberg, *Science,* 156:488–493, 1967.

13. EWG papers, VUMC Archives, Box B, File 10.

14. Cochrane, 209.

15. *Science,* 289:1443, 2000.

16. Zachary, *Endless Frontier,* 112.

17. Baxter, *Scientists against Time,* 14.

18. Zachary, 112.

19. Ibid., 115.

20. Ibid., 129.

21. EWG papers, VUMC Archives, Box C, File 15 (Palmer report).

22. Baxter, 27. OSRD was directly responsible for our victory in World War II, as Germany, predicting a short war, had restricted its research efforts, and Japan did not effectively mobilize its scientists. See Baxter, 8–10.

23. Obituary, *New York Times,* June 29, 1974.

24. Zachary, 226.

25. EWG papers, VUMC Archives, Box 11, Blake correspondence.

26. Dr. Goodpasture also served on a NRC—Division of Medical Sciences Subcommittee on Infectious Diseases, with Doctors O. T. Avery, Chester Keefer, and Kenneth Maxcy. Francis Blake was chairman. See EWG, Box A, File 25. The functions and meetings of this subcommittee probably overlapped with the S.G.O. committee, providing liaison with the NRC and NAS.

27. The name of this board was subject to frequent change. Beginning as the Board for Investigation of Infectious Diseases, it was called the Board on Epidemic Disease at the organizational meeting, and shortly was changed again.

28. *Army Medical Bulletin* 64:1–22, 1942.

29. The Public Health Association initially acted as the agent giving this award for the Lasker Foundation. EWG papers, Blake correspondence and *Am. J. Pub Health,* 37:112, 1947, but since 1946 the Lasker Foundation itself has given highly prized awards for basic research.

30. The AEC came into existence on August 1, 1946, after an intense political battle led by scientists over the extent of security provisions and the degree of military control. Cochrane, 456.

31. EWG papers, VUMC Archives, Box B, File 15.

32. Ibid.

33. EWG papers, VUMC Archives, Box B, File 13 (Report to Warren.)

34. EWG papers, VUMC Archives, Box B, File 14.

35. In the years to come, leukemia proved to be one of the major long-term consequences of atomic bomb radiation, just as it is in civilian exposures to irradiation.

36. EWG papers, VUMC Archives, Box B, File 12.

37. These questions have been paraphrased in several forms and in differing order. The text and order here are those found in England's article in *Science,* 176:41–47, 1976, as they are perhaps closest to the original. A different version may be found in Barfield, *Science in the Twenty-First Century,* 2.

38. This letter has acquired considerable mystique because of its significance, with conflicting information as to its authorship. Bush's close associate Carroll Wilson was interviewed by J. Merton England, historian of the National Science Foundation, for his article in *Science,* 176:41–47, 1976 titled: "Dr. Bush writes a report: Science—the endless frontier." Wilson is quoted as saying: "Bush did not write it nor did he ask for it." Zachary thirty-three years later gives evidence on 439 that Bush claimed authorship.

6

39. EWG papers, VUMC Archives, Box C, File 15.

40. Other members were Secretary Dr. Homer Smith, professor of physiology, New York University College of Medicine; Assistant Secretary Dr. Kenneth Turner, assistant professor of medicine, College of Physicians and Surgeons, Columbia University; Dr. William Castle, professor of medicine, Harvard Medical School; Dr. Edward Doisy, professor of biochemistry, St. Louis University School of Medicine; Dr. Alton Ochsner, professor of surgery, Tulane University School of Medicine; Dr. Linus Pauling, professor of chemistry, California Institute of Technology; and Dr. James Waring, professor of medicine, University of Colorado School of Medicine.

41. One of the issues was institutional overhead, in the discussion of which we learn that OSRD probably initiated the practice of paying overhead to educational institutions as remuneration for floor space, depreciation, and use of facilities. The routine for OSRD was to provide 50 percent of total salary expenditures as overhead. Dr. Palmer noted "The Universities have tasted money and it is questionable if they will welcome or accept Government funds without an overheard charge . . ." Overhead allowance is standard practice in 2002 but was not prior to World War II.

42. There was an "Executive Meeting" in Denver in mid-March, as well as an earlier meeting in New York. EWG, VUMC Archives, Box C, File 15.

43. EWG papers, VUMC Archives, Box C, File 15 (Palmer Report) 10.

44. EWG papers, VUMC Archives, Box C, File 15.

45. Bush considered the Palmer Committee's recommendation of an independent medical research foundation unnecessary, presumably because he intended to recommend an independent foundation as the parent organization. Zachary, 225.

46. Barfield, 1–2.

47. Zachary, 223. Both Bush and Roosevelt liked the word *frontier*; Bush writing that the "quest for knowledge could replace the vanishing geographical frontier as the new source of America's freedom and creativity" and Roosevelt writing in his letter requesting the Bush Report: "New frontiers of the mind are before us, and if they are pioneered with the same vision, boldness and drive with which we have waged this war we can create . . . a fuller and more fruitful life."

48. Barfield, 1.

49. Zachary, 223.

50. Barfield, 5.

51. Barfield, 10. Matters did not improve over time. In 1966, research and development expenditure by the Defense Department totaled $8.5 billion, by NASA $7.2 billion, by AEC $1.8 billion, while NSF spent $0.4 billion. Total basic research funding by all of these agencies and HEW was $400 million. See Schaffter, 149.

52. Barfield, 37.

53. It was Bush's judgment that our success in World War II was not so much a factor of winning technologies; instead he identified the "nation's political inventiveness as its unique strength." Zachary, 225.

54. More academic-type names were tried early on, specifically in 1948, when the NIH created two new institutes: the Experimental Medicine and Biology Institute, and the National Microbiological Institute. Less than two years were required for this mistake to be recognized, and by 1950 the current practice of naming institutes for diseases was in full flower.

55. Other members were Doctors Edward Doisy, A. Baird Hastings, Charles Huggins, Colin MacLeod, C. Philip Miller, and Wendell Stanley.

56. Oveta Culp Hobby was secretary from April 11, 1953, until July 31, 1955, and Secretary Folsom from August 1, 1955, to July 31, 1958. It would be interesting to know why Dr. Hobby requested such a potentially damaging study two months before she stepped down.

57. EWG papers, VUMC Archives, Box 10, 1955 Report of Special Committee contains report and Hobby's letter. The purpose of the deadline was to have the report available at the NSF annual meeting.

58. EWG papers, VUMC Archives, Box D, File 2.

59. EWG papers, VUMC Archives, Box A, File 14, letter to Long, 6.

60. EWG papers, VUMC Archives, Box A, File 14, letter to Long, 8–10.

61. EWG papers, VUMC Archives, Box A, File 14.

62. Ibid.

63. EWG papers, VUMC Archives, Box 10, Special Committee Report, 54–55.

64. EWG papers, VUMC Archives, Box 10, Blue Sheet, 1957, Volume 1, Number 1.

65. EWG papers, VUMC Archives, Box 10, Blue Sheet, 1957. The Bayne-Jones report was presumably published, but attempts to find a copy in the Tulane papers of Bayne-Jones or in National Library have been unsuccessful.

66. *Science*, 291:1903–1904, 2001.

67. The position of secretary then and now was a powerful one in the association, as it was held for several years. The secretary was responsible for arranging meetings, programs, and providing continuity, while the presidency was held for one year and had many ceremonial duties. The council was advisory to the officers of the association, and universally contained the senior leaders. These letters are in EWG papers, Karsner correspondence.

68. Dr. Goodpasture on this visit was able to enlist the aid of Dr. M. R. Abell, associate professor of pathology at the University of Michigan, as an editorial consultant. The other key person was Miss Seiferlein, assistant to Dr. Weller. This correspondence is in EWG papers, VUMC Archives, Box 11, Gall correspondence.

69. *Oxford English Dictionary*.

Chapter Seven

1. See chapter 6 for a discussion of the National Research Council and its relationship to the National Academy of Sciences.

2. As of 1962, there were twenty-seven registries, all sponsored by civilian national societies of various medical specialties. One of the major functions of each registry is to serve as a point of collection and study of tumors or unusual diseases. In particular, the collections of

ophthalmic diseases, bone tumors, and soft tissue tumors are unequalled in size and documentation of clinical information. Analysis of cases in these and other registries has provided guidance as to standardization of diagnosis and prognosis worldwide.

3. Long, *History of Pathology*, 126.

4. The six-volume account of the medical and surgical aspects of the Civil War is titled *The Medical and Surgical History of the War of the Rebellion 1861–65*, under the direction of Surgeon General Barnes, United States Army, Washington: Government printing office, 1875–83.

5. The Army Medical Museum became the site of vaccine production for the Army. Proper sanitation and vaccination sharply reduced the incidence of typhoid fever, which had frequently been a disastrous problem for encamped troops.

6. Henry, *The Armed Forces Institute of Pathology: Its First Century 1862–1962*.

7. Sternberg's biography by Martha Sternberg, American Medical Association, Chicago, 1920 was purchased by Dr. Goodpasture for his personal collection and is available in the VUMC Archives.

8. *A Manual of Bacteriology*, published in 1892.

9. The pictorial services of the museum were even used to prepare the reward posters for the capture of Booth and Sarratt. Stranger yet, the museum was housed for several years in the Ford Theatre, perhaps because no other agency wished to use that site.

10. EWG papers, VUMC Archives, Box 10.

11. A foundation dedicated to study and prevent diseases in horses. This particular meeting was on the Dupont estate near Washington.

12. General DeCoursey arranged VIP treatment, beginning with tooth extraction by a colonel and follow-up penicillin injections.

13. EWG papers, VUMC Archives, Box 10 to DeCoursey Sept. 29, 1954.

14. Paperwork finalizing this appointment was not completed until April 1955, when Mr. Bennett, chief of the Personnel Office of Walter Reed Army Medical Center, came to Nashville for that purpose. See EWG papers, VUMC Archives, Box 11, letter to Dr. Robert Moore, May 2, 1955.

15. *Military Medicine*, 117:177–201, 1955.

16. President Eisenhower also felt that unification of the (armed) services in this building was laudatory.

17. Original plans called for a twelve-story building with 228,108 square feet of usable space—see EWG papers, VUMC Archives, Box 10, 1956, Correspondence from Capt. Silliphant, and Collins papers, VUMC Archives, Box 1, AFIP file.

18. The 1955 AFIP Annual Report notes that 17,000 square feet of storage was required off-site, and that ventilation of rooms housing formalin-fixed gross tissues was inadequate. Building plans had been considerably tailored by cold-war mentality, reducing useful space to offset perceived need for blast—as in atomic bomb—resistance. All of the Annual Reports are now in Eskind Library, Special Collections, EWG papers.

19. Autopsy rooms are usually windowless and isolated but are rarely relegated to sub-basements.

20. This laboratory was connected by pneumatic tubes with the operating rooms of the hospital.

21. These specialists were members of the medical, dental, and veterinary professions and were probably chosen by recommendation of the directorate or their peers on the Scientific Advisory Board, and had a term of five years.

22. 1955 AFIP Annual Report.

23. 1957 AFIP Annual Report.

24. EWG papers, VUMC Archives, Box 9, speech to AFIP Staff, Jan. 1956.

25. 1956 AFIP Annual Report. The 1955 Annual Report shows a Dynamic Pathology Division and Basic Laboratories Division, which were fused by 1956 into the Division of Experimental Pathology.

26. EWG papers, VUMC Archives, Box 9, Jan. 20, 1956, speech to staff.

27. Apparently the less direct terminology was chosen so as not to appear condemnatory of the system. In any case, Dr. Goodpasture immediately recognized that the mindless warehousing of tissue samples was not productive.

28. EWG papers, VUMC Archives, Box 9, Jan. 20, 1956, speech to staff.

29. Ibid.

30. Ibid.

31. Ibid.

32. This memorandum is available as a rough draft in EWG papers, VUMC Archives, Box 10, and consists of handwritten notes. It was probably prepared early in 1956.

33. EWG papers, VUMC Archives, Box 9, 1956 speech to NMRI staff.

34. Dr. Goodpasture obviously recognized it would be politically insensitive to criticize the surgeon general, and substituted vaguer wordage.

35. Annual Reports, AFIP, 1954–57, Henry's *The Armed Forces Institute of Pathology*, 1964. Archived material relating to Dr. Goodpasture's 1955–59 role as scientific director has apparently not been saved, according to the historian, AFIP, 12/11/2000.

36. EWG papers, VUMC Archives, Box 10, 1956 address by Silliphant.

37. Henry, 354.

38. EWG papers, VUMC Archives, Box 9, 1958 letter to Silliphant.

39. EWG papers, VUMC Archives, Box 11, letter to Dr. Sam Clark, November 22, 1957.

40. Record Group 300, Box 197, File 14, for this letter and subsequent correspondence of Branscomb and Youmans.

Chapter Eight

1. We are indebted particularly to Dr. Goodpasture's daughter and son-in-law, Sarah and Dr. Joseph Little, as well as grandchildren, nieces, nephews, and close friends of the Goodpastures for source materials. See Collins papers, VUMC Archives, Box 1, Elizabeth Collins notebooks.

2. Thomas Rivers's *Memoir of Ernest William Goodpasture (1886–1960)*, American Philosophical

Society, 111–120, 1964; the same story is given in less detail in John Youmans's *Memoir* published in the *Transactions of the Association of American Physicians*, 74:21–24, 1961. The original source for this story is not known.

3.   Esmond Long's *Memoir*. See Collins papers, VUMC Archives, Box 1, Memoirs.

4.   Family lore has no uniform explanation for the name Ernest William. Ernest's siblings bear easily identified and often used family names. The William in Ernest's name probably came from Stephen William Dawson, Ernest's maternal grandfather, who died one year after Ernest's birth. There are two distant cousins named Ernest who are mentioned in the genealogy in the biography of Jefferson Dillard Goodpasture but an appropriate predecessor for the three Ernests has not been identified. Family lore also has it that Ernest at birth was not given a middle name and that he later requested the name William. This possibility could not be proven by review of his birth certificate, as such certificates were not uniformly available in Tennessee before 1900. There is no christening record for Ernest at the Episcopal Church in Clarksville.

5.   *American Heritage Dictionary*, Third Edition, 1992.

6.   See Collins papers, VUMC Archives, Box 1, EWG relatives file and biography of J. D. Goodpasture.

7.   *Memoirs of Henry Goodpasture*, 1979, Tennessee State Archives, File 436.

8.   Mules are the sterile offspring of a male donkey (*equus asinus*), known colloquially as jacks, and a female horse. Henry Goodpasture states that jacks were in "enormous demand" because mules were needed for cotton farming. For other tasks, mules worked harder and longer than horses and had the reputation of being smarter and healthier.

9.   There were four children by this second marriage.

10.   We do not know why his birth occurred in Livingston, as the family home was at Hilham.

11.   Their reason for choosing Clarksville is not given in the memoir of Henry Goodpasture nor in the genealogical section of the biography of Jefferson Dillard Goodpasture.

12.   One of the most influential of the Dawson physicians, at least from our perspective, was Stephen William Dawson who sparked the intention of Ernest Goodpasture to become a physician. The last one in this line to become a physician is Joseph Alexander Little III, Dr. Goodpasture's grandson.

13.   Details about the Dawson family were provided by an unpublished manuscript called Country Life Before the Civil War by A. V. Goodpasture, filed in Collins papers, VUMC Archives, Box 1, Goodpasture relatives. Also see the account by Katherine Goodpasture prepared in 1987 and filed in Collins papers, VUMC Archives, Box 1, Katherine Goodpasture file.

14.   *Memoirs of Henry Goodpasture*, 1979. Tennessee State Archives, File 436.

15.   Choosing the word *Company* for this enterprise was deliberate, knowing the owner's command of

language. The intention presumably was to convey the spirit of companionship available there, in contrast to the usual store.

16.   Assisting in the store was A. V.'s son Ridley Rose Goodpasture. William Henry, known as "Uncle Bill" to the family, was the coauthor with A. V. Goodpasture of the biography of James Dillard Goodpasture, their father.

17.   Sarah Goodpasture's theme for Dr. Mims; see Collins papers, VUMC Archives, Box 1, Sarah Little file.

18.   This magazine was the predecessor of the current *Tennessee Historical Quarterly*; it had been started by Peabody Normal College American history Professor William Garrett, with whom Goodpasture coauthored the school text *History of Tennessee*.

19.   *Tennessee Encyclopedia of History and Culture*, 368.

20.   Sarah Goodpasture's theme for Dr. Mims; see Collins papers, VUMC Archives, Box 1, Sarah Little file.

21.   The original octagonal house burned and was not replaced. The "summer home" was more modest and lacked many of the usual facilities including plumbing. See Sarah Goodpasture's theme and conversation with Ann Wilson Goodpasture. See Collins papers, VUMC Archives, Box 1, Elizabeth Collins notebook.

22.   Dunbar Cave at the time was six miles from the city limits of Clarksville. It is a "blowing cave," emanating a cooling breeze that was particularly welcome in the summer. A wooden dance floor was built in the cave entrance to take full advantage of the natural air-conditioning. Friday and Saturday night dances were a tradition in Montgomery County and very popular with young blades and their dates. In the summer, whole families would come out to spend the day, picnic, or partake of the healing waters from the adjacent mineral springs.

23.   All of A. V. Sr.'s children had nicknames. Mattie was "Tier" or "Dutchess" or "Dutch;" Ridley was "Rid;" Ernest was "Doc" or, later after Hopkins, "Parson;" Albert was "Sim;" and Sarah was "Sook."

24.   The *Clarksville Leaf Chronicle* of August 11, 1915 (Tennessee State Archives) contains other details: present were Misses Marion and Margaret Catlett, Miss Susie Ferguson, Miss Barry Rogers, Richard Catlett and B. A. Patch, of Clarksville (Marion, Margaret, and Richard were Sarah's siblings). An adjacent article in the *Leaf Chronicle* has details of "a brilliant evening reception" at the home of Mr. and Mrs. James H. Smith Jr. "in compliment to" Miss Sarah Catlett. Other details about the wedding and reception may be found in Collins papers, VUMC Archives, Box 1, Elizabeth Collins notebooks.

25.   Sarah Little's handwritten notes about her mother and family have been filed in Collins papers, VUMC Archives, Box 1, Sarah Little file.

26.   A syndicated newspaper columnist, who was a friend of Sarah Catlett Goodpasture and was related by marriage.

27.   For the first year, they rented a home on Woodmont Boulevard.

28.   William Wemyss was one of the founders of the shoe company Genesco; Donald Davidson was a professor of English at Vanderbilt and a member of the Fugitives; Hugh Morgan was professor of medicine;

Beverly Douglas was a prominent surgeon; and Walter Morgan was a prominent dentist.

29. The Sims lived on Honeywood Avenue in Belle Meade.

30. Joe Little Jr. was an excellent basketball player in those long ago times before jump shots, dunks, and similar advances had been invented.

31. Sarah Goodpasture called her husband "Doc," and objected to his nickname "Chick" for daughter Sarah, stating "She has a perfectly good name."

32. This event is described in Sarah Little's letter to Tom Rivers in 1961. See Collins papers, VUMC Archives, Box 1, Sarah Little file.

33. The cottage had been named Wisteria by previous owners. Lavender was Sarah Senior's favorite color and was used for her stationery.

34. Mark Twain's observation about law on this occasion was, "I suppose nobody in the world knows less about law than I do, unless it is my brother Orien who is practicing out West!"

35. Home Avenue was originally the driveway to the home purchased in 1891 by Asahel Huntington Patch, daughter Sarah's maternal grandfather. Contemporary families had built their homes along this street, so the neighborhood in 1936 contained about forty young people. Sarah's comment to Dr. Mims was: "Such a sociable environment there never was, I suppose, before nor since. Just the mere fact that there were always four or five sisters and brothers around, and possibly three cousins besides, seems like a party to me, for I was an only child."

36. They are reported to have kicked pebbles across the street all the way to their fathers' offices, on more than one occasion!

37. Sarah's theme for Dr. Mims.

38. Collins papers, VUMC Archives, Box 1, Family friends, letter from Mary Jane Evans.

39. Ibid.

40. Personal communication from Sarah Little. Mrs. Goodpasture also belonged from 1929–33 to the Centennial Club, which was founded in 1905 and has been responsible since for many civic and cultural activities.

41. Sarah's theme for Dr. Mims.

42. A home in Nashville for unwed mothers.

43. See Collins papers, VUMC Archives, Box 1, Elizabeth Collins notebooks.

44. Sarah ("Sook") Goodpasture attended Hopkins Nursing School and became nursing supervisor at Hopkins in 1922–1923. She married Dr. Karl Martzloff, Hopkins graduate and surgeon, in 1923 before moving to Portland, Oregon.

45. EWG papers, VUMC Archives, Box 11, Martzloff correspondence.

46. Ibid.

47. In 1939, in the same summer as the trip to Yale for Dr. Goodpasture's honorary degree, Sarah and Grace Benedict drove to Mackinac Island with Mrs. Benedict to attend the Delta Delta Delta convention. Their driver was Tom Fite Paine. Sarah as president of the local chapter and Mrs. Benedict as delegate apparently had more administrative responsibilities than their companions.

48. See *Vanderbilt Alumnus*, June 1940. Mrs. Morris also attended as guest of the university. Her full name was Mrs. Alice Vanderbilt Shepard Morris; she was the great-granddaughter of Commodore Cornelius Vanderbilt and was the first descendant of Commodore Vanderbilt to attend a Vanderbilt commencement.

49. They were both undoubtedly pleased that Dr. Goodpasture was inducted as an alumnus into ODK at the Alumni Dinner on the previous Monday night.

50. Collins papers, VUMC Archives, Box 1, Sarah Little file.

51. The foursome routinely included Mrs. Morford Whitson, Mrs. Oren Oliver, and Mrs. Ann Warner.

52. EWG papers, VUMC Archives, Box 11, Burwell correspondence dated April 1, 1940. On April 10, Dr. Burwell was notified that Sarah would not be able to accompany Dr. Goodpasture on his upcoming trip to Boston, and that "Sarah has not felt like writing her [Edith Burwell] but will do so when she can."

53. Dr. Goodpasture sold the cottage in Monteagle within one or two years. As noted in correspondence with Watson Sellards—see EWG papers, VUMC Archives, Box 11, Sellards correspondence—he also attempted to sell the house on Fairfax in 1942, but the purchaser backed out in February 1942 "because of the war."

54. Sarah Jr. and Dr. Goodpasture took a trip to New York from the 9th to the 16th of December 1940. Watson Sellards joined them "to participate in the Christmas spirit." In a letter to Sidney Burwell on December 27, Dr. Goodpasture noted: "It was the first real visit she [Sarah] had made to New York and we had a real good time. The shops were festively bedecked and she had her Christmas shopping to do when we were not at the theatre, opera, ballet, hockey game or dining at interesting places, sometimes with her friends Mary Jane Brooks, Peggy Fountain and Marjorie Bell. Watson Sellards came down for the week and took us to see Life with Father and to dinner at the Harvard Club." See EWG papers, VUMC Archives, Box 11, Burwell and Sellards correspondence.

55. Conversation with Margaret Dawson, Sarah and Joe Little, 1998. See Collins papers, VUMC Archives, Box 1, Elizabeth Collins notebook.

56. EWG papers, VUMC Archives, Box 11, EWG to Dawson, May 17, 1955, closing with "You will never know Jim what a comfort you were to me during sad and difficult days and always. Ernest."

57. See Collins papers, VUMC Archives, Box 1, Joe Little's file, for details about this trip and other fishing adventures with Doctors Dawson and Goodpasture.

58. Personal communication to author from Dr. Robert Merrill.

59. Remedial lessons in fishing continued after their marriage. There was a memorable trip to the Buffalo River, one hundred miles to the west of Nashville, in the fall of 1941. An overnight stay was arranged in a farmhouse near the river, the lady of the house promising to "do the best I can" for the requested breakfast of toast and coffee. Wake-up was at 4:00 A.M., followed by a country breakfast of coffee, scrambled eggs, fried chicken, country ham, bacon, fried potatoes, grits, and

hot biscuits! Their generous hosts were the parents of nine children, the last of whom had left the farm three months previously. The breakfast was the high point of the trip, as later the two younger outdoorsmen managed to dump the elder fisherman into the river. See Collins papers, VUMC Archives, Box 1, Joe Little file for details.

60. Grace and Tom went first, enabling Sarah to be Grace's maid-of-honor. Unfortunately, Grace could not reciprocate the following weekend, as she and Tom were still on their honeymoon—somewhere on the Skyline Drive or at Mountain Lake, Virginia.

61. For communications from Joe Little, see Collins papers, VUMC Archives, Box 1, Joe Little file.

62. Neither were members of this church, but his cousin Henry Goodpasture had probably made the essential arrangements. Their wedding was attended by his sister Sarah and her mother Mrs. H. O. Anderson Sr. Her brothers were in the Pacific in the armed forces.

63. Bertha referred to the Goodpastures as "Doctor" and "Miss Katherine." In 1955, she went to work for Peggy Wemyss and Tom Kelly Connor, a position she held for thirty-five years.

64. It was the custom for visitors to the university to stay in the homes of their hosts and be entertained there until well into the 1960s. This custom reflected Southern hospitality and institutional penury. Very little money was available for entertainment then, and "upscale" facilities were limited as well. For example, Nashville had surprisingly few good restaurants until liquor by the drink was legalized in 1967. There was no University Club. It is difficult to know how much we lost or gained when our customs changed to the present arrangements of institutional rather than personal hospitality. In that regard, Sir MacFarlane Burnet was still writing in 1968—see Burnet's *Changing Patterns*—about his stay in Sam Clark's home for the seminar on immunology in which he participated in 1958.

65. There were nicknames, of course. Dr. Goodpasture was called "Gran," and Katherine was "Kafun."

66. There are several tributaries of the Harpeth in or near Nashville: the West Harpeth lies to the south of Nashville, flows by Leiper's Fork and enters the Harpeth near the antebellum home called Meeting of the Waters; the Little Harpeth flows through Percy and Edwin Warner Parks before entering the Harpeth; the South Harpeth enters the Harpeth near Kingston Springs thirty miles to the west of Nashville. In addition to these tributaries, the Harpeth receives several large creeks before draining into the Cumberland River fifteen to twenty miles below Nashville.

67. The post office was discontinued on June 15, 1905. The route ran from Franklin in Williamson County to Charlotte in Dickson County. The Goodpastures tried in vain to obtain a letter carrying a Basin Spring postmark. See Collins papers, VUMC Archives, Box 1, Basin Spring.

68. Dr. Goodpasture had inherited one-third of the Dawson-Goodpasture farm in Montgomery County when his father died in 1942, Sarah Martzloff giving her part to her brothers Ernest and A. V. Jr., and Mattie

obtaining the house and adjacent property. See conversation with Ann Wilson Goodpasture, January 16, 2001, Collins papers, VUMC Archives, Box 1, Elizabeth Collins notebook. Dr. Goodpasture apparently gave his part to A. V. Jr., to help in the raising of his young family, although there is correspondence in 1942 with Watson Sellards in which Dr. Goodpasture writes: "I am now trying to sell my farm." The farm to which Dr. Goodpasture was referring was in Montgomery County.

69. These logbooks were found in Katherine's home on Hopkins Lane by her good friend and frequent birding companion, Ann Tarbell. They are now in the possession of Dr. Joe Little III of Murfreesboro. Entries were made by Katherine in the logs from memory or notes and were apparently kept current. A separate notebook was used each year. The 1949 log was transcribed by Joe Little III, a copy of which is deposited in the Goodpasture papers in Special Collections, Eskind Library. The 1950–51 books have presumably been lost, but there are books for 1952, 1953, 1954, and the first three months of 1955 (they left for Washington in July 1955). After Dr. Goodpasture's death, books were kept for 1962, 1973, and 1975.

70. For those unfamiliar with the specifics of fencing, a line must be established, usually by cutting brush or small trees; post holes two feet deep must be dug at ten to twenty foot intervals (depending on the terrain), along the line; in point-to-point fencing, trees along the line may be substituted for posts; the posts (of red cedar, osage orange, or black locust) must be cut, trimmed to size, brought to the site, and set in place by tamping dirt around the base; three or four strands of barbwire must be strung, stretched with a "come-along," and fastened. The roll of barbwire weighs seventy-five to eighty pounds. These details about fencing were provided by Osgood Anderson, Katherine's brother. See Collins papers, VUMC Archives, Box 1, Basin Springs.

71. A floral assay of Basin Spring was carried out by Earl Bishop, Ph.D., University of Hawaii, probably in the summer of 1974. This botanist compiled a ten-page list of the flora, citing frequency and site, the results of camping at Basin Spring for "a few summer months." Consequently, spring and late fall plants may not have been recorded. The list was prepared by Ann Tarbell after Katherine Goodpasture's death and is found in Collins papers, VUMC Archives, Box 1, Basin Spring.

72. Reminiscences from Sarah, Susan, and Joe Little, Collins papers, VUMC Archives, Box 1, grandchildren.

73. On the other hand, they made very good use of their free time in the Washington area. Katherine became a skillful ornithologist, and together they explored Goodpasture family history, particularly the Dawson and Willson lines—Dr. Goodpasture's mother was descended from Stephen William Dawson and Martha Lucretia Willson. Katherine described their investigations in a manuscript dated 1987 and filed in Box 1, Collins papers, VUMC Archives, Katherine Goodpasture: "We worked deep into the early history of Maryland and Virginia. On week days I sallied forth to the Court Houses at Rockville, to State Archives at Annapolis, to the Library of Congress, to the beautiful

homes of Montgomery County described by Farquar. On Saturdays, bright and early, we both trekked back to review wills that gave family history, to cemeteries that gave marriage records and life-dates. We made many turns into blind alleys but the avenue would eventually lead to St. Bethlehem and Montgomery County, Tennessee."

74. Ann Tarbell's Remembrance at the memorial service for Katherine Goodpasture, 1995. See Collins papers, VUMC Archives, Box 1, Katherine Goodpasture file.

75. Her feathered friends apparently reciprocated in a limited way. Ann Tarbell relates in her Remembrance that when the turn was taken into Basin Spring, "There the chickadees and song birds who loved her sunflower seed treats met her at the gate with excited calls . . ." The explanation given was that they recognized the sound of the car. It seems more likely that they recognized Katherine.

76. Graveside services were held at Rose Hill Cemetery in Columbia, Tennessee, where she is buried.

77. Collins papers, VUMC Archives, Box 1, Katherine Goodpasture file.

78. Anne was valedictorian of Fogg High School (later merged with Hume grammar school to form present Hume-Fogg High School), ranked first in all subjects at Vanderbilt, was captain of the girl's basketball team, and through intervention with Chancellor Kirkland initiated the hiring of the first dean of women (Ada Belle Stapleton) and construction of the first residence hall for women—McTyiere Hall. Scales Chapel at West End Methodist Church was given by her in memory of her parents. Scales Hall (in the Branscomb residential complex for women) on the Vanderbilt campus was named in her honor.

79. Mr. Benedict, as a successful banker at Nashville Trust Company, bought as an investment a controlling interest in Ward-Belmont in 1927. After the stock market crash, he was principally involved in management of that school until 1941. He began to assist Chancellor Kirkland with overseeing the endowment in 1933 and became a full-time employee as treasurer of the university in 1941.

80. The Paines were from Aberdeen, Mississippi, but had long affiliations with Vanderbilt. Bishop Robert Paine had dedicated the cornerstone of Old Main (now Kirkland Hall) in 1875 as a senior bishop of Methodist Church South and friend of Bishop McTyiere. Tom Fite Paine Jr., Bishop Robert's great-grandson, attended Vanderbilt as an undergraduate and medical student. Tom Fite was asked by Secretary Robert McGaw to participate in the rededication of the Kirkland Hall cornerstone at centennial ceremonies in 1975.

81. Collins papers, VUMC Archives, Box 1, Elizabeth Collins notebook.

82. These daughters were centers of attention in both families. Dr. and Mrs. Brooks had tragically lost a seven-year-old son to the complications of scarlet fever while they lived in St. Louis. See Louis Rosenfeld's memoir of Dr. Brooks, 23.

83. Collins papers, VUMC Archives, Box 1, Student correspondence.

84. This and the following memoirs are filed in Collins papers, VUMC Archives, Box 1, Memoirs.

85. A poker game on a long train trip might do equally as well. Canby Robinson attributed some of his success in bonding with the faculty at Vanderbilt to his facility with the cards and accompanying libations on a train ride to New Orleans in 1920, immediately after he was introduced as the new dean. See Jacobson, 108.

86. See 45, of Kampmeier's *Recollections*. The photographs were later published in Kampmeier's *Vanderbilt University School of Medicine the Story in Pictures*, 67.

87. Collins papers, VUMC Archives, Box 1, Family friends file. See Mary Jane Evans letter.

88. Collins papers, VUMC Archives, Box 1, Physiology.

89. EWG papers, VUMC Archives, Box B, File 17.

90. Collins papers, VUMC Archives, Box 1, Memoirs.

91. EWG papers, VUMC Archives, Box 11, Clark correspondence.

92. Bill Gunter and his sons worked at Vanderbilt until they started the William Gunter and Sons Funeral Home on Jo Johnston Street in 1946 that is now managed by Marcus Gunter. For a complete description of Bill Gunter's role in the educational program, see Harris Riley "In praise of dieners," *Vanderbilt Medicine*, Winter 1987, and Sam. L. Clark "Medical education from the ground up," *Jour. Med. Education*, 37:1291–1296, 1962.

93. Harvey writes that Sellard's strain of yellow fever virus was used by Theiler to develop an effective vaccine. See 52, *Bull JHH*, 144:45–55, 1979.

94. A. M. Harvey, *Bull JHH*, 144:45–55, 1979.

95. See EWG papers, VUMC Archives, Box 11, Burwell and Sellards correspondence. There are no letters of condolence from Watson Sellards on file after Sarah's death in July 1940. Their absence indicates that Dr. Goodpasture did not save all personal correspondence with his other papers.

96. EWG papers, VUMC Archives, Box 11, Sellards correspondence. The rest of his letter read: "Instead of those beautiful fields on the farm, I am thinking of opening a Ramos gin and fizz emporium in Nashville. . . . The new emporium will send up fizzes ad lib for your rummy in the evening. Just tell that to Sarah and Joe. . . . A pit bull terrier is something new to me. Don't let them get out of hand."

97. EWG papers, VUMC Archives, Box 11, Burwell correspondence.

98. The Burwells stayed with the Morgans on this occasion, although they had other invitations, including one from the Goodpastures. The portrait was formally presented to Chancellor Carmichael by Dr. Goodpasture.

99. EWG papers, VUMC Archives, Box 11, Burwell correspondence.

100. Ibid.

101. F. M. Rackemann, *The Inquisitive Physician: The Life and Times of George Richards Minot*, Harvard University Press, Cambridge, Massachusetts, 1956, 115–116.

102. Collins papers, VUMC Archives, Box 1, Social clubs.

8

103. The three volumes of minutes of the Medical Exchange Club covering the period 1920 to 1955 were in Dr. Goodpasture's library and are now housed in the Eskind Library, Special Collections.

104. Stahlman papers, Heard Library, Coffee House file.

105. This club was formed, or had its first meeting, on October 17, 1909, as we are informed by Ridley Wills, who is currently a member. Papers are given monthly but apparently have not been systematically archived. Dr. Goodpasture's papers contain a picture of the Coffee House Club taken in 1942, a list of the twenty-nine members for 1947–48, and several papers he gave to the club.

106. Addresses of the Ernest Goodpasture family: 1908–12: 518 N. Broadway, Baltimore, Maryland; 1918–21: Reading, Massachusetts; 1921–22: 5 Cortibitarte (Judge Streets's house, rented), Manila, Philippines; 1922–24: 6915 Thomas Boulevard, Pittsburgh, Pennsylvania; 304 Chestnut Road, Sewickley, Pennsylvania; 1924–25: Vienna, Austria; 1925–26: Woodmont Boulevard, Nashville, Tennessee; 1926–55: 408 Fairfax Avenue, Nashville, Tennessee; 1955–59: 4810 Cumberland Avenue, Chevy Chase, Maryland; 9716 Elrod Road, Kensington, Maryland; 1959–60: 106 Woodsia Lane, Jackson, Mississippi; 1960–93: 3407 Hopkins Lane, Nashville, Tennessee.

Dr. Goodpasture's Social Security Number: 411-38-3938.

Chapter Nine

1. Computerization facilitates computation of a "citation index," which is the number of times other authors cite a publication and is a measure of its perceived value. Articles with high citation indices are publicized as indicators of accomplishment of individuals and their institutions.

2. Please see chapter 1 for descriptions of his recruitment by other institutions and success of trainees. Leadership positions as chairman and dean are described in chapters 4 and 5. Leadership positions in professional societies are described in chapter 6.

3. The comparison process requires a cadre of faculty who, serving without pay in their own institution as well as nationally, are delegated to judge academic accomplishments and potential. Locally, faculty sit on committees that review faculty candidates for initial appointment as well as for promotion and determine the suitability of candidates for doctoral degrees. Professorial appointments, with judgements as to tenure, are generally made by an intramural group that for upper-level appointments solicits opinions of outside referees. Faculty also routinely become formal or informal mentors of juniors just entering the system, serving thereby as judge, jury, promoter, and guide as to the vagaries of the academic process. Nationally, faculty sit on editorial boards or grant review committees and nominate or judge candidates for prizes and awards.

4. This ubiquitous expression was apparently coined by Logan Wilson in the book *The Academic Man*

published in 1942. See Eugene Garfield, *The Scientist,* 10:11, 1996.

5. Decimus Junius Juvenalis (A.D. circa 55–circa 130). The quote is from Satires.

6. The only cv in Dr. Goodpasture's papers was prepared in 1958 and apparently was assembled, at least in part, from memory. There are some differences in dates and wordage between this cv and information in his correspondence files. The cv in Appendix A of this biography has been slightly amended from the 1958 version on the basis of correspondence or other records.

7. Dr. Graham Lusk, *The Harvey Society*, in Harvey Lectures, 25:207, 1931.

8. See EWG papers, VUMC Archives, Box 11, Correspondence with Canby Robinson.

9. This lecture drew extensively on his review of fowlpox prepared the previous year for the book *Filterable Viruses,* edited by Thomas M. Rivers, and on ongoing research, some of which had been published in the *Am J Pathol* in January 1929 by Woodruff and Goodpasture.

10. Harvey Lectures, 24:45, 1930. Incidentally, another lecture in the 1928–29 series was given by Dr. Wade Brown, of the Rockefeller Institute. Dr. Brown had been a contender for the professorship at Vanderbilt—see chapter 4 for details.

11. Harvey Lectures, 25:81, 1929–30.

12. EWG papers, VUMC Archives, Box 11, Canby Robinson correspondence.

13. See Appendix A for EWG, *Diplomate*, 5:251–263, 1933.

14. Collins papers, VUMC Archives, Box 1, Speeches file.

15. His balanced and historical analysis of the past and future of medicine on Ivy Day contrasts with the slightly negative biography of Vanderbilt University by Professor Paul Conkin. *Gone with the Ivy* is a title apparently selected for the evolution of Vanderbilt from its traditional past, as stated on vi: "As a historian, I found the first fifty years easier to chronicle than those that followed. This reflects not only the advantages of perspective and hindsight but also the greater unity and simplicity of the early, literate, classical, pious, securely southern Vanderbilt. The luxurious ivy that enveloped Old Main before the 1905 fire well symbolizes this early Vanderbilt and the ideals it exemplified. But that Vanderbilt has gone with the ivy. In a sense it had its final, belated apotheosis in the work of the Fugitives and Agrarians. The building that now houses the medical school symbolizes the modern Vanderbilt, one in which strong professional schools and specialization in traditional disciplines have diluted the literary and humanistic ideals of the past. A little nostalgia for that past is in order."

16. Lady, *Journal of Higher Education*, 38:197–205, 1967.

17. Other recipients of honorary degrees were A. F. Fischer, forester; W. A. Delano, architect; George Stewart, minister; A. Macleish, poet; R. G. Harrison, scientist; Hans Zinsser, bacteriologist; A. N. Hand, jurist; H. R. Wilson, diplomat; and Eduard Benes, statesman

and late president of Czechoslovakia. See EWG papers, Eskind Library, Special Collections.

18. EWG papers, VUMC Archives, Box 11, letter to Sidney Burwell, June 29, 1939.

19. Citation enclosed with degree, Eskind Library, Special Collections, Box 1.

20. Chicago degree, Eskind Library, Special Collections, Box 1.

21. Dr. Goodpasture was also the official representative of Vanderbilt University.

22. Dr. Goodpasture was at table thirteen, directly before the speaker's table; his companions were Dr. and Mrs. Paul Cannon, Dr. and Mrs. Ludvig Hektoen, and Dr. and Mrs. Robert Millikan. Doctors Cannon and Hektoen were pathologists at the University of Chicago. Dr. and Mrs. Millikan's son would later come to Vanderbilt as chairman of physiology. Please see chapter 5, Dean.

23. Awardees included Doctors Linus Pauling, Thomas Rivers, Donald Van Slyke, Edward Doisy, Evarts Graham, and Robert Williams.

24. Dr. Goodpasture's paper was titled: "Some aspects of twentieth century research on infectious diseases." Papers were also given by two of the other three awardees, Dr. Edwards Park and Dr. Charles Huggins, the former a distinguished pediatrician from Hopkins, and the latter a future Nobel laureate for describing the sensitivity of prostatic cancer to hormonal influence. Mr. Abraham Flexner was the fourth recipient of an honorary degree on this occasion.

25. You may remember these sentences from the Kober Medal acceptance speech, quoted in full in chapter 1, The Measure of the Man.

26. American Philosophical Society web site, home 2001.

27. EWG papers, VUMC Archives, Box 11, correspondence file with Loranz, 1928.

28. Previous awardees were Doctors Kenneth Lynch, J. Shelton Horsley, Evarts Graham, and William deB. MacNider.

29. A copy of this speech was sent to his father in 1938; preserved in its original envelope, it was in the memorabilia in Sarah Little's home in January 2001.

30. Sarah's telegram read: "Here's to the world's greatest daddy from a mighty proud daughter." EWG papers, Eskind Library, Special Collections, Personal memorabilia, green notebook.

31. Burwell's presentation speech, *Trans Assn Amer Physicians*, 48:45, 1944.

32. Several winners were close friends and/or colleagues of Dr. Goodpasture, including Alfred Blalock and Helen Taussig (1948), Oswald T. Avery (1949), John Enders (1953), Homer Smith (1954), Stanhope Bayne-Jones (1959), and Rene Dubos (1960).

33. See EWG papers, Eskind Library, Special Collections, 1946, Announcement section.

34. EWG papers, Eskind Library, Special Collections, Passano brochure.

35. EWG papers, VUMC Archives, Box 11, Gill correspondence.

36. This award probably enabled purchase of the Basin Springs Farm in 1948.

37. National Academy Sciences web page, Kovalenko Medal, 2001.

38. EWG papers, VUMC Archives, Box A, Folder 22, letter from Dryden, February 11, 1958. Other recipients from the web were Doctors Alfred Richards (1952), Peyton Rous (1955), Eugene Opie (1959), Karl Meyer (1961), George Whipple (1962), Rufus Cole (1966), Karl Link (1967), and Thomas Francis Jr. (1970).

39. EWG papers, VUMC Archives, Box A, File 22.

40. *Am J Pathol*, 77:189s, 1974.

41. *Am J Pathol*, 77:188s, 1974.

42. *Laboratory Investigation*, 7:284, 1958.

43. The recipients immediately after Dr. Goodpasture were: Doctors Eugene Opie (1960), George Whipple (1961), William Boyd (1962), Peyton Rous (1964), and Paul Cannon (1965). The Association apparently moved to a yearly award in 1964. See *Am J Pathol*, 77:197s, 1974.

44. A. McGehee Harvey, "One hundred years of clinical science—an overview of contributions through the association of American physicians." *Trans Assn Amer Phys*, 49:clvi-clxvi, 1986. The goal of the association is "the advancement of scientific and practical medicine," as described in J. Claude Bennett, "The Association of American Physicians: Conception and Renewal of Purpose," *Proc Assn Am Physicians*, 109:489–491, 1997.

45. There was a long interval until the next pathologist Arnold Rich received the Kober Medal in 1958 and then a longer one until Lewis Thomas in 1983. For a list of all recipients, see *Proc Assn Am Physicians*, 109:492–493, 1997.

46. See yearbooks, The American Philosophical Society, Heard Library, for geographical distribution of membership. In 1959, Dr. Goodpasture was listed by his hometown of Williamsport, Tennessee, a distinction few of the larger cities in the South enjoy.

47. There are only a handful of Southerners on the roster in 2001. Former President Carter is undoubtedly the best known. See web page, American Philosophical Society, for active members by state and institution.

48. BOT Minutes, November 14–15, 1997, Vanderbilt's Goal: To become one of the top ten research and teaching universities in America and to be admired for its service to the community. Board of Trust's Mission: The Board of Trust's Mission is to help Vanderbilt University achieve its goal. As fiduciaries of the University, the Board of Trust shall work through the Chancellor to: 1. Determine the university's strategy. 2. Guarantee its fiscal soundness including providing leadership to its development efforts. 3. Establish appropriate policies. 4. Assure adequate human resources exist to implement the university's strategy. 5. Review progress toward the university's goal.

49. www.vanderbilt.edu

50. Heard Library, Record Group 300, Box 197, File 14.

51. It is worth reflecting that the battle and lawsuit between the bishops of the Methodist Church and Chancellor Kirkland over the control of Vanderbilt's board began when Ernest Goodpasture was an undergraduate. See Conkin's *Gone with the Ivy*, 154–184, and

9

the opinion on the suit released by the Tennessee State Supreme Court on March 21, 1914.

52. Rules then and now state that employees of the university, the chancellor excepted, may not be members of the board.

53. The correspondence about Dr. Goodpasture's resignation may be found in Heard Library Special Collections, Record group 300, Box 197, File 14.

54. See chapter 7, AFIP for a description of the correspondence between Dr. Youmans and Chancellor Branscomb about Dr. Goodpasture's return to Vanderbilt.

55. EWG papers, VUMC Archives, Box 10, 1956 correspondence.

56. Correspondence about this appointment may be found in EWG, VUMC Archives, Box A, File 14, and in Box 10, 1959 and 1960 correspondence.

Chapter Ten

1. Dr. Goodpasture's wish to study fowlpox had been anticipated by Doctors Elliot and Shapiro. The former, a veterinarian, had obtained the affected cock, the head of which had been maintained frozen in the freezer in Dr. Shapiro's laboratory.

2. Some of you may be unaware this is a small bird.

3. This notebook is currently housed in the Eskind library, Special Collections.

4. Collins papers, VUMC Archives, Box 1, Sarah Goodpasture Little file, letter from EWG September 14, 1960.

5. Local and national papers state that he was raking leaves, but Sarah Little recalls differently.

6. Sarah Little states that Dr. Goodpasture smoked cigarettes until age fifty-five (when the Surgeon General reported that smoking might be harmful). Until that time he may have smoked 20–25 cigarettes a day but had no known smoking-related illnesses other than gingivitis and caries. He was hospitalized at Hopkins in 1909 for presumed tuberculosis; consequently, as described in chapter 2, he spent three months at Lake Saranac but the diagnosis of tuberculosis was never established. Dr. Goodpasture was admitted on two occasions to Vanderbilt Hospital. The first of these admissions was on October 5, 1931, when he had radiographic examinations for unexplained upper abdominal pain. He was discharged on October 8 without a specific diagnosis and apparently had no recurrence. He also was admitted for food poisoning or colitis in 1937 after a trip to New Orleans. His correspondence mentions an undefined "illness" in 1953, an abscessed tooth in 1954 (as well as a history of a previous abscessed tooth treated in Colorado), and a "series of

infections" in 1960. His correspondence also describes episodes of "flu" in 1929, 1931, 1940, 1943, and 1944. See Collins papers, VUMC Archives, Box 1, Health file for details. His Vanderbilt chart number is 43220.

7. The specific obituaries, memoirs and resolutions in the paragraph below may be found in Collins papers, VUMC Archives, Box 1, Memoirs file.

8. Sarah Little thanked Chancellor Branscomb in a letter dated November 15. The family had appreciated having the services in Benton Chapel when Chancellor Branscomb had kindly analyzed Dr. Goodpasture's influence as a faculty member. She especially cherished her memory of visiting Benton Chapel the previous May with her father. Sarah had returned then for her twentieth reunion, and Dr. Goodpasture was giving her a special tour. Benton Chapel was included as "the most significant new building on the campus." See Record Group 300, Box 197, File 14, letter from Sarah Little to Branscomb.

9. However, the initial statement about prophets and honor through double negatives states the reverse. This statement is attributed to Matthew, one of the Twelve Apostles: "A prophet is not without honor, save in his own country."

10. Acceptance of Kober Medal. See chapter 1.

11. Letter to Branscomb. See chapter 5, note 56.

12. Ivy Day address at Tulane. See chapter 9, notes 14 and 15.

13. Spirit of Inquiry address, 1943. See chapter 4, note 36.

14. From a handwritten manuscript titled "Alma mater for the spirit of inquiry." For the full text see Collins papers, VUMC Archives, Box 1, Speeches. This manuscript was not published, nor is there a record that the speech was given. However, his papers contain a 1958 manuscript titled: "An alma mater for pathologist's spirit of inquiry," and presumably the manuscript quoted was from the same time.

15. Clinical training in contrast has been extended a minimum of four years for most graduates. This time is used for residency training. Fellowships or specialty training extend the period of clinical training before graduates assume direct responsibility for patient care. It should be noted that the first two years in most medical schools contain a variety of clinical experiences in addition to the basic sciences, and in some cases basic sciences have been compressed into a single year.

16. See Ludmerer's *Time to Heal* for a general discussion of the malaise of academic medical centers and of the profession of medicine.

SELECTED SOURCES

ESKIND BIOMEDICAL LIBRARY ARCHIVES
A. Goodpasture Papers
B. Robinson Papers
C. Leathers Papers
D. Youmans Papers
E. Henry Clarke Papers
F. Rudolph Kampmeier Papers
G. Collins Papers

JEAN AND ALEXANDER HEARD JOINT UNIVERSITY LIBRARY ARCHIVES
A. Annuals
B. *Hustler*
C. Papers of Chancellors Kirkland, Carmichael, and Branscomb

REFERENCES, ALPHABETICAL BY AUTHOR

Anderson, Katherine. "The encephalitogenic property of herpes virus." *Science* 1939 Nov. 24, 90(2343): 497.

Anderson, Katherine. "The cultivation from granuloma inguinale of a micro-organism having the characteristics of Donovan bodies in the yolk sac of chick embryos." *Science* 1943 June 18, 97(2529): 560–61.

Anonymous. "Armand Max Souby." *The Vanderbilt Alumnus* 1922 March, 8:117–18.

Avery, O. T., C. M. MacLeod, and M. McCarty. "Studies on the chemical nature of the substance inducing transformation of pneumococcal types." *Journal Experimental Medicine* 1944, 79: 137–58.

Barfield, Claude E., ed. *Science for the Twenty-First Century: The Bush Report Revisited*. Washington, D.C.: The AEI Press, 1997.

Bashford, E. F., and S. A. Murray. "The significance of the zoological distribution, the nature of the mitoses and the transmissibility of cancer." *Proc R Soc Lond* 1904, 73: 66–76.

Bashford, E. F. "The comparative study of cancer." *J R Sanitary Institute Lond* 1904–1905, 25: 852–56.

Batts, William O. *Private Preparatory Schools for Boys in Tennessee Since 1867*. Nashville: Parthenon Press, 1957.

Baxter, James P., III. *Scientists Against Time*. N.p.: Little, Brown and Co., 1946.

Beecher, Henry K. and Mark D. Altschule. *Medicine at Harvard: The First Three Hundred Years*. Hanover, N.H.: The University Press of New England, 1977.

Bliss, Michael. *William Osler: A Life in Medicine*. Oxford; New York: Oxford University Press, 1999.

Branscomb, Harvie. *Purely Academic: An Autobiography*. Nashville: Vanderbilt University Press, 1978.

Burnet, F. M. "The use of the developing egg in virus research." *Special Report Series* 1936, 220: 3–53.

———. *Virus as Organism: Evolutionary and Ecological Aspects of Some Human Viral Diseases*. Cambridge, Mass.: Harvard University Press, 1946.

———. *Changing Patterns: An Atypical Autobiography*. Melbourne and London: Heinemann, 1968.

Chesney, Alan M. *The Johns Hopkins Hospital and the Johns Hopkins University School of Medicine: A Chronicle*. Vol. 3. Baltimore: The Johns Hopkins Press, 1963.

Cochrane, Rexmond C. *The National Academy of Sciences: The First Hundred Years 1863–1963*. Washington, D.C.: National Academy of Sciences, 1978.

Cohen, D. "The canine transmissible venereal tumor: A unique result of tumor progression." *Adv Cancer Res* 1985, 43: 75–112.

Conkin, Paul K. *Gone with the Ivy: A Biography of Vanderbilt University*. Knoxville: University of Tennessee Press, 1985.

Corner, George W. *George Hoyt Whipple and His Friends: The Life-Story of a Nobel Prize Pathologist*. Philadelphia: J. B. Lippincott Company, 1963.

Craighead, John E. *Pathology and Pathogenesis of Human Viral Disease*. San Diego: Academic Press, 2000.

Dalldorf, G. *Introduction to Virology*. Springfield, Ill.: Charles C. Thomas, 1955.

Dixon, Thomas W. *The Rise and Fall of Alderson, West Virginia*. Parsons, W.V.: McClain Printing Company, 1967.

Evans, Alfred F. "Causation and disease: The Henle-Koch postulates revisited." *Yale J Biol Med* 1976, 49: 175–95.

Feldman, B. *The Nobel Prize: A History of Genius, Controversy, and Prestige*. New York: Arcade Publishing, 2000.

Fenner F., A. Gibbs, and Canberra, eds. *Portraits of Viruses: A History of Virology*. Basel, N.Y.: Karger, 1988.

457

Galbraith, John K. *The Great Crash 1929*. Boston and New York: Houghton Mifflin Company, 1954–1997.

Habel, Karl. "Cultivation of mumps virus in the developing chick embryo and its application to studies of immunity to mumps in man." *Public Health Rep* 1945 Feb. 23, 60(8): 201–12.

Henry, Robert S. *The Armed Forces Institute of Pathology: Its First Century, 1862–1962*. Washington: Office of the Surgeon General, Department of the Army, 1964.

Huebner, Robert J. "The virologist's dilemma." *Ann NY Acad Sci* 1957, 67: 430–38.

Jacobson, Timothy C. *Making Medical Doctors: Science and Medicine at Vanderbilt since Flexner*. Tuscaloosa, Ala.: University of Alabama Press, 1987.

Johnson, Richard T. "The pathogenesis of herpes virus encephalitis." *J Exp Med* 1964, 119: 343–54.

Kampmeier, Rudolph H. *Recollections: The Department of Medicine, Vanderbilt University School of Medicine 1925–1959*. Nashville: Vanderbilt University Press, 1980.

———. *Vanderbilt University School of Medicine: The Story in Pictures from Its Beginning to 1963*. N.p., 1960

Kharsany, A. B. M., A. A. Hoosen, P. Kiepiela, T. Naicker, and A. W. Sturm. "Culture of calymmatobacterium granulomatis." *Clin Infect Dis* 1996, 22: 391.

Klingaman, William K. *1929: The Year of the Great Crash*. New York: Harper and Row, 1989.

Levine, Arnold J. "The origins of virology." In: B. N. Fields, D. M. Knipe, P. M. Howley, et al., eds. *Fields Virology*. 3rd ed. Philadelphia: Lippincott-Raven Publishers, 1996.

Long, Esmond R. *A History of American Pathology*. Springfield, Ill.: Charles C. Thomas Publishers, 1962.

Ludmerer, Kenneth M. *Time to Heal: American Medical Education from the Turn of the Century to the Era of Managed Care*. N.p.: Oxford University Press, 1999.

Luria, S. E., and M. Delbruck. "Mutations of bacteria from virus sensitivity to virus resistance." *Genetics* 1943, 28: 491–511.

Mims, Edwin. *History of Vanderbilt University*. Nashville: Vanderbilt University Press, 1946.

Murphy, Frederick A., Sally P. Bauer, Alyne K. Harrison, and Washington C. Winn. "Comparative pathogenesis of rabies and rabies-like viruses. Viral infection and transit from inoculaton site to the central nervous system." *Lab Invest* 1973, 28(3): 361–76.

Murphy, James B. "Transplantability of malignant tumors to the embryos of a foreign species." *JAMA* 1912, 59: 874–75.

O'Farrell, Nigel. "Donovanosis." In: K. K. Holmes, P. A. Mardh, P. F. Sparling, S. M. Lemon, W. E. Stamm, P. Piot, and J. N. Wasserheit, eds. *Sexually Transmitted Diseases*. New York: McGraw-Hill, 1999.

Plotkin, S. L. and S. A. Plotkin. "A short history of vaccination." In: S. A. Plotkin, and W. A. Orenstein, eds. *Vaccines*. Philadelphia: Saunders, 1999.

Rackemann, F. M. *The Inquisitive Physician: The Life and Times of George Richards Minot*. Cambridge, Mass.: Harvard University Press, 1956.

Rivers, Thomas M. "Some general aspects of filterable viruses." In: Thomas M. Rivers, ed. *Filterable Viruses*. Baltimore: Williams and Wilkins, 1928.

———. "Viruses and Koch's postulates." *J Bacteriol* 1937, 33(1): 1–12.

Robbins, Frederick. "The history of polio vaccine development." In: S. A. Plotkin, and W. A. Orenstein, eds. *Vaccines*. Philadelphia: Saunders, 1999.

Robinson, G. Canby. *Vanderbilt University School of Medicine History and General Description*. New York: The Rockefeller Foundation, 1929. (Methods and problems of medical education; 13.)

Rosenfeld, Louis. *Barney Brooks, M.D. (1884–1952)*. Vanderbilt University Medical Center, 1986. In Eskind Library, Special Collections.

Sanders, Murray. "Cultivation of the viruses: A critical review." *Arch Pathol* 1939, 28(4): 541–86.

Schaffter, Dorothy. *The National Science Foundation*. New York: Frederick A. Praeger, 1969.

Smith, Theobald. *Parasitism and Disease*. New York: Hafner Publishing Company, 1963.

Theiler, Max and M. D. Smith. "The use of yellow fever virus modified by invitro cultivation for human immunization." *J Exp Med* 1937, 65: 787–800.

van Helvoort, Ton. "When did virology start?" *ASM News* 1996, 62(3): 142–45.

van Rooyen, C. E., and A. J. Rhodes. *Virus Diseases of Man*. 2nd ed. New York: Thomas Nelson and Sons, 1948.

Williams, Greer. *Virus Hunters*. New York: Alfred A. Knopf, 1967.

Winternitz M. C., Isabel M. Wason, and Frank P. McNamara. *The Pathology of Influenza*. New Haven: Yale University Press, 1920.

Zachary, G. Pascal. *Endless Frontier: Vannevar Bush, Engineer of the American Century*. New York: The Free Press, 1997.

GUIDE TO THE
COMPANION COMPACT DISC

T he attached CD contains a recording of a lecture given by Dr. Goodpasture in 1955 to second-year students in pathology. The lecture room was on the third floor of the C corridor, a room that now carries the number C 3213, and is used as a laboratory. I was chief resident in pathology in 1955 and taped the lectures simply because I was aware of Dr. Goodpasture's role in the development of Vanderbilt Medical School and that I was witnessing the end of an era; he was the last of the professors appointed by Canby Robinson in 1924–1925.

The subject of this lecture was "Virus Diseases." It was the first in a series of several lectures on that topic. This lecture is important for historical reasons, in that Dr. Goodpasture describes herein several of the major studies performed in his laboratory that made him and his coworkers leaders in the field. In particular, he describes his work in which fowlpox inclusions were shown to contain active viral particles, and he briefly mentions the development of the chick embryo as a culture medium for viruses. A transcript of this lecture is filed in the Special Collections section of the Eskind Library (Goodpasture file).

This lecture was apparently interrupted by the entrance of students and residents on two occasions when you may hear the door squeaking open. These interruptions were presumably due to conflicts with an ongoing autopsy, as only autopsies took precedence over one of Dr. Goodpasture's lectures. The resident shepherding the students in and apologizing for their late entrance is Dr. Judson Randolph, a 1953 graduate of Vanderbilt Medical School.

There are two tracks on this CD. Track two contains some descriptive material followed by Dr. Goodpasture's lecture. Track one contains the classroom sounds and greeting of my last lecture in pathology on December 9, 1998. Between us, Dr. Goodpasture and I had the privilege of teaching pathology and related matters at Vanderbilt Medical School from the class of 1929 to that of 1999, excepting the classes of 1956 to 1959.

INDEX

461

466